Playgoing in
Shakespeare's London

Playgoing in Shakespeare's London

ANDREW GURR

Professor of English
University of Reading

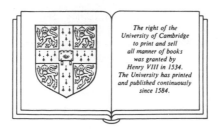

The right of the
University of Cambridge
to print and sell
all manner of books
was granted by
Henry VIII in 1534.
The University has printed
and published continuously
since 1584.

CAMBRIDGE UNIVERSITY PRESS

Cambridge
New York   Port Chester
Melbourne   Sydney

Published by the Press Syndicate of the University of Cambridge
The Pitt Building, Trumpington Street, Cambridge CB2 1RP
40 West 20th Street, New York, NY 10011-4211, USA
10 Stamford Road, Oakleigh, Victoria 3166, Australia

First published 1987
First paperback edition 1988
Reprinted 1989, 1991

Printed in Great Britain at the
University Press, Cambridge

British Library cataloguing in publication data
Gurr, Andrew
Playgoing in Shakespeare's London.
1. Theatre audiences – England – London
– History – 16th century 2. Theatre
audiences – England – London – History
– 17th century
I. Title
792'.09421   PN2596.L6

Library of Congress cataloguing in publication data
Gurr, Andrew.
Playgoing in Shakespeare's London.
Bibliography.
Includes index.
1. Theatre – England – London – History – 16th century.
2. Theatre – England – London – History – 17th century.
3. Theatre audiences – England – London – History – 16th century.
4. Theatre audiences – England – London – History – 17th century.
5. English drama – Early modern and Elizabethan, 1500–1600 – History
and criticism. 6. English drama – 17th century – History and criticism.
7. Shakespeare, William 1564–1616 – Contemporary England.
8. London (England) – Social life and customs.
I. Title.
PN2596.L6G87   1987   792'.09421   86-23276

ISBN 0 521 25336 5 hardback
ISBN 0 521 36824 3 paperback

CE

'The action of the theatre, though modern states esteem it but ludicrous, unless it be satirical and biting, was carefully watched by the ancients, that it might improve mankind in virtue; and indeed many wise men and great philosophers have thought it to the mind as the bow to the fiddle; and certain it is, though a great secret in nature, that the minds of men in company are more open to affections and impressions than when alone.'

Francis Bacon, *The Advancement of Learning*

The work that has gone into this book,
and a good deal more beside,
is dedicated to
Muriel Bradbrook

Contents

viii   *Contents*

Illustrations

Acknowledgements

We should like to thank the following for permission to reproduce the illustrations: the Guildhall Library, City of London (nos. 1, 4, 6 and 9); the Bibliotheek der Rijksuniversiteit, Utrecht (3 and 5); the Master and Fellows of Magdalene College, Cambridge (17); the National Portrait Gallery (7, 16, 20 and 21); the Provost and Fellows of Worcester College, Oxford (8); the Royal Library, Windsor (10); the British Library (11, 13, 14, 15, 18 and 19); the Society of Antiquaries of London (12); and the President and Fellows of St John's College, Oxford (22).

Preface

This book is about the drama of Shakespeare's time. It examines the evidence for the nature of playgoers and playgoing at the commercial playhouses in London from 1567 to 1642. Essentially it is a history of playgoing, because in those seventy-five years not only was the kind of play offered at the different playhouses transformed by Marlowe, Shakespeare, Jonson and their followers but the conditions of playgoing changed radically too. In the early years plays were tolerated reluctantly in London by the City of London magistrates, and more willingly by the great lords who used the playing companies for their own greater glory at Court. From that modest start the leading companies rose in esteem until they enjoyed the patronage of the king himself. James gave royal titles to four companies in 1603. Under Charles in the last fifteen years playgoing, playwriting and discussion of the art became a serious courtly pastime. Charles himself annotated his playbooks and intervened to correct the government censor. That rise in social status was partly the cause and partly the effect of changes in the nature of playgoing amongst London's residents and visitors. Those changes need to be studied carefully if the context for the plays is to be understood. Plays relate far more intimately and immediately to their audiences than the printed word, and the interaction between their givers and receivers is much more direct. The history of the writing of plays in Shakespeare's time is not really complete without an account of the audiences.

I must confess to some discomfort over the title. For reasons which are set out in Chapter 4 the word 'audience' is less than an ideal term for a playgoer in Shakespeare's time. The more neutral word 'playgoer' is preferable, but implies the person and not the conditions of playgoing. Also it was used by Ann Jennalie Cook in her *The Privileged Playgoers*, with which in some respects this book takes issue. The first book on the subject, Alfred Harbage's *Shakespeare's Audience*, comes near to my purpose, but it suggests a homogeneity which did not exist and a narrower scope than the period of history needed for a proper coverage.

Despite that last reservation, the term 'Shakespearean' is used here to cover a period in London's history which began when William Shakespeare was three and ended twenty-six years after his death, an act of generosity towards him which is justified by the scale of his achievement and his signal influence in transforming the nature of the plays written in that time. While Marlowe was a more overt early influence and Jonson a more aggressive later influence on their times, Shakespeare's contribution can be found almost everywhere, and the quality of the written play-texts which have survived and which are the principal justification for this kind of history owe a bottomless debt to his work. Shakespeare's own plays are the magnet which attracted this accumulation of bits and pieces of evidence and inspired the labour of trying to put them into a coherent shape.

The other impetus to write this kind of history grew out of my feeling that the final chapter of my earlier book, *The Shakespearean Stage, 1574–1642*, was far too compact for the material it professed to contain. The book itself was written as a conspectus of the conditions of play performance in Shakespeare's time, to simplify the labours (and correct some misapprehensions) entailed in studying all that has become known about that complex subject in the present century. I am fairly unrepentant about the book and its usefulness, but have always felt that the chapter about the audiences said either too little or too much. Audiences are from one perspective an irrelevant nuisance, the ancients who, because they were different from us, wanted different things from the Shakespearean poets and therefore got in the way of what we would like them to have written. They are dead and gone and it is pointless to try resurrecting them. From the other view audiences are an active part of the performance text, that intricate social exchange in which the immediate playhouse occasion is a conjunction of many inflowing streams of thought. Not to try to know it better is to accept falsification of the whole exchange. From this prejudiced account of the two alternatives, it will be clear that I favour the latter.

This book, in so far as it tries to develop the brief survey of Shakespearean playgoers in the earlier book, in part depends on the rest of that book to supply a context and a basis for this one. This is not intended to be any sort of conspectus. It surveys all the available evidence about playgoing, thoroughly in the physical and more tentatively in the mental features of the phenomenon, and tries to set all the evidence in its historical place with a lengthy final chapter which surveys the radical changes that happened across the span of seventy-five years, and the social and cultural diversification which accompanied those changes.

Because it is a history and because it uses very largely written evidence about playgoing, all the texts quoted other than Shakespeare's own are quoted in the original spelling, with only the typographical accidents (i for j. initial v and medial u) modernised. Money is cited in the original pounds, shillings and pence. All the illustrations, of playgoers and the conditions of playgoing, are taken from the period. Dates are silently modernised to avoid the confusion which sometimes stems from the old habit of starting to date a new year in March. Books which are frequently cited in the notes are abbreviated in the form given at their first mention in the notes. Most of the significant evidence on which the book is based is gathered in the two appendices. Appendix 1 names and describes the 162 real persons known to have attended playhouse performances. Appendix 2 is a comprehensive list of the evidence about audiences, real and fictional, which can be found in contemporary comments, given in chronological order. Where such comments are cited in the text, reference is made by the number of the quotation as it appears in Appendix 2.

Parts of Chapter 4 appeared, in a different form, in *Essays in Theatre*, and I should like to thank the editors for permission to reproduce the material here. Accumulating the evidence has taken a long time, and my debts to friends along the way have accumulated too. My thanks are due to all, and especially to Lilian Argrave, Charles Barber, Philip Brockbank, Cedric Brown, Martin Butler, Theo Crosby, Henk Gras, E. A. Gurr, E. R. Gurr, Christopher Hardman, Richard Hosley, Marion Lomax, Carolyn Lyle, Michael Neill, John Orrell, Michael Shapiro, Angela Smith and Alan Wardman, all of whom gave me more support than I deserve, and more help than perhaps they knew. The faults are, inescapably, all mine. To Sarah Stanton of Cambridge University Press I owe particular thanks for a long period of warm and congenial association, and simply offer her Middleton's sentiment, in the preface to a book he published in 1603: 'I never wisht this Booke better fortune, then to fall into the hands of a true spelling Pritter.'

Reading, 1986

I
Introduction

In the argument about satire and raillery which occupies the Induction to Jonson's *Every Man out of his Humour*, the principal railer Asper is prodded by his friends into expressing the poet's ambition for his play and its reception:

> To please, but whom? attentive auditors,
> Such as will joine their profit with their pleasure,
> And come to feed their understanding parts.

Asper is not Jonson, but here he voices the hope Jonson put into his prologues in the plays he wrote between 1599 and 1626. Ignorance, says Asper at the end of his speech, is the enemy to art. A good playhouse audience will listen to the poetry and be properly rewarded in the mind. A poet wants auditors, listeners, not spectators, mere viewers of the scene.

Every Man Out was performed at the Globe in 1599. Some time later in that year Jonson left Shakespeare's company for the company of boys at the newly opened Blackfriars playhouse. His reasons may not have been entirely divorced from the Globe audience, and the wrong kind of 'understanding' which he felt a large proportion of them displayed. The prologue to his first play for the boys, *Cynthia's Revels*, openly appeals to the 'learned eares' at the new venue. There can be no doubt that he expected a better educated and more attentive audience at the smaller and more expensive playhouse. It would be nice to know how far this new 'auditory' met his expectations. By 1626 he was looking to the Court to give him the audience of 'Schollers' who might understand his play. We might also wonder how many of his fellow poets wrote for scholars.

Drama, and especially Shakespearean drama, is a performance art. Francis Beaumont called the printed text of a play a 'second publication' after the first on the stage (see Appendix 2, no. 84). Shakespeare himself was evidently not concerned to immortalise his plays by a second publication, and rested content with the transient fame of his company's performances. As performance texts, the plays were composed for a tighter grouping of people, a more immediate and

readily recognisable social entity, than any audience for a printed
text. Performed texts of course also supply an immediate response
from the recipients, so that playwrights engage in a form of communication which is more nearly intercommunicative than any other
publication. The more intimately you know your audience, the less
simply verbal will the communication be.

For Shakespeare's contemporaries, moreover, this intimacy was an
extraordinary and uniquely rewarding novelty. London playgoers in
the 1580s and 1590s created the unprecedented phenomenon of an
audience paying money to hear poetry. For the poets this novelty
gave them the first direct and regular contact with a large and
committed crowd of hearers that poets in England had ever enjoyed.
For the poets who were also players it must have been a revelation:
poetry as a performing art speaking directly to an expectant crowd
who had paid money to enjoy the offering. Audience response could
be directly manipulated, known audience tastes could be catered for,
new devices could be tried in the confidence that they would be
welcomed as novelties. What we see in the texts of plays composed
between about 1590 and 1610 is very largely an exploration of the
new possibilities seen in this direct relationship between poet and
playgoer.

All we have now of these novelties of course is their second
publication. It is a commonplace for criticism that the written
play-texts of Shakespeare's time need supplementing and amplifying
through knowledge of the stage conventions and the iconography of
performance, what has been called the 'art of orchestration' of the
performance text.[1] It is an approach which has brought substantial
dividends both to our understanding of the texts in detail at the
verbal level and to the larger dimensions. Mostly however it has
worked by identifying conventional techniques of staging evident
either implicitly in the play-texts themselves or explicitly in the
stage structures. We know a great deal now about how Shakespeare
was staged at the Globe in 1600. What we do not know is how the
players and playgoers interacted to create the performances of 1600.
Indeed, without taking the contemporary audiences into account,
the full complex of intercommunication through performance for
which Shakespeare designed his plays must remain uncertain. We
know that *Hamlet* was first staged at the Globe in about 1600, in the
broad daylight of what was probably an autumn afternoon on the
Bankside. We do not know how the audience in the daylight of that
London afternoon received the news, delivered in the play's opening
lines, that it was supposed to be shortly after midnight and bitterly

cold. We know that they would recognise Hamlet's pun about the distracted Globe he finds himself in, and possibly connect it with the 'distracted multitude' which Claudius later says loves Prince Hamlet. We cannot be so sure how they would receive Hamlet's soliloquies, spoken ostensibly in solitude when in fact he was visibly surrounded by three thousand people, some of whose heads were literally at his feet. A performance text is a transmission tuned to a highly specific wavelength, and a specific set of atmospheric conditions. The receivers are a part of the mechanism of transmission, and need careful consideration in the business of trying to recompose the performance text for what it can add to our knowledge of Shakespearean dramaturgy.

Shakespearean receivers were far from passive objects. They are likely nowadays to be invoked all too often in a vicious circle of internal evidence, as arbiters of this or that otherwise inexplicable or undesired feature of the plays. Understandably, because they are the most inconstant, elusive, unfixed element of the Shakespearean performance text, their contribution is presented as an easy means of explaining away features of the dramaturgy which seem incongruous to modern audiences. Shakespearean theatre is such a complex phenomenon that historians have found it all too easy to persuade the evidence to reflect their own wishes for an ideal performance text by means of the shapes they give to that plastic entity the audience.

In the last fifty years there have been two major scholarly assessments of the nature of the audiences for London's drama through the seventy or so years up to 1642. Alfred Harbage, working in the 1930s and 1940s when the political climate encouraged him to identify Shakespeare as a truly 'popular' playwright appealing to a whole and united nation, used demographical analysis and contemporary comments to shape the characteristic playgoer of 1600 into a London artisan, a city worker.[2] Later he refined this analysis by distinguishing what he called the 'rival traditions'. On the one hand Shakespeare wrote popular fictions for a middle and working class audience, while on the other the 'coterie' playwrights of the boy companies wrote for an elite class, select, satirical and decadent in their theatrical tastes. Harbage's evidence for the predominance of the artisan class at the Globe was demolished in 1974 by Ann Jennalie Cook, in an article which showed the fragility of his demographic evidence.[3] Seven years later she followed this demolition with a book which proposed instead that the characteristic playgoer of Shakespeare's time was precisely the elite or 'privileged' audience whom Harbage had confined to the boy company playhouses. She replaced Harbage's stereotype of the idle artisan with the equally oversimplifying stereotype of the idle rich. Using similar evidence to Harbage, though with better help from the demographers, she maintained that

London's large and lively privileged set ruled the playgoing world quite as firmly as they ruled the political world, the mercantile world, and the rest of the cultural world. Their own ranks were tremendously varied, reaching from bright but impoverished students, younger sons of gentry families set to a trade, and minor retainers in noble households all the way up to lords, ambassadors, merchant princes, and royalty itself. Though the clever, the ambitious, and the newly rich enormously expanded the ranks of the privileged under Elizabeth and James, they still stood firmly apart from the mass of society. Most people ate, dressed, worked, and lived as best they could. The fortunate wrote music and poetry. They made the laws. They ruled the government and the church. They monopolised education. They led armies. They claimed estates and controlled companies. They elevated dining and dress and decor to an art. And they were avid playgoers, men and women alike.[4]

This is rather less than a part of the truth. Over the years between the 1560s, when the first purpose-built playhouses were established, and 1642, when all playhouses were closed, well over fifty million visits were made to playhouses. Even by Cook's very generous definition of the privileged as including 350,000 of the London population[5] they could not have provided more than a small part of that total. Of course even a small section of the privileged in any audience might have exercised a disproportionate influence over the whole. Cook's is a more plausible stereotype than Harbage's, but it is still a thorough oversimplification. By insisting that only the one species of playgoer predominated, she ignored the variety which existed between one playhouse and another and eliminated the wealth of evidence about changing patterns of playgoing. The stereotype of the 'privileged' playgoer needs dissecting into its component parts by factors more intricate than numbers or social status.[6]

Of all the complicating factors which make assessing the nature of Shakespearean audiences difficult the chief one is historical change. The seventy-five years between the building of the first amphitheatre playhouse in 1567 and the closing of the three hall playhouses and three amphitheatres operating in 1642 saw huge changes, not only in audience tastes but in the physical nature of the auditorium and the social composition of the playgoers. The reopening of the hall playhouses in 1599, which Jonson tried to exploit for the learned ears he expected them to provide, entailed a transformation of priorities in the auditorium, for instance. Where at the

Globe and the other amphitheatres the people closest to the stage were the poorest, paying a minimal penny for the privilege of standing on their feet next to the stage platform to view the players, at the Blackfriars and the other hall playhouses the wealthier a patron was the closer he or she could come to the action, and the cheapest places were put at the rear. That transfer reflects a social shift in playgoing priorities which splits the period in two. The gentlemen students of the Inns of Court and the City's artisan apprentices were equally prominent as playgoers throughout the period, but not always in the same proportions, the same positions, or the same playhouses. And just as the social composition of playgoing crowds varied, so did their mental composition and their expectations. The establishment of a popular repertory by the end of the 1580s gave the poets a chance to build an intimate framework of allusion to familiar traditions and conventions which by the very process of building became subject to constant change. A historical perspective, applied to the physical structure of playhouse auditoriums and to the varying social and mental structure of the playgoers, stresses the importance for studies of Shakespearean drama not just of the play as performance text but of the original performance text. A properly detailed historical perspective is a necessary component in any analysis of the original audiences and their contribution to performance.

The evidence about audiences falls into four main categories. The first and most tangible is the physical circumstances of performance, the shape of the auditorium, the numbers in an audience, and the consequent behaviour patterns characteristic of Shakespearean playgoing, down to the material provision the playhouses made for the playgoer's physical comfort in such things as cushions and toilets. The second body of evidence is largely demographic. It entails identifying the main social groupings in Elizabethan and Jacobean society, and among them those elements most likely to have provided the playgoers. This can be supplemented with a detailed analysis – audience sampling – of the people known to have attended plays at the time, whether real people or types identified by contemporary comments. The third body of evidence is the kind of contemporary comment which makes or implies a statement about the type of playgoer who would be regarded as a normal (or exceptional: the distinction is important) member of the audience at a particular playhouse at a particular time in its history. Finally, most elusive but potentially by far the most rewarding is the evidence for the mental composition, the collective mind of people in company, of the kind of playgoer the hopeful poet might expect to find in the crowd at the venue intended for his play. The hermeneutics of the theatre, the complex interactive communication between stage and audience, depends as much on the audience's state of mind as it does on the author's and the players' expectations of what, mentally, their audience will be prepared for. That 'mindset' is a consequence of the mental furniture the Shakespeare playgoer might have been equipped with much more than it is a consequence of his or her state of stomach or bladder. It comprises the education, the routine prejudices, the playhouse traditions, and everything the playgoer expected from the playgoing experience. That kind of evidence needs to be anchored firmly in the more solid matter of the preceding kinds. It has to be approached with the reservation that the detail is fragmentary, and that even when framed carefully in its historical place it can more easily lead to misinterpretation than any other sort of evidence. This study takes only the most tentative steps towards the final kind of evidence. Perhaps, though, the solidity established with the other three may provide an anchorage for further exploration of this fourth kind, and a reduction in the speculation which has stood in for it in the past.

The majority of the available evidence is contemporary comment. It may be useful to cite one example as a measure of what can reasonably be extracted from any one comment when properly located in its context. It should also indicate the importance of that context. A not untypical comment appears in a small pamphlet written by Henry Peacham the younger and published in 1642. It must have been written before March of that year, when the playhouses were closed, because it gives no hint that playgoing was not currently available, but it was probably made not long before since the pamphlet was clearly written for publication and there is no reason why the printing should have been delayed. It made a small supplement to Peacham's *Compleat Gentleman*, originally published in 1622 and reprinted in 1625, 1627 and 1634. Its title is *The Art of Living in London*, and basically it describes the dangers of London life for a gentleman newly arrived from the country. The principal dangers of course were the idle pastimes of gambling, drinking and playgoing, together with their attendant costs. Near the end of the pamphlet Peacham offers a little story.

A tradesman's wife of the Exchange, one day when her husband was following some business in the city, desired him he would give her leave to go see a play; which she had not done in seven years. He bade her take his apprentice along with her, and go; but especially to have a care of her purse;

Marchants wife of London

Ciuis Londinensis melioris qualitatis Vxor.

2

1. A merchant's wife, one of a series of engravings by Wenceslas Hollar made in the early 1630s (Catalogue no. P1893)

which she warranted him she would. Sitting in a box, among some gallants and gallant wenches, and returning when the play was done, returned to her husband and told him she had lost her purse. 'Wife, (quoth he,) did I not give you warning of it? How much money was there in it?' Quoth she, 'Truly, four pieces, six shillings and a silver tooth-picker.' Quoth her husband, 'Where did you put it?' 'Under my petticoat, between that and my smock.' 'What, (quoth he,) did you feel no body's hand there?' 'Yes, (quoth she,) I felt one's hand there, but I did not think he had come for that.'

There is more than a hint in this anecdote of Peacham's gentlemanly contempt for a money-conscious citizen and a citizen's wife who is little more than a foolish and vulnerable sex object. But there is a good deal more too, and when it is stitched into the pattern made by equivalent pieces of evidence it makes a surprisingly strong fabric.

The wife's seat in a box, for instance, means that she was at one of the indoor playhouses, which in the 1630s customarily maintained their boxes for ladies and their escorts. Squeezed in amongst the gentry and their ladies ('gallants and gallant wenches') she might well have felt a little ill at ease, sufficiently so to give her one reason for not objecting in public to the intrusive hand. A seven-year absence from playgoing might well have intensified her discomfort, even though it is apparent from Massinger's *City Madam* that the wives of the wealthier London citizens did try to imitate the behaviour of Court ladies in boxes at playhouses. This city madam was certainly the wife of a magnate, since her husband was busy at the Royal Exchange, which meant that he was either a merchant trader or a goldsmith-banker, one of the affluent City families living on the borderline between citizenship and gentrification which was the subject of Massinger's play. No respectable lady went alone to a playhouse, so in the absence of her husband her escort, her husband's apprentice, was aping the pages whom Court ladies took with them to playhouses. He might possibly have had a pretension to being gentry himself. One third of the apprentices in the Goldsmith's Company were younger sons of gentry. The wife was clearly an affluent City madam, since her purse had four 'pieces' of gold in it. The cheapest gold coins were marks or nobles, at three to a pound, or royals at two to a pound, so she seems to have taken at least £2 in cash to the playhouse, plus the crown which admission to the box would have cost the two of them. Finally it is evident that the box was crowded enough for the cutpurse to have got his hand inside the wife's dress without being noticed by anyone else, and that not all gallants were as gentlemanly, either in their thieving ways or in the lecherous groping which the wife expected, as Peacham's own

Compleat Gentleman would have us assume. The wife's reaction to the groping hand says something about how usual it was for lechery to thrive in playhouse crowds and perhaps how unusual it was for cutpurses to operate in those conditions.

If we were to milk this possibly fanciful anecdote for rather more than it can reasonably be expected to give, we might associate Peacham's City madam with the wife of the Citizen in Beaumont's *Knight of the Burning Pestle*. In the play's Induction the wife explains that she has been trying for twelve months to get her husband to bring her to a play, and subsequently entertains the gentry amongst whom she sits by her thoroughgoing ignorance of dramaturgy and her innocently lecherous double entendres. Her taste is for romance and old-fashioned tales of knight errantry, and she enjoys the stage spectacle with comic literalmindedness. After seven years without seeing plays it would not be inconceivable that Peacham's City madam should also be romantic in her tastes and gullible in her enjoyment of the spectacle.

This anecdote is useful, then, for deducing tangible details about the physical conditions the wife endured in her box, somewhat less tangible details about her social circumstances, and markedly fragile conclusions about her mental outlook. These can be related to the repertory of the indoor playhouses in the early 1640s, though the fact that it is the wife's first visit to a play for seven years would hardly make her a typical or normative figure. In itself the anecdote offers only a tiny sampling of audience types. If several hundred such pieces of evidence are put together, though, the fabric becomes both long and finely detailed. The anecdote does tell us something about the normal expectations of playgoing for the wealthier citizens and citizens' wives in the 1630s and early 1640s. It also indicates that there should be some constraints about the increasingly speculative nature of any deductions we make as we move from the tangible details of the physical setting into attempts to calculate what might have been in the particular playgoer's head on that visit.

These possibilities and constraints, weaving the evidence into a fabric and limiting speculation over the precise mental processes, have established the structure of this analysis of Shakespearean playgoing. It begins with the physical circumstances of the playgoing exercise, as the playhouses developed and changed through the seventy-five years between 1567 and 1642 when there were specially-built commercial playhouses in London, and the varied provisions at the different playhouses. It continues with an analysis of the social structure and an attempt to identify the social types who are known to have been playgoers throughout the period. It investigates the more tangible pieces of evidence for the composition of the minds of different playgoers, both the learned ears and the 'Nutcrackers, that only come for sight', as Jonson called them in the Court prologue to *A Staple of News*, and tentatively identifies some of the doors to further investigation which the evidence leaves open. Finally it seeks to emphasise the strength of the pressure for continual change inherent in the exercise of playgoing, by sketching a history of the changing tastes and the different kinds of repertory offered by the different playhouses. That history is also, by implication and rather covertly, an attempt to flesh out some of the questions raised by the chapter on the mental composition of playgoers. A history of the evolution of playgoers' tastes in plays has some value in suggesting the preferences which made one kind of play more popular at a given time than another. It also provides an outline of the interaction between the poets and their audiences.

The closing date for the period covered by this study is obvious. Parliament may not have intended to do more in March 1642 than to batten down the hatches in a time of political storm by ordering the closure of all places of public assembly such as playhouses.[7] The order explicitly offered the judgement that the times were too seriously disturbed for such frivolities as plays to be tolerable. It was in its macabre way a repetition of the lengthy closures ordered when Elizabeth and James I died. Charles was not to die for another seven years, but the interim was not unlike a long wake so far as the lighter distractions of town life were concerned. Nobody could have anticipated in 1642 that the storm would last for eighteen years. Nonetheless, it was the longest interval in theatre history, and whatever flickers of life lit up the closure the lamp was of a different kind when Davenant set it going again at the Restoration. Both the amphitheatres and the version of their open stage-playing which the hall playhouses maintained went out of existence in 1642, and that cessation provides the terminus for this study.

The opening date is necessarily a more arbitrary point in the evolution of playgoing. Most histories still fix on 1576 as the significant date, since Burbage's Theatre and the first Blackfriars both opened in that year. But we know that Burbage's brother-in-law and partner John Brayne built the Red Lion playhouse on the pattern followed by the Theatre and the later playhouses as early as 1567.[8] If the significance of the Theatre is that it indicates the size of the potential market for popular plays, leading Brayne and Burbage to invest money in an auditorium like those of the animal-baiting arenas where the owners could take money at the door and accommodate thousands of paying Londoners, then the building of its predecessor the Red Lion makes 1567 the watershed. At first this watershed was probably more important for the impresarios than the plays. It gave them better control of their income than they had passing a hat around in a market place or hiring an innyard or baiting arena to put on their shows. But it must also have made a difference fairly rapidly to the playgoers. By enclosing the plays inside a special building players made the customers who paid to see what was on offer more selective, and no doubt more demanding. Only those who paid got in. They got in for the exclusive purpose of seeing a play, and they handed their money over to the impresarios and players whose sole interest was in satisfying their demand for entertainment. Moreover a single fixed venue needed a much larger turnover of plays than was needed when the players were on their travels from one town to another. So the London playhouses became a massive stimulus to the production of new plays.

The first commercial playhouses offered a system for playgoers which differed significantly from the earlier arrangements. Players who performed in market places had to take a hat around for their income, and were likely to be paid by results, haphazardly, rather than systematically in advance. Players who secured an innyard venue were dependent on the innkeeper's willingness and the variable physical facilities he could provide. Players who performed in halls, whether at the behest of the local mayor or the lord of the manor, were paid by their host to use the facilities and to entertain the guests he provided. Such audiences did not have any direct financial link with the pleasures the players gave them. To that extent the first purpose-built playhouses signal not just an escalation of impresario investment in playgoing but a change of motive and circumstance for the playgoers. They were a rationalisation of the growing fashion for seeing plays for money at the inns more than they were a radical innovation, but they made as precise a growth point in the evolution of London playgoing as any in that rather obscure region of theatre history. The vicinity of 1567 is therefore the best starting date.

A study of the evidence about Shakespearean playgoing cannot afford to be hopeful about reconstructing a Shakespearean performance with any amplitude. Performances are ephemeral, audiences are disparate, and the poet, especially if he was of the tribe of Ben, was likely to have aimed more at the individual intellect than the collective emotion. Identifying the relative proportions in a playhouse crowd of artisan 'understanders', City madams and gallants sitting on their benches in judgement does not throw much light on those darker problems of the performance text. But it does light up the context, and that kind of illumination is certainly worth having. Shakespeare reads rather differently once the evidence set out in this kind of study is taken into account. The question of wordplay, for instance, and the learned 'lusus' or witty allusion seems of primary importance to the reader, but is treated with heavy scepticism by those who take seriously the physical circumstances of high-speed performances in noisy open-air amphitheatres.[9] Even in the relative quietness of a hall like the Blackfriars a Shakespeare play, without serious cuts and with four short intervals for candle trimming between the acts, that took well under three hours to perform as it did in Shakespeare's time, could have given its audience little time to take either breath or thought. And yet that restriction need not be overstated. We have our own limitations which a knowledge of the context for Shakespearean performance can help to minimise. It is not only the actors who take Shakespeare more slowly these days. Sitting in padded armchairs in an artificially darkened auditorium is not good training for anyone's experience of Elizabethan plays. If we were habituated to hearing sermons, if we stood in a muddy yard or even sat on wooden benches by candlelight, we might perhaps be more alert to many features that Elizabethans would have taken for granted. The metatheatrical and 'all the world's a stage' aspects for instance are easier to recognise when the auditorium is not darkened from view, and the audience is as visible a presence as the players. The verbal tropes and quibbles are quicker of access when listening is a more natural habit than reading. Knowing the context helps us to be more attentive to such factors and to give them better weight.

In the epistle which accompanied the printed text of a sermon he gave at Paul's Cross in October 1578, the Cambridge divine Laurence Chaderton apologised for the defectiveness of his second publication.

Let no man thinke, that the reading of this can be half so effectuall and profitable to him, as the hearyng was, or might be. For it wanteth the zeale of the speaker, the attention of the hearer, the promise of God to the ordinary preaching of his word, the mighty and inwarde working of his holy spirite.

(Epistle, 'To the Christian Reader', A3r)

Whether or not we want to think of Shakespeare as a sacred spirit, the player's zeal and the playgoer's attentiveness were essential elements in the collective process that created a performance text in the Shakespearean playhouse.

2
Physical conditions

(A) THE AMPHITHEATRE PLAYHOUSES

There were two quite different types of commercial London play-house, one beginning in 1567, the other in 1576. The 'public' playhouses or open amphitheatres, the first of which seems to have opened in 1567, were versions of the animal-baiting houses and galleried innyards. The 'private' playhouses or halls were built in large rooms on the model of the banqueting halls in the royal palaces and great houses where plays were provided for banqueting guests. The terms 'public' and 'private' were not used to differentiate the two types until about 1600, and they indicate more about the social antecedents of each type than any difference of commercial function. The terms 'amphitheatre' and 'hall' are better indications of their character. The value of the terms 'public' and 'private' lies chiefly in the way they indicate the social snobbery which separated the two kinds.

The 'public' amphitheatres were built in the suburbs. The first of them (so far as we know) was the Red Lion, built in Whitechapel in 1567, and replaced in 1576 by the Theatre in Shoreditch, on one of the main roads north out of the city. The dimensions of the Red Lion's stage are known, but nothing about its auditorium. Much of what we know about the Theatre and its near neighbour, the Curtain, built in the following year, has likewise to be inferred from the evidence for the later playhouses, which are rather better documented. The Theatre was dismantled in 1599 so that its timbers could be used as the frame for the Globe, and in its basic layout and audience capacity it must have closely resembled the later play-house. A little more is known about the Rose (1587) and much more about the Swan (1595), built on the Bankside in Surrey close to Paris Garden, which was the chief bear-baiting house. We know about the Swan largely thanks to the drawing which the Dutchman Johannes De Witt made of its interior on a visit in 1596. Different kinds of evidence, including builder's instructions and lawsuits, give infor-

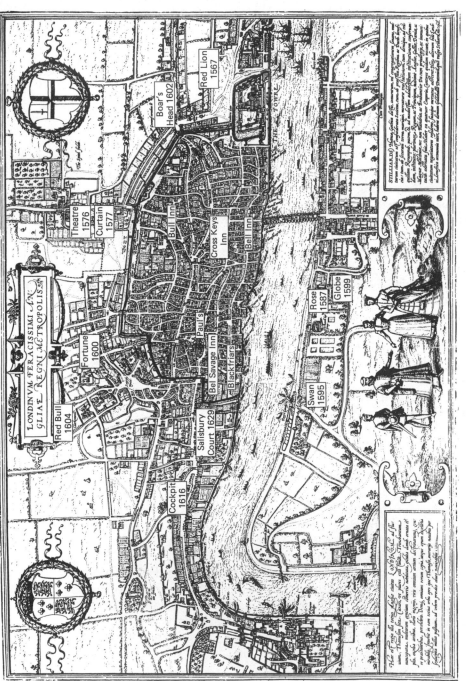

Red Lion
1567

Boar's
Head 1602

Theatre
1576

Curtain
1577

Bull Inn

Cross Keys
Inn

Bell Inn

Rose
1587

Globe
1599

Fortune
1600

Paul's

Bel Savage Inn

Blackfriars

Swan
1595

Red Bull
1604

LONDINVM FERACISSIMI AN
GLIAE REGNI METROPOLIS

Salisbury
Court 1629

Cockpit
1616

STILLIARD

2. A map of London, showing its playhouses built between 1567 and 1629. The engraving is from Braun and Hogenberg's *Civitates Orbis Terrarum*, first edition, 1572. The playhouses and inns used for playing are marked in their approximate locations, with the date of building where known. In the seventy years from 1572 London expanded to cover most of the periphery shown here.

mation about the last five major amphitheatres, the Globe (1599) on the Bankside, the Fortune (1600) to the north, the Boar's Head (1601) in Whitechapel to the east, the Red Bull (1604) in Clerkenwell to the north-west, and the Hope, built on the Bankside to double as a baiting house and playhouse in 1614.[1] The main features of the auditorium seem to have been basically similar in all the amphitheatres, and it is possible to identify something like a typical setting for seeing a play at any of the 'public' venues. John Brayne, who built the Red Lion playhouse in 1567, partnered James Burbage in building what was probably its replacement, the Theatre, in 1576. Most likely all of these earliest amphitheatres had an auditorium similar in structure to the galleried animal-baiting rings which had stood on the south bank of the Thames for the previous forty or more years. They probably also resembled the great coaching inns, which had square yards and surrounding galleries. In fact two later playhouses, the Boar's Head and the Red Bull, were converted from inns, and the square-built Fortune may have been similar to them. The 1576 edition of William Lambarde's *Perambulation of Kent* describes playgoing at the Bel Savage Inn in Ludgate, and the 1596 edition adds the Theatre to the account without otherwise altering what is described. The arrangements for playgoing at the two venues were evidently similar. The inns and playhouses provided standing-room in the 'yard' around the stage, an area obviously not available to audiences at the baiting houses, but apart from that extra space the auditorium layout probably did not differ in any fundamental way.[2] The playhouses certainly copied their three levels of galleries from the baiting houses.

Samuel Kiechel, a German merchant visiting London in 1584, reported that both of the playhouses then had three levels of galleries.[3] These served as the chief accommodation for playgoers, offering seating on wooden 'degrees' or steps, and a roof to fend off the London weather. The stage itself, jutting from one side into the middle of the yard, was also protected by a cover or 'heavens', but the yard itself was open to the sky, and the playgoers who gathered there closest to the stage had nothing but their legs to uphold them. This minimal provision – no seating, and no protection from the rain – helps to explain one of the curious features of the earliest playhouses which seems to have been altered when the new generation appeared in the 1590s. Admission to the earliest playhouses was a gradual progression from the minimal comfort of the yard to the better and more sheltered places in the galleries. As Lambarde put it in his 1596 edition (p. 233):

such as goe to *Parisgardein*, the *Bell Savage*, or *Theatre*, to beholde Beare baiting, Enterludes or Fence play, can account of any pleasant spectacle, [if] they first pay one pennie at the gate, another at the entrie of the Scaffolde, and the thirde for a quiet standing.

Thomas Platter, a young Swiss visitor in 1599, described the same system with the added detail that the best seats were cushioned (2.32). You went in by the entrance doors directly to the yard, as you would entering a coaching innyard through its great double gates. Once in the yard you could choose to enter the galleries for a seat, and if you wanted more privacy and a cushion you could pay once again for a room in the galleries closest to the stage. This arrangement, a sequence of choices, may have owed something to the design of the inns, and it must have been acceptable to the players familiar with the traditions of the booth stages in market squares, where the entire audience simply stood around the booth stage. It can hardly have been used in the baiting houses, where the yard became the baiting arena, but in the playhouses it was an arrangement which must have seemed entirely natural to those who assumed that a normal audience would principally be a crowd of men and women clustered on their feet around the stage platform. So you were admitted to the yard, and could go elsewhere only if you chose to separate yourself from the principal audience, the crowd standing around the stage platform. If it rained, you had the choice of getting wet or paying a second penny for the shelter of the galleries.

The second generation of playhouses, including possibly the Rose (1587), and the Swan (1595) and certainly the Globe and Fortune, seem to have been designed with a less clumsy system of admission which acknowledged from the start that the gallery sitters were different from the standers of the yard. De Witt's drawing of the Swan has caused some debate about this, because the openings marked 'ingressus' in the gallery walls surrounding the yard seem to mark the same cumbrous sequential system as the Theatre, where the first penny gaining entrance to the yard required the gallery-goer to push his or her way through the crowd before surrendering another penny for a seat and a roof. But the Globe and the Fortune, built as exact rivals – James Burbage transported the timbers of his Theatre from the northern suburb to the Bankside near to Philip Henslowe's Rose, and Henslowe promptly built the Fortune in the north not far away from the old Theatre site, using as his builder the man who had just completed the Globe – had a more sophisticated admission system. Access to the galleries in these playhouses did not entail passing through the yard. Once in one of the two entrance-ways you chose

3. The Swan playhouse, a drawing by Arendt van Buchel from
Johannes De Witt's sketch made in 1596

either to enter the yard or to mount the stairs which rose in towers above the entrance-ways directly into the galleries.[4] The 'twopenny galleries' in fact could accommodate more than twice as many playgoers as the yard, so it is understandable that the players eventually came to feel that gallery patrons deserved better treatment than to be siphoned through the crowd who were paying least for their pleasure.

The 'two small doors', which were all that the audience at the Globe had to escape by in 1613 when a performance of *Henry VIII* set the thatching over the galleries alight and destroyed the playhouse, could admit more than three thousand people in all. When the house was full, the crowding was intense. At the Fortune, built in an 80-foot square, probably out of an existing building, the yard measured 55 feet along each side, with the stage jutting into the centre from a tiring-house front occupying 43 of the 55 feet on the side opposite the entry gates. It thus gave the standers in its yard a

4. The second Globe (1614–44), a detail from Wenceslas Hollar's 'Long View' of London. In the original the names of the two Southwark amphitheatres, the Globe and the 'beere baiting house' or Hope, were accidentally reversed. In this reproduction the name has been transferred to the correct building, the second Globe, built in 1614.

total space of 1,842 square feet. The Boar's Head playhouse, converted from an innyard in 1599, had rather less than that, and only two levels of gallery. The Globe, built on a circular or polygonal frame almost exactly 100 feet in outside diameter, and with a yard about 70 feet in diameter, offered nearly 2,500 square feet.[5] There is no firm evidence about how many people this space could hold, and it would not have been really packed very often. But it could be enough of a squeeze to be an uncomfortable experience, if we are to judge by Marston's reference to being 'pasted to the barmy Jacket of a Beer-brewer', and Dekker's frequent mentions of garlic-breathed stinkards.[6] The only actual figures we have allocating a set number of standing spectators to a fixed space come from documents about the king's visit to Oxford in 1605 and the play performed for him at Christ Church.[7] There 400 square feet were allowed for 130 standers. But that ratio – 3 square feet each – was actually more than the average gentleman or lady was allowed for sitting at the same play (2¼ square feet), and cannot bear much relation to the level of crowding acceptable at the Globe or Fortune. Calculations of 600 or 800 in the yard at these playhouses probably rather underestimate the maximum capacity. At the nine performances of *A Game at Chesse* at the rebuilt Globe in 1624 the squeeze must have been fearsome, and there could hardly have been less than a thousand people in the yard for each performance, since the Spanish Ambassador claimed that there were 'more than 3000 persons there on the day that the audience was smallest'.[8]

The change in the admission system for the later playhouses probably indicates a shift in priorities to favour the gallery audience over the 'understanders' in the yard. The wealthiest patrons most likely always had separate access to their places, since the 'lords' rooms'[9] which were on the balcony immediately over the stage must have been reached through the tiring-house. The sixpence which a lord's room cost would have been paid at the tiring-house door at the back of the playhouse. The revised entry system devised for the Globe and Fortune went some distance towards giving comparably separate access for the gallery patrons. This system, a major stairway with doors leading off to each gallery level, may have been devised for the Rose. Sir John Harington wrote an epigram, about a lady who was caught on the stairs by a pair of thieves, which dates from the 1590s and clearly indicates that access to the galleries at that time was no longer through the yard. We need not assume that the anecdote in the epigram really happened, since Harington is clearly developing a bawdy pun on the stock term for stealing, 'cony-catching' (catching rabbits), but the material circumstances of the stairway must be genuine.

> A lady of great Birth, great reputation,
> Clothed in seemly, and most sumptuous fashion
> Wearing a border of rich Pearl and stone,
> Esteemed at a thousand crowns alone,
> To see a certaine interlude, repaires,
> To shun the press, by dark and privat staires.
> Her page did beare a Torch that burnt but dimly.
> Two cozening mates, seeing her deckt so trimly,
> Did place themselves upon the stayres to watch her,
> And thus they laid their plot to cunny-catch her:
> One should as 'twere by chance strike out the light;
> While th'other that should stand beneath her, might
> Attempt (which modestie to suffer lothes)
> Rudely to thrust his hands under her clothes.
> That while her hands repeld such grosse disorders,
> His mate might quickly slip away the borders.
> Now though this act to her was most unpleasant,
> Yet being wise (as womens wits are present:)
> Straight on her borders both her hands she cast,
> And so with all her force she held them fast.
> Villaines, she cryde, you would my borders have:
> But I'll save them, tother it selfe can save:
> Thus, while the Page had got more store of light,
> The coozening mates, for fear slipt out of sight.
> Thus her good wit, their cunning over-macht,
> Were not these conycatchers conycatchd?[10]

If this anecdote relates to a public playhouse, as its dating indicates it must, then it suggests a few additional points about gallery audiences. Wealthy noblewomen could expect to see plays there unescorted except by their pages. Cutpurses were regularly in attendance. Nor did crowds come to the playhouse so thick and so fast that a gallery-goer might not climb the stairs alone. This last point fits in with the implications of Philip Henslowe's takings from the galleries of the Rose. His average income was less than half the maximum.[11] Overcrowding, except at new plays and exceptionally scandalous events like *A Game at Chesse*, was not usually the playgoer's main problem.

By John Orrell's calculations, allowing an 18-inch spread and also 18 inches fore and aft for each person on the 'degrees', the Globe's galleries could hold almost 1000 on each of the two lower levels, and on the third level where sight lines would have required a steep rake and less depth of degrees, about 750.[12] By the same criterion the Fortune galleries could hold 880 in the lower galleries and 660 in the

upper tier. The allocation of space for the Christ Church performance in 1605 which Orrell uses to obtain his figures in fact allocated
18 inches in width for everyone, but gave a relatively generous 30
inches fore and aft for lords and 24 inches fore and aft for Court ladies
and the king's servants. The gentlemen in the upper tier were
confined to 18 inches each way. It seems plausible to assume that
the public amphitheatres would provide the minimum spacing for
all their customers, though of course Lambarde's third penny 'for a
quiet standing'[13] (i.e. a seat) might have given access to a more
spacious arrangement, like the Oxford allocation for Court ladies,
close to the stage. If so, the totals for the lower galleries would be less
than a thousand each. The lords' rooms must have been spacious,
with benches or stools. On the Swan's balcony De Witt sketched not
more than two people to a room. A reference from about 1609 to a
gallant who 'Plays at Primero over the stage'[14] indicates that there
could easily be space for a card-game in the lords' rooms. Primero
was a gambling game rather like poker involving three or more
players.

5. The audience in the 'lords' rooms' at the Swan, a detail from
De Witt's sketch

This disposition, with space for about 800 in the yard and over 2000 in the various galleries, matches the contemporary estimates for the total capacity of the amphitheatres. The Spanish Ambassador reckoned over 3000 at the second Globe, which being built on the same foundations as the first must have had a similar total capacity. De Witt gave the same total for the Swan in 1596.[15]

(B) THE HALL PLAYHOUSES

The capacity of the amphitheatres, and their open yards, comprised the main obvious differences of the 'public' playhouses from the 'private' halls. Francis Beaumont spoke of the Blackfriars in 1609 as a court where 'a thousand men in judgement sit' (2.84). Modern estimates put its capacity rather lower, and the set of drawings for a playhouse which Inigo Jones made in about 1616, almost certainly for the Cockpit, provided seating for less than 750 people, at 18 inches per bottom.[16] There was no yard or standing area of any kind in the hall playhouses – the 'pit' was filled with bench seating – so it is possible to make a reasonable estimate of their capacity using the Christ Church figures. On that basis none of the indoor playhouses would accommodate more than about a quarter of the amphitheatre capacity.

The first 'private' playhouses came into use in the decade follow-ing the first public amphitheatre. Paul's choir school was using a small playhouse adjacent to the Chapter House in 1575.[17] It accommodated perhaps less than 200 people, and was in use inter-mittently between 1575 and 1590 and again from 1600 to 1606. The master of the rival company to Paul's, the Chapel Children, built a playhouse in a hall in the Blackfriars precinct in 1576, soon after Paul's started using their commercial venue. Little is known about it, and it was in use only for eight years, up to 1583–84, when for a brief season a combined company of Chapel and Paul's Children under John Lyly played there. From 1590 to 1600 no boy companies and no indoor playhouses, except possibly the occasional hall at a City inn, were available in London. The durable beginnings of hall playhouse use came towards the end of the century, through a peculiar combination of circumstances.

The most famous of the hall venues, the second Blackfriars playhouse, was built in 1596 by James Burbage, builder of the original Theatre, for his adult players, Shakespeare's company. By 1596 the twenty-one-year lease of the ground he had built the Theatre on was

Paulus wharfe

6. A section of Hollar's 'Long View' of London, printed in 1644. According to R. A. Foakes, *Illustrations of the English Stage 1580–1642*, Scolar Press 1985, pp. 39–41, the roofline below and to the right of St Bride's tall, four-spired tower, with two slender chimneys or lanterns rising from the centre, is most likely to be the roof under which Burbage constructed the second Blackfriars playhouse in 1596

nearly up, and he had good reason to doubt whether he would be able to renew it. Moreover the City authorities were winning their battle to exclude players from the inns inside the City limits where they sometimes sheltered in the winter. In 1594 Lord Hunsdon had to seek specific permission from the City authorities for his new company, the Chamberlain's Men, which included Shakespeare among its sharers, to play at the Cross Keys Inn at Gracechurch Street, up from London Bridge, through the winter months.[18] No such permission was given after 1595. That constraint, which left the players only with the open-air amphitheatres in the suburbs for winter playing, probably persuaded Burbage into the gamble of building a new hall playhouse inside the City walls in place of the lost City inns.

He chose his site advisedly. He bought an imposing building in the 'liberty' of Blackfriars, an area on the fashionable western side close to the City of Westminster, inside the London walls but free of the City of London's jurisdiction because of its ancient status as a monastic precinct. There he had no more need to worry about the City authorities than he did with his Theatre in the suburbs of Middlesex. Moreover the smaller hall playhouse was much closer to the area where the wealthiest playgoers lived. Potentially it was an ingenious solution for the problem of replacing the Theatre, and an emphatic shift up-market, from the amphitheatre serving primarily the penny-paying standers in the yard to the 'private' or 'select' kind of audience which expected seats and a roof over their heads.

Sadly for Burbage he miscalculated his popularity among the wealthy. After he had spent £600 on the acquisition of a great chamber, once used for meetings of Parliament, and converted it into his playhouse, the wealthy and influential residents of Blackfriars petitioned the Privy Council to forbid the players using it, on the grounds that it

will grow to be a very great annoyance and trouble, not only to all the noblemen and gentlemen thereabout inhabiting but allso a generall inconvenience to all the inhabitants of the same precinct, both by reason of the great resort and gathering together of all manner of vagrant and lewde persons that, under cullor of resorting to the players, will come thither and worke all manner of mischeefe, and allso to the great pestring and filling up of the same precinct...and besides, that the same playhouse is so neere the Church that the noyse of the drummes and trumpetts will greatly disturbe and hinder both the ministers and parishioners in tyme of devine service and sermons. (2.24)

This last point of objection reveals some of the grounds for the petition. It was not just the standard view that churchgoing and playgoing were antithetical – plays were officially forbidden at times of divine service anyway – but that the characteristic noises of adult players at the public amphitheatres were about to be imported into a neighbourhood which had previously tolerated only the Chapel Children in a hall playhouse. The martial noise of drums and trumpets was an affliction the amphitheatres visited on their neighbours, but not the small enclosed playhouses and their boy company repertoire. 'Public' playing was trying to penetrate a superior residential area. Such effrontery roused the opposition even of Burbage's own noble patron, who happened to live close by the new playhouse. As the petition carefully noted,

one Burbage hath lately bought certaine roomes in the...precinct neere adjoining unto the dwelling houses of the right honorable the Lord Chamberlaine and the Lord of Hunsdon...

and in case anyone thought that this signified the Lord Chamberlain's personal protection for his company's new venture, he himself signed the petition to the Privy Council, of which he himself was the executive member for all matters concerning playing. It was either a great betrayal, or a total failure of consultation. Burbage miscalculated disastrously the willingness of the nobility and especially of his own patron to tolerate adult players in that vicinity.

Had the times not been so prosperous for the two adult companies which then monopolised London playing, the ban on using the Blackfriars would probably have destroyed the Chamberlain's Men. Burbage, violently at odds with the owner of the land on which his Theatre stood, had purchased, not leased, the Blackfriars property, a heavy financial commitment even before he added the cost of converting it into a playhouse. He was about to lose the Theatre and now his money was trapped in the abortive Blackfriars venture. Moreover the other lucrative central City locations were firmly barred to the players. As the Blackfriars petition protested,

now all players being banished by the Lord Mayor from playing within the Cittie by reason of the great inconveniences and ill rule that followeth them, they now thincke to plant themselves in liberties.

Once the inhabitants of the Blackfriars put a stop to that idea, the players had to retreat to their suburban amphitheatres. Out of that retreat, and out of Burbage's financial straits, came a rather desperate, second-best expedient, the Globe.

The Globe was an afterthought in the wake of the Blackfriars disaster. Burbage himself died in 1597 and his two sons and heirs, Cuthbert and Richard, had to invent a new arrangement to finance the rebuilding of the old Theatre as the Globe. They offered shares in the building to the five leading players in the company, including Shakespeare.[19] The leading sharers thus became the first and only co-owners of the playhouse in which they performed. This arrangement, arising as it did out of the Burbage misfortunes, perhaps as much as anything else guaranteed the stability and security of tenure which Shakespeare's company enjoyed all the way to the closure of the playhouses in 1642. Not for them the mere three-year tenancies allowed to their rivals under Henslowe, Alleyn, Beeston and the other playhouse-owning impresarios. They themselves were both impresarios and tenants. The Lord Chamberlain in 1596 did more for Shakespeare's art, and his income, than he knew.

But the success of Shakespeare's company at the Globe must not be allowed to obscure the fact, with its implications about audience preferences, that it came second to the Blackfriars in James Burbage's planning. Since the Blackfriars swallowed up his available funds he could not have been planning in 1596 to provide both an indoor City playhouse and a suburban amphitheatre for his players.[20] He considered that the future of the adult playing companies lay in the City's hall playhouse exclusively. The Globe was a retreat in the face of the unexpected opposition by Burbage's patron and the nobility in the west of the City, a reluctant renewal of the old style of playhouse originally erected thirty-two years before.

The 1596 Blackfriars playhouse differed from the Red Lion and the Theatre in three major ways.[21] Each of the three differences indicates the drastic shift which took place between 1567 and 1596 in the kind of playgoer at whom Burbage's company aimed its plays. The first difference was in the sharply reduced size of the auditorium, and the switch of allegiance from the 'public' tradition to the 'private' tradition of playing in halls. The second was the sharp increase in admission prices. Where the basic price at the Theatre was one penny, and sixpence could buy a lord's room, at the Blackfriars once it came into use as a playhouse the minimum admission price was set at sixpence, and a box alongside the stage cost five times the minimum, two shillings and sixpence or half a crown.[22] For apprentices, who earned no wages and were dependent on their master's generosity even for the pennyworth of admission to an amphitheatre or baiting house, the hall playhouses were quite out of reach. Contemporary comments acknowledge the occasional 'shops *Foreman*...That may judge for his *sixe-pence*' (2.83), but the main clientele must have been the privileged, principally gallants, law students, the wealthier citizens and the nobility. They were a 'select' audience, as Marston called them,[23] selected by their affluence, who could relish the fiction that they attended a 'private' playhouse, away from the common throng.

The third difference of the Blackfriars from the Globe reflected the shift in priorities even more precisely. In the amphitheatres the poorest patrons were closest to the stage, standing at its rim while the wealthier sat behind them in the galleries. In the hall playhouses not only were the boxes given a better position than the lords' rooms in the amphitheatres, flanking the stage instead of behind it, but also the more you paid the closer you were to the stage. One shilling and sixpence gave you a bench in the pit immediately in front of the stage. All that the minimal sixpence provided was a space in the topmost gallery, farthest from the stage. The Blackfriars auditorium established for the first time in England the disposition of seat prices which still rules in every modern indoor theatre. The highest prices are for the stalls and boxes, and the lowest for the balcony or the 'gods' at the top and rear of the house. If proximity to the stage is any reflection of priorities, Burbage's reversed themselves between his building the Theatre for the common penny-payer in 1576 and setting up the Blackfriars for the wealthy in 1596.

The upper frater at the Blackfriars where Burbage constructed his playhouse was a long hall 46 feet wide by 100 feet in length. He built his auditorium not in the round but longitudinally, setting the stage across the shorter dimension to make a playhouse measuring altogether 66 feet by 46 feet. A great circular stone stairway gave admission at the end farthest from the stage. The central pit was approximately 28 feet square, probably the same width as the stage itself. On each flank of the stage were boxes, and along the two long sides and over the stone stairway, all round the pit, ran curved galleries, either two or three levels – the hall had a very high roof – which would have been about 8 feet 6 inches in depth.[24] The pit and the boxes flanking the stage could not have seated more than about 200 people. Three galleries of 8 feet 6 inches depth with four degrees each and some walkway space at the back could take another 200 at each level. The total capacity of a two-gallery house would thus have been barely 600, and of a three-gallery house (allowing for fewer degrees in the top level because of steeper sight-lines) perhaps 700. The boxes, judging by Peacham's story, appear to have accommodated more than the lords' rooms shown in the Swan drawing, though the wealthiest patrons might well have reserved exclusive use of a box for themselves by paying more. There is a record of an affray at the Blackfriars in 1632 which tells us that the Countess of

Essex occupied a box there, squired only by her stepson Captain
Essex. The Essex affray on the Blackfriars stage tells us a number of
things about the more aristocratic patrons at this type of playhouse,
and their behaviour. The lady was the Earl of Essex's new wife, who
had an already-established reputation for sexual indiscretions. Her
stepson and escort was a soldier on leave from the Dutch army. In the
civil conflict of the 1640s he was to command a foot regiment in the
Parliamentary army under his cousin the Earl. His opponent at the
Blackfriars in 1632, the Irish Lord Thurles, was about twenty-one,
and newly arrived in London from Edinburgh. He became the Earl of
Ormond only three weeks after the affray, and in later years served as
the King's commander in the field and Lord Deputy of Ireland.

The Essex version lays the blame on the younger man. According
to the record,

This Captaine attending and accompanying my Lady of Essex in a boxe at the
playhouse at the blackfryers, the said lord coming upon the stage, stood
before them and hindred their sight. Captain Essex told his lordship they had
payd for their places as well as hee, and therefore intreated him not to deprive
them of the benefitt of it. Whereupon the lord stood up yet higher and
hindred more their sight. Then Capt. Essex with his hand putt him a little by.
The lord then drewe his sword and ran full butt at him, though hee missed
him... [25]

The affray's immediate outcome was a hearing in Star Chamber and
a verbal apology from Lord Thurles. What is revealing about Blackfriars audiences in all this, though, is not just the social background
of these two truculent rufflers but the stations they took up for
watching the play.

Captain Essex was with the Countess in a box flanking the stage, at
stage level. Lord Thurles chose the position which the most exhibitionistic of gallants tended to adopt in the indoor playhouses, on
the stage itself. The practice of hiring a stool for an extra sixpence and
emerging with it from the tiring-house to sit and watch the play on
the stage itself was a long-established custom at the Blackfriars. In
this case whether out of ignorance, being new to London, or because
other young sprigs had already taken all the limited number of stools,
Lord Thurles was on his feet, standing in front of the box occupied by
the Essex party.[26] Captain Essex's attempts to shift him so that the
box-holders could see the play were what provoked the quarrel. The
whole affair was an ironic endorsement of Dekker's advice to a
gullible gallant in *The Gull's Hornbook*:

let our Gallant. . .presently advance himselfe up to the Throne of the Stage. I
meane not into the Lords roome (which is now but the Stages suburbs): No,

7. The Duke of Ormonde (Lord Thurles), from a portrait in the
National Portrait Gallery (Catalogue no. 370)

those boxes, by the iniquity of custome, conspiracy of waiting-women and
Gentlemen-Ushers, that there sweat together, and the covetousness of
Sharers, are contemptibly thrust into the reare, and much new Satten is there
dambd, by being smothred to death in darknesse. But on the very Rushes
where the Comedy is to daunce, yea under the state of *Cambises* himselfe,
must our fethered *Estridge*, like a piece of Ordnance, be planted valiantly
(because impudently) beating downe the mewes and hisses of the opposed
rascality... [27]

Dekker goes on to advise his gull to wait until the play is about to
begin before appearing with stool and sixpence to occupy the most
conspicuous position on the stage. Captain Essex was bound to
occupy a box, since he had a lady with him, and ladies did not sit on
the stage itself. Lord Thurles was positioning himself where any
noble and wealthy young man-about-town visiting the play on his
own would think of going, especially if he was newly arrived and
keen to show himself to his peers in London.

The practice of allowing the most important patrons to sit on the
stage began with the first boy companies probably as early as the
1570s. The adult players never offered it at the open amphitheatres.
There the interference which the stool-sitters created for everyone
else's vision would have been rather worse, given the greater height
of the stage, and the numbers occupying the flanking galleries and
standing at the sides of the stage. Moreover the public stages, lacking
the rails which divided the actors from the audience in the hall
playhouses, and raised five or more feet above the ground, would
have seemed more precarious even without the mews and hisses of
the penny-payers standing close up against the stage platform.
Webster wrote an induction for a play which Shakespeare's company
took from the Blackfriars boys in 1604, in which he burlesqued the
behaviour of two gallants who insist on importing to the amphitheatre the hall playhouse custom of viewing the play from stools on
stage.[28] Contrariwise Beaumont's Induction for *The Knight of the
Burning Pestle* for the Blackfriars boys in 1607 burlesqued the
expectations of the Grocer and his wife and apprentice by bringing
them up onto the stage and seating them on stools to comment on
the play. Sitting on stools on stage was clearly taken to be a very
distinct mark of the difference between the audiences for the adult
plays in the amphitheatres and those for boy plays in the hall
playhouses through the decade when they were rivals. That immediate rivalry faded in 1609 when Shakespeare's company took over the
Blackfriars. Stool-sitting remained as a divide thereafter, but more as
a mark to distinguish the types of playhouse and their clientele than
the kinds of company using them.

Once James was on the throne, and had graced the leading companies with his family's patronage, the impresarios who built the playhouses concentrated almost exclusively on the hall type. Henslowe replaced the old Bear Garden in 1614 with the Hope, intending it to function in the old multipurpose way as both playhouse and baiting-house. But the bears won against the players, as Hollar's label in his 'Long View' engraving indicates, and all the other new projects were indoor playhouses. When the tiny Paul's playhouse finally closed in 1606 a boy company set up in a hall in Whitefriars. Once the King's Men started the practice of adult companies offering daily performances at Blackfriars several attempts were made to emulate them. A plan for a playhouse at Porter's Hall in 1615 failed, but a year later Christopher Beeston opened the Cockpit in Drury Lane with an adult company, and in 1629 Richard Gunnell opened a third, Salisbury Court. Near the closure Davenant was prevented from launching a grandiose scheme for an indoor playhouse in Fleet Street even closer to the Inns of Court. The acting companies for all these projects were adult, and some companies changed from amphitheatre to hall – for instance from the Red Bull to the Cockpit – as readily as the King's Men switched between the Blackfriars and the Globe. Whatever the company, and whatever its repertory, the trend went emphatically towards the hall type of playhouse. The distinctive features of the hall playhouses, their all-seat auditorium, the roof, the higher prices which kept apprentices away, and the opportunities for display which stools on stage provided, were part of that trend. Hot-blooded young men jockeying for social prominence were always likely to regard the crowds in the amphitheatre yards and the lack of stools on their stages as tokens of an alien environment. By the time the king was provoked into banning the use of stools at the smallest hall playhouse, Salisbury Court, in 1639, the division between aristocratic hall and plebeian amphitheatre was nearly complete.

(C) PERFORMING CONDITIONS

The physical conditions of the two types of playhouse did not change widely between 1576 and 1642. There was evidently some improvement in the design of the amphitheatres, particularly in the system of admitting people to the different sections of the auditorium, and there may have been some changes also in the private playhouses. Burbage built the Blackfriars in 1596 as a replacement for his Theatre, and must have designed it along familiar lines, at least at the

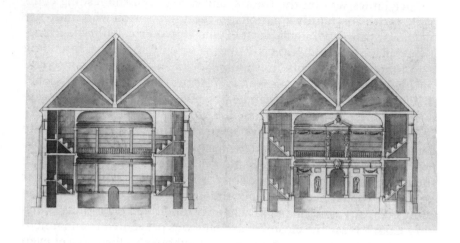

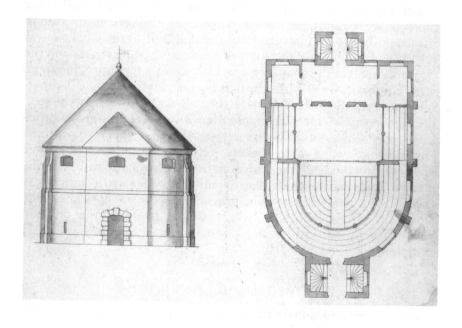

8. Plans made in about 1616, probably for Beeston's Cockpit
playhouse in Drury Lane, by Inigo Jones

stage and tiring-house end. Certainly Shakespeare's company had no trouble alternating between the Globe and Blackfriars with the same plays, even though the Blackfriars stage was half the size of the Globe's. The Blackfriars auditorium was very different from the Globe's, having seating for everyone and putting the cheapest places furthest from the stage. But it was still spartan by modern standards, more functional than ornate. Even Inigo Jones's design for an indoor playhouse, made probably in 1616 for Beeston's rival to the Black-friars, the Cockpit or Phoenix,[29] seems colourful in its decoration but conservative in other provision, and certainly made no allowance for such comfort stations as a bar or toilets. The whole playgoing experience with all its physical discomforts calls for detailed comment.

The amphitheatres needed optimum daylight for their plays, so they established a pattern of performances starting at 2 p.m. which prevailed even when the principal playhouses became candle-lit halls. In October 1594 the Lord Chamberlain wrote to the Lord Mayor on behalf of Shakespeare's company, assuring him

that, where heretofore they began not their Plaies till towards fower a clock, they will now begin at two, & have don betwene fower and five.[30]

This offer effectively closed an issue which had run for some time. Afternoon church services began at 2 p.m., and the clash between churchgoing and playgoing was a constant irritant to the more puritanical divines and city fathers. A 4 p.m. start for the perform-ances, and shorter performance times, was one solution. The Lord Chamberlain's was the other.

Perhaps it was in oblique response to this that most playwrights insisted that performances did not usually last more than two hours. Whetstone wrote in 1578 that plays took 'three howers', and Dekker in 1609 mentioned players 'glad to play three houres for two pence',[31] but most of them, even Shakespeare, refer to 'these two short hours', or the 'two hour's traffic of the stage'.[32] In the absence of watches, of course, and the kind of precise timekeeping which only became necessary when railway timetables were invented, an hour was a fairly flexible device. The likely duration of most performances, which at the amphitheatres were followed by a jig and in the halls were preceded by music, was nearer three hours. Some such time, allowing for the arrival and dispersal of the crowd of playgoers, is indicated by a petition sponsored by the Puritan minister of the church adjacent to the Blackfriars playhouse in 1619. It spoke of unruly crowds gathering 'almost everie daie in the winter tyme (not

forbearinge the tyme of Lent) from one or twoe of the clock till sixe
att night, which beinge the tyme alsoe most usuall for Christeninges
and burialls and afternoones service, wee cannot have passage to the
Church for performance of those necessary duties, the ordinary
passage for a great part of the precinct aforesaid being close by the
play house dore'.[33] John Davies' courtier 'Fuscus' usually spent from
1 p.m. till 6 p.m. at a play in the 1590s, confirming the claims of the
Blackfriars petitioners. It is probably a token of the prestige now held
by Shakespeare's company, which by this time was alternating
between the Blackfriars in winter and the Globe in summer, that it
could sustain against this kind of pressure its old amphitheatre
tradition of afternoon performances even at Blackfriars. In later years
some evening performances were put on at Blackfriars, but they were
probably special occasions, such as Queen Henrietta Maria's visits,
for which the Master of the Revels picked up the bill.[34]

The practice which Shakespeare's company introduced at the
Blackfriars after 1609, of performing on every afternoon in winter in
contrast with the boy company's once-weekly performances, must
have been a major reason for its predominance as the most highly
regarded of the London playhouses. In the first decade of the century
adults playing daily in the amphitheatres gradually prevailed over
the boys playing weekly in the halls. Once the adults could play daily
in the halls their success was beyond question. But it was also a
major cause of discomfort to the local inhabitants. The regular daily
flow of large numbers of playgoers was an unpleasant novelty in
London, which had no real means of policing it. So long as the
amphitheatres were in the fields to the north of the city, accessible
on foot, there was no major difficulty. The land across London Bridge
too, having supported bull- and bear-baiting houses and whorehouses
for most of the century, could carry the flow of playgoers easily
enough. The poorest crossed the bridge, while the wealthier patrons
paid sixpence for a boat to get them to the Globe, or the Rose, since
the Thames wherries offered the nearest thing to a taxi service
London had at the time. In 1604 a prodigal gallant had the choice, as
Middleton described it, to

venture beyond sea, that is, in a choice paire of Noble mens Oares, to the
Bank-side, where he must sit out the breaking up of a Comedie, or the first
cut of a Tragedie; or rather (if his humour so serve him) to call in at the
Black-fryers, where he shall see a neast of Boyes able to ravish a man.[35]

There was a playhouse of some kind within two miles of nearly every
Londoner.

So long as the boy company occupied Blackfriars Middleton's

latter choice only produced difficulties for the locals once a week. But from 1609 it became a daily event, and by that time the relatively novel habit which drew the privileged to travel by coach had created a fresh problem, the traffic jam. The petition of 1619 described it in these terms:

> there is daylie such resort of people, and such multitudes of Coaches (whereof many are Hackney Coaches, bringinge people of all sortes) that sometymes all our streetes cannott containe them. But that they Clogg up Ludgate alsoe, in such sort, that both they endanger the one the other breake downe stalles, throwe downe mens goodes from their shopps. And the inhabitantes there cannott come to their howses, nor bringe in their necessary provisions of beere, wood, coale or haye, nor the Tradesmen or shopkeepers utter their wares, nor the passenger goe to the common water staires without danger of their lives and lymmes.[36]

Coaches were an uncommon nuisance. In January 1634 George Garrard wrote about a Privy Council attempt to control the parking of coaches:

> Here hath been an Order of the Lords of the Council hung up in a Table near *Paul's* and the *Black-Fryars*, to command all that Resort to the Play-House there to send away their Coaches, and to disperse Abroad in *Paul's Church-Yard, Carter Lane*, the Conduit in *Fleet-Street*, and other Places, and not to return to fetch their Company, but they must trot afoot to find their Coaches, 'twas kept very strictly for two or three Weeks, but now I think it is disorder'd again. (2.168)

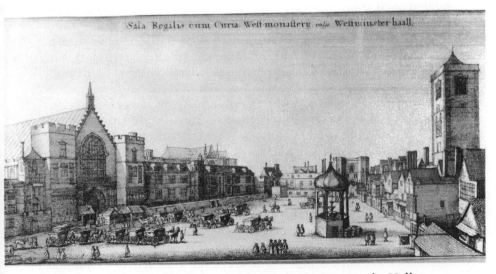

9. Coaches in Whitehall, an engraving from the 1630s by Hollar
(P1040)

The City authorities never had much reason to be grateful to the players.

Once at the playhouse, whether summoned by flag, trumpet and drum to the suburbs, ferried across the river or carried by coach into the City, the two or three hours' traffic of the stage would be jammed in with a variety of other distractions: the weather, food and drink, smells, noise, cutpurses, and occasionally riots. Of all these the weather seems to have been the least irksome difficulty. Edmond Howes' extension of Stow's *Annales* mentions prolonged bad weather through eleven periods up to 1631, and yet there is not a single reference in the entire seventy-five years of playgoing to the deterrent effect of rain or snow.[37] The galleries of course could shelter more than two-thirds of the total capacity from rain, and the stage itself was covered. Overcast wintry weather blighted the first performance of *The White Devil* at the Red Bull in 1610, by reducing the available daylight, but that was always potentially a problem. All the open-air amphitheatres aligned their stages with their backs to the midsummer solstice, so that the players would have a uniformly shadowed stage to work on.[38] It is possible that a low winter sun, shining from just above the roof behind the stage, would have bothered spectators in the upper galleries even more than rain. On the whole it seems probable that playgoing at the open-air play-houses was troubled more by acoustic problems than by bad weather. A large open auditorium with a good proportion of the audience on its feet would certainly generate a level of background noise much greater than the smaller gatherings, all seated, in the hall playhouses. The players must have had remarkable volume control if they managed the transfer from amphitheatre to hall without damaging a few eardrums.

Once settled in place it was possible for playgoers at an amphi-theatre to distract themselves with refreshments while the play was in progress. Until the hall playhouses, which had a practical need for pauses between the acts so that the lights could be trimmed, began to predominate over the amphitheatres, performances were con-tinuous. Food and drink and the need for toilets consequently became a distraction from the play while it was in performance. Thomas Platter reported in 1599 that 'during the performance food and drink are carried round the audience, so that for what one cares to pay one may also have refreshment' (2.32). The food seems prin-cipally to have been apples (there are several references to 'pippins' being used as ammunition), and nuts. Jasper Mayne spoke of the audience in the cheapest gallery of a hall playhouse who 'sixpence pay and sixpence crack'.[39] Fletcher has a character in *Wit Without Money* (1614) describe youths who 'break in at playes like prentices for three a groat, and crack Nuts with the Scholars in peny Rooms again, and fight for Apples' (2.102). John Tatham mentions pears (again used as ammunition) in 1641, and Overbury's Character 'A Puny-Clarke' (a puisne or junior law clerk) 'eates Ginger bread at a Play-house' (2.196, 105). The drink offered was either water (see 2.105) or bottle-ale. In 1615 John Stephens, writing a set of 'Characters' in imitation of Overbury's recently published collection, included among the features of 'a base Mercenary Poet' that 'when he heares his play hissed, hee would rather thinke bottle-Ale is opening'. Webster, who probably composed many of the 'Characters' in Overbury's volume and who wrote a reply to Stephens' character of 'A Common Player', was the likely target of this jibe. Henry Fitzgeoffery describes him in the gallery at Blackfriars in 1617, where bottled ale was presumably available, although the restricted circulation at the indoor playhouses where all the audience were seated must have made life difficult for the itinerant sellers.

The consequent form of distraction to refreshments, the need for toilets, is a feature of playgoing for which there is regrettably little evidence. There is no provision for it anywhere in Inigo Jones's two sets of theatre plans. We have to look for such circumstantial evidence as we can find, and even this is patchy. Harington's

Palatium Archiepiscopi Cantuariensis propæ Londinum   vulgo   Lambeth House.

10. A view of Lambeth (with the Archbishop, Laud, embarking) by Hollar (P1038). The sheds hanging over the river on the right are possibly privies

celebrated *Metamorphosis of Ajax* gives a hint of the likely provision at playhouses, by its clear differentiation between the defecation of solids, the subject of his treatise, and urinating. The former required elaborate constructions. The latter was too trivial a business for Harington to bother with. Platter offers some help here by describing what was available for that purpose in the central pedestrian precinct in London, St Paul's. It was, to put it mildly, minimal.

> Outside one of the doors is a hewn stone, and a standard nearby where water may be obtained, and often a vessel stands by it for passing urine, giving a pleasant odour to the passers-by![40]

I would suspect that the Globe offered no privy for the defecation of solids closer than the river,[41] and that buckets served for the passing of urine. Privacy there was none, and how women managed we can only guess.

Smells were the subject of comment in a number of ways. Predictably when the hall playhouses were resurrected in 1599 and 1600 their supporters made the point that the more select audiences there were freed from the occupational smells that artisans carried with them. Marston wrote about the audience at Paul's in 1600 that 'A man shall not be choakte / With the stench of Garlicke, nor be pasted / To the barmy Jacket of a Beer-Brewer.' (2.40). Dekker first published his dislike of garlic-breathed 'stinkards' in 1606 and used the term regularly thereafter.[42] By implication all such stinkards were

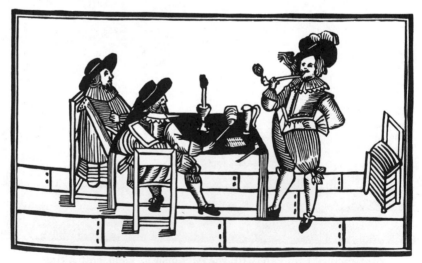

11. A woodcut from a broadside ballad, showing gallants taking tobacco

gathered in the yards of the amphitheatres. The distinctive smell at the indoor playhouses, and in the lords' rooms at the amphitheatres, was tobacco. Sir John Davies praised it ironically in an epigram written in or about 1593:

> ...that vile medicine it doth far excell,
> Which by sir Thomas Moore hath bin propounded,
> For this is thought a gentleman-like smell.[43]

The equally ironic More had recommended eating onions to take away the smell of leeks and then garlic to take away the smell of onions. Guilpin recorded the gentleman-like feature at an amphitheatre playhouse in 1598:

> See you him yonder who sits o're the stage,
> With the Tobacco-pipe now at his mouth?   (2.29)

and in the same year Henry Buttes commented on the cheaper local form of tobacco which was being tried as an alternative to the novelty from Virginia:

> It chaunce'd me gazing at the Theater,
> To spie a Lock-Tobacco-Chevalier
> Clowding the loathing ayr with foggie fume
> Of Dock-Tobacco, friendly foe to rume.   (2.31)

Presumably it was rheum, not room, of which tobacco was the enemy. The meticulous Thomas Platter described the habit with his customary detail at the time of his visit to the newly-opened Globe in 1599.

In the ale-houses tobacco or a species of wound-wort are also obtainable for one's money, and the powder is lit in a small pipe, the smoke sucked into the mouth, and the saliva is allowed to run freely, after which a good draught of Spanish wine follows. This they regard as curious medicine for defluctions, and as a pleasure, and the habit is so common with them that they always carry the instrument on them, and light up on all occasions, at the play, in the taverns or elsewhere, drinking as well as smoking together, as we sit over wine, and it makes them riotous and merry, and rather drowsy, just as if they were drunk.[44]

Dekker inevitably made his gullible gallant follow the habit, and Fitzgeoffery included a complaint about smokers in his survey of the Blackfriars audience in 1617. In 1631 Richard Brathwait spoke of ruffians smoking and making themselves offensive in other ways in the twopenny gallery of an amphitheatre playhouse (2.151).

Sitting on stools to display their fine clothes and smoking to show their wealth were not the only marks that distinguished gallants at playhouses. By no means the least obtrusive feature of any Elizabethan gathering was the headgear. Hats were worn indoors as well as out, and there is no reason to suppose that a gallant minded like Lord Thurles would bother to lower his feather for the sake of the multitude behind him. Hats were worn in a descending social order of obtrusiveness. Gallants wore crowned hats with feathers which might be as broad and opaque as an ostrich plume. Citizens, and most ladies, wore shorter hats with smaller or no feathers. Artisans wore flat caps or woollen bonnets.[45] You were likely to suffer least from finding yourself behind obtrusive headgear if you stood in the yard. In the galleries hats could get in the way, but the steep rake of the degrees and the relative narrowness of the galleries would have made the problem fairly manageable. The worst position must have been in a box at Blackfriars in the dark behind half a dozen stool-sitting gallants in their ostrich plumes and tobacco clouds.

Human beings, even when long-haired, lose more than 30% of their body heat from the head, and in the little ice age of Elizabethan times it must have seemed sensible to keep the head covered for most of the day and night. Hats, in the whole range from royal crowns to domestic night-caps, were a particularly prominent feature of Elizabethan costume. Philip Stubbes saw them as a sign of the evil times in 1583:

Sometymes thei use them sharpe on the crowne, pearking up like the spere, or shaft of a steeple, standying a quarter of a yarde above the croune of their heades...Othersome be flat, and broad in the croune, like the battlementes of a house. An other sorte have round crounes, sometymes with one kinde of bande, sometymes with an other, now blacke, now white, now russet, now red, now grene, now yellowe: now this, now that, never content with one colour or fashion two daies to an ende...some are of silke, some of Velvet, some of Taffetie, some of Sarcenet, some of Wooll, whiche is more curious, some of a certain kind of fine haire...And so common a thing it is, that every Servyng man, countreiman, and other, even all indifferently, do weare of these hattes...And an other sort (as phantasticall as the rest) are content with no kind of Hat, without a great bunche of feathers of divers and sundrie colours.

Women were equally liable to suffer from the urge to show colourful variety:

Then, on top of these stately turrets (I meane their goodly heads wherein is more vanitie then true Philosophie now and then) stand their other capitall ornaments...according to the variable fantasies of their serpentine minds.
(*The Anatomy of Abuses*, D7v–8r, F4v)

It would have been an unusually modest, or considerate, or warm-blooded playgoer in any of the playhouses, indoors or out, who removed his or her headgear during the performance.

The 'plumed dandebrat' as Fitzgeoffery called him, with his feather and his sword, was a constant presence in the playhouses throughout the period. As early as 1563 Lawrence Humphrey noted the idler who 'licentiously roames in ryot, coasting the stretes with wavering plumes, hangd to a long side blade, & pounced in silkes...haunteth plaies, feastes, bathes and banketings' (2.1). Feathers were not popular with most observers. Samuel Rowlands wrote in 1600 of a gallant's feather as 'his heades lightness-proclaymer',[46] a jibe which Middleton elaborated a few years later:

His head was drest up in white Feathers like a Shuttle Cock, which agreed so wel with his braine, being nothing but Corke, that two of the biggest of the Guard might very easily have tost him with Battledores, and made good sport with him in his Majesties great Hall.   *(Father Hubburds Tale.* C2r–2v)

Webster in his Induction to *The Malcontent* makes the point that the feather-merchants lived in the Blackfriars district. It was probably outside the Blackfriars playhouse in 1620 that the target of the anonymous *Haec-Vir: or the Womanish-Man* prepared himself for his grand entry:

(in the midst of his pride or riches) at a Play-house...(before he dare enter) with the *Jacobs*-staffe of his owne eyes and his Pages, hee takes a full survey of himselfe, from the highest sprig in his feather, to the lowest spangle that shines in his Shoo-string.   (2.130)

Since the highest sprig in a gallant's feather was likely to be a good foot or more above eye-level for the unfortunates sitting behind, there was some point in the unpopularity of this fashion.

Feathers in the playhouses were not only on hats, and hats were not worn only by gallants, of course. Davenant's prologue for *The Unfortunate Lovers* (1638), a Blackfriars play, speaks of the citizenry in the twopenny galleries at the amphitheatre playhouses of a previous generation.

> ...they...to th' Theatre would come
> Ere they had din'd to take up the best room;
> Then sit on benches, not adorn'd with mats,
> And graciously did vail their high-crowned hats
> To every half-dress'd Player, as he still
> Through th'hangings peep'd to see how th' house did fill.
> Good easy judging souls, with what delight
> They would expect a jig, or target fight.   (2.182)

Citizenry in high-crowned hats are visible in the picture of an audience for one of the celebrated open-air sermons at St Paul's Cross in 1620. Citizens' hats did not include the frivolity of feathers, but women, even citizens' wives, not infrequently came to the play-

12. Detail from a painting of a sermon at Paul's Cross in 1620.
The audience are all in the clothing of citizens.

13. A woodcut from a broadside ballad, showing Elizabethan use of feathers and fan

house with fans made of feathers which no doubt could in a crowded hall prove as obtrusive as a plumed hat. They also wore starched ruffs around their necks. Their attire bulked them out to the point where a box would certainly have been more convenient for them than the eighteen-inch buttock space of the Christ Church Oxford entertainment, or the degrees in the galleries of Inigo Jones's 1616 plan. Rowlands described the trappings for a woman in 1600 as

> A Buske, a Mask, a Fanne, a monstrous Ruffe,
> A Boulster for their Buttockes and such stuffe.
> (*The Letting of Humours Blood*, F2r)

Jonson in 1609 wrote of the indoor playhouse '*Lady*, or *Pusill*, that weares maske or fan, / *Velvet*, or *Taffeta* cap' (2.83). The woodcuts attached to broadsheet ballads of the time show the fans and the bolster, and Hollar's engravings made in the 1630s show masked ladies. In the prologue to *Rule a Wife and have a Wife* (1624) Fletcher indicated one use for the fans:

> Nor blame the Poet if he slip aside,
> Sometimes lasciviously if not too wide.
> But hold your Fannes close, and then smile at ease,
> A cruel Sceane did never Lady please.

Such ladies seem to have characteristically placed themselves in the boxes of the indoor playhouses, like the Countess of Essex in 1632 at Blackfriars, though by the 1620s the term 'boxes' may have been extended to include what were originally known as the 'lords' rooms' over the stage in the amphitheatres. Thomas May's *The Heir*, written for the Red Bull in 1620, has an elegiac passage about Richard Burbage, who had died the previous year, which says

> ...Ladies in the boxes
> Kept time with sighs, and teares to his sad accents
> As had he truely been the man he seem'd   (*The Heir*, I.i)

May was probably thinking of the Blackfriars boxes, but the same ladies frequented the Globe in summer, where the equivalent places were on the balcony over the stage. In the Praeludium to Thomas Goffe's *The Careless Shepherdess* at Salisbury Court in 1638, a country gentleman summarises the place of ladies fairly precisely. After an exchange with a courtier and a gallant, they go offstage to take their places, and the gentleman suppresses his worry about the expense and announces

> I'le follow them, though't be into a Box.
> Though they did sit thus open on the Stage
> To shew their Cloak and Sute, yet I did think
> At last they would take sanctuary 'mongst
> The Ladies, lest some Creditor should spy them.
> 'Tis better looking o're a Ladies head,
> Or through a Lettice-window, then a grate.   (2.186)

The grate was the window in a debtors' prison.

(D) AUDITORIUM BEHAVIOUR

The final matter for consideration among the physical conditions of Shakespearean playgoing is not strictly physical, though on occasions it could have an emphatically physical impact. Audience behaviour, in individuals and in crowds, is a complex but vital part of the physical environment for playgoing. It is also more easily notable in its extreme forms than its everyday features. The extremes, of course, give some hints by their very notability about where the lines for good behaviour were usually drawn. It is certainly possible to identify some of the normative as well as the extreme features of audience behaviour, and even to see how behaviour changed between different playhouses.

Whether because of the greater numbers, the quantity of people standing on their feet close to the stage, or the broader social catchment, the crowds at the amphitheatres were markedly noisier than those in the hall playhouses. Nor, if John Lyly is to be believed, was the noise so much a matter of incidental shuffling or coughing as a direct vocal response to the performance. Lyly's prologues written in the 1580s for boy plays at Blackfriars and Paul's more than once express the hope that the gentlemanly audience in the halls would react with 'soft smiling, not loude laughing', or at worst would be too courteous to hiss. These were evidently common reactions elsewhere. Applause too was delivered with voice as well as hands. Drayton has a sonnet written in about 1600, which refers to his writing plays for Henslowe at the Rose amphitheatre and sitting in the 'thronged Theater' listening to the 'Showts and Claps at ev'ry little pawse, / When the proud Round on ev'ry side hath rung' (2.41). Shakespeare, Marston, Dekker and many other poets used epilogues to appeal for applause at the end of their plays, but it was clearly not only at the end that applause came. Moreover it was not just *'Brawny hands'* which delivered the audience's opinion.[47] William Fennor, bringing to the reader's eye in 1616 the text of a performance recently given to a royal audience, offered a pained account of his play's original reception at the Fortune amphitheatre:

> Yet to the multitude it nothing shewed;
> They screwed their scurvy jawes and look't awry,
> Like hissing snakes adjudging it to die:
> When wits of gentry did applaud the same,
> With silver shouts of high lowd sounding fame:
> Whil'st understanding grounded men contemn'd it,
> And wanting wit (like fooles to judge) condemn'd it.
> Clapping, or hissing, is the onely meane
> That tries and searches out a well writ Sceane,
> So it is thought by *Ignoramus* crew,
> But that good wits acknowledge's untrue;
> The stinkards oft will hisse without a cause,
> And for a baudy jeast will give applause.
> Let one but aske the reason why they roare
> They'll answere, cause the rest did so before. (2.114)

Hearing this kind of doggerel it is perhaps hardly surprising that audiences would feel free to applaud or hiss at any point throughout the performance. In 1640 John Tatham characterised the behaviour of audiences at the Fortune as 'a noyse / Of *Rables, Apple-wives* and Chimney-boyes, / Whose shrill confused Ecchoes loud doe cry, / Enlarge your *Commons*, We hate *Privacie'*. Crowds strengthen their sense of identity, their collective spirit, by vocal expression of their shared feelings. The audience was an active participant in the collective experience of playgoing, and was not in the habit of keeping its reactions private.

Tatham was a judge no less biassed than Fennor. His lines were written for a company expelled from the Fortune and forced to play instead at the Red Bull, and therefore understandably hostile to the Fortune and its playgoers. Not that the Red Bull, the other citizen playhouse in 1640, was noticeably quieter. Tatham's verses confirm the suspicion that when an audience was addressed as 'Gentlemen' or 'Gentles' the poet was likely to ask for less riotous behaviour than he had reason to expect.

> Here Gentlemen our Anchor's fixt; And wee
> (Disdaining Fortunes mutability)
> Expect your kinde acceptance; then wee'l sing
> (Protected by your smiles our ever-spring;)
> As pleasant as if wee had still possest
> Our lawfull Portion out of Fortunes brest:
> Onely wee would request you to forbeare
> Your wonted custome, banding *Tyle*, or Peare,
> Against our *curtaines*, to allure us forth.   (2.19)

Tatham evidently called them gentlemen because their wonted custom was so markedly ungentle.

Other commentators suggest that missiles might be used not only to hasten the beginning of a performance but to stop it, and even to make the players offer a different play, though this was an extreme and probably rare example of the customers insisting on getting what they wanted.[48] The usual form of audience behaviour is better indicated by the rare cases when authority laid down its laws for proper conduct. When the Court visited Cambridge in March 1632, for instance, and a play was provided for Charles's entertainment, the university authorities issued an order prescribing exactly what the student audience might and might not do.

Item: That no tobacco be taken in the Hall nor anywhere else publicly, and that neither at their standing in the streets, nor before the comedy begin, nor all the time there, any rude or immodest exclamations be made; nor any humming, hawking, whistling, hissing, or laughing be used, or any stamping or knocking, nor any such other uncivil or unscholarlike or boyish demeanour, upon any occasion; nor that any clapping of hands be had until the *Plaudite* at the end of the Comedy, except his Majesty, the Queen, or others of the best quality here, do apparently begin the same.[49]

The performance for which this instruction was issued entailed a seven-hour play, *The Rival Friends*, by the ambitious young academic Peter Hausted. The performance was a disaster, and helped drive the university's Vice-Chancellor to suicide on 1 April following the royal visit. His directive over student behaviour reads rather naively in retrospect. But it does indicate that even a student audience at Cambridge in the presence of the king was expected to react vocally in the course of a performance, and to maintain a distracting level of background noise and activity.

At the amphitheatres the vastly greater crowds, the packed mass of 'understanders' and the open-air acoustics could generate a higher intensity of audience reaction and hubbub than the halls with their padded benches and seated clientele. Small and darker as the candle-lit halls were, though, they did not change the most basic feature of the amphitheatre auditorium. They had windows to let in some light, and although at the 'Torchy Fryers' (2.145) the auditorium might not have had the candle power of the Globe's daylight, at neither playhouse was there any thought of using darkness to conceal the playgoers from the players and from themselves. Thus at every performance, while the play was on, Dekker's gull and his fellow gallants in the audience were free to distract themselves and others by their attention-seeking antics. Not surprisingly, there was a good deal of comment on their behaviour.

In the 1590s before the halls reopened gallants occupied the lords' rooms, or the front places in the galleries. Jonson's *Every Man Out* (1599), written for Shakespeare's company, identifies a gallant

> Who (to be thought one of the judicious)
> Sits with his armes thus wreath'd, his hat pull'd here,
> Cryes meaw, and nods, then shakes his empty head... (2.33)

in visible response to the action on the stage platform. This kind of self-conscious criticising was taken by Marston a year or two later at Paul's to be a matter for words as well as gestures. In the induction to *What You Will* (1601) Phylomusus, friend of the author and speaker of the prologue, complains of 'some halfe a dozen rancorous breasts' who come to the play to advertise their hostility to the poet. The outcome would be that

> ...some juicles husk,
> Some boundless ignorance should on sudden shoote
> His grosse knob'd burbolt, with *thats not so good*,
> *Mew, blirt, ha, ha, light Chaffy stuff*...

Deliberate interjections of that kind were probably most fashionable during the early years of the revived boy companies, when the so-called War of the Theatres harnessed the fashion for poetic railing, and put the attacks by poet against poet in front of titillated playgoers. Outside that phase, which did not outlive the boy companies of 1599–1608, the gallants in the hall playhouses would have made their peacock display as Jonson has Fitzdottrell describe it in *The Devil is an Ass* (1616):

> Today I goe to the *Blackfryers Play-house*,
> Sit i' the view, salute all my acquaintance,
> Rise up betweene the *Acts*, let fall my cloake,
> Publish a handsome man, and a rich suite
> (As that's a speciall end, why we goe thither,
> All that pretend, to stand for't o' the *Stage*)
> The Ladies aske who't that?

It may serve as a rough measure of the changes in behaviour at the playhouses which developed through the seventeenth century if we set Jonson's parody of a gallant at Blackfriars in 1616 against what Clitus-Alexandrinus (the Inns of Court poetaster Richard Brathwait) wrote about an amphitheatre playhouse in the 1620s. His Theophrastan character 'A Ruffian' is a belligerent swaggerer who attends plays on his own terms.

> ...To a play they will hazard to go, though with never a rag of money: where after the *second Act*, when the *Doore* is weakly guarded, they will make *forcible entrie*; a knock with a Cudgell is the worst; whereat though they grumble, they rest pacified upon their admittance. Forthwith, by violent assault and assent, they aspire to the two-pennie roome; where being furnished with Tinder, Match, and a portion of decayed *Barmoodas*, they smoake it most terribly, applaud a prophane jeast unmeasurably, and in the end grow distastefully rude to all the Companie. At the conclusion of all, they single out their *dainty Doxes*, to cloze up a fruitlesse day with a sinnefull evening.
> (2.151)

According to Brathwait such rufflers, probably paid-off soldiers, wore the swords and spurs of would-be gentlemen, though their behaviour was a crude burlesque of the gallants whom Jonson and Fitzgeoffery claimed to see at Blackfriars in 1616.

Playhouse crowds, for all their violence and exhibitionism, seem to have adopted an effective if anarchic regime of self-regulation. Authority of any kind was signally absent. If a pickpocket was caught, for instance, he could expect to be dealt with by a form of mob rule. Will Kempe in 1600 wrote of cutpurses being tied to one of the stage pillars 'for all the people to wonder at, when at a play they are taken pilfring' (2.37, 67). Cutpurses had to be expected at plays as readily as the whores whom Brathwait's ruffians looked for, not only in the amphitheatres. Dekker described their favourite localities as 'the antient great grandfather Powles, & all other little churches his children, besides Parish Garden, or rather (places of more benefit) publick, & by your leave private play houses.'[50] All the attendant characteristics of large gatherings could be found there, from the secretive thief to the gentleman and whore. Such figures, though, were a fairly small proportion of the total throng, parasites as they were upon the many whose first purpose was to see the play.[51]

3
Social composition

(A) SOCIAL CLASSES IN ENGLAND

Renaissance societies were much more sharply divided into distinct social roles and functions than modern societies. Money, dress, education, the entire pattern of living enforced a rigid social identity from which there was little chance of escape. The range in London was enormous, from the Earl of Salisbury, whose income in the central years 1608–12 was almost £50,000 a year, much of it exploiting his status as James's Lord Treasurer, down to the wife (and hence dependant) of a glover or shoemaker who might earn for his family no more than £3.6s.8d. a year.[1] There was nothing like the amorphous 'middle class' which provides the great bulk of modern theatre audiences. Within the broad social process which Louis B. Wright identified as a rising middle class in Elizabethan England[2] there were distinct individual growths: a large urban artisan class, chiefly in London; a citizen class of merchants and manufacturers in the major cities and ports; an increasingly literate class of schoolmasters, scriveners and clergy. Such growths imply a fairly high level of social mobility. But each class was distinct from the others in education, occupation, dress and income, and would have been shocked to find itself lumped in with any of the others. Almost all of these distinct classes in the middle stratum can be found amongst Shakespearean playgoers. Their composition broadly defines the composition of a majority in the London playhouse audiences, though the complete social range goes all the way from earls and even a queen to penniless rogues (Brathwait's rufflers) and the unemployed.

The Elizabethans who wrote about their society agreed in distinguishing four principal classes. Sir Thomas Smith, utilising his years of service representing England to the French court, wrote his account in the 1560s.[3] William Harrison contributed his 'Description' of England to Holinshed's *Chronicles* of 1577.[4] The two accounts agree to such an extent that one must be largely a copy of the other, a fact which is probably better seen as a confirmation of the accuracy of the first account than a sign of laziness in the second

49

writer. Thomas Wilson's account of 'The State of England, Anno
Dom. 1600'[5] broadly agrees with the two earlier descriptions, though
it supplies enough additional categories within the four principal
classes to suggest that there had been changes between the 1560s and
1600, and that Wilson was hardening against the social mobility
which the broadness of Harrison's and Smith's categories tended to
conceal. Whatever the shifts that the process of social change
imposed on contemporary commentators, it seems sensible to base a
picture of Elizabethan society on the four main classes of Harrison
and Smith. Modern analyses of social process suggest anyway that in
the first half of the seventeenth century social divisions were if
anything strengthening the separate identity of the main categories.[6]
It is probably also fair to say that the polarisation of social groupings
which helped promote the war between king and parliament was one
reason why the cultural appeal of the repertories in the different
types of playhouse came to vary so distinctly. There is no direct
evidence of links between social polarisation and the playhouse
repertories favoured by different classes of playgoer, but the two
phenomena are well worth setting alongside each other.

William Harrison's four classes were, in order of income and
status, first the nobles and gentlemen, next citizens and burgesses,
thirdly yeomen, the rural smallholders, and finally artisans and
labourers. These categories reflect the extent to which land more
than money was seen as the great divider, and they are therefore less
precise than is really helpful in reflecting the class divisions of urban
and suburban London, which provided almost all the Shakespearean
playgoers. In all the seventy-five years up to 1642, for instance, I
have found only two references to a yeoman going to a playhouse.
On the other hand there are quite a few to young heirs of landed
estates selling their patrimonial land for the sake of a high life in
London. The transfer of wealth from land to what Wemmick called
portable property, the growth of a cash nexus based in London, made
a by no means insignificant contribution to the rise of playgoing.
The newly rich and the big spenders alike used playhouses to advertise their status, whether their social mobility was upward as a
prosperous citizen, or downward as a young and extravagant gallant.[7] That consideration – the distorting effect of London's magnet-
ism on the wealthy – should be borne in mind when looking at
Harrison's or Wilson's categories. London's population doubled,
from 100,000 to 200,000 between 1580 and 1600, and doubled again
by 1650, to 400,000, at a time when the total population of England
grew only about 20%, from a little over four million in 1600.[8]

London's dynamism attracted the wealthy and the unemployed alike.

The nobles and gentry comprised all social ranks below the monarch down to, as Harrison put it, 'they that are simplie called gentlemen'.[9] The nobles were all called 'lords' — 'the prince, dukes, marquesses, earls, viscounts, and barons' – and the bishops. Amongst the lesser gentry of knights, esquires and simply gentlemen Harrison included lawyers, doctors, and army captains, provided that a man with those qualifications 'can live without manuell labour, and thereto is able and will beare the port, charge, and countenance of a gentleman'. If he does so, 'he shall for monie have a cote and armes bestowed upon him by heralds ... and thereunto being made so good cheape be called master, which is the title that men give to esquiers and gentlemen, and reputed for a gentleman ever after'. Shakespeare, knowing Harrison as he did from the volumes of Holinshed in which Harrison's *Description* appeared, was evidently not bothered by these sarcasms about being made so good cheap when he secured a gentleman's coat of arms for his father in 1596.[10]

John Shakespeare's elevation to the gentry was a piece of vanity illustrating the upward shift from citizen to gentleman which was one of the principal forms of mobility in this period. If a citizen bought himself a new status it was most likely a reflection of his financial wellbeing. Rather more often entry to the rank of gentleman came through that commonest of mobilising forces, education. Barnaby Rich, in *Roome for a Gentleman* (1609) defined the categories of people just above the boundary between gentry and citizenry in terms almost as sceptical as Harrison's:

there are comprised under the title of Gentry, all Ecclesiastical persons professing religion, all Martial men that have borne office, and have commaund in the field; all Students of Artes and Sciences, and by our English custome, all Innes of Court men, professors of the Law: it skilles not what their Fathers were, whether Farmers, Shoomakers, Taylers or Tinkers, if their names be inrolled in any Inne of Court, they are all Gentlemen.

(*Roome for a Gentleman*, E1r)

Rich, himself a soldier, was partly reacting to the threefold increase at this time in students of the London Inns, which deposited eight hundred young gentlemen at a time on Fleet Street and its environs.[11] Members of the Inns who wrote plays, such as Marston and Beaumont, were gentlemen more automatically than the products of citizen households like Middleton and Webster, and even the son of a bishop like Fletcher. Shakespeare, despite the coat of arms bought for his father, was no gentleman, less honoured in fact than the shoemaker's son Marlowe, who was gentrified by his Cambridge degree. Shakespeare, Jonson, Dekker, Heywood, Webster and others never secured the right to put 'Gent.' after their names on the titlepages of their books.[12] Henslowe, Alleyn, Burbage and Beeston likewise could never comfortably claim to be more than citizens. Still, the distinction between a gentleman and a citizen was most unclear when the citizen was a wealthy merchant or from a family of merchants, and especially when he was educated.

Harrison acknowledged this blurred boundary in his account of the second class. Technically citizens were 'those that are free within the cities, and are of some likelie substance to beare office in the same'. In this sense 'free' meant a member of a City guild who was an employer as distinct from an employee. Among citizens Harrison included merchants, with the proviso that merchants 'often change estate with gentlemen, as gentlemen doo with them, by a mutuall conversion of the one into the other'. Barnaby Rich's point about law students indicates one method for this conversion. The other method is indicated by the fact that of the 8,000 apprentices in the fifteen London livery companies through the period 1570–1646, 12.6% were the sons of knights, esquires and gentlemen.[13] Younger sons had to find other means than a patrimony to keep themselves in London. In the wealthiest companies, such as the goldsmiths', nearly a third of apprentices were the sons of gentlemen. Gold was the principal alchemy for converting citizenry into gentry. Lack of it, for younger sons, worked the opposite way.

The third class, yeomen, were the country equivalent of citizens in being also 'free'. Harrison's definition makes them 'free men borne English, and may dispend of their owne free land in yearelie revenue, to the summe of fortie shillings sterling, or six pounds as monie goeth in our times'. Their freedom gave them 'more estimation than labourers & the common sort of artificers', but placed them below gentlemen, on whose behalf they might work as farmers. At their best, 'with grasing, frequenting of markets, and keeping of servants (not idle servants, as the gentlemen doo, but such as get both their owne and part of their masters living) do come to great welth, in somuch that manie of them are able and doo buie the lands of unthriftie gentlemen, and often setting their sonnes to the schooles, to the universities, and to the Ins of the court; or otherwise leaving them sufficient lands whereupon they may live without labour, doo make them by those meanes to become gentlemen'. It is worth noting that these examples of social mobility did not really blur the distinctions between classes. They were transfers from one distinct class to another.

The fourth and final class in Harrison's account was made up of 'daie labourers, poore husbandmen, and some retailers (which have no free land) copie holders, and all artificers, as tailers, shomakers, carpenters, brickmakers, masons, &c'. Apart from the 'poore husbandmen', who farmed land they did not own, most of these categories were employees, men who sold their labour or its products to the larger retailers and employers. The grades in the London livery companies reflect this distinction. Citizens were 'free' of their company, and employed skilled artisans as day labourers or journeymen while training their apprentices to become day labourers. Apprentices were trained for seven years or more in return for their board and lodging before they could rise to the level of wage earners. The employer-citizens were in Harrison's second class, the employees in the fourth class.

Near the bottom of the fourth class was a group much in evidence at the playhouses. Artisans and apprentices who took an afternoon off to see a play were cutting their working time. The same was not so true of the last category Harrison distinguished in this class, house servants. Harrison took a low view of 'our great swarmes of idle serving men', devoting a lengthy paragraph to their evil ways. They were the unskilled workers, taking board and lodging as part of their wage. Below them lay only the depths of beggary and vagabondage, the unhoused and unemployed layer who ranked nowhere in Harrison's busy commonwealth and for whom he found no place at all.

Vagrants and vagabonds, according to the City of London authorities, had a great deal to do with the playhouses. The Lord Mayor's steady stream of complaints to the Privy Council about how playhouse audiences were largely made up of vagrants needs some explanation. Vagrants were basically the unemployed. Most of them were young men – thirty out of the thirty-seven vagrants registered at Bridewell in 1602 were aged between eleven and twenty. Three-quarters of them were unemployed servants or apprentices.[14] Most of the London vagrants were immigrants from country areas. London's fourfold growth in the seventy years from 1580 produced an even larger growth in vagrancy, eightfold between 1560 and 1601 and twelvefold by 1625.[15] Most of the unemployed lived in the suburbs where the playhouses were, since the suburbs were the poorest parts of London. That fact possibly swayed the minds of successive Lord Mayors, whose jurisdiction did not extend to the suburbs, and who would naturally assume that most troubles were generated in areas outside their control. But they must also have made the assumption that playgoing, being an occupation for the idle, must also be largely a recreation of the unemployed. Nashe in 1592 pointedly ignored the fact that an 'afternoon's man' was a euphemism for a drunkard, and characterised such idlers as 'men that are their owne masters (as Gentlemen of the Court, the Innes of the Courte, and the number of Captaines and Souldiers about *London*)'. These man 'do wholy bestow themselves upon pleasure, and that pleasure they devide (howe vertuously it skils not) either into gameing, following of harlots, drinking, or seeing a Playe' (2.15). This observation, together with the multitude of evidence for 'mechanicals' or working men at the playhouses, suggest that the City definition of vagrancy was a little simple minded.

Harrison does give a chapter to the poor, among whom, understandably, he includes all the known varieties of thief. In this chapter, and in the section on the twenty-three types of thief, he makes his only acknowledgement of the female half of his commonwealth. Women had no property rights, and little in the way of employment. Even women with respectable jobs, like fishwives or Ursula the pig-woman in *Bartholomew Fair*, were assumed for Harrison's purposes to be attachments or extensions of their husbands' business affairs. The only women overtly self-employed were whores. The absence of women from the active members of Harrison's commonwealth is the most conspicuous example of a number of ways in which Harrison's picture of the four classes in the nation differs from the evidence we have for the identity of a Shakespearean playhouse audience. Those differences are important.

(B) SOCIAL CLASSES IN LONDON

London itself of course was in many ways different from the nation at large, and the distinctive character of the London population as a whole obviously makes it more like the character of its playhouse audiences than the nation as a whole. Literacy, for instance, was markedly higher in London than elsewhere. Only 18% of London apprentices and 31% of servants in this period were unable to sign their names, whereas in the country the same class appears to have been little more literate than husbandmen and labourers, of whom 73%–100% were unable to sign their names.[16] In the country as a whole the gentry and clerics were most literate, tradesmen and yeomen next, labourers and women least. Amongst the citizenry of London and Middlesex there was a distinct hierarchy:

At one end the civic elite of merchants, joined by the pen-wielding scriveners, wholesale dealers and polite shopkeepers, had complete possession of literacy. Specialist distributors and craftsmen came next, followed by a miscellany of people in servicing and processing trades. Industrial workers and craftsmen occupied the fourth metropolitan cluster, with less-skilled craftsmen and outdoor workers at the bottom. Most of these people were more literate than their provincial and rural counterparts.[17]

London could provide the playhouses with an exceptionally high number of literate urban workers, as well as a huge population of the unemployed, and by far the greatest concentration of gentry and rich citizenry in the country. It is a reasonable presumption that London's playgoers had a similarly exceptional level of literacy, wealth and poverty.

Literacy, however, like the other general components of London's population, is by no means a straightforward guide to the make-up of playhouse audiences. Playgoing must have had a special appeal as a leisure activity to the illiterate, since the playgoer's involvement with the written word need have gone no further than the playbills posted to advertise performances. The high proportion of women at the playhouses testifies to the popularity of playgoing for the illiterate, since few women of any class, even in London, could write their names. Illiteracy among women in the country as a whole approached 90%, and did not drop significantly until the last quarter of the seventeenth century.[18] A few women were very thoroughly educated. Queen Elizabeth herself established the model, having gained the benefit of a Tudor experiment in allowing well-born women to follow the teaching programme laid down for boys. This novel practice, especially promoted by Thomas More's circle, gave its benefits in the next generation to both Elizabeth and Mary, and Lady Jane Grey. In 1562, when she was Queen, Elizabeth spent time reading Latin and Greek with Roger Ascham every day. Thanks to the example of Elizabeth the practice grew. Lord John Russell, a scholar who taught Edward VI, announced his belief that 'sexes as well as souls are equal in capacity',[19] and taught his five daughters Latin and Greek. That, of course, was a conscious eccentricity. Henry Peacham in *The Compleat Gentleman* (1622) wrote of Russell's daughters as a rare marvel.[20] Learning for women was the exception, though not entirely a rarity. In the second decade of the seventeenth century when Joseph Swetnam published his notorious *Araignment of lewde, idle, and unconstant women* (1615), three women published pamphlets in reply, citing quite as many classical and biblical texts as he had. But these were all privileged women.

Their kind could have supplied a far smaller proportion of playgoers than the generally illiterate housewives. Some could certainly write, and evidently supplied much of the market for the romances of knight-errantry which grew as light reading through the sixteenth century. Joan Alleyn, daughter of citizen Philip Henslowe, could write an easy letter to her husband Edward when his playing company was on its travels. The appetite for reading and writing was certainly there. But time to read meant leisure, and leisure required money. Magnates' wives would have been much more thoroughly literate than artisans'.

Citizens' wives were a noteworthy presence in the playhouses. Respectable citizens treated women as a protected species, and their playgoing was a worry. The restrictions on their range of activities and the assumption that their proper habitat was the home are attested by many writers besides the author of *A third blast of retrait from plaies and Theaters* (1580), who wrote about women playgoers that

Some citizens wives, upon whom the Lord for ensample to others hath laide his hands, have even on their death beds with teares confessed, that they have received at those spectacles such filthie infections, as have turned their minds from chast cogitations, and made them of honest women light huswives.

(2.6)

John Lane in 1600 wrote of 'light-taylde huswives' at the Bankside playhouses wearing masks – 'Though unseene to see those they faine would know' (2.38). Even Samuel Rowlands, a regular frequenter of plays himself, certainly saw playgoing as the mark of an immodest woman. In his *The Bride* (1617), he says of a 'good wife',

> At publike plays she never will be knowne,
> And to be taverne guest she ever hates,
> She scornes to be a streete-wife (Idle one,)
> Or field wife ranging with her walking mates.
> She knows how wise men censure of such dames . . .   (2.121)

though it should be noted that this poem appeared in the middle of the Swetnam controversy. Beaumont's Citizen's wife in 1607 and Peacham's in 1642 both imply that their husbands went to the playhouse more often than their wives did, and that it was not because the wives were reluctant. In such a tame society it was obvious that most men expected only the wilder species of woman to be a playgoer. The author of the *retrait* gave the motive as well as the character for such wild creatures:

Whosoever shal visit the chappel of Satan, I meane the Theater, shal finde there no want of yong ruffins, nor lacke of harlots, utterlie past al shame:

who presse to the fore-front of the scaffoldes, to the end to showe their impudencie, and to be as an object to al mens eies. (2.6)

But harlotry is an easy charge to lay where there is no foundation. Playgoing could be a family occasion. In November 1587 the Admiral's Men accidentally fired a loaded gun and 'killed a chyld, and a woman great with chyld', according to Philip Gawdy.[21] The presence of women playgoers is much easier to establish than their motivation. Spenser's reference to 'a troublous noyes' of 'womens cries, and the shouts of boyes, / Such as the troubled Theaters oftimes annoyes' (2.23) suggests that women were certainly capable of reacting in numbers and vocally to what they saw on stage.

The prevalence of whores – perhaps, given their commercial motive in attending, we should say the availability of whores – at the playhouses is attested throughout the seventy-five years. But such testimonies need to be treated with even more caution than evidence about the literacy of women playgoers. Any meeting-place for large numbers of people was likely to be regarded as a market for their goods by most of London's itinerant whores. How much they went to playhouses in order to combine the pleasures of being a spectator with the business of marketing themselves there is no way of knowing. The suburban playhouses stood surrounded by brothels, and gallants tended to choose between them, like Davies' Fuscus, whose daily round varies only when

> ... sometimes he comes not to the play
> But falls into a whore-house by the way. (2.19)

On the one hand many a brothel-worker might have taken a holiday from her work to become a genuine playgoer. On the other hand, the playhouses were the obvious place to solicit custom for the neighbouring brothels. According to Guilpin the plays themselves fired some playgoers to look for whores. He wrote in 1598 of 'an old gray-bearded Cittizen ... Who comming from the Curtain sneaketh in, / To some odde garden noted house of sinne' (2.28). This of course suggests that brothel whores did not need to get work by attending the playhouses.

Women playgoers provide the hardest evidence for the social composition of Shakespearean playgoers. They were, as a whole, the least literate section of society. Their reasons for playgoing were most open to question and most subject to attack. And yet women from every section of society went to plays, from Queen Henrietta Maria to the most harlotry of vagrants. Evidence for a plentiful supply of women playgoers is there throughout the period, although little of any assertion beyond the bare fact that women were present can be trusted. Hardly any statement on such an emotive question as the morals of women playgoers tells as much about audiences as it does about the man making the statement. John Lane wrote of 'light-taylde huswives' at the Globe in 1600, but Francis Beaumont brought onto the Blackfriars stage in 1607 a citizen's wife of utter if comic respectability, who has been begging her husband for years to take her to a play, like Peacham's housewife in the 1640s. They were probably a more orthodox example of women playgoers than the whores, though both types were expected by Fitzgeoffery to be present at Blackfriars in 1617. *The Actors Remonstrance*, written in 1643 after the closure, acknowledges both too:

> ... we shall for the future promise, never to admit into our sixpenny-roomes those unwholesome inticing Harlots, that sit there meerely to be taken up by Prentizes or Lawyers Clerks; nor any female of what degree soever, except they come lawfully with their husbands, or neere allies ...   (2.200)

Clearly women were presumed to be respectable if they were accompanied by a man, and to be whores if alone. Ann Halkett recalled that she was the first woman, in the 1630s, to organise a group of girls who paid for themselves and had no male escort. She started the custom

> for 3 or 4 of us going together withoutt any man, and everyone paying for themselves by giving the mony to the footman who waited on us, and he gave itt in the playhouse. And this I did first on hearing some gentleman telling what ladys they had waited on to plays, and how much itt had cost them.[22]

Such a group still had a footman to escort them and hand over their money to the playhouse gatherer, the footman presumably attending them from their coach, and waiting with the coachman to collect them after the performance. Ann Halkett's innovation needed its safeguards. Her motive was to free herself and her friends from laying financial obligations on their male escorts, but that was not to be bought at the cost of any doubts about their morality. There is no indication of which playhouses the group went to, but they were not likely to have been the suburban amphitheatres.

That last statement is more an assumption than a deduction. The pattern of women's playgoing probably changed with time, but the principal change most likely came with the return of the halls in 1599. The admission price for the indoor playhouses meant that only the richest whores would have gone there seeking custom. All the private playhouse writers in the 1630s acknowledged the presence of 'ladies' as a large proportion of their audience, and ladies must by then have certainly predominated over the whores. That seems a reasonable assumption, but it has little tangible support from the hard evidence about who went to which playhouses, and in which decades. It is to this evidence, in a mildly despairing effort to establish something like a statistical basis for this analysis of the social composition of playgoers, that I now turn.

(c) WHO WENT WHERE

Appendix 1 gives the name and a brief description of every person who can be identified as having seen a play in a commercial playhouse in London between 1567 and 1642. Appendix 2 lists the major references I have been able to locate about playgoers real or fictional, their social identity, and the general features of playgoing. The first list amounts to no more than 162 names, the second a total of 205 entries. Since on a conservative estimate the playhouses in their seventy-five years probably entertained their customers with close to fifty million visits, that is a very small sample for statistical purposes. Still, it is all we have, and treated with the right kind of scepticism it can be revealing. Well over half the references are to real people, tangible if fortuitous evidence, and the distribution amongst the social classes provides a few surprises which modify some of the easier assumptions. There are, for instance, almost as many references to women playgoers as to the artisan and apprentice class. Predictably the gentry are most conspicuous, with over 100 real names and half the total number of references, but that apparent predominance is undermined by the striking paucity of references to citizens. No more than eleven real citizens can be identified as playgoers, and of the eleven four were playwrights and three were players. Of the remaining four, two went on the same occasion for a similar reason (Howe and Flaskett to Paul's in 1603), one was a regular playgoer in 1611 (Simon Forman) and the last is known, like Howe and Flaskett, only because of his involvement in a notorious legal case (Dr Lambe in 1626). This number is so small we have to seek an explanation for it. Even including all the fictional comments about citizens at playhouses the total of references to citizens is still less than half the number for women or workingmen. Most oddly, in the decade 1590–99 when London had only the two amphitheatres there is barely more than a single reference to citizens as playgoers. The only real clear-cut references are Guilpin's 'old gray-bearded Cittizen' at the Curtain, and Sir John Davies' to the non-selective gathering at the public playhouses, where 'A thousand townsemen, gentlemen, and whores, / Porters and serving-men together throng' (2.17). Either townsmen were notable absentees, or they were such a constant buyer on the playhouse market that their presence was completely unremarkable.

Some evidence does exist to support the latter view, since the opposite seems to have happened later, when the poets of the indoor playhouses gave attention to citizens between 1636 and 1641, usually in the form of comments about their discomfort in coming to such an alien venue. Citizens were evidently a noteworthy presence at that time in the hall playhouses. The inference is that citizens were the standard kind of playgoer in the 1590s, but that they were a distinctly less normal feature of the later indoor playhouse audiences. This is, regrettably, a fairly loose calculation. The evidence which names real playgoers is highly selective – almost the only names we know of real artisans who were playgoers, for instance, were recorded for their part in affrays – and needs very careful scrutiny if it is to produce any valid inferences.

Women, whether because of the high proportion of illiterates among them, or because of the employment opportunities for whores, stood to gain a particularly advantageous return from play-going, so it makes sense to examine the evidence for their presence first. Of the real women known to have gone to playhouses, one was a queen (Henrietta Maria; Anne of Denmark was said to have enjoyed seeing plays mocking her husband, but these may not have been at public playhouses), two were countesses, four others were titled, one was an ambassador's wife, eight were ladies, including the wife of the Dean of St Paul's, a noted flirt, and one a famous transvestite. No citizens' wives are named, but references to their presence appear as early as 1577, and are distributed fairly evenly throughout the whole period, in 1582, 1600, 1601, 1611, 1616, 1632, 1636, 1640 and 1643, for instance, as a look through Appendix 2 will indicate. Attendances by known individuals (listed in Appendix 1) strengthen the pattern suggested by the more general references. The assumption, or the accusation, that such wives went for harlotry or adultery belongs to the earlier period, up to about 1600, and some of the later references distinguish the women at the Fortune or Red Bull as fishwives or apple-wives, whereas the references to women playgoers at the indoor playhouses are almost exclusively, apart from Massinger's fictional City Madam and Peacham's merchant wife, to ladies.

There are in all more references to ladies than to wives, though for the most part they appear later than the references to the citizenry.

Lyly addressed the ladies of his courtly audience in 1584, while
Harington's lady of 'great birth, great reputation' is the first, in about
1595, to be mentioned at a public playhouse. Other references appear
in 1599 (the epilogue of *As You Like It*), 1601, 1610, 1614 (Mrs
Elizabeth Williams, the married sister of Sir Dudley Carleton's wife,
seeing a play at the rebuilt Globe), 1615, 1616, 1617, 1624, 1628,
1630, 1632, 1637, 1638, 1639, 1640 and 1641, besides a number of
ladies, including wife and sister-in-law, whom Sir Humphrey
Mildmay escorted to plays in the years between 1632 and 1640, and
the parties of unmarried women whom Ann Halkett organised in the
same decade. A little surprisingly, there was much less noting of
whores than either citizens' wives or ladies. The more sensational
nature of such identifications has possibly given them more prominence than their true number among playgoers really warrants. Even
if we admit as whores the companions of soldiers, whom Peter
Heylyn in 1621 advised to 'fly to ye Globe or Curtaine with your
trul', or Richard Brathwait's ruffians identified in 1631 with their
'dainty Doxes', the total number of such references is still less than
ten. Davies in c.1593, Platter in 1599, Dekker in 1608, Jonson in
1610, Heylyn in 1621, Brathwait in 1631 and the *Remonstrance* in
1643 are the chief instances. The only real presence of this type
besides those noted by Platter, who as a traveller was marginally less
ready to write fictions than the others, was Marion Frith at the
Fortune in 1611.

Marion Frith, or Moll Cutpurse as she was popularly known, is a
special case which says more about the value of playgoing for
publicity seekers than about the presence of likely whores. Pressed
by the Bishop of London's court in 1612,

to declare whether she had not byn dishonest of her body & hath not also
drawne other women to lewdnes by her perswasion & by carrying her selfe
lyke a bawde, she absolutely denied yt she was chargeable with eyther of
these imputations.[23]

Her misdemeanour was much less routine. The Ecclesiastical Court
record reported that she had appeared on stage dressed as a man at a
performance of a play, Dekker and Middleton's *The Roaring Girl*, in
which she was the central figure. The court record states

This day & place the sayd Mary appeared personally & then & there
voluntarily confessed yt she had long frequented all or most of the disorderly
& licentious places in this Cittie as namely she hath usually in the habite of
a man resorted to alehowses Tavernes Tobacco shops & also to play howses
there to see plaies & pryses & namely being at a play about three quarters of a
yeare since at ye Fortune in man's apparel and in her boots and wth a sword

62

The Roaring Girle.

OR
Moll Cut-Purse.

As it hath lately beene Acted on the Fortune-stage by
the Prince his Players.

Written by *T. Middleton* and *T. Dekkar.*

My case is alter'd, I must worke for my liuing.

Printed at London for *Thomas Archer*, and are to be sold at his
shop in Popes head-pallace, neere the Royall
Exchange. 1611.

14. Moll Frith, from the titlepage of *The Roaring Girl*, 1612

at her syde, she told the company then present yt she thought many of them were of opinion that she was a man, but if any of them would come to her lodging they shoulde finde she is a woman and some other immodest and lascivious speaches she also used at yt time. And also sat upon the stage in the public viewe of all the people there presente in man's apparel & played upon her lute and sange a song. (2.88)

Such bravado and such publicity created a major stir. The play itself, its publication in 1612 with an accurate woodcut of Moll Cutpurse herself on the titlepage, references in other plays and pamphlets and even an account by Chamberlain for Dudley Carleton, all testify to her notoriety. But a professional whore this twenty-six-year-old was not. She went to the playhouse for her own pleasure, not for profit. Her offences were partly the alleged lewdness of her display at the Fortune, but mainly a later affray in St Paul's Cathedral on the night of Christmas Day 1611, when her offence was to flaunt the fact that she was a woman in man's dress openly by showing her tucked-up petticoats under her cloak. The Bishop remanded her in Bridewell for that pending further examination. She seems not to have been punished by anything more than her stay in Bridewell.

The chief general conclusion from this evidence must be that the wives of citizens were regular playgoers throughout the whole period, though with some social division in the later years which directed the poorer 'apell-wyfes' to the Fortune, and the wealthier 'Cheapside Dames' or City madams to the Blackfriars. Dekker mentions whole audiences of penny-paying fishwives at the Fortune in 1611 (2.93). Ladies went relatively rarely to the common playhouses before 1600, but were in numbers at the Globe from 1599 to 1614, and became a major section of the audience at the indoor venues by Caroline times. References to the adulterous intentions of playgoing housewives faded with the quietening of the Puritan protests by 1600, but the assumption that female playgoers were motivated by sex, whether for pleasure or money, remained a male prejudice throughout the period. There may well have been fewer professional whores looking for custom than there were 'trulls' or 'doxies' accompanying their menfolk for the pleasure of seeing a play. They clearly did not make so much of their presence that they deterred more respectable playgoers. Glapthorne, in the prologue to 'a Reviv'd Vacation Play' of about 1636, wrote urging citizens 'as you have done today, / To bring your Wives and Daughters to a play' (2.180).

Evidence for the presence of citizens' wives at plays confirms the inference that citizens themselves were likewise regular playgoers, since no respectable wife could easily attend a play without a male escort. I am inclined to believe that despite the infrequent reference to their presence citizens were the staple, at least of amphitheatre audiences, throughout the period. They attracted far less attention than the gallants, the Inns of Court students, or even the foreign visitors, who took in the playhouses much as they took in the river and a view of royalty, and noted their impressions accordingly. Given the number of citizens in London, their relative affluence, and their proximity to all the playhouse venues, it may not be wildly wrong to think of them and their lesser neighbours the prosperous artisan class as a kind of silent majority in the playhouses.

The artisan class and those socially below them were usually described by occupation rather than by name, except in court records about affrays. Gosson in 1582 identified tailors, tinkers, cordwainers (shoemakers or leather-workers) and sailors in a list intended to be more contemptuous than comprehensive. In 1589 Nashe wrote of 'every mechanical mate' as a would-be playwright, more ambitious in their urban setting than the rude mechanicals and their play in *A Midsummer Night's Dream*. He also wrote of playgoing apprentices in 1592. Davies wrote of porters and servingmen a year or two later, and in 1602 Philip Gawdy included servingmen in his conspectus of an audience at the amphitheatres. A drover features in a poem of 1605 by Rowlands about a playhouse incident, and in 1609 there is a reference to 'grooms', a dismissive term for the most lowly. In this decade Dekker and others began to deride artisan garlic-chewing and the smellier occupations such as beer-brewing in their increasingly frequent references to audiences of 'stinkards'. In 1610 an affray at the Red Bull involved a butcher and four feltmakers. Two other butchers were in an affray at the Fortune in 1611, 'abusing certen gentlemen', in the same year that Dekker wrote about a 'Greasie-apron *Audience*' at the same playhouse. Heywood wrote of an 'unlettered' audience at the Red Bull in 1613, the year of an eccentric visit by the Venetian Ambassador to the Curtain where he stood in the yard amongst 'the gang of porters and carters'. An apprentice, John Gill, was wounded by an actor on stage at the Red Bull in 1622. In 1626 the Privy Council took action over an affray at the Fortune involving nine sailors and their associates from Stepney. In 1631 Brathwait wrote of ruffians and their '*Doxes*'. In 1632 Jonson in *The Magnetic Lady* scorned the 'sinful sixpenny mechanicks' and the ignorance of a 'Trewel, or a Hammer-man', and Alexander Gill, joining the hostile chorus raised by Jonson's play, suggested that he would have done better 'If to the Fortune you had sent your ladye /

Mongst prentizes and apell-wyfes' instead of to the Blackfriars with its 'silkes and plush'. A silkweaver was arrested for menaces at the Red Bull in 1638. In 1640 Tatham wrote dismissively of the '*Rables, Applewives* and Chimney-boyes' at the Fortune, in contrast to the 'Gentlemen' of the Red Bull. The gentlemen there still had to be asked not to throw tiles and pears at the hangings, which suggests that the Red Bull's audience had not changed its habits, and therefore probably not its composition, as much as Tatham's flattery suggests. The *Remonstrance* of 1643 names 'Prentizes' as still the most conspicuous element in the amphitheatre audiences at the closure.

Conycatchers, and more specifically cutpurses, were also regular playgoers. It might be expected that the crowd in the yard gave them better pickings with less chance of detection than the ranks in the galleries seated on the 'degrees', or the playgoers on benches in the pit at the indoor playhouses. In fact, though, their favourite hunting ground seems to have been the amphitheatre galleries. There are signally few references to nips or cutpurses except at the amphitheatres, and the main legal record relates to the Fortune, when the Middlesex magistrates invoked the presence of cutpurses together with the 'tumultes' at the end of plays as their reason for banning jigs there, in 1612.[24] This general allegation is supported in *The Roaring Girl* of 1611, where Moll Cutpurse identifies a well-dressed nip in the twopenny galleries of the Fortune, though of course Peacham's wife was robbed at a hall playhouse. Apart from that the only legal records are about the theft of a purse at the Curtain in 1600 and at the Red Bull in 1614.[25] Other allusions to cutpurses at playhouses, probably only marginally more reliable than allusions to the presence of whores, appeared in 1590, c.1595 (Harington's 'great lady' and her conycatchers), 1600, 1605 and 1606. These all belong to the amphitheatres, including Rowlands' cutpurse who robbed a drover in the yard, though Moll's gentlemanly cutpurse also had fictional counterparts, and some factual support in a thief executed when seized at the Chapel Royal during a Court performance for the Christmas festivities of 1611.[26] Nips evidently did not keep to the company of what Harrison saw as their proper class.

Up to the revival of the boy companies and the hall playhouses in 1599 the artisan and servant classes joined with the citizens and gentry at playhouses. Those few descriptions which suggest that the full range of society was present at plays come from around the 1590s, when only the amphitheatres were open. Sir John Davies in about 1593 was clearly trying to include all comers in his epigram 'In

Cosmum'. He uses the crowd struggling out of the playhouse at the
end of a play as a metaphor describing the confusion of thoughts
falling over one another when Cosmus struggles to express them all:

> For as we see at all the play house dores,
> When ended is the play, the daunce, and song:
> A thousand townsemen, gentlemen, and whores,
> Porters and serving-men together throng,
> So thoughts of drinking, thriving, wenching, war
> And borrowing money, raging in his minde,
> To issue all at once so forwarde are,
> As none at all can perfect passage finde.   (2.17)

In the 1590s, at an amphitheatre play with its concluding jig, this is
the range of society Davies thought characteristic among playgoers.
Henry Chettle suggested a similar range in 1592: gentlemen, citizens, the servants of both classes, and apprentices (2.14). A slightly
different story, though with similar implications, was told by Philip
Gawdy in 1602. Gawdy, a lawyer of Clifford's Inn, wrote to his elder
brother at Redenhall in Norfolk about the illegal impressment by the
City authorities of soldiers for the war in the Low Countries. To
Gawdy the Lord Mayor's mismanagement of the affair was a great
joke because he took it as an opportunity to organise a raid on the
playhouses. The outcome was a test for his annual complaint to the
Privy Council that the amphitheatre playhouses were chiefly places
where vagrants gathered together. Gawdy exulted in the spectacular
failure of the test.

Ther hath bene great pressing of late, and straunge, as ever was knowen in
England, only in London, and my L. Mayor and the rest of the Londiners have
done so contrary to their Instructions from the Lordes of the councell as this
last sondaye your good frend Mr Wade told me that their wer letters that day
directed from the L. of the councell to Sr Jhon Payton, and Sr. Jerom Bowes,
with others to examyne the Londiners indiscreat proceedinges, and all suche
as had cause to complayne shold be hard, and their causes redressed. So that
uppon the Tuesday following their was a proclamation in London that no
gentleman, or serving man should any more be impressed, for the weake
before they did not only presse gentlemen, and sarvingmen, but Lawyers,
Clarkes, country men that had lawe causes, aye the Quenes men, knightes,
and as it was credibly reported one Earle, quight contrary to that the
councell, and especyally my L. Cheif Justice intended. For their meaning was
that they should take out of all ordinaryes all cheting companions, as suche
as had no abylyty to lyve in suche places, all suche as they cold fynd in bawdy
houses, and bowling allyes, wch they never went to any but only to the
bowling allyes. All the playe howses wer beset in one daye and very many
pressed from thence, so that in all ther ar pressed fowre thowsand besydes
fyve hundred voluntaryes, and all for flaunders. Ther was a Cheshire
gentleman called Mr Manwaring that hathe this three weekes expected to be

a Knight, but both he, and all others besydes have myssed as yet their
expectation.   (2.45)

Gawdy, as an Inns of Court man, evidently had no love for Guildhall
and its citizen Lord Mayor. His account may therefore over-
emphasise the number of gentry and nobility rounded up at the
playhouses to embarrass the Lord Mayor. But the numbers involved –
four thousand impressed from three amphitheatres and a few
bowling alleys – seem accurate. And his range, from servingmen to
knights and other gentry, broadly matches the society described by
Davies and Chettle. The only oddity is that the hall playhouses seem
to have been exempted from the round-up. Gawdy's letter does not
mention the Blackfriars and Paul's, and from his account of the Lord
Mayor's expectation of rounding up vagrants and 'cheting companions' seems to refer only to the amphitheatres. Since the boy
companies only performed once a week while the adults played daily,
and since the Guildhall complaints against vagrants were always
aimed specifically at the suburban amphitheatres, it may have been
that the raids took place when the boys were not on show, or else
were directed only at the amphitheatres. In either case, it seems, the
gentry, knights and earl were willing patrons of the adults along with
the servingmen.

   Gawdy's evidence for 1602 casts a little doubt on the assumption,
perhaps too easily made, that by 1600, on Rosencrantz's evidence,
gentlemen had separated from the citizens and mechanicals and
were going only to the hall playhouses. The question of a division
between the popular and the privileged, when it came into existence
and what playhouses it separated people into, is the most knotty
item in this whole history of playgoing. The most reliable evidence
comes not from rumour-mongers like Hamlet's fellow student but
from the record of what real people went to which playhouses and in
what years.

   Inns of Court students were regular playgoers from the start, and a
conspicuous presence at the amphitheatres from early on. Twice, in
1580 and 1581, students got into quarrels with players. The Privy
Council minutes for the summer of 1580 concern three of the Earl of
Oxford's players, two of whom were imprisoned briefly 'for committing of disorders and affrays appon the gentlemen of the Innes of the
Courte'.[27] The following summer it was Lord Berkeley's players who
were attacked by 'a dysordered companye of gentlemen of the Innes
of Courte & others'. This time both players and gentlemen were
committed, possibly because it was not the Privy Council but the

City authorities who now handled the affair. Lord Berkeley had to answer for his players. This hostility must have had a social origin, the common players facing the arrogant and idle young gentlemen in a hot summer.

Over the next twenty years affrays grew less, and some distinguished young names can be found among the playgoers. Edmund Spenser and Gabriel Harvey were enthusiasts, along with more regular London residents such as Davies, Donne, Drayton, Joseph Hall, Marston and Henry Peacham and other Inns of Court students such as Everard Guilpin and Francis Meres. William Lambarde, Keeper of the Tower, and John Chamberlain, Sir Dudley Carleton's friend and correspondent, also went to the amphitheatres. One rather less eminent but literate man, James More, secretary to the country gentleman William Darrell of Littlecote, cost his master sixpence when he saw a play at Paul's in 1589. The foreign visitors, Samuel Kiechel in 1584, Prince Lewis of Anhalt-Cöthen and Johannes De Witt, both in 1596, and Thomas Platter in 1599, all went to the amphitheatres.

In the 1590s while only the amphitheatres were open the 'gallant' established himself as the most noteworthy playgoing presence. Within this broad category of gallants the three types Nashe distinguished in his account of 'afternoones men' followed different patterns of behaviour. Davies differentiated the courtier from the student, for instance:

> *Rufus* the Courtier, at the Theater,
> Leaving the best and most conspicuous place,
> Doth either to the stage himselfe transferre,
> Or through a grate, doth shew his double face,
> For that the clamorous fry of Innes of court
> Fills up the private roomes of greater price:
> And such a place where all may have resort,
> He in his singularity doth despise.   (2.18)

Davies' point is that Rufus' singularity does not stop him from visiting 'common' whores. Samuel Rowlands linked the same activities in his book of satires in 1600, where one gallant says 'Speak gentlemen, what shall we do today? . . . / Or shall we to the Globe and see a play? / Or visit Shoreditch for a baudy house?' (2.36). The pattern of gallant behaviour was already something of a stereotype. And in 1600 the Globe was still a routine alternative to the bawdy houses in its neighbourhood and the Blackfriars in the City.

Between the early 1580s when the clamorous fry of law students fought with the common players and the 1590s when Burbage and

Alleyn were worshipped as models for gallant behaviour, playgoing for the students and gentry clearly transformed itself. By the end of the 1590s the amphitheatres became not only the market place for gallants to show their personal wares but even the models for such displays. From the depths of the Middle Temple Marston made fun of the apish behaviour of his contemporaries in 1597, as they copied the players:

> *Luscus* what's playd to day? faith now I know
> I set thy lips abroach, from whence doth flow
> Naught but pure *Juliat* and *Romio*.
> Say, who acts best? *Druscus*, or *Roscio*?
> Now I have him, that nere of ought did speake
> But when of playes or Plaiers he did treate.
> H'ath made a common-place booke out of plaies,
> And speakes in print, at least what ere he sayes
> Is warranted by Curtaine *plaudeties*,
> If ere you heard him courting *Lesbias* eyes;
> Say (Curteous Sir) speakes he not movingly
> From out some new pathetique Tragedie? (2.27)

Alleyn at the Rose, Burbage at the Curtain playing Romeo (Drusus and Roscio), together with their suppliers Kyd, Marlowe and Shakespeare, by this time had evidently established more than just a sound financial footing in London society.

After 1599, when the hall playhouses reopened, the numbers of gentry going to the amphitheatres probably shrank, since at least once a week they had other venues open to them and at the hall playhouses they ran less risk of being pasted to brewers' jackets. Most of the comments on audiences at this time, however, were made by interested parties, especially Marston writing for his employers at Paul's. The poets' reports are notably biassed towards the 'select' hall playhouse clientele. The only real members of the gentry known to have attended playhouses in the decade up to 1610 divided themselves equally, two at the Blackfriars and two at the Globe. Frederic Gerschow, a visitor to London in the Duke of Stettin-Pomerania's entourage, went to the Blackfriars on 18 September 1602. Like other foreigners with little English he was chiefly impressed by the preliminary concert and the singing, though he also commented on the number of gentlewomen present.[28] In 1603 Sir Richard Cholmley also went to the Blackfriars. A dashing twenty-three-year-old, who had been embroiled in the Essex conspiracy, he claimed to be a little embarrassed to find himself so late for the performance that the only seat available for him was a stool on the stage. He was still more embarrassed when at a pause between the acts he stood up to stretch his legs and another young gallant took his stool. Sir Richard by his own account behaved most properly, leading the other young man, some 'Lady's eldest son', out of the playhouse where he challenged him to a duel. When the young man said he had no sword, Sir Richard offered to buy him one, presumably an offer meant as an insult rather than to make the duel possible. The affray ended when the watch arrived and Sir Richard had to satisfy himself with 'two or three good blows' on his offender.[29] Both Gerschow's and Cholmley's evidence confirms the genteel, if not gentle, attendance at the boy company performances at Blackfriars.

There is no evidence apart from Rosencrantz's 'little eyases' reference about how the Globe players may have suffered while their intended playhouse at the Blackfriars was leased out to the boys. It is unlikely that the gallants gave up filling their commonplace books with lines from Shakespeare altogether, and in 1607–08 the Globe received one thoroughly distinguished visitation. Giorgio Giustinian, the Venetian Ambassador in London from January 1606 to November 1608, made up a party with among the chief guests the French Ambassador and his wife together with the Secretary of the Florentine embassy to see *Pericles* at the Globe. The party took over the lords' rooms over the stage, at a cost to Giustinian of more than twenty crowns.[30] An entourage only slightly smaller went with Prince Frederick Lewis of Württemberg in 1610 to the Globe to see *Othello*.[31]

The practice of ambassadors going to the common amphitheatres seems to have begun at the Globe, but it carried on well beyond the time when Shakespeare's company repossessed the Blackfriars playhouse, and extended to the other amphitheatres. Sir Robert Rich and Sir Henry Wotton took the Ambassador from Savoy, the Marchese di Villa, to an amphitheatre in May 1613, and more grandly Gondomar, the Spanish Ambassador, took a party to the newly rebuilt Fortune in 1621. This was clearly a political act of ambassadorial self-display, complete with a banquet for the players after the performance. The banquet was not likely to have been prompted by simple gratitude for the entertainment offered, and given the ignorance of English which most embassies enjoyed the most likely explanation is that Gondomar was concerned to fly the Spanish flag where the maximum number of people could see it. The position of the lords' rooms over the stage made the amphitheatres much better for this purpose than the halls, quite apart from the larger number of spectators.

There is another piece of evidence about ambassadorial ventures among amphitheatre audiences which suggests a second motive indirectly related to the first: spying on the crowds to discover popular sentiments. Unlikely though that would be for a grandee with no command of the language, it seems to have been the idea behind the eccentric behaviour of Foscarini, the Venetian Ambassador, in 1613. Antimo Galli, a Florentine reporting home with caustic gusto about his neighbour, gives a startlingly vivid account of Foscarini's visit to the Curtain in August 1613.

... my Pantalone often goes out now all alone, though with a faithful interpreter who walks a little in front to show him the way. He goes about saying that he's travelling incognito, and goodness knows where he ends up. He often goes to the plays in these parts. Among others, he went the other day to a playhouse called the Curtain, which is out beyond his house. It is an infamous place in which no good citizen or gentleman would show his face. And what was worse, in order not to pay a royal, or a scudo, to go in one of the little rooms, nor even to sit in the degrees that are there, he insisted on standing in the middle down below among the gang of porters and carters, giving as his excuse that he was hard of hearing – as if he could have understood the language anyway! But it didn't end there because, at the end of the performance, having received permission from one of the actors, he invited the public to the play for the next day, and named one. But the people, who wanted a different one, began to call out 'Friars, Friars' because they wanted one that they called 'Friars'. Then, turning to his interpreter, my Tambalone asked what they were saying. The interpreter replied that it was the name of a play about friars. Then he, bursting out of his cloak, began to clap his hands as the people were doing and to yell 'Friars, Friars'. But at this racket the people turned on him, thinking him to be a Spaniard, and began to whistle at him in such a fashion that I don't think he'll ever want to go back there again. But that doesn't stop him frequenting the other theatres, and almost always with just one servant. (2.101)

Galli's story reveals a number of things besides his own dislike of the audiences at the old Curtain. The clothing worn by this mixture of fool (*pantalone*) and Tamburlaine-like grandee (*Tambalone*) once he shed his cloak, for instance, was evidently as alien to the 'porters and carters' in the yard as his foreign speech and conduct. The yard was for working men and the unemployed poor only. Their hostility to Spain gives point to the display which Gondomar laid on at the Fortune in 1621, and suggests how predictable was the success of *A Game at Chesse* at the Globe in 1624. Galli also implies that the not so respectable citizens and gentlemen who did go to the Curtain paid their extra scudi to avoid the mechanicals and sit in the galleries, if they attended that amphitheatre at all. The Curtain was thirty-six years old in 1613, and did not command the leading repertories available on Bankside or at the Red Bull and Fortune. Foscarini was venturing into the lowest reaches of playgoing in his incognito exploration of London's crowds.

(D) DIFFERENT KINDS OF PLAYGOER

It has long been a standard assumption that the two decades from 1599 to 1619 saw major changes in playgoing. The records of gentlemanly playgoers give no direct indication of the nature of these changes, and since all the changes relate to the gentry, the privileged section of society, the other kinds of evidence need cautious analysis. In essence the standard assumption is that once the boy companies reopened at Paul's and the Blackfriars after 1599 some version of what Harbage called rival traditions developed – rival repertoires, distinct preferences for types of play and types of staging, and audiences from different sections of society. The boy companies drew their support from courtiers, gallants and law students, and were satirical about the City and citizens. The amphitheatre companies drew their support chiefly from citizens and upheld the values of the City. The courtiers were served one kind of play, the citizens another. Once the boy companies fully established themselves at the hall playhouses in 1600 they developed a distinct repertoire of new plays while the amphitheatre companies in the main clung to the old favourites such as *The Spanish Tragedy* and *Faustus*. When Shakespeare's company acquired the Blackfriars from the boys in 1609 they too developed a courtier repertoire and perpetuated the division, so that the halls played for courtiers and the amphitheatres for citizens.[32]

There is no doubt that this is too simple a history. It is based partly on the intensely competitive publicity campaign which the boy company poets mounted in the early years of the seventeenth century, and partly out of the fact that, because the chief buyers of playbooks were courtiers and law students, many more plays from the courtier end of the range have survived than have plays from the Red Bull and Fortune repertoire. Some of the features in this history have a basis in fact, and confirm the broad assumption that from 1599 on the composition of audiences at different playhouses did diverge quite markedly. But the divergences were more a branching out than a simple fork. Paul's boys differed from the Blackfriars boys. The Globe differed from the Red Bull. The Cockpit differed from the King's Men at Blackfriars. None of these differences remained constant. The evidence needs sifting with particular care, and merges eventually into the history of changing play fashions which is the subject of Chapter 5.

Poets writing for the boy companies, especially the boys at Black-friars, went to great lengths to emphasise what a different clientele they enjoyed compared with the crowds at the Shoreditch or Bank-side playhouses. Marston started by calling the Paul's audience a 'choice selected influence' (2.40) in 1600, and brought in the point about freedom from the stench of garlic there which Dekker took up and repeated throughout the decade in his references to stinkards at the amphitheatres. In 1607 Beaumont's *Knight of the Burning Pestle* for the Blackfriars boys based itself entirely on exploitation of the indoor playhouse's gentlemanly affiliations to make fun of naive citizens. His Induction even made a game of exploiting the play-house's reputation for mocking the City in its opening lines. The prologue begins

> From all that's neere the Court, from all that's great,
> Within the compasse of the Citty-wals
> We now have brought our Sceane.[33]

and is immediately interrupted by the angry Grocer who climbs on stage to voice his objection to the idea that City affairs are not great, giving it point by the nature of his objections. The boy prologue speaks of 'the noble City' and of the Grocer as 'an understanding man' without him grasping any inkling of the sarcasm:

CITIZEN. Hold your peace good-man boy.
PROLOGUE. What do you meane sir?
CITIZEN. That you have no good meaning: This seven yeares there hath beene playes at this house, I have observed it, you have still girds at Citizens; and now you call your play, *The London Marchant*. Downe with your Title boy, downe with your Title.
PROLOGUE. Are you a member of the noble Citty?
CITIZEN. I am.
PROLOGUE. And a Free-man?
CITIZEN. Yes, and a Grocer.
PROLOGUE. So Grocer, then by your sweet favour, we intend no abuse to the Citty.
CITIZEN. No sir, yes sir, if you were not resolv'd to play the Jacks, what need you study for new subjects, purposely to abuse your betters? why could not you be contented, as well as others, with the legend of *Whittington*, or the life and death of sir *Thomas Gresham*? with the building of the Royal Exchange? or the story of Queene *Elenor*, with the rearing of London bridge upon wool-sackes?
PROLOGUE. You seeme to be an understanding man.

Beaumont certainly thought that the 'sweet favour', or face, of the sugar-selling Grocer was a sufficiently unfamiliar sight at the Black-friars in 1607 to warrant introducing him as a stranger to the hall playhouses, and the butt of their audiences. The play, however, did not succeed at its one performance because, according to its publisher in 1613, the audience 'not understanding the privy mark of *Ironie* about it ... utterly rejected it'. From this it could be inferred that there were too many citizens present to enjoy such an anti-citizen joke, though other views are possible. Harbage thought that the mockery of citizens was not savage enough to satisfy an exclusively 'gentle' audience. More evidence is needed.

Some of the boy company plays certainly did have girds against citizens, but they also satirised gallants, lawyers and women. Tucca's recantation in the epilogue of *Satiromastix*, performed at Paul's and the Globe, includes an apology for 'the opinion which I helde of Courtiers, Ladies, and Cittizens, when once (in an assembly of Friars) I railde upon them' (2.35). The Poetomachia or War of the Theatres, to which *Satiromastix* belongs, promoted a particular fashion for 'railing'. It flourished, especially in some of the city comedies of the whole period from 1599 to 1619, and its targets included many more types than citizens and their wives. They included the puritanical Mistress Purge of *The Family of Love* (1602), who complains

> Hither I come from out the harmless fold
> To have my good name eaten up by wolves:
> See, how they grin! (2.47)

but these wolves were not courtiers deriding citizens. In the Induction to Day's *Isle of Gulls* a set of gallants whose taste is said to be for 'rayling, and invectives' ask of the play 'ist any thing Criticall? Are Lawyers fees, and Cittizens wives laid open in it: I love to heare vice anotomizd, & abuse let blood in the maister vaine, is there any great mans life charactred in it?' The prologue-speaker of course denies that there is any such material in his play, though the published text suggests that the censor did not agree with him.

Jonson was the first promoter of the fashion for railing, as he acknowledged in his prologue to *Volpone* in 1605. There he denies the claim that 'All he writes, is rayling' while clinging to his disapproval of the more common fashions:

> ... thus much I can give you, as a token
> Of his PLAYES worth, No eggs are broken;
> Nor quaking Custards with feirce teeth affrighted,
> Wherewith your rout are so delighted.

Jonson was technically a citizen, and *Volpone* was written for Shakespeare's company at the Globe. His contribution to the divergence of playhouse repertoires was not a matter of simple alignment with courtiers and gallants at the indoor playhouses.

The fashion for railing lost much of its impetus when the boy companies faded from the scene. Heywood gave it a valediction in his *Apology for Actors*, and a similar disclaimer on behalf of the King's Men was offered to the king in the epilogue to the revival of *Mucedorus* which Shakespeare's company presented at Whitehall in February 1611.[34] Railing was a fashion most visible in the writing, and there is not a great deal of evidence to show how closely it reflected audience tastes or the social composition of playgoers. Since the poets railed at courtiers and lawyers as well as at citizens it would be wrong to single out the 'girds at citizens' as a thorough confirmation of Beaumont's expectations about the non-citizen audience at Blackfriars. There is no firm evidence in the repertory to indicate that citizens stayed away from the boy company playhouses. The Blackfriars boys' plays made fun of citizen tastes often enough, but the Paul's company seems to have expected a strong citizen presence at their plays.

The strongest material basis for assuming that there was a divergence in the social composition of audiences at the different types of playhouse remains the price of admission. Galli's comments on the audience at the Curtain in 1613 indicate that single pennies were enough to divide the porters and carters in the yard from the citizens and gentry in the galleries. Such a division must have been far more acute when a playhouse had no standing-room at all and charged for the cheapest seat in the furthermost gallery the same price as could gain the best place at an amphitheatre. Merchants and wealthier citizens could afford the indoor playhouses (Beaumont's Grocer is tricked into paying more than £1 in all for his pleasure at the Blackfriars), but distinctly few of the apprentices and servingmen could. Circumstantial evidence (presented below) suggests that a mob of apprentices which smashed the Cockpit in 1617 were driven by the removal of its plays beyond their capacity to pay for them. Jonson mentions a 'shop's foreman' paying sixpence at Blackfriars for a place in the top gallery, but this minimum price could bother even a gentleman. Ann Halkett's decision to arrange parties of ladies to go to the plays was spurred by her overhearing some gentlemen complain how much it cost them.

A link between the divergent repertories and divergent playgoers after Shakespeare's company began using the Blackfriars can be charted to some extent. It may not have been gentlemen whom Jonson particularly had in mind when he mocked the playgoers at the

Hope who stayed loyal to *The Spanish Tragedy* and *Titus Androni-cus* twenty-five or thirty years after their first success (2.103). On the other hand it was probably not a feeling that their social territory had been invaded that drew two butchers into trouble for 'abusing certen gentlemen' at the Fortune in 1611.[35] Shakespeare's company used both Blackfriars and the Globe in alternate seasons for thirty-three years up to the closure. Companies proved capable of moving from the Red Bull amphitheatre to the Cockpit's hall with no sign of social discomfort except perhaps to the apprentices who could not follow them. The divergence was gradual and unemphatic. But it grew more and more distinct as the number of hall playhouses increased. The gentry who kept commonplace books with tags from plays and who paid the price of a bench at the rear of the Blackfriars or Cockpit certainly bought far more of the Blackfriars productions than Red Bull plays. Of the five hundred or so plays published in Charles's reign, one hundred and fifty name the playhouse at which the play was performed on the titlepage. Most frequently named was the Blackfriars. The Red Bull was named only six times, four of them for old plays from the period before 1619.[36] Inns of Court students in particular seem to have confined themselves to the hall playhouses and their repertoire of playbooks. Of the few students who have left catalogues of their books, four had Jonson's folio *Works*. Francis Lenton's account of an idle law student asserted that

> Instead of *Perkins* pedlers French, he sayes
> He better loves Ben: Johnson's books of Playes.

The same young idler, according to Lenton, always kept to the expensive urban playhouses (2.145). Lenton's parodic account is confirmed with some precision by John Greene's diary of 1635, which records numerous visits by groups of students to the Black-friars and the Cockpit, but no others.[37] Edward Heath's scrupulously kept accounts, which note the purchase of ten playbooks, and forty-nine visits to playhouses between 1629 and 1631, list sums never less than one shilling and sixpence or two shillings each time, which are hall prices.[38] Sir Humphrey Mildmay through the 1630s went to the Globe when the King's Men were playing there instead of the Blackfriars, but otherwise seems never to have gone to an amphitheatre. He specifies eighteen visits to Blackfriars, four to the Globe and four to the Cockpit amongst his fifty-seven visits.[39]

The evidence consistently says that by 1630 – though not much before – the amphitheatres in the northern suburbs, the Red Bull and Fortune, served a distinctly less gentlemanly clientele than the hall

15. An audience for William Alabaster's *Roxana* (1632). Possibly
it depicts a hall playhouse, most likely the Cockpit

playhouses in the City, the Blackfriars, Cockpit and Salisbury Court, and in summer the Globe on Bankside. The fact that the hall playhouses could perform plays from the amphitheatres – not only Globe plays at the Blackfriars but Red Bull plays at the Cockpit – suggests that the division was more of social class than audience taste. That in turn implies that the price of admission had more effect than any class loyalty shown in the specific repertoires.

Evidence for the preferences of real playgoers such as Greene, Heath and Mildmay is supported by a resurgence in the 1630s of jibes at citizens and the Red Bull repertory. This resurgence, startlingly close to Beaumont's satire in *The Knight of the Burning Pestle*, which was revived and reprinted in 1635, may help to explain the new crop of references to citizen playgoers and their tastes in those years. The Red Bull in particular became a joke to the hall playhouse patrons for its old-fashioned repertoire of heroic military plays. Cowley's play *The Guardian*, written for performance at Cambridge as late as 1642, speaks of someone roaring 'like *Tamerlin* at the Bull'.[40] It was a distinct and vivid tradition, which Edward Howard remembered after the Restoration as a mark of 'the Red Bull writers, with their drums, Trumpets, Battels, and Hero's' (2.203). This was the fashion which repelled the erudite sons of Ben such as Jasper Mayne (2.181). A verse written in 1638 for Thomas Randolph's posthumous collection of his poems, speaks of 'some vaine City gull' at the Red Bull, in contrast (like Massinger's City Madam) to the Court gulls who went to the Blackfriars and Cockpit. This too must have been largely socially inspired criticism rather than condemnation of a feeble repertoire, since the gentry welcomed Red Bull plays such as *The Jew of Malta* and *The Rape of Lucrece* at the Cockpit. The question will be studied more deeply in Chapter 5.

Citizen and working-class playgoers by this time had their own playhouses and their own repertoire in some distinctive features. It was predominantly masculine and heroic, though it was by no means entirely old-fashioned. Its favoured plays formed part of the nostalgic worship of Elizabethan glories which was rooted firmly in present troubles. The difference in social composition of this audience from those of the hall playhouses can be registered by setting against it Aston Cockayne's *Obstinate Lady*. This play was written before 1639, probably for the Salisbury Court playhouse (in III.ii. a character speaks of escorting a lady to the Blackfriars or Cockpit). Its prologue emphasises the contrast between amphitheatre plays and the fare for ladies and gentlemen which Cockayne's hall playhouse provides.

'Troth Gentlemen, we know that now adayes
Some come to take up Wenches at our Playes;
It is not in our power to please their sence,
We wish they may go discontented hence.
And many Gallants do come hither, we think
To sleep and to digest there too much drink:
We may please them: for we will not molest
With Drums and Trumpets any of their rest.
If perfum'd Wantons do for eighteen pence,
Expect an Angel, and alone go hence;
We shall be glad with all our hearts: for we
Had rather have their Room then companie;
For many an honest Gentleman is gon
Away for want of place, as looke you yon!
We guess some of you Ladies, hither come
To meet your Servants, wh' are at dice at home.   (2.187)

By the time the playhouses were ordered to be closed the social range branched from the boxes at Blackfriars, which might contain the Countess of Essex, the Duke of Lennox or the Lord Chamberlain himself (see 2.179), to the nameless chimney boys and apple-wives in the yard of the Fortune or Red Bull.

How early after 1599 this division of playhouse clientele began is not easy to fix, if only because the branching was gradual and intricate. The hall playhouses, notably Blackfriars, started high in the market and remained at the top with the King's Men, though the company never changed its practice of closing the Blackfriars from May to September while the Court was in the country and the lawcourts were not in session, when they played instead to the broader spread of audience at the Globe. The amphitheatres which stayed in use through the winter enjoyed audiences which stayed more constant than the companies which played to them. Some plays, familiar as the typical fare of one particular playhouse, seem to have stayed at the playhouse even when the playing company changed. The amphitheatre companies, however much they changed playhouses, seem to have settled as early as 1611 into the type of repertoire which they sustained until the closure and which fixed the identity of their audiences as consistent with the poorer working-class suburbs where they were lodged. They retained the traditional jig at the end of their plays, for instance, a practice the hall playhouses never indulged in and which the Globe company abandoned before 1614. That distinction, though, belongs more to the history of audience tastes, which will be considered in Chapter 5. It is only secondary evidence for the division of social classes between the playhouses.

4
Mental composition

(A) THE MENTAL RANGE

Michael Drayton begins a verse epistle to his friend Henry Reynolds, written some time near the end of James's reign, with reminiscences of the long talks they used to enjoy by the fireside in winter. They would

> Now talk of this, and then discoursed of that,
> Spoke our own verses, 'twixt our selves, if not
> Other men's lines, which we by chance had got,
> Or some Stage pieces famous long before,
> Of which your happy memory had store.　　(2.112)

Drayton had written plays for Henslowe at the turn of the century. Reynolds was the author of *Torquato Tasso's Aminta Englisht* (1628) and other works in verse. This game of quoting verse from memory, whether of written texts or performed texts, was not at all unusual. Jonson had a formidable memory for poetry and drama. In *Discoveries* he claimed that 'I my selfe could in my youth, have repeated all, that ever I had made; and so continued, till I was past fortie: Since, it is much decay'd in me. Yet I can repeate whole books that I have read, and *Poems*, of some selected friends, which I have lik'd to charge my memory with.'[1] Learning by rote was a widespread practice in schools, though not one uniformly recommended. It led to attainments of the kind John Manningham recorded when visiting his cousin Richard, the squire of Bradbourne, in March 1602:

My cosen repeated *memoriter* almost the first Booke of Virg[ils] AEniads. And this day he rehersed without booke verry neere the whole 2[n]d booke of the Aeneads, viz. 630 verses without missing one word. A singular memory in a man of his age: 62.[2]

Possibly it is a measure of the mental capacity of Elizabethan playgoers that Manningham's cousin's feat should be thought 'singular', even with the impoverishment that Jonson acknowledged comes with age. If so, the feat of an Alleyn or Burbage, who had to memorise up to 800 lines for each play in a repertory which presented as many as fifteen different plays each month must have been singular indeed.

What these feats of memory chiefly indicate about playgoers is their habitual assumption that poetry was words for speech rather than the page.[3] Education and literacy were still rare enough and the price of books high enough to make the spoken word much more the central mode of communication than it is now. It was not only the illiterate housewives who went to plays because they could hear stage fictions more easily than they could read them. Poets wrote to be heard much more than to be read. The hearing of plays, a concept implicit in the Latin origin of the word 'audience', was a basic expectation in the minds of Shakespearean playgoers.

Yet even hearing and the capacity to memorise long passages of verse was a quality which varied across the social range of playgoers. Poets certainly wrote to be heard, and to be heard by people like John Manningham, whose diary contains one brief reference to a play (*Twelfth Night*) amongst forty-seven summaries of sermons he heard. The summaries run to as much as two thousand words for each sermon, giving the gist of the whole argument as Manningham remembered it some time after the event, a notable feat both of concentration and memory. He clearly heard and thought about the sermons much better than Lucius Cary, Lord Falkland, heard the plays he went to in Caroline times. Cary wrote to Thomas Carew thanking him for the printed text of a play, the reading of which improved on the performance because 'at the single hearing...mine eares could not catch half the wordes'.[4] Both of these educated playgoers, whatever their strength of memory or hearing, thought of the essential medium as words. That, perhaps, was one consequence of education. At the less educated levels, even as early as the 1570s, spectacle rivalled poetry as the main playhouse attraction. The 'understanding' men of the yard and their preference for visual treats over wit or poetry became a familiar jibe amongst the learned in the seventeenth century.

The mental composition of any playgoer must have varied according to an enormous complex of factors, ranging from the physical condition of the playgoer's feet or stomach, or the hat worn by the playgoer in front, to the hearer's familiarity with Ovid or Holinshed. Education and taste in reading, the contrasting social and political allegiances of blue apron and flat cap culture against the court gallants and law students, all influenced the kind of play written for the different playhouses and must to some extent therefore reflect at least the poets' and players' expectations of their customers. It needed a fair degree of confidence about social distinctions, for instance, to allow the King's Men at the Blackfriars under Charles to direct the final speech of Massinger's *The City Madam* at the women in their audience. Massinger bluntly underlined his moral that 'our city dames' should learn the decorums of their modest social means and not try to imitate the ladies of the Court.

> ...and willingly to confesse
> In their habits, manners, and their highest port,
> A distance 'twixt the City, and the Court.

Massinger's title, 'The City Madam', was coined as an antonym to define a species the opposite of the Court lady, and the play is in large part an attempt to assert the more modest pattern of behaviour proper to the wife of a City merchant. She was, for instance, expected not to occupy a box at Blackfriars where she could be ogled by gallants. Such eminence was reserved for ladies of the Court. It is not entirely clear whether Massinger expected his moral to be registered by an audience made up of Court ladies who would applaud his point, or alternatively an audience of shamefaced City madams, like Peacham's merchant wife with her apprentice, boxed in amongst the gallants. Probably he expected both. What is certain is that he expected both kinds to accept his moralising.[5] There were prejudices as well as influences in the Shakespearean playgoer's mind, as divergent as the playgoers themselves.

Unfortunately perhaps, social prejudices like Massinger's are more accessible in the plays than they are apparent in the playgoers. Consequently apart from the anti-Spanish prejudice evident in Galli's account of the Curtain audience in 1613 and at *A Game of Chesse* at the Globe in 1624 most of the evidence says more about the poets than their hearers. Far more tangible is evidence about the range in education. It might be expected, for instance, that Webster's social allegiance as the crabbed citizen 'playwright-cartwright' held him among Henslowe's collaborators at first, and ensured that *The White Devil* appeared at the Red Bull in the winter of 1610–11. Possibly not just the poor conditions of its staging but its author's intellectual pretensions brought his next play, *The Duchess of Malfi*, to the Blackfriars in 1614. His resentment over the amphitheatre performance in winter ('so open and black a theatre', 2.92) and its dull audience might have sent him to a hall playhouse for his next play in any case. But some features of *The Duchess*, and one learned echo in particular, suggest that he hoped to cater specifically for learned hearers at Blackfriars.

Webster's plays are full of verbal echoes, ranging from such standard gentlemanly reading as Sidney's *Arcadia* through the slightly more esoteric philosophical musings of Montaigne to the decidedly intellectual rarity of William Alexander's *Four Monarchic Tragedies* published in 1607. He could have expected few of the quotations from these sources to be identified by even the most alert and well-read hearer. Even at Blackfriars where Fletcherian tragi-comedy took much of its strength from that most popular book with gentlemanly hearers, *The Arcadia*, precise verbal echoes would not have been easy to catch. But Webster put one especially emphatic echo into the final couplet of *The Duchess of Malfi* which is distinct from all the others, and which Webster almost certainly did expect a few hearers to understand. Ostensibly the couplet offers a routine epigrammatic summary of the play's moral:

> *Integrity of life is fame's best friend,*
> *Which nobly, beyond death, shall crown the end.*

The Duchess, in other words, will live on in human memory because her life had integrity, whereas the evil characters such as the Cardinal will be laid by and never thought on. The first quarto printed the couplet in italics as a moral apophthegm. It expresses the sentiment we find also in the Lord Mayor's pageant *Monuments of Honour* which Webster composed in 1624 and which includes this memorial for Prince Henry:

> Such was this prince, such are the noble hearts,
> Who when they dye, yet dye not in all parts:
> But from the *Integrety* of a Brave Mind,
> Leave a most Cleere and Eminent Fate behind.[6]

This alludes quite unambiguously to the opening of Horace's ode, Book 1, no. 22, which would have been familiar to anyone who had stayed at school until the sixth form under the Winchester syllabus or the fifth form of the Eton syllabus.[7] On its own the phrase would evoke Horace to any educated hearer. But a recollection of the original ode should also bring to mind a point which horribly complicates the epigram as it rounds off the play. The ode begins 'Integer vitae...' and says that a pure life will keep a man immune from mortal harm since not even a wolf will attack a man possessed of *integer vitae*. An audience which picked up that allusion might also recall that in the play Ferdinand, the brother who killed the Duchess, was a wolf; he died of lycanthropy. With Horace in mind, that oddly macabre detail about Ferdinand's death suddenly gains a new resonance. It is hard not to believe that Webster expected the more educated in his audience to pick up the context of his allusion to Horace and realise that it reverses the ostensible point of the couplet. If the Duchess had died by a wolf then she could hardly have been possessed of the true integrity of life which Horace was writing about. What Webster clearly does seem to have been doing was aim at a split-level audience, offering one thing, the routine epigrammatic moral, for the main audience, and an oblique *lusus*, whether a complex final irony or not, to the learned.[8]

Webster certainly found his element at Blackfriars. Burbage made Ferdinand one of his better-known parts, and Webster's own presence in the Blackfriars audiences became regular enough to get him included in Fitzgeoffery's *Notes from Blackfriars* in 1617. The problem is what we can make of the evidence that he was writing for two levels of education in the audiences there. When he re-used the phrase from Horace on behalf of the London citizens in 1624 he intended it unambiguously, since in an elegy for Prince Henry he had no reason to do otherwise. Conceivably he meant to be equally unambiguous in *The Duchess*, though I think it unlikely. On the whole, Webster aside, there is more evidence of playwrights making covert allusions to contemporary people and events than there is of allusions to passages or phrases from familiar books. The 'application' which Jonson called a menial trade was the characteristic style of the War of the Theatres at the turn of the century, and made great use of familiar phrases from plays written by the contestants in the War. Such allusions were of course to current plays fresh in the memory of the playgoers, and expected no greater form of education in the audience than frequent playgoing. The same applies to the echoes and parodies of famous plays like *Tamburlaine*, *The Spanish Tragedy* and *Hamlet*. Jonson's *The Alchemist* expects the spectators to know Kyd's play much better than Broughton or the writers on alchemy. This kind of echo extends, at its farthest reaches, into the exploitation of familiar stage stereotypes like Touchstone's inversion of the country clown type in *As You Like It*, the exchange of types between the simple but black soldier Othello and the black-hearted soldier Machiavel Iago, or more broadly the adaptation of Shakespearean models of character and situation in the early Beaumont and Fletcher. Playwrights used much more allusion to the familiar stage repertoire than to even the most standard of the schoolbooks.

The wealth of allusion in Shakespearean drama, where it does not point to stage plays, has in all likelihood much more to say about the poets than their hearers, and probably more still about modern readers. To assess this likelihood it is necessary to scan the evidence, first about the conflict between hearers of the words and beholders of the spectacle, next about the minds of the learned few, then about the few opinions of plays in performance which Shakespearean playgoers have actually recorded.

(B) AUDIENCES OR SPECTATORS

English lacks an adequate word for the feast of the senses which playgoing ought to provide, and the inadequacy is reflected in its words for playgoers. 'Audience' harks back to its judicial sense of giving a case a hearing. 'Spectators' belong at football matches where the eye takes in more information than the ear. There is no English term which acknowledges the full experience of both hearing and seeing the complete 'action' of a play.

This lack is a simple consequence of the fact that all the relevant terms in Latin and English relate to specific senses. From the Latin *audire*, to listen, come *audiens*, hearing, *audientia*, an audience or the act of giving a hearing to something, and *auditor*, a hearer or student. From *specere*, to see, and *spectare*, to watch, come *spectaculum*, a show or play, or theatre, and *spectator*, a spectator or critic. English kept these Latin roots, despite a campaign for English alternatives waged in the later sixteenth century when the drama was beginning to demand a new vocabulary. Even then all that George Puttenham and the enemies of 'inkhorn terms' could come up with were 'hearers' and 'beholders'.[9] They never managed to evolve a term encompassing the feast of the conjoined senses which drama began to offer in Shakespeare's time. Their and their successors' struggles to find a terminology appropriate to playgoing tell something about the mental dispositions of the crowds at the Shakespearean playhouses.

The survival of 'audience' today as the nearest thing to an all-embracing term for playgoers is an oddly Pyrrhic victory for the poets. They valued their poetry much more than the 'shows' of the common stage, and consequently rated hearing far above seeing as the vital sense for the playgoer. Every time Jonson called his audience 'spectators', as he almost invariably did, he was covertly sneering at the debased preference for stage spectacle rather than the poetic 'soul' of the play, which he claimed they could only find by listening to his words. The eventual predominance of what the poets, alert as they all were to the Latin terminology, felt was the respectable term 'audience' conceals what Jonson and others thought was a

heavy defeat for poetry at the hands of Inigo Jones with his spectacular masques, and of the players with their mindless 'shows'.

Jonson's quarrel with Inigo Jones, who served his royal master by
reducing the secrets of universal harmony to mathematical tables, is
deservedly well known.[10] But Jonson's scorn for Jones's principles is
soaked in the bitterness of a defeat which had set Jonson against the
common stage even before he turned against the architect of the
royal masques. His contempt, which led him in 1626 to hail Jones's
work for the eye as mindless decoration – 'Oh, to make Boardes to
speake! There is a taske / Painting & Carpentry are ye Soule of
Masque.'[11] – is implicit in the theory of art which he voiced as early
as *Poetaster*, and in his prologue to *Cynthia's Revels* in 1600. This
latter play, written as a kind of exhibition for the talents of the new
boy company at Blackfriars, he designed as an emphatic departure
from the traditions the adult players of the Globe pandered to. He
hoped that the wealthier audience filtered in at the Blackfriars by the
higher admission prices might be more receptive to his poetry.

> ...if gracious silence, sweet attention,
> Quicke sight, and quicker apprehension
> (The lights of judgements throne) shine any where;
> Our doubtful author hopes this is their sphere.
> And therefore opens he himselfe to those;
> To other weaker beames, his labours close:
> As loth to prostitute their virgin straine,
> To ev'ry vulgar, and adult'rate braine.
> In this alone, his MUSE her sweetnesse hath,
> Shee shunnes the print of any beaten path;
> And proves new wayes to come to learned eares:
>   ...his *poesie*, which (he knowes) affoords
> Words, above action: matter, above words.[12]

The vulgar and adulterate brains which throng the amphitheatres are
debarred from judging the poetry which only learned ears can
apprehend. The poet's hierarchy begins on a basis of 'action', which
is all the 'weaker beames' see, ascends to the words which 'learned
eares' can understand, and culminates in the 'matter', the idea which
elsewhere he calls the 'soule' of his play.

By the time Jonson wrote *The Staple of News* in 1626 his view was
simpler and more blunt. In the two plays he had written before he left
playwriting for the ten-year silence which *The Staple of News*
brought to an end, especially *Bartholomew Fair*, he had given the
amphitheatre audiences a thoroughgoing test of their role as judges,
and predictably found them deficient. His prologue for *The Staple of
News* has all the despairing last-chance hopefulness of a writer who

expects the worst but still after ten years feels obliged to make the
effort.

> Would you were come to heare, not see a Play.
> Though we his *Actors* must provide for those,
> Who are our guests, here, in the way of showes,
> The maker hath not so; he'ld have you wise,
> Much rather by your eares, then by your eyes.[13]

The poet was at odds with his medium, and bluntly admitted it.
Poetry was losing to shows on the public stages. Spectators were
triumphing over hearers.

Jonson's was an extreme view, and he was going against traditions
both classical and modern in upholding it. Some of his contemporaries knew and approved his principle: Dekker and Heywood
explicitly made the same point, and Marston, Beaumont and others
implied it. Shakespeare evidently knew it, but was less committed.
As an issue it developed first in the 1570s and 1580s when the
professional acting companies began to set themselves up perma-
nently in London. It grew into a question of the proper terminology
for playgoing, usually as a choice between one sense and the other,
and one term or another. There was a surprising range of terms
available, and the blanket word 'audience' was not nearly so predominant as it is now. The concept of huge and regular urban
gatherings at plays was new enough to provoke a sensitive and
discriminating range of terms which only slowly narrowed down to
the current usage. The shifts in terminology tell us something about
the poets and their patrons in the playhouses.

The idea that poets wrote plays more as poetry than as spectacle
and more as a treat of intellectual inventiveness than a traditional
festival started early in the sixteenth century, and was mostly
attached to Court plays. It was a narrow concept, generating plays
like *Magnyfycence, King Johann* and *Gorboduc*, the staging of which
kept close to the traditions of academic drama and the plays composed in Latin at the universities for audiences trained to listen
intelligently. Their chief requirement was eloquent speech, not
dramatic action or scenic extravagance. As a tradition it survived
well into the seventeenth century in university drama and the
Senecan closet plays of Kyd, Fulke Greville, Daniel and other poets
who never descended so low as to be regular providers of plays for the
public stages. In education drama was customarily treated as an
instrument for the teaching of rhetoric. It was a handmaiden of
oratory, and its 'action' was technically only the gestures which
accompanied the orator's 'pronunciation' of his speeches. Richard

Edwardes, Master of the Chapel Children in the 1560s, described the
requirements for a stage play as no more than 'speeches well
pronounste, with action lively framed' in the prologue to *Damon and
Pithias*, written for the Court in 1565. Academic circles would have
given strong backing to Jonson.

Support from the classics was decidedly mixed. The theories of
human physiology deriving from Galen and ultimately Aristotle
made sight the primary sense, more than hearing, and were quite
unequivocal about it. Andreas du Laurens, writing a treatise about
vision, was understandably partial when he started his third chapter
'*That the sight is the noblest of all the rest of the sences*':

Amongst all the sences, that of the sight, in the common judgement of all the
Philosophers, hath been accounted the most noble, perfect, and admirable.
The excellencie thereof is to be perceived in an infinite sort of things: but
more principally in foure: as first, in respect of the varietie of the objects
which it representeth unto the soule: secondly, in respect of the meanes of
his operation, which is (as it were) altogether spirituall: thirdly, in respect of
his particular object, which is the light, which is the most noble and perfect
qualitie that ever God created: and lastly, in respect of the certaintie of his
action.
(*A Discourse of the Preservation of the Sight*, trans. Richard Surphlet, 1599,
pp. 12–13)

Du Laurens was of course giving his subject a puff. But in *The
Anatomy of Melancholy* Burton, also basing his case on the classics
and always keen to record any disagreements among his sources, is
equally positive about the superiority of sight over hearing. Sight
'sees the whole body at once; by it we learn and discern all things...'
and consequently it 'is held to be most precious, and the best'.
Hearing is 'a most excellent outward sense, *by which we learn and
get knowledge*', but it is less precious than sight.[14] The only support
for Jonson in Elizabethan physiology was the concept that the sight
had a special role in enslaving the reason. As du Laurens put it,

Yea, tell me, how many soules have lost their libertie through the sight of the
eyes? Doe not men say that that little wanton, that blind archer doth enter
into our hearts by this doore, and that love is shaped by the glittering glimces
which issue out of the eyes, or rather by a certaine subtile and thin spirits,
which passe from the heart to the eye through a straite and narrow way very
secretly, and having deceived this porter, doe place love within, which by
little and little doth make it selfe Lord of the house, and casteth reason out of
the doores?   (*A Discourse of the Preservation of the Sight*, p. 12)

Jonson might well have thought that the seductions of love and the
seductions of stage action did the same job of deceiving the rational
porter.

Classical drama gave little more help than classical physiology. In Latin 'auditor' was the term commonly applied to the students and others who came to hear philosophical lectures. Plautus, however, the best known Latin playwright to Elizabethans, called his audiences watchers rather than hearers. In the prologue to *Amphitruo* and in the final line of the play when he urges them to applaud he calls them 'spectatores'. The Romans do not seem to have had a settled idea of what name belonged to their playgoers. Writing in the fourth century in his *Confessions* about the plays he saw as a young man, St Augustine used both 'spectator' and 'auditor'. His subject was the falsity inherent in the fictions of the 'spectacula theatrica', where playgoers got pleasure from the fictional miseries of the stage characters. He thought that eyes and ears could be equally deceitful.[15]

The uncertainty of the Latin terminology is not unimportant, because every Elizabethan writer knew the classical writers, and at the time Puttenham wrote his *Arte of English Poesie*, at the beginnings of commercial London theatre, serious efforts were made to find exact English equivalents for the Latin terms. Eventually of course the anti-Catholic prejudice against the use of Latin faded, but it left its mark, and serves us by clarifying the precise denotations of the terms which became interchangeable. 'Plays' and 'players', for instance, gained in credibility and in definition by their exact equivalence to 'interludes' and 'lusores'. 'Actors' entered only later, with the qualification 'stage-actor', because of the place 'action' held in oratory. Similarly 'shows' stood in for spectacles. Puttenham translated 'redeunt spectacula mane' as 'early the shewes returne'.[16]

Although the concern of the stages became a matter of offering 'shows' to the 'beholder' who gradually became a 'spectator', the English 'hearer' and later its Latin equivalent 'auditor' held on with surprising strength. With the advantage of hindsight we might feel that the contest between speech and spectacle was a foregone conclusion. Long before proscenium arch staging and fixed sets the eye was bound to overcome the ear. In 1616 Thomas Gainsford pointed out that 'as an Orator was most forcible in his ellocution; so was an actor in his gesture and personated action'.[17] The actor's resources in visible action, role-playing, movement and interplay between characters, besides costume and the standard stage properties, let alone the more openly exhibitionistic 'shows' of swordplay, fireworks and 'discovered' set-pieces, all assumed that the eye was a stronger sense than the ear. So the spectator should have replaced the auditor with ease. But if we make such assumptions we ignore not only the survival of 'audience' as the standard word but the vastly greater readiness of Elizabethans to use their ears for all forms of learning. Varro's use of the term 'auditor' for a reader should remind us how normal it was to read aloud, for instance. Hamlet, who enters before his 'To be or not to be' speech reading silently, was as exceptional in this as in so many of his other habits. Both the collective 'audience' and the singular 'auditor' enjoyed a much longer currency in English than 'spectator', and in Shakespeare's time the competition was on fairly even terms.

The Oxford English Dictionary records 'audience' and 'auditory' from the 1370s, and 'auditor' from the 1380s, when Chaucer used it.[18] While 'audience' tended to hold the judicial connotation of a hearing, in both the king's court and in lesser lawcourts, 'auditor' meant simply a listener. We have to look beyond OED to locate the terms used specifically for playgoers. In about 1533 a stage direction in the closet interlude *Love* describes a stage trick with fireworks which survived for more than a century:

Here the vyse cometh in ronnynge sodenly aboute the place among the audiens with a hye copyn tank on his hed full of squybs fyred.[19]

I have found no other applications of the judicial term to playhouse audiences in the earlier sixteenth century. Edwardes wrote of the 'lookers on' in his prologue to *Damon and Pithias* in 1565, and Puttenham favoured 'hearers and beholders', as a kind of doublet. In about 1580, though, Nathaniel Woodes used the term for hearing which seems to have run parallel to 'spectator' up to the closure in 1642. The prologue to his morality interlude *The Conflict of Conscience* gives as its author's objective 'to refresh the myndes of them that be the Auditors'. For a while 'auditor' was more current than 'audience', in Gosson and others of the more academically-trained writers. Shakespeare also used the word through the 1590s. In *A Midsummer Night's Dream* III.i.79–80 Puck applies it precisely: 'What, a play toward? I'll be an auditor, / An actor too perhaps'. In *Love's Labours Lost* V.i.138 and *A Midsummer Night's Dream* I.ii.26 the royal playgoers are quite properly called the 'audience', in a combination of their judicial and playgoing functions. Hall in his satire *Virgidemiarum II* (1597) wrote of a playhouse with a 'dead stroke audience', and Marston in his satire *The Scourge of Villainy* a year later registered the influence of university Latin when he described a Cambridge student actor as 'Yon Athens Ape (that can but simperingly / Yaule *auditores humanissimi*)'. He called the playgoers at Paul's for *Antonio and Mellida* (1600) 'select, and most respected Auditours'. In 1603 Middleton wrote in *Father Hubburd's Tale* of 'a dull Audience of Stinkards sitting in the Penny Galleries of a Theater', and Chapman, retaining the distinction of singular from plural, referred to 'many a moist auditor' in *The Widow's Tears* IV.i.42 (1605). Even Jonson began with an 'auditory' in *The Case is Altered* (1597), and 'auditors' in *Every Man Out*.

Early in the new century, though, Jonson's point about poetry being for the ear had registered, and a more selfconscious usage developed. Poets wrote for ears while players merely offered shows. The Blackfriars audience was expected to display its superiority by using its ears. In the Induction to *The Isle of Gulls* (1606) Day has a character react in mock horror to the idea of a claque amongst the playgoers, using the exact terminology. 'Doe Poets use to bespeake their Auditory?' A foolish gallant in III.ii also speaks of fashioning his discourse 'fit to the ears of my auditorie'. And in the prologue Day emphasises the alleged gentility of the audience expected to attend the boys at Blackfriars by pretending to disclaim any 'bawdy and scurrill jests, which neither becomes his modestie to write, nor the eare of a generous Auditory to heare'. Bawdy jokes of course are the antithesis of what a poetically-inclined audience would wish to hear. The opening of the Blackfriars playhouse along with Paul's had sprung the social divide amongst playgoers which made the different kinds of fare on offer more clearly distinct than they had been before. There was now such variety that the choice of what to listen for as well as the choice between hearing and seeing was now an issue.

Curiously the first writer to use the term 'spectator' appears to have been that most critical of educated and gentlemanly playgoers, Philip Sidney. The first use recorded by OED is in the revised *Arcadia*, in an account of a character concerned to watch an 'action':

Plexirtus (so was the bastard called) came thether with fortie horse, onely of purpose to murder this brother; of whose comming he had some advertisement, and thought no eyes of sufficient credite in such a matter, but his owne; and therefore came him selfe to be actor, and spectator.

(Prose Works, ed. Feuillerat, 1.210–11)

Sidney made his revision in 1584. The word 'spectator' does not occur in the earlier version of 1580, nor in the *Apologie for Poetry*, written 1581–83. Nonetheless in the *Apologie*, writing of comedy, Sidney speaks of the 'beholder', the same term Puttenham was using a few years earlier, and he assumes that playgoing is more for the eye than the ear:

And litle reason hath any man to say, that men learne the evill by seeing it so set out, since as I said before, there is no man living, but by the force truth

hath in nature, no sooner seeth these men play their parts, but wisheth them
in *Pistrinum*.   (*Prose Works*, III.23)

Sidney goes on to mention the anecdote of the tyrant Alexander
Pheraeus who was moved to tears by 'hearkening' to a tragedy, but
broadly his assumption is that the eye is the principal instrument at a
play. On stage illusion, possibly referring back to his initial trans-
lation of Aristotle's *mimesis* as 'a speaking picture', he declares 'the
Poets persons and dooings, are but pictures, what should be'.

Spenser was not far from Sidney in these years, and he was a keen
playgoer in London in his youth. He too, despite his academic
training, accepted the primacy of the eye. In *The Faerie Queene*
II.iv.27 he launched the new word into the drama, with the phrase
'the sad spectator of my Tragedy'. At about the same time Nashe in
Pierce Penilesse (1592) described the fourth of the standard leisure
activities for young men in London as '*seeing* a Playe', and adopted
the Latinism in his description of brave Talbot 'newe embalmed with
the teares of ten thousand spectators' (2.15). Perhaps it was the
arrival of the new term which stimulated awareness in the 1590s of
what the alternatives implied. Certainly John Weever chose the right
one when he wrote a characteristically crabbed epigram about
Hieronymo in *The Spanish Tragedy* biting out his tongue and
continuing to speak.

> *Ruffinus* lost his tongue on stage,
> And wot ye how he made it knowne?
> He spittes it out in bloudy rage,
> And told the people he had none:
>   The fond spectators said, he acted wrong,
>   The dumbest man may say, he hath no tongue.[20]

By 1599 when this was written the difference between hearing and
seeing an actor or an action had registered itself firmly. Shakespeare
changed his own terminology in 1600, in *Hamlet*.

In *Coriolanus* (1608) Volumnia gives patrician instructions to her
son on how to perform his second attempt at winning the plebeian
votes, in these terms:

> Thy knee bussing the stone (for in such business
> Action is eloquence, and the eyes of th' ignorant
> More learned than the ears).

Arrogant Volumnia claims that ignorance uses eyes more than ears.
The same patrician assumption sits in Hamlet's mind when he
warns the players against giving their clowns too much licence, 'that
will themselves laugh to set on some quantity of barren spectators to

laugh, too'. In 1600, with the boy companies competing for the more educated audiences, the populist clowns attracted, as the educated Hamlet sees it, merely spectators, observers of spectacle designed for the eyes of the ignorant.

From 1600 onwards Shakespeare abandoned the idea of an auditory in favour of spectators. In *The Winter's Tale*, where theatre illusion is precisely set out to deceive the eye with bears on stage and statues that come to life,[21] Hermione uses the term for seeing a play as the appropriate one for deception. Her life, she says, was a happy tale and is now sad, 'which is more / Than history can pattern, though devis'd / And play'd to take spectators'.[22] The same kind of 'taking' is there also shortly after, in Time's invitation to the credulous:

> ...imagine me,
> Gentle spectators, that I now may be
> In fair Bohemia.

The ease with which sight can be confused by mere appearance, affirmed in Paulina's declaration about the moving statue, 'It *appears* she lives', has been anticipated by the gentleman of the preceding scene when he describes the reunion of Leontes and Camillo:

A notable passion of wonder appear'd in them; but the wisest beholder, that knew no more but seeing, could not say if th' importance were for joy or sorrow.[23]

Shakespeare evidently gave some ear to Jonson's grievance against unlearned spectators.

The poets who openly adopted Jonson's view chiefly voiced their opinion in the first two decades of the seventeenth century. It is hardly surprising that poets should speak out for the hearing of their verse against the distracting shows of the stage, but it is certainly noteworthy that the complaints can be found across the whole range, from the poets who wrote university plays to Heywood with his spectacles at the Red Bull. Curiously, in view of the later reputation the Red Bull gained for spectacular shows, it seems to have been more of an issue at the Red Bull and Hope amphitheatres in the period 1610–14 than anywhere else.

All the poets agreed that there were two kinds of playgoers, divided according to the priority of eye or ear, but they did not always agree over who represented which. Jonson differentiated in his 'prologue for the Court' of his *Staple of News* between the 'Schollers, that can judge, and faire report / The sense they heare' and the 'vulgar sort / Of Nutcrackers, that onely come for sight'. Thomas Tomkis on the other hand, writing for Cambridge scholars in 1602, suggested that at the university it was not the groundlings cracking nuts but women who came only for what they could see. After a display of *'the olde kinde of Pantomimick action'*, Communis Sensus comments that such acting is absurd 'unless we should come to see a Comedy, as gentlewomen to the commencement, only to see men speake.'[24] University orators may not have been quite as unwavering in their concern to put elocution before action as Gainsford assumed. Marston, writing for Paul's boys at about the same time as Tomkis was writing for Cambridge, seems equally sceptical about the capacity of gentlewomen to listen while they watched. The Induction to *What You Will* (1601) brings on three gallants, who are carefully described as 'three of the most to be fear'd *Auditors'* of the poet's verses. When the Prologue finally gets to his prepared opening for the play he is told to address it to 'the kinde Gentlemen, and most respected Auditors'. But in the meantime some ladies have been noted in the gathering, and for them the word is 'we straine the spectators patience'. Marston implies that only the respected gentlemen are attending for the poetry.

The hall playhouses, however much they raised Jonson's hopes for a full and understanding auditory, did not live up to expectation. Day wrote of an 'auditory' at Blackfriars in *The Isle of Gulls*, but the same playhouse disappointed Jonson's followers Beaumont and Fletcher over their reception of Fletcher's *Faithful Shepherdess* in 1608. Beaumont, who knew Jonson intimately enough to have read his plays in manuscript and to write commendatory verses for them, made use of Jonson's complaint in verses he wrote for the published text of Fletcher's unfortunate play. Printing the play as a 'second publication' would allow the original playgoers 'to see the thing they scorn'd', if only half of them had not been illiterate anyway. Their brains were in their eyes:

> ...it was thy happe to throw away,
> Much wit, for which the people did not pay,
> Because they saw it not... (2.84)

The joke is Tomkis', about seeing men speak, but the inspiration is Jonson's.

Writing for the more pretentious repertory and clientele of the boy company at the Blackfriars, poets might reasonably be irked if their verse was misunderstood, though Fletcher had more grounds for grief than most since the playgoers at Blackfriars seem to have expected a traditional and populist kind of play with May-games and rural clowns, not at all the usual Blackfriars pretension. But the same thing happened to Webster's *White Devil* in 1610 at the populist Red Bull, and he combined with Dekker to voice the same grievance as Fletcher, this time over the amphitheatre audience. Wester's epistle complained that it failed on stage because the playhouse was dark and the play therefore 'wanted (that which is the only grace and setting out of a tragedy) a full and understanding auditory'. The same incapacity to hear verse was Dekker's target in the dedication to his *If This Be Not a Good Play, the Devil Is In It*, which appeared in the same year as Webster's play, 1612. Dekker dedicated his play to the Queen's Men at the Red Bull, apparently because they took it when it was rejected by the Prince's Men at the Fortune. He was careful first to wish them 'a *Faire* and *Fortunate Day*' for their next new play, and went on to express the hope that 'my *Worthy Friends Muse*. . .deserve a *Theater* full of very *Muses* themselves to be *Spectators*. To that *Faire Day* I wish a *Full, Free*, and *Knowing Auditor.*' In the prologue to the play itself he implies that poetry has been made to suffer in conflict with other priorities, and hopes that the '*Banished* Auditor' might be recalled from his exile by poetry, and enforce '*Rare silence*' on the playgoers. The Red Bull was beginning to get a name for spectacle, and its poets evidently felt they were losing by it. Heywood, the Red Bull's resident actor-playwright, presumably knew the trend he was facing when he half-heartedly proclaimed in 1613 in the prologue to the first of his four stage spectaculars, *The Brazen Age*, that 'more than sight / We seek to please'.

The central text of all this dispute is the set of Articles which Jonson drew up in the Induction to *Bartholomew Fair* for the audience at the Hope in 1614. Essentially a parodic exhibition of the duty of wise judging which Jonson wanted all playgoers to accept, the 'ARTICLES of Agreement' named all the varieties of audience:

. . .the said *Spectators*, and *Hearers*, as well the curious and envious, as the favouring and judicious, as also the grounded Judgements and understandings. . .

Apart from the very early *The Case is Altered* and *Every Man Out*, this was the only occasion when Jonson used more than the contemptuous 'Spectators' as a term for his audience. The hearers are 'favouring and judicious' while the spectators are merely 'curious and envious', and everyone knew how much could be expected of the understanding men and groundlings at the Hope. Since legalistic language prefers two terms where one will do, Jonson adds 'hearers' to his usual 'spectators', expanding the oxymoronic 'judging Spectators' to whom he had appealed sarcastically in the prologue to *The Alchemist* in 1610.[25]

From the time of *The Alchemist* onwards, the distinction between hearers and spectators gradually lost its point, though by no means in a uniformly downward slide. The Master of the Revels, Henry Herbert, used Jonson's phrase from *The Alchemist* without the least consciousness of its bite in 1633, when he recorded his admiration for Shirley's play *The Young Admiral*. If other poets imitated that play, he wrote, it 'shall speak them masters in their art, at the first sight, to all judicious spectators'.[26] Such an injudicious echo belies the care with which others used the terms in those decades. Heywood, who had used 'spectators' and 'Audients' indifferently in his *Apology for Actors* before 1610, showed discomfort in *The Brazen Age* (1613), and openly displayed the divide in the same year as Herbert wrote about *The Young Admiral*. Preparing his *Londini Emporia*, an account of his City pageants, he wrote that the third show

is a modell devised to humour the throng, who come rather to see than to heare: and without some such intruded anti-maske, many who carry their ears in their eyes, will not sticke to say, I will not give a pinne for the Show.
(*Dramatic Works*, IV.324)

Writing of his *Iron Age* in 1632 he again used the poet's word, 'auditories'. Richard Flecknoe even carried the point into the Restoration, when scenic staging was in its first bloom. Stage decorations, he noted,

now for cost and ornament are arriv'd to the heigth of Magnificence, but that which makes our Stage the better makes our Playes the worse perhaps, they striving now to make them more for sight than hearing, whence that solid joy of the interior is lost.[27]

Flecknoe heralds the scenic staging which paradoxically accompanied the triumph of the term 'audience'. It is the more paradoxical in that its triumph was never certain before the Restoration.

In the last three decades before the London playhouses were closed the whole range of terms remained current, and were usually employed with precision. Gainsford used 'auditor' with reference to a player's speaking.[28] The printer of the 1620 text of *The Two Merry Milkmaids* used it of the poet's audience.[29] John Gee, writing of the late Richard Burbage's speaking in 1624, claimed that he was 'the *Loadstone* of the Auditory'.[30] On the other hand, a funeral elegy written in 1619 put the sight of him first:

oft have I seene him, play this part in jeast,
soe livly, that Spectators, and the rest

of his sad Crew, whilst he but seem'd to bleed,
amazed, thought even then hee dyed in deed.　　(2.124)

And an equally emphatic writer, commenting on the 'shows' at the
Red Bull in 1615, also used the more apt word. Thomas Greene, the
Red Bull clown, he wrote, used to 'flash choaking squibbes of absurd
vanities into the nosthrils of your spectators'.[31] Presumably they
flashed in people's noses more than they banged.

The term 'audience' did recur throughout the period. Marston used
it in *Antonio's Revenge* (1600) and *Jack Drum's Entertainment*
(1602). It was used of the Blackfriars playgoers in 1617 and of
Shakespeare's faithful in Leonard Digges' verses for the First Folio. It
was applied to an amphitheatre audience (called 'Audients') in
1638.[32] But more often writers used the kind of word available for
any crowd, 'assembly', 'throng', or in the more aristocratic mouths
'multitude'.[33] The most congenial and commonplace word between
about 1594 and 1640 was 'company'. The eventual triumph of
'audience' after the Restoration was certainly not a tribute to the
judging role or the sensitive ear for poetry of the majority of playgoers.

(C) LEARNED EARS

In a little treatise he wrote in 1598 Sir John Harington considered
three kinds of 'Playe': devotional, wanton, and recreational. He
counted playgoing in the second category, and underscored the
correctness of its inclusion among the wanton pastimes. Still, he
added,

for my part...I thinke in stage-playes may bee much good, in well-penned
comedies, and specially tragedies; and I remember, in Cambridge, howsoever
the presyser sort have banisht them, the wyser sort did, and still doe
mayntayn them.[34]

A few years later he echoed one particularly well-penned comedy in a
way which says something about the use of familiar allusions
amongst courtiers. By 1605, under James, he was much nearer the
rim of the Court circle than he had been under Elizabeth. On 20 April
of that year he wrote to Cecil, the Lord Treasurer, asking him for help
in securing the posts of Archbishop of Dublin and Chancellor of
Ireland. Both Harington and Cecil were keen playgoers,[35] so the
principal allusion in Harington's letter must have had a familiar air
to it. On the verge of rural exile, Harington in 1605 made an excellent
melancholy Jacques.

that the world is a stage and we that live in it are all stage players...I playd my chyldes part happily, the scholler and students part to neglygently, the sowldyer and cowrtyer faythfully, the husband lovingly, the contryman not basely nor corruptly...Now I desyre to act a Chawncellors part hollyly.[36]

However modest Harington was here in confessing his negligence as a student, however reluctant his scholarship had been in translating Ariosto and however tongue in cheek he was invoking so many sources to make his *Metamorphosis of Ajax* seem respectable, his use of *As You Like It* in this letter to Cecil indicates his facility with allusion. More to the point, he implies that allusions to contemporary stage plays were as acceptable in such a weighty context as were allusions to Horace or the other well-known classics. The question of allusion in stage plays is at least in part one of accessibility. If learned courtiers like Harington and Cecil could allude to poems from the common stage so familiarly, how readily might they pick up more scholarly allusions when they heard them on stage? How far could a poet go in exploiting the common ground of education and reading, and how many shared such common ground?

Horace is one author whom the learned would certainly recognise. Access to such a major author from the schools, though, was a privilege granted not only by the grace of education but by mastery of Latin. It would have been available to relatively few among the penny-payers in an amphitheatre audience. If Webster could use Horace, as he seems to have done in *The Duchess of Malfi*, in a consciously divisive way so as to differentiate the learned elite from the many-headed commoners, the likelihood is that every allusion to a classical author, and every Latin quotation of the kind which abounds in *The White Devil*, would have served similarly as a deliberate piece of flattery to the elite, a calculated separation of the few from the many, the hearers from the spectators. Such an attitude to audiences might be expected in Jonson, given his contempt for the common run of judging understanders, and evidently in Webster too, for all his early training as a collaborative writer for Henslowe. But it was not Shakespeare's own mode, and it is not easy to identify in many other writers. Allusions have to be recognisable to someone if they are not to be kept within the wholly restricted circle of the writer's private conception. To be sure that an allusion, the learned *lusus*, is designed as a calculated hint to the most intellectually alert in a Shakespearean audience, we have to be confident that Shakespearean sensibilities had the capacity and disposition to receive it.

Most notably amongst the recent analysts of the ironic mode of allusion in Shakespearean drama, Richard Levin has compiled a

16. William Drummond of Hawthornden, from a painting (NPG 1195)

daunting body of evidence about contemporary audience responses. All of it casts doubt on the existence of a predominantly allegorical or allusive reading of the drama by Shakespearean playgoers.[37] Some consideration will be given to this evidence in the next section of this chapter. A possibly more helpful alternative kind of evidence is the capacity of scholars to pick up echoes or allusions in their reading. Reading being a more leisured form of assimilation than playgoing, the quiet of a study ought to provide some kind of high tidemark for the capacity of Shakespeareans at this learned game.

There is a little evidence in at least one location for this tidemark. The personal library of William Drummond of Hawthornden, much of which has survived intact and which bears evidence about his reading in the marginalia he wrote in many of his books, gives us an insight into the nature of closet learning in the early seventeenth century. After graduating from Edinburgh University in law, Drummond went to France, like many gentlemanly Scotsmen, to continue his studies. On the way he spent some time in London. He was there in 1606 during the visit of King Christian of Denmark, and reported home that 'there is nothing to be heard at Court but soundings of Trumpets, Haut-boys, Musick, Revelling and Comedies'. While enjoying these soundings and playgoings he read *The Courtier, The Mirror of Knighthood*, and *A Midsummer Night's Dream* amongst other works, and bought a copy of Lodge's *Phyllis* to take with him to France. In 1610 he was back in Britain again, with the beginnings of a handsome library of literary works. After his father died in 1611 he settled as the laird of Hawthornden and became the major book collector and minor poet we now know. He was a gentleman of leisure and learning. Since his books and papers have largely survived they reveal some of the effects of such a gentlemanly playgoer's reading.

Drummond was learned in several languages. He could manage Greek as well as Latin, and he read in the original the French works of Passerat, Desportes, Ronsard, Pontus de Tyard, Tabourot, Pasquier and Jodelle. He read Volpi, Zanchi, Castiglione, Virgil and Horace in Latin, Boscan and Garcibasco in Spanish, and Petrarch, Bembo, Groto, Sannazaro, Paterno, Guarini, Bonardo, Belli, Guazzo, Tasso, Marino, Moro and others in Italian. Principally he was a master of the Romance languages, French, Italian and Spanish, on the basis of his excellent grasp of Latin. His English books of literature included first and foremost Sidney, Daniel, Drayton, Shakespeare, Spenser, Peele, Watson and William Alexander. In the Arcadian tradition he read Montemayor and Gil Polo in English and French as well as the original Spanish. Sannazaro's *Arcadia* he read in Italian and French. His favourite Shakespeare plays were, not surprisingly, *A Midsummer Night's Dream, Love's Labours Lost*, and *Romeo and Juliet*, though he knew another four or five, including *Hamlet*, pretty well.[38]

A test of how his learning affected his reading and probably his hearing of plays can be found in his copy of William Alexander's *Four Monarchic Tragedies* now in the National Library of Scotland (MS 1692). It contains an autograph sonnet to Alexander dated about

1614, and a good few marginal notes also in Drummond's own hand. The copy has been cropped at some time and some of the annotations are lost, but they are clearly all citations of parallels which Drummond noted between Alexander's verses and their sources. Most of the parallels are from Sidney's *Arcadia*, and they vary from simple points of vocabulary to broad parallels of rhetorical conceits. At sig. F3r in Alexander's *Tragedie of Darius* III.ii, for instance, where there is a couplet reading

> And from the height of Honour to digresse,
> To womanise with courtly vain delights...

Drummond has picked up the verb, and noted in the margin 'S.P.S. Lib. 1. [i.e. Book 1 of *Arcadia*] this effeminat Loving of a woman doth womanize a man'. Sidney's point was well known in Jacobean times. It is the basis for Donne's epigram 'Manliness', for instance. Drummond, however, was concerned with the specific word, and knew its context. Besides such echoes of Sidney he picked up du Bartas (citing the parallels in French), Montemayor in Spanish, Ariosto in Italian, and specifically in *The Tragedie of Darius*, 'Jacques de la Taille, who wrote Darius tragedie in french'. Drummond was tracing deliberate utilisations of the sources, not any kind of plagiarism. The point is that for the most part he could pick them up out of his own memory. He had a copy of Jean de la Taille's poem in his library, and probably checked in it to verify the echoes he found, but he quoted at least the Sidney parallels direct from his memory.

Alexander's tragedies were closet dramas, just as Drummond was a closet audience. The circumstances at the Blackfriars or at Court could hardly have afforded anyone the leisure to make connections in the detail that Drummond's marginalia provide. I would think that he might stand as an extreme, the most well-read, the most multilingual, and the most undistracted corner of a potential Jacobean audience. In his reading, if not in his hearing of plays, he could detect a good number of literary echoes.

How common Drummonds with their *Arcadia* and their Alexander might have been in any of the playhouses we do not know. Gabriel Harvey, another playgoer, had a similar library to Drummond's and wrote similar marginalia in it, but like Drummond he never lived regularly in London. It is not likely that such scholars existed in large numbers, and even Jonson's description of a scholarly audience at Court amongst the Haringtons and the Cecils cannot have been much more than an unavailing hope, to judge by the accounts we have of audience behaviour at Court masques. Jonson,

Dekker and the other professional poets had to use print to make sure that their elaborate ceremonial allegories became accessible to the enlightened few for whom they had been composed. Carleton and Busino have left accounts of masques in which the rush for food and the consequent collapse of the banquet tables seem to have been the most memorable incidents on each occasion.[39] Webster's allusion to Horace in *The Duchess of Malfi* assumed that the learned who would pick it up were only a select few, even at the most select of the playhouses. If he wrote the play specifically for the King's Men at the Blackfriars he designed it for the only indoor playhouse then operating, the top of the market. And since the allusion only works by swimming against the current of its superficial meaning, Webster evidently expected most playgoers even at Blackfriars to hear the words only at the superficial level.

There is rather more evidence for divisions between audiences in their social and cultural character than in their learning or intellect. Massinger probably assumed that the women at Blackfriars near the end of the 1620s would be predominantly ladies of the Court rather than merchants' wives. Beaumont made the same kind of assumption, probably with rather less justification, at Blackfriars in 1607, close to the middle of the seventy-five years of Shakespearean playgoing. The comic Grocer and his wife in *The Knight of the Burning Pestle* are set up as objects of ridicule for the 'Gentlemen' among whom they sit on the stage. The play therefore has to serve as the most extreme mark of the division, real or at least assumed by Beaumont, between citizen tastes and gentlemanly values. The gentlemanly Beaumont set his marker down in a mood of elitist satire and genial contempt for citizens, and it has already been noted that in 1607 the audience missed the point of his satire. The portrait of the citizens in the play may therefore be not merely satirically overcoloured but overstated to the extent that there were not enough gentlemen present at Blackfriars to share Beaumont's joke.[40] Nonetheless Beaumont did expect sympathetic laughter from the gentry against the merchant class of playgoers, so it is worth noting in some detail what he presented as ridiculous in their culture.

As we have seen, the play begins with the Citizen, an employer-member of the Guild of Grocers, climbing on stage to stop the performance of the advertised play, *The London Merchant*. He evidently suspects that a play with such a title, echoing citizen plays like *The London Prodigal*, which was printed in 1605 as having been acted by the King's Men at the Globe, must when performed at the Blackfriars be intended as a burlesque of the citizen genre. The prologue's opening, announcing that they have transferred their scene from all that's great at Court to the City, confirms his suspicion. In fact *The London Merchant* when the boys do eventually present it does prove to be a burlesque of *The London Prodigal* and its like. Both plays have a heroine called Luce, but the Globe play emphasises the mercantile interpretation of the prodigal son parable, customary in citizen plays by then, which puts its moralistic emphasis on the errant son's reform and his return to the ways of financial prudence. Beaumont's play reverses this moral by forcing the miserly characters to convert themselves into the ways of prodigality. Instead of a prodigal son *The London Merchant* has a prodigal father, and the hero is his penniless son who wins the fair Luce from a grasping father, who at the end is forced to forgive and accept his new son-in-law along with the new principle of prodigality. Beaumont's play directly challenges the standard mercantilist interpretation of the Biblical parable of the prodigal, and offers 'mirth' as the alternative principle to miserliness.[41]

The Citizen Grocer by his contribution to the performance shows how mercantilist values are embodied in citizen tastes for literature. He objects to the boy players' policy of offering plays with 'new subjects, purposely to abuse your betters', and proposes the old favourites instead, such as the story of Dick Whittington, which had grown into a London legend at the end of the sixteenth century, or Heywood's *2 If You Know Not Me* (1606), which celebrated Sir Thomas Gresham, builder of the Royal Exchange. What the Grocer wants is something 'notably in honour of the Commons of the Citty', like the Royal Exchange or the feats of apprentice gallantry staged in Heywood's *Four Prentices of London* and Day and Wilkins's *The Travels of the Three English Brothers*. The boy prologue's opinion of these is indicated by his mock-proposal to stage 'the life and death of fat *Drake*', not Sir Francis but a citizen's dinner, or 'the repairing of Fleet-privies'. This, not exactly an alternative to Gresham's Royal Exchange, was a current business in the City. In 1607 citizens were being levied for contributions to build several new waterworks, notably Sir Hugh Middleton's New River project.

The Grocer's idea of honour and citizen plays were by no means Beaumont's only targets. The Grocer's wife and apprentice join him on stage, and each reveals a distinctly different taste in contemporary drama. The wife favours escapist romances about characters like Jane Shore, the citizen wife who was loved by Edward IV and who features in *King Edward IV*, a play which appears in Henslowe's records. She wants the apprentice, Ralph, to take the romantic lead

as a knight-errant in the play, like the Palmerin stories from which
Ralph quotes at length and almost verbatim, except where Beaumont changes Palmerin's horse into an elephant. She wants Ralph to
kill a lion with his grocer's pestle, in the fashion of *The Travels of
the Three English Brothers*. Ralph shows his acting mettle with
Hotspur's huffing speech (1 *Henry IV*, I.iii.201ff), and is claimed as
the star in a version of *Mucedorus*, another Globe play, and *Jeronimo*. In the play itself Ralph appears principally as an apprentice
errant performing deeds of gallantry like the Red Bull's *Travels*,
which is named at IV.i.33–5. He also appears as a Maylord in the
fourth Interact, dressed in bells and scarves and carrying a gilded
staff, and in the final act becomes the leader of a town band of citizen
militia.

Besides this mockery of citizen tastes and spectacle in their
favourite plays the boy players also make sure that the Grocer
himself and his understanding are thoroughly guyed. He completely
misses the boy prologue's sarcasms about 'the noble Citty' and fat
Drake, just as his wife misses all the bawdy jokes she innocently
broaches. They both display a Dogberry-like ignorance. In the Interact between Acts II and III the wife asks her husband if the painting
on the hangings shows 'the confutation of Saint *Paul*'. The Grocer
corrects her by declaring it to be '*Raph* and *Lucrece*'. In III.ii the wife
refers to the biblical story of '*Jone* and the Wall'. Their capacity for
understanding spectacle too is as defective as their hearing. In both
The London Merchant and the play which Ralph tries to perform,
The Grocer's Honour,[42] the Grocer and his wife invariably mistake
the fiction for reality. The wife asks Ralph if he has slept well after a
night is supposed to have passed, and both speculate about the
progress of the lovers as they wander through Waltham Forest. They
accept the adventures of Ralph which they demand he be allowed to
perform as true events as soon as they are performed, and are
disappointed by the boys' refusal to adopt their proposals for spectacular Red Bull-type events on stage. Just as they invariably identify
themselves with the mercantile values which are guyed in the main
play and as a result misconstrue everything they see, so they accept
the spectacularly ludicrous knight-errantry of Ralph as stage realism.
If there is any degree of truth in Beaumont's picture of citizen
playgoers at the Globe and Red Bull, the only surprise is that Jonson
should ever have left the boy company to take *Volpone* to the Globe,
as he did in 1605. Beaumont's picture certainly reflects the pressure
to favour spectacle over poetry which Jonson fought from the
Blackfriars stage in 1600 and 1601.

(D) PLAYGOER REACTIONS

It is easier to identify the length and breadth of audience tastes than the height of their mental capacity or the exact shape of the mental constructs they took into the playhouses. The plays which lasted in the various repertories, the plays which became the most popular and came to characterise different playhouses, define the tastes which singled them out. These tastes, of which there is more to be said in Chapter 5, by their nature remained passive. They allowed the attractions of *Faustus* and *The Spanish Tragedy* to hold steady for fifty years in the northern amphitheatres. It is a fairly straightforward exercise, using that kind of evidence, to identify what audiences liked in the mass and as passive tasters of what was set before them. On the other hand the poets by their nature had more active tastes, always on edge to provide novelty. It is not really surprising that all the contemporary commentators who found occasion to mock old-fashioned tastes in playgoing were themselves stage poets (Middleton, Dekker, Jonson, Massinger and Brome: see 2.89, 103, 147 and 185). While playgoers certainly did vote with their feet in following the poets' activities in particular directions, so that the evolution of tastes in playgoing is an indication of audience preferences on a very broad perspective, their reactions to the novelties which poets kept offering form markers of a more localised kind.

Sadly, very few accounts of playgoing exist, and the writers of those few accounts did not feel obliged to make much more than a few jottings about the plays they saw. There were neither theatre reviews nor journals to print them in, so the accounts are all personal and perfunctory. They all dwell on plot rather than other features such as character, poetry or staging, and have consequently led modern commentators such as Richard Levin to use them as indications that Shakespearean playgoers took their plays literal-mindedly and for the story alone.[43] This misjudges the evidence. There are, taken altogether, many more quotations of famous verses, praises of actors for their characterisations, comments on the 'application' which became a trade by 1605, and comments on stage spectacles than there are summaries of plots. A comprehensive survey of audience reactions to the plays of this period suggests a complex and wide-ranging responsiveness which makes the eyewitness accounts of plays seem almost simple minded.[44] They need to be examined, but rather as narrowly normative accounts than as expert analyses.

Before looking at the three accounts of plays seen in performance, special note needs to be taken of the period's most celebrated critique of plays, Sidney's extended condemnation of stage realism in the *Apology for Poetry*. Written in about 1582, and widely circulated in manuscript (Lyly seems to have been familiar with it), Sidney's little treatise did not appear in print until 1595. Between the writing and the publication much had changed. Strikingly, though, little that Sidney objected to had shifted, and even more strikingly there was little care taken for his criticisms either in 1582 or in the years following 1595 except possibly by Ben Jonson. The flow of popular fashion swept Sidney's criticisms aside not so much because they seemed out of date as because they lacked a cutting edge. His condemnation of stage realism and his objections to popular clowning have a place in the history of audience taste, but it is academic and evidently marginal to the main currents. He was attacking something too strong to be affected by his arguments.

There is no direct evidence that Sidney ever went to the public playhouses. The only play he specifically mentions, *Gorboduc*, was first staged in the hall of the Inner Temple in 1561, and may never have appeared on the amphitheatre stages, though Sidney's knowledge of it suggests that it was performed through the 1570s. The characteristics of other plays which he condemns might also have been shown at Court or in the Inns of Court as readily as at the Theatre or Curtain. On the other hand his familiarity with plays shows the sort of everyday ease which can hardly have been cultivated exclusively by the irregular offerings of the law students or the festive season at Elizabeth's Court. His dislike of clowns, paper dragons breathing fire and smoke, and four swords representing two armies suggests either weariness at the debased level of popular taste or a more personal contempt for courtly taste. The former is the more likely. Sidney's critique stands, therefore, as the expression of a sophisticated and learned courtier's distaste for popular and self-indulgent standards of dramaturgy in the early years of commercial playgoing in London.

Sidney objects principally to three things. The first is doggerel rhyming, a matter which allows him the transition from printed poetry to stage poetry. Secondly he objects to stage poets flouting the classical rules for the unities of time and place, a fault even in the play he regards as well written.

But if it bee so in *Gorboducke*, howe much more in all the rest, where you shall have *Asia* of the one side, and *Affricke* of the other, and so manie other under Kingdomes, that the Player when he comes in, must ever begin with telling where he is, or else the tale will not be conceived. Now you shall have three Ladies walke to gather flowers, and then we must beleeve the stage to be a garden. By and by we heare newes of shipwrack in the same place, then we are too blame if we accept it not for a Rock. Upon the back of that, comes out a hidious monster with fire and smoke, and then the miserable beholders are bound to take it for a Cave: while in the meane time two Armies flie in, represented with foure swords & bucklers, and then what hard hart wil not receive it for a pitched field.   (*Prose Works*, III.38)

Time is misused as violently as place. The hard-hearted stand against the credulous, divided over stage realism and the plausibility of the fiction. It is not just a question of poets flouting the classical precedents, but of their feeble challenge to human credulity. Other decorums are similarly ignored, notably by the placing of clowns in company with kings. This last point brings out Sidney's major grievance, the use of clowns to generate mindless laughter. Comedy is mixed into tragedy, and debases it. 'Laughter almost ever commeth of thinges moste disproportioned to our selves, and nature. Delight hath a joy in it either permanent or present. Laughter hath onely a scornfull tickling...For what is it to make folkes gape at a wretched begger, and a beggerly Clowne: or against lawe of hospitalitie, to jeast at strangers, because they speake not English so well as we do?' Delight is not the same as laughter, and the stage poets abuse the nature of poetry by aiming for the cruder form of pleasure. Sidney ends by apologising for spending too many words on stage poetry, which he did on the grounds that 'as they are excelling parts of *Poesie*, so is there none so much used in England, and none can be more pittifully abused'. Even as early as 1582, it seems, stage plays were the pre-eminent vehicle for poetry in London. Sidney was trying to raise standards among stage poets. His criticisms never altered the liberality with which they treated time and place, and only in one company do his strictures against clowns appear to have sounded a sympathetic chord, as the next chapter will try to indicate.

   The three main accounts of plays by playgoers are spread across thirty-four years, and two of them deal principally with perform-ances of Shakespeare. Two are from personal diaries and one from a letter. John Manningham's diary describes a performance of *Twelfth Night*, not at the Globe but at the Middle Temple in February 1602. Although it was not at the usual amphitheatre, the performance must have been by Shakespeare's company, bought by the law students for an evening's entertainment. Manningham's entry reads

At our feast wee had a play called 'twelve Night, or what you will'; much like the commedy of errores, or Menechmi in Plautus, but most like and neere to that in Italian called *Inganni*. A good practise in it to make the Steward beleeve his Lady widdowe was in Love with him, by counterfayting a letter, as from his Lady, in generall termes, telling him what shee liked best in him, and prescribing his gesture in smiling, his apparaile, &c., and then when he came to practise, making him beleeve they tooke him to be mad.[45]

Manningham's knowledge of Italian drama seems to have been less solid than his study of Plautus at school. The play closest to *Twelfth Night* is the *Ingannati*, not any of the group known as the *Inganni*. The plot device of identical twins seems to have prompted the comparison, although the different sexes of *Twelfth Night*'s twins brought no comment. Evidently the most noteworthy feature of the performance was the gulling of Malvolio. Apart from that, a reasonable comment to make, the entry shows that Manningham missed the point about Olivia mourning for her brother and saw the play instead in the more conventional shape of a widow being wooed by her steward. Widows were commonly thought to be vulnerable, and several popular ballads tell tales of rich ladies when widowed being seduced by their servants. Manningham conceived of the play as a stereotype joke situation where for once the villain is tricked in a way that satisfied conventional morality. It is a version of the play at some distance from modern readings.

Simon Forman, the fortune-telling quack who kept an extended diary of his activities around the turn of the century, went to four plays in April 1611 and included an account of each of them in his diary. He headed it 'The Booke of plaies and Notes hereof per formans for Common pollicie'. The four plays were *Macbeth*, *Cymbeline*, a play about Richard II (not Shakespeare's) and *The Winter's Tale*. All four must have been seen at the Globe, since Forman marked three 'at the Glob' and the fourth was *Cymbeline*.[46] Forman summarises the plot of each play in less than five hundred words, fairly accurately. Some indication of his intention in writing them out for 'Common pollicie' is given by the brief moral drawn at the end of the last two. After his account of the Richard II play he cites an example of the Duke of Lancaster's (John of Gaunt's) double dealing, and concludes 'Beware by this Example of noble men, and of their fair wordes, & sai lyttell to them, lest they doe the like by thee for thy good will.' At the end of his briefer account of *The Winter's Tale* he describes Autolycus, lists his cozening devices in the play and concludes 'Beware of trustinge feined beggars or fawninge fellouss.'

Forman's summary of *Macbeth* is accurate down to the details of the witches' prophecies to Macbeth and Banquo, the aftermath of Duncan's murder, and Banquo's ghost at the feast. No moral is drawn from this play. *Cymbeline*'s story is told like a narrative from the old romances which Beaumont burlesqued. Again the plot is summarised accurately, and no moral is drawn. The treatment of the four plays is similar except for the morals drawn after the last two. Both morals are based on details in the play, about single characters whose practices might prove dangerous to anyone innocent of 'Common pollicie'. All that can be deduced from the four accounts is that Forman thought of each play as if it was a dramatised romance narrative, with incidental lessons to be drawn from the activities of the bad characters for the unlearned at whom his account was probably aimed. The idea that plays were educative was nothing new. It underlies Sidney's critique, and Heywood makes the point strongly in his *Apology for Actors*, published very close to the time Forman wrote his summaries. Forman shows himself to have been attentive to the narrative sequence of events and to have picked up the details with nearly complete accuracy. His moralisings seem to be afterthoughts. He should probably serve as an example of one fairly ordinary type of playgoer, more absorbed in the story than the verse or the characterisation, not at all interested in symbols or application, inclined to moralise only in the conventional way as a response to the depiction on stage of villainy at work.

The third account of a play is of a performance, again at the Globe, in mid August 1634. It appears in a letter written from London by Nathaniel Tomkyns to his friend the landowning politician Sir Robert Phelips in Somerset. Tomkyns had done some business in London for Phelips over a legal case involving some men living on a royal manor of which Phelips was steward. The first third of the letter covers the business, and the remainder deals with current gossip in London. The last item Tomkyns offers as 'some meriment' to soften the sad news of a death.

Here hath bin lately a newe comedie at the globe called *The Witches of Lancasheir*, acted by reason of ye great concourse of people 3 dayes togither: the 3rd day I went with a friend to see it, and found a greater apparance of fine folke gentmen and gentweomen then I thought had bin in town in the vacation: The subject was of the slights and passages done or supposed to be donc by thesc witchcs sent from thence hither and other witches and their familiars; Of ther nightly meetings in severall places: their banqueting with all sorts of meat and drinke conveyed unto them by their familiars upon the pulling of a cord: the walking of pailes of milke by themselves and (as they say of children) a highlone: the transforming of men and women into the shapes of several creatures and especially of horses by putting an inchaunted bridle into their mouthes: their posting to and from places farre distant in an incredible short time: the cutting off a witch-gent woman's hand in the forme of a catt, by a soldier turned miller, known to her husband by a ring thereon, (the onely tragicall part of the storie:) the representing of wrong and putative fathers in the shape of meane persons to gentmen by way of derision: they tying of a knott at a mariage (after the French manner) to cassate masculine abilitie, and ye conveying away of ye good cheere and bringing in a mock feast of bones and stones in steed thereof and ye filling of pies with living birds and yong catts &c: And though there be not in it (to my understanding) any poetical Genius, or art, or language, or judgement to state or tenet of witches (wch I expected,) or application to vertue but full of ribaldrie and of things improbable and impossible; yet in respect of the newnesse of ye subject (the witches being still visible and in prison here) and in regard it consisteth from the beginning to the ende of odd passages and fopperies to provoke laughter, and is mixed with divers songs and dances, it passeth for a merrie and excellent new play, *per acta est fabula. Vale.*[47]

The play was Heywood and Brome's *The Late Lancashire Witches*. It was written over the summer of 1634 to capitalise on the trial of four women and the family who accused them of witchcraft, who had been brought to London because of some well-justified doubts among Privy Councillors about the correctness of the hearings in Lancaster. The play sensationalised the accusations by wholeheartedly taking the side of the accusers. Its use of details from the Lancaster hearings in fact makes it likely that Brome and Heywood were supplied with copies of the major depositions made against the accused, probably by the faction of the Privy Council which believed the charges and wanted to raise an outcry to strengthen the likelihood that the witches would be convicted. Tomkyns' account is of a performance designed as a rabble-rousing case for the prosecution.

It has been suggested that Laud, the Archbishop of Canterbury and the dominant Privy Councillor, would have been the leader of the faction sceptical of the accusations. Pembroke, the Lord Chamberlain, was his chief opponent and had easy access to the leading acting company at the Globe as well as to the accusers' depositions on which the play was based.[48] He certainly blocked another play about the witches from being performed at Salisbury Court until the Globe play had finished its run. Tomkyns' account suggests that neither the writers nor the players took their propagandising task very seriously. Tomkyns himself can have known little or nothing about the backstage machinations over the play, but his scepticism seems quite as deep as Laud's. He declares that the play showed 'the slights and passages done or supposed to be done by these witches', and that they were 'things improbable and impossible'. It was mere clowning about a topical piece of news.

In the event the accusations against the witches, shaky though they were, led to the women being returned to prison in Lancashire. Three of them were still there three years later.[49] Tomkyns' view of the play therefore needs to be set in the context of the profoundly divided feelings of the Privy Council on the one hand and the cheerfully credulous clowning of the players on the other. He preserved his independent judgement more worthily than the players or the Pembroke faction on the Council. He was certainly not the kind of judging spectator Jonson derided. But his sceptical response to the stage witchery was only a part of his response to the performance. His regret at the lack of 'poetical Genius, or art, or language' puts him in the Sidney class of playgoer, valuing poetry above the 'ribaldrie' and the 'fopperies to provoke laughter'. His scepticism was not only exercised over the case against the witches. Presumably such a delicate judgement should be weighed against the credulity of the other 'fine folke gentmen and gentweomen' who surprised him by their presence in the playhouse out of their usual season.

None of these three accounts of plays in performance offers anything really distinct as a characteristic audience reaction. Manningham saw *Twelfth Night* in stereotyped terms, Forman followed the plots and Tomkyns watched the knockabout from a standpoint which would clearly have made him prefer a more poetic offering. To these accounts we should add the kinds of audience reaction noted by Richard Levin: an interest in 'the portrayal of intrinsically interesting personalities and their actions',[50] with an expectation that actions can be viewed as real and that they should evoke the appropriate emotions of tears or laughter. These reactions lead Levin to sum up Shakespearean audiences as expecting chiefly 'a literal representation of individual characters and actions that were meant to be interesting and moving in their own right, and to embody the primary significance of the play'.[51] None of the evidence considered in this chapter runs seriously counter to that conclusion, though one important reservation should be made. The normative way of describing a play need not have been particularly close to the normative response to it in performance. Descriptions of this kind tend to be conventional, to obey familiar prescriptions. The plays are being summarised as a whole, and their most distinctive features identified. There is some evidence which suggests that these descriptions, especially those of Manningham and Forman, reflect the convention for accounts of plays more exactly than they indicate the writer's whole response.

It was standard practice for booksellers to paste titlepages on posts in the city when they wanted to advertise their latest products.[52] Quartos of plays were advertised in this way, and in terms not unlike Manningham's account of *Twelfth Night*. This is how *Richard III* was described on its first publication in 1597:

The Tragedy of King Richard the Third. Containing his treacherous Plots against his brother Clarence: the pittiefull murther of his innocent nephewes: his tyrannicall usurpation: with the whole course of his detested life, and most deserved death. As it hath beene lately acted by the Right honourable the Lord Chamberlaine his servants.

Whoever wrote that had seen the play in performance and registered the emotions appropriate to the main incidents in the plot. Similarly, if more crudely, the publisher of the quarto of *The Merchant of Venice* in 1600:

The most excellent Historie of the *Merchant of Venice*. With the extreame crueltie of *Shylocke* the Jewe towards the sayd Merchant, in cutting a just pound of his flesh: and the obtayning of *Portia* by the choyse of three chests. As it hath beene divers times acted by the Lord Chamberlaine his Servants. Written by William Shakespeare.

There is perhaps more of the advertisement here, in the hint that Shylock gets his bloody pound of flesh, than a fair report of the play. A more detailed account of a play's plot appeared on the titlepage for *Arden of Feversham* in 1592, giving not only the play's lurid story but its moral:

The Lamentable and True Tragedie of M. Arden of Feversham in Kent. Who was most wickedlye murdered, by the meanes of his disloyall and wanton wyfe, who for the love she bare to one Mosbie, hyred two desperat ruffins Blackwill and Shakbag, to kill him. Wherein is shewed the great mallice and discimulation of a wicked woman, the unsatiable desire of filthie lust and the shamefull end of all murderers.

The similarity of these advertisements to Manningham's and Forman's descriptions supplies ground for two suspicions: that they all followed a conventional pattern for describing plays in a brief, summarising form, and that such a convention gives only a small part of the full range of possible responses to the plays by the playgoers of the time. A great deal of room is left for memorable poetry and Jonsonian 'application' in the hinterland of audience responses. But there is sadly little tangible evidence there.

Before leaving this area, where in a sense the real study of the Shakespearean poets ought to begin, I should like to sketch in one line of speculation about these uniquely privileged playgoers. Stage plays became such a popular feature of London's culture by 1600 that it is impossible they could not in various ways have influenced the society which harboured them. These influences must be intangible, but they are a part of the mental composition of playgoers in their time, and some speculation about them might be justifiable before the final full stop is put to this chapter. Since the mind and actions of monarchs have been most closely studied in this period, I shall confine my speculations to two of them, and two incidents which affected them.

When the Essex rebels asked for *Richard II* to be staged on the day before their rebellion they revealed some of the misconceptions which made their rebellion such a sickly miscalculation of London's mood at the time. Censorship had removed the scene in which Bullingbrook takes the crown from Richard out of all three texts of the play printed in Elizabeth's lifetime. She herself had seen the point of the analogy which the Essex rebels tried to draw between Richard and herself, and commented on the frequent performance of the deposition on the public stages. Since Elizabeth saw herself as Richard, it was not surprising that the rebels saw Bullingbrook in Essex, a descendant of the Duke of Gloucester whose murder is held against Richard in the play, and dreamed of their leader successfully deposing Elizabeth and acceding to the crown like Bullingbrook. Only some such faith in stage fictions as political realities can explain the romantic impracticalities of the Essex plot.

Some comparably romanticising notion of princes living in an Arcadian world and riding gallantly into histrionic action must have sent Charles and Buckingham, disguised and athletic as they rode swashbuckling through foreign territories, off to Spain in 1623 on their ludicrous quest for a bride to reconcile the two hostile kingdoms. Charles's adventures in France and Spain have in their extravagance and impulsiveness the exact mode of Fletcherian tragicomedy. The Arcadian practices, love, disguise, princely errantry, and the happy ending necessary to love dramas were all part of the mental constructs out of which Charles and Buckingham undertook their political adventure. Its painfully ridiculous outcome, like the more plainly tragic consequence of the Essex rebellion, measures the distance of its protagonists from political realities. The old truism that when Charles became king the displays at Court of masques and dramas helped to conceal knowledge of his real position from him has a particularly sharp point in the misconception which prompted the Spanish adventure.

Essex and his followers, like Charles and Buckingham, tried to repeat familiar fictions and make them become political realities. Their minds must have been made suggestible by the evidence the playhouses provided of how the minds of men in company, as Bacon put it, can be swayed by the sight of great actions. The part played by the different playhouse repertories in the history of English society at this time will probably never be known with much precision, but since it was the only major medium for social intercommunication, the only existing form of journalism and the only occasion that existed for the gathering of large numbers of people other than for sermons and executions, it was certainly not cast in a minor role. The fictional presentation of affairs of state, in a city devoted to the art and trade of 'application', is probably a sharper guide to popular and even governing modes of thought about politics and society in Shakespearean times than is the case today. The fictions of the stage were certainly not so marginal to the affairs of state, because imaginative thought had few other outlets, and none with the coerciveness of the minds of men in company. It seems appropriate, as a final step in this history, to trace the history of playgoing tastes, the fashions in plays and playgoing, as they developed, changed and diversified between 1567 and 1642.

5
The evolution of tastes

Once it took on a plainly commercial function, as it did when the Red Lion came into existence in 1567 and the Theatre replaced it in 1576, London playgoing quickly became a settled institution. Its settled place in London's commerce, however, paradoxically meant that it became subject to rapid and incessant change. Regular attendances at a fixed venue required the impresarios to offer a constant supply of novelty. Whereas when travelling the players could sustain themselves with the same plays repeated in constantly changing venues, once the venue was fixed the repertory had to keep changing. As the chief determinant of this novelty there had to be an intimate interaction between the settled expectations of the playgoers and the fare they fed on. The result was constant, pressurised evolution in the players' repertoire of plays, a kind of aesthetic Darwinism, with the poets and their audiences as parents and the plays as their offspring. Henslowe's *Diary*, which records the financial labours of half of London's theatrical parentage at the peak of evolution in the 1590s, is above all an account of how intimate the interaction was between what the playgoers enjoyed and what the impresarios bought for them. Henslowe processed more than three hundred plays to feed London's appetite between 1592 and 1600. The history of Shakespearean playgoing has to start with the repertories which are the principal fossil record of this evolutionary process.

Most of the evidence about the repertory James Burbage planted in his playhouses through the 1570s suggests that it had little new to offer at first. The amazing changes which took place at the end of the first twenty years, in 1588, look like a belated response by the impresarios and poets to the new demands the London venues had stimulated. There was certainly no stock of plays already in existence before the 1580s which could have satisfied the tastes revealing themselves in 1588. Plays like *Common Conditions* (printed in 1576), *The Conflict of Conscience* (c.1572), and *Clyomon and Clamydes* (c.1570) all share a distinctly ungainly medley of moral teaching and romantic escapism, as if the bare commercial motive for enter-tainment could not walk out comfortably without the overcoat of morally instructive pretensions. The release from this overcoat which the professional London playhouses provided must have been due principally to their captive audiences. Only when the plays were offered to a crowd which had gathered and paid exclusively to enjoy a play were the poets made free to create offerings like *The Spanish Tragedy* and *Tamburlaine*. In the 1560s use of an open market place or a banqueting hall meant that authority's frown was a recurrent danger. Moreover audiences in halls and even at markets usually gathered for reasons more weighty than seeing a play. Plays in banqueting halls were a garnish to the feast supplied by a generous host. Brayne's and Burbage's commercial playhouses thus created the first regular means for every playgoer to buy just the garnish of his or her own entertainment. The plays designed to feed such a well-focussed hunger came afterwards.

Romantic narratives or 'gallimaufreys' like *Clyomon and Clam-ydes* were evidently the staple of the amphitheatre playhouses at first, and their popularity evoked enough protests from the more educated end of the audience range to give early notice of a social division in tastes. George Whetstone in 1578 and in the 1580s Stephen Gosson, Philip Sidney and John Lyly all poured scorn on the medleys of romantic fantasy staged with cardboard monsters and knockabout clowns. The vigour of the protests might be taken as an acknowledgement of the popular hold such plays had, and also of the players' aim to attract a mass rather than a select audience.

Brayne and Burbage of course built to supply an appetite they well knew already existed. The medleys or 'hybrid plays', as Anne Barton has called them, were based on assumptions about theatrical illusion which had grown to accompany a gradual swing in the mid century from the didactic to the entertaining.[1] By the 1580s Burbage could probably tell from his gatherers that a new market was developing. There was a new middle zone of public taste, fixed in London and offering new possibilities for an urban audience somewhere between the taste of the Court and the knockabout moralising of the country market places. The 'hybrid plays', Sidney's 'mungrell Tragy-comedie', had developed in the gap created at the beginning of the century between the community play of medieval religious drama and the 'self-contained play' of banqueting hall and Court enter-tainment.[2] Now there was a new body of urban playgoers who could begin to impose their presence and their preferences on their sup-pliers. Gosson in 1582 objected to the new body:

the common people which resorte to Theatres being but an assemblie of
Tailors, Tinkers, Cordwayners, Saylers, olde Men, yong Men, Women,
Boyes, Girles, and such like. (2.8)

Ordinary citizens, he felt, needed protection from corrupting experiences like playgoing. But such citizens, even boys and girls, had the pennies to pay for their corruption, and money was power.

There was another reason for starting captive playgoing in London besides the growth of an urban body of payers, a reason which might well be credited more directly to the poets than to the impresarios or the swell of social change. In the 1570s presenting plays at Court was a conspicuous sign of the power and influence of the nobles whose companies presented them. The Earl of Leicester and the Lord Chamberlain, Sussex, played no small part in the sponsorship of the new playhouses and their London playgoers. J. Leeds Barroll has produced evidence to show that the status at Court of major members of the Privy Council between 1573 and 1583 determined which companies were employed to perform the Christmas entertainments each year.[3] The plays and players must have proved entertaining enough to reflect the status of their sponsors at Court to everyone's satisfaction. That mutual benefit no doubt also helps to explain why Leicester got his company a royal patent in 1574, and why the position of Master of the Revels as the chief organiser of Court entertainment was regularised in 1579. The potential tensions in such rival displays of ostentatious nobility may also explain why when the Lord Chamberlain, Sussex, died in April 1583 the Master of the Revels, acting on Walsingham's orders for the Privy Council, immediately set up the Queen's Company by making a clean sweep of all the star players from the leading nobles' companies, as if to stop the rivalry with a royal monopoly.

Underlying these courtly manoeuvrings is the point that theatre had now become baldly a matter of secular entertainment, and a conspicuous one. The religious and folk rituals of Easter and May-games were a distant memory, and the transitional didactism of 'morality' plays was also going fast. Playgoers, now themselves paying directly for their entertainment, were motivated exclusively by the pleasure they expected for their pennies. Their taste in pleasure meant that they preferred to swallow the fantasies of romantic knight-errantry on stage which they were already familiar with in print. The Vice of the morality plays turned into a clown entertaining through foolery. The moral requirement faded as the commercial incentive grew.

Like all evolutionary trends, many factors combined to alter the

fare which playgoers consumed in the 1580s. Commercial security
made possible larger companies and longer plays, for instance.
Clyomon and Clamydes at 2220 lines was a consequence of the
growth of the standard company from the five who played Skelton's
Magnyfycence in the 1520s or the eight in *Cambises* (c.1561) to the
eleven men and four boys of *Tamburlaine* (1587) and *Edward II*
(1592). An even greater stimulus to change was the fact that playing
at the one fixed venue created a hugely enlarged demand for new
plays. So long as the companies travelled through the country they
needed barely three or four plays to satisfy their geographically
dispersed clients. In London by the 1590s Henslowe's company
performed as many as thirty-five different plays in a year.[4] Whether
or not the playgoers truly needed novelty, with a repertory committed to staging a different play every day of the week they certainly got
it. A third factor which must have influenced what playgoers saw
was the poets' new familiarity with what they could expect of their
regular customers, and possibly more directly useful, with the
companies for which they wrote their new plays. *Tamburlaine* was
not written by accident to include the number of parts which with
doubling could be handled by a company of precisely the standard
London size. And with that size went quality. *Tamburlaine*'s verse
must have been written for players who had shown something of
what could be done on a stage once poulter's measure and rhyming
fourteeners were replaced by decasyllabic verse. The Queen's
Company in 1583 had in Knell and Bentley as well as in Tarlton
players who had developed a level of professional expertise well
capable of encouraging other kinds of development.

Who were the paying playgoers at the first public playhouses in
London? The outcry against them from the pulpits and Guildhall,
which ran as a campaign with City funding from 1580 to 1584 and
only stopped when the Privy Council set up the Queen's Men as a
monopoly, makes it likely that there were few playgoing clerics or
aldermen of the City, certainly not the more puritanical of either
group. In 1580, 1581 and 1584 there were 'affrays' which give rather
more positive evidence, as well as indicating some of the tensions
which the playhouses and the outcry against them generated. Three
Privy Council minutes of April to July 1580 dictate the action
required over a scuffle which took place at a playhouse between men
of Oxford's company, and some law students. In April two players
from Oxford's, Robert Leveson and Lawrence Dutton, were lodged in
Marshalsea Prison 'for committing of disorders and frayes appon the
gentlemen of the Innes of the Courte'. In July a letter ordered a bond

for a year's good behaviour to be taken from Thomas Chesson, a former Oxford's player, to secure his release from prison.[5] This and the next incident are the only records of players actually coming to blows with playgoers in the entire history of the stage up to 1642, except for the attack by apprentices on Beeston's playhouse in 1617, which had a special cause, as we shall see. The 1580 affray was repeated the following summer, when once again a band of law students came to blows with a playing company. A City of London order of 11 July 1581 marked down

Parr Stafferton gentleman of Grayes Inne for that he that daye brought a dysordered companye of gentlemen of the Innes of Courte & others, to assalte Arthur Kynge, Thomas Goodale, and others, servauntes to the Lord Barkley, & players of Enterludes within the Cyttye . . . (2.7)

Despite the fact that Stafferton evidently took the initiative, the players were detained along with the gentlemen. Lord Berkeley himself intervened, asking the Lord Mayor to release the players and making himself answerable for their conduct. Players were now a mark of status, and needed the kind of care which valued possessions usually receive. We know nothing of the reasons for either of these summer affrays between the players and their customers, but it is unlikely to be part of the hostility either of the pulpit or Guildhall. It might have been a distant reflection of the rivalry between the noble patrons at Court, or it may simply reflect at some remove the excitement generated by a major novelty in London's society. The Inns of Court students who made such a conspicuous section of later audiences must have joined the crowds at the new amphitheatres early on, and the affrays might have been little more than crude ways of making their presence known. Certainly the documents about the affrays of 1580 and 1581 do indicate that law students were a conspicuous presence in the first audiences.

The third affray was between a servingman and a group of handicraft apprentices at the Theatre in 1584. A few years later Henry Chettle commented that house servants and apprentices formed rival groups in playhouses, and handicraft boys were usually the poorest apprentices. Elizabeth's chief minister, Lord Burghley, received a vivid report of this affray from William Fleetwood. Again, it happened in summer.

Uppon Weddensdaye one Browne, a serving man in a blew coat, a shifting fellowe having a perrelous witt of his owne, entending a spoile if he cold have browght it to passe, did at Theatre doore querell with certen poore boyes, handicraft prentises, and strook some of theym, and lastlie he with his sword wonded and maymed one of the boyes upon the left hand; where upon there assembled nere a ml people.

... This Browne is a common cossiner, a thieff, & a horse stealer, and colloreth all his doynges here about this towne with a sute that he haithe in the lawe agaynst a brother of his in Staffordshire. He resteth now in Newgate ...

(2.9)

Fleetwood went on to report that the Lord Mayor had issued an order to suppress the playhouses, and that James Burbage, owner of the Theatre, had resisted, claiming immunity as Lord Hunsdon's man. Hunsdon was the new Lord Chamberlain, and Burbage was evidently hoping that the Court would protect him against the City. Such disturbances could not have eased the Lord Mayor's displeasure against the amphitheatres, which technically were outside his jurisdiction in the suburbs, even though the Privy Council held him responsible for civil disorders in their vicinity.

Concern over the disorderly behaviour of the crowds at the public amphitheatres might have been intensified by the apparently contrasting docility of the gentlemen and ladies who attended the indoor playhouse in the Blackfriars, which opened in 1576. The prologue to Lyly's *Campaspe* (c.1584) concludes with the hope 'that although there bee in your precise judgements an universall mislike, yet wee maye enjoy by your woonted courtisies a general silence' (2.10). A similar plea in the prologue to *Sapho and Phao* (c.1584) suggests that Lyly wanted to remind his listeners that an audience made up exclusively of gentry should not behave in the manner of amphitheatre audiences. A gathering of gentlemen and ladies (the epilogue to *Gallathea* of about the same period is addressed to 'You Ladies') ought not to give voice to any disapproval. The artfully diffident prologue for *Midas* (1589) suggests that true gentlemen would never actually hiss at what they disliked. Servingmen, apprentices and Inns of Court students at the Theatre and Curtain evidently did not behave like gentlemen.

Lyly's concern to differentiate the behaviour of the playgoers attending boy company plays from the crowds at the amphitheatres is to some extent a reflection of the narrowness of his ambitions. His eye was always on the Court rather than the commercial theatre. For years he manoeuvred to obtain the post of Master of the Revels which Edmund Tilney had secured in 1579. His plays at the first Blackfriars playhouse in 1583–84 and later at Paul's through 1587–90 were aimed precisely at courtiers and the gentry who were familiar with the Court's major preoccupations. *Endimion* (1588) and *The Woman in the Moon* (c.1590), for instance, both make use of the stock courtier image of Elizabeth as Cynthia, the moon, and exploit the dogma of the king's two bodies as phases of the moon.[6] Partly he did this because the traditional identity of the boy companies as choristers who acted only for the improvement of their education and the incidental recreation of their betters gave him a claim to the top end of the market. Partly he did it as a means of holding the regular patronage of the courtiers through this specialised set of interests. The limited capacity of the boys, who could speak his lucid prose and exploit his wit-play, but who would be an obvious second best to the adult players at romantic heroics or the clowning of a Tarlton, made him offer decidedly different fare from the rumbustious popularism of the amphitheatres, and cater openly for more selective appetites. That the boy companies did not outlive the 1580s, that the Privy Council itself ordered them to be suppressed, and that Lyly died in penury is perhaps as much a measure of the strength of the competition as of Lyly's hazardous gamble.

(B) TARLTON'S FOLLOWERS (1576–88)

'Rumbustious popularism' is a term which, however evocatively designed, needs some definition. 'Popularism' is an overused term when applied baldly to the Shakespearean repertory. For Harbage the chief distinction of the Globe was its artisan audience, which he called 'popular' as distinct from the 'select' or elite audiences of the indoor playhouses. Some Elizabethan writers gave him a precedent for this with their equally tendentious distinction of the 'private' halls from the 'public' amphitheatres. I would prefer to rescue the term 'popular' from the associations Ancient Pistol gave it ('base, common, and popular'[7]) and keep it for those few phenomena like Tarlton and *Hamlet* which seem to have been truly popular in their capacity to 'please all'[8] at every level of English society.

Tarlton's fame, which made him a legend for sixty years after his death, is significant more for the phenomenon he represented than any jokes he actually created. It is hardly too much to say that, as much as the Virgin Queen herself, he became the chief emblem of the emerging national consciousness at the end of the sixteenth century. What Gabriel Harvey in a typically inventive doublet called 'piperly extemporising and *Tarletonising*'[9] became the hallmark of success as a professional entertainer. There had been professional jesters and fools before, both at Court and in the May-games of peasant and artisan holidays. But Tarlton was the first to become a national figure, and most significantly his fame was equally potent at Court, in the playhouse and in provincial towns. The book of *Tarlton's Jests*, produced posthumously and including some chestnuts which Tarlton himself certainly never invented, marks the range of his popularity by dividing its stories about him into three categories. The titlepage records them as

1. His Court-witty Jests
2. His sound City Jests
3. His Countrey-pretty Jests.[10]

His popularity ran through the whole nation and through every social rank.

What probably says more than anything else about adult players and their clients in the 1570s and 1580s is the relationship between Tarlton and Sir Philip Sidney. Tarlton was a Londoner, born in Ilford, almost within sound of Bow Bells, and first came to general notice as a comedian in the 1570s in the playing company of the Lord Chamberlain, the Earl of Sussex. In 1576 he gave the press a serious poem, *Tarlton's Tragical Treatises*, which he dedicated to Frances Mildmay, Sussex's daughter, in an epistle describing himself as the Lord Chamberlain's servant. The intriguing thing about the fragment of this poem which survives is that it is a defence of poetry. As such it is a far cry from the arguments Sidney was to compose a few years later:

> Seth verse and I so different are,
> I'll press with ragged rhyme
> To manifest the mere goodwill
> That I to learning owe,
> No painted words but perfect deeds
> Shall my invention shew.[11]

It is curious that a player and ballad-maker (his first ballad appeared in 1570) should spring to the defence not of playing but of poetry, at a time when the new public playhouses had begun to stir up the City's animus. Perhaps it is accidental that Sidney should have written his *Apology* only three or four years later, under the prompting of Gosson's misapplied dedication of his anti-player *School of Abuse* to him in 1579. It is certainly odd that Sidney should have been so dismissive in the *Apology* of plays which mingled clowns and kings when he knew Tarlton so well that in 1582 he agreed to be godfather to Tarlton's son.

Sidney's links with popular theatre and particularly with Tarlton are something of a mystery. Sidney evidently was a playgoer, and knew enough of London's current repertory in 1580 to incorporate an extended condemnation of the 'gallimaufrey' plays in the *Apology*. But the attitude he adopts in the essay clearly did not extend into his friendships in life. Like Whetstone, from whose *Promos and Cassan-*

17. Richard Tarlton with his stage trappings, from a sepia wash
drawing in the Pepys Library, Cambridge

dra he probably took his attack on clowns consorting with kings, his position was ambivalent. Whetstone's prefatory epistle for the publication of his play in 1578 objected to the adult companies using clowns:

not waying, so the people laugh, though they laugh them (for theyr folleys) to scorne: Manye tymes (to make mirthe) they make a Clowne companion with a Kinge; in theyr grave Counsels, they allow the advise of fooles ...

And yet in *Promos and Cassandra* itself a character, John Adroynes, is the 'clown' of the subplot and plays a rustic fool at Court in exactly the mode of Tarlton. Sidney, whether he met Tarlton in the amphitheatres or at Court, was no more consistent than Whetstone.

Tarlton's link with Sidney was by no means his only access to Court circles. When he was dying in 1588 he appealed to the Queen's most powerful factotum, Sir Francis Walsingham, to protect his six-year old son, whose godfather Sidney had died two years before.[12] Like all the material relating to social patterns at this time the evidence for Tarlton's links with the aristocracy is more plentiful than his links with the rest of the nation. But all three categories in the *Jest Book* say the same thing. His capacity to inspire laughter was universal, and his fame as a comedian guaranteed his welcome at all social levels.

His comedy was rumbustious in degrees which varied according to his venue. At Court and in his extemporising in the playhouses his act seems to have been more witty than knockabout, though wit survives more readily in print than knockabout does, and that assessment must be partly conditioned by the fact that the only surviving evidence is in print. The anecdotes in the *Jest Book* which report his extempore verses, especially two which he produced when apples were thrown at him by spectators, seem rather to be dependent for their humour on his reputation than to be justifications for it. A better mark of his rapport with his audiences is two accounts of how the first sight of his face alone, peeping through the hangings at the back of the stage, could start people laughing. His stocky figure, peculiar squint and flat nose could set an audience off even without the pipe and tabor which announced his routine. Henry Peacham has a verse which speaks from first-hand experience:

> Tarlton when his head was onely seene,
> The Tire-house dore and Tapistrie betweene,
> Set all the multitude in such a laughter,
> They could not hold for scarse an houre after.

Nashe in *Pierce Penilesse* (1592) tells how when Tarlton was with the Queen's Men on tour he reduced a country audience similarly,

much to the annoyance of a local magistrate who felt the Queen's
servants deserved more respect than to be laughed at.[13]

His rumbustious knockabout and his exploitation of the comedy
inherent in separating the clown from his stage parts in plays can be
seen in Tarlton's first entry as a Kentish mechanick in the Queen's
Men's play *The Famous Victories of Henry V*. The first scene
presents Henry and various courtiers, and the second scene intro-
duces the watch, four London citizens. They chat about what a
peaceful night it is, until Tarlton breaks in on them. The stage
direction reads *Enter Dericke roving*. He shouts 'Who there, who
there?' and gallops off, re-entering a few moments later in the same
manner.

> DERICKE. Who there, who there, who there?
> COBLER. Why what ailst thou? here is no horses.
> DERICKE. I alas man, I am robd, who there, who there?
> ROBIN. Hold him neighbor *Cobler*.
> ROBIN. Why I see thou art a plaine Clowne.
> DERICKE. Am I a Clowne, sownes maisters,
>   Do Clownes go in silke apparrell?
>   I am sure all the gentleman Clownes in Kent go so
>   Well: Sownes you know clownes very well:
>   Heare you, are you maister Constable, and you be speake?
>   For I will not take it at his hands.

The comedy starts with Dericke charging past the four members of
the watch while calling out for the watch to come because he has
been robbed. It progresses into a joke about his rustic dress and the
stock comedy of a countryman in the city. Between Robin's two
speeches there must have been some wrestling, since the last line of
this passage indicates Dericke's hostility to Robin. Broad comedy of
this kind – physical knockabout, incongruous dress, comic stereotypes – warrants the term 'rumbustious'.

Playgoers could engage in this kind of comedy, with its extra-
dramatic tactics of direct address to the audience and the clown
speaking out of character or playing as Dericke does a part claiming
not to be a clown. It depends largely on the audience knowing
Tarlton as himself, and his speciality after the play when he versified
extempore on subjects given him by the audience. This backchat
might easily spill into the play itself, as two of the *Jest Book*
anecdotes indicate. Because both of them give some sense of the
intimate kinship which existed between players and audience, they
are worth quoting at length.

> How *Tarlton* and one in the Gallery fell out.
> It chanced that in the midst of a Play, after long expectation for *Tarlton*,

being much desired of the people, at length hee came forth. Where (at his entrance) one in the Gallerie pointed his finger at him, saying to a friend that he had never seene him, That is he. *Tarlton*, to make sport at the least occasion given him, and seeing the man point with one finger, he in love againe held up two fingers: the captious fellow, jealous of his wife (for he was married) and because a Player did it, took the matter more hainously, and asked him why he made hornes at him? No (quoth *Tarlton*) they be fingers:

> For there is no man, which in love to me,
> Lends me one finger, but he shall have three,

No, no, sayes the fellow, you gave me the hornes. True (sayes *Tarlton*) for my fingers are tipt with nailes, which are like hornes, and I must make a shew of that which you are sure of. This matter grew so, that the more he medled the more it was for his disgrace; wherefore the standers by counselled him to depart, both hee and his hornes, lest his cause grow desperate. So the poore felow, plucking his hat over his eyes, went his wayes.

An excellent jest of *Tarlton* suddenly spoken.

At the Bul at Bishops-gate was a Play of Henry the 5 wherein the Judge was to take a box on the eare: & because he was absent that should take the blow, *Tarlton* himself (ever forward to please) took upon him to play the same Judge, besides his own part of the Clowne: and Knel then playing *Henry* the 5 hit *Tarlton* a sound boxe indeed, which made the people laugh the more, because it was he: but anon the Judge goes in, and immediately Tarlton (in his Clownes cloathes) comes out, and askes the Actors what newes? I (saith one) hadst thou been here, thou shouldst have seene Prince Henry hit the Judge a terrible box on the eare. What, man, said *Tarlton*, strike a Judge? It is true y faith, said the other. No other like, said *Tarlton* and it could not be but terrible to the Judge when the report so terrifies me, that me thinkes the blow remaines still on my cheek, that it burnes againe. The people laught at this mightily: and to this day I have heard it commended for rare.

The first of these anecdotes suggests something of the crowd psychology in such gatherings. If Tarlton picked on an individual it became a contest of wit where the crowd cheered the winner and jeered the loser, as they might in a physical struggle. Several of the 'sound City jests' have this outcome, mostly during a bout of extemporising in the playhouse. The crowd felt itself to be homogeneous, a gathering of familiars out to enjoy their pennyworth. Possibly the men in the galleries took more part in the extemporising backchat than the crowd in the yard. Certainly the gallery was a more conspicuous place from which to conduct an exchange with the player. But there does not seem to have been any firm sense of social division between the standers in the yard and the sitters in the galleries of the kind which is shown later by the derisive references to 'understanders'. Tarlton made his audiences a single unit through the cohesion of laughter.

More than any other player in this history Tarlton seems to have been a positive influence on the evolution of his medium and the development of audience tastes. He probably invented, and certainly made famous, the figure of the cunning rustic clown. The word 'clown' first appears in English in the 1560s. Related to the Low German for a farmhand ('yokel' is probably the nearest equivalent) and perhaps helped by the courtly pastorals of the 1570s which used 'Colin' as a shepherd's name, it meant a country fool or cunning innocent. Tarlton put the stereotype on stage, dressing himself in country clothes, a buttoned cap, baggy slops in russet, a bag at his side and the pipe and tabor (a small side drum) commonly used in country May-games. Chettle in *Kind Harts Dream* identifies Tarlton's ghost by 'his suit of russet, his buttond cap, his tabor, his standing on the toe, and other tricks'.[14] He thus had a persona, the innocent abroad whose guileless front makes him the butt who always wins in the end. As Dericke in *The Famous Victories* he is a countryman from Kent who copes with the affairs of London and the Court by virtue of his native wit. He made the stereotype of the guileless rustic so popular that several commentators after his death claimed that real countrymen were imitating Tarlton.[15] Touchstone in *As You Like It*, the urbane Court fool entering Arden's country world of rustics, performs his part as a very self-conscious opposite to Tarlton, and enjoys a sophisticated game of reversed clowning against the stereotype which his audience clearly knew well, even though by the time *As You Like It* came to the stage its originator had been dead for ten years.

In one sense Tarlton was old-fashioned even in the 1580s. He based his act on direct address to the audience and exploited the gap between the player and his play-role at a time when plays were generally moving towards the more illusionistic mode of the self-contained play. Comedy seems always to have been slower to discover new fashions than tragedy. Captive audiences encourage illusion, the separation of the stage spectacle from its beholders and the consequent identification of players with their roles. As a trend it never went so far as cinematic realism allows today. Richard Burbage as Hamlet could still step outside his role to joke about Polonius having previously played Caesar and his killer playing the 'brute' part. That kind of in-joke aside, though, Burbage evidently did convince his audiences of the reality of the roles he played. His elegist's account in 1619 tells of him playing the death of Hamlet in so lifelike a way that not only the spectators but his fellow players thought he was truly dying (2.124). This is an exaggeration, but the terms the elegist chose for praising Burbage were echoed by Thomas May and others and show how fully the power of dramatic illusion in the self-contained play took over from Tarltonising. In the 1590s the word 'personation' came into the language of playing for the first time. Tarlton's kind of audience, drawn by his fame and united by comedy into intimacy with the players, did not long outlast the 1580s.

Tarlton himself was by no means the only star of his company. The clown had his special extra-dramatic act, which could easily force its way into the play itself as it did when Tarlton took the Chief Justice's role in *The Famous Victories*, but he was also a member of the team. He took smallish parts in such plays as *King Leir* and *The Trouble-some Raigne of King John*, both of which the Queen's Men were playing in 1588. All three plays were closer to being star vehicles for the tragedians than for Tarlton or his fellow comic Robert Wilson. Nashe called Tarlton a king, and the ruler of traditional and popular audience taste he certainly was. But his successors as clowns or fools found the scope of their acts narrowing and by Tarlton's death the tragedians were recognised as the chief drawcard. Marlowe's Tamburlaine was ready to replace Tarlton when he died in 1588. In that year the shift in audience priorities from knockabout to tragic poetry was voiced with all its author's arrogance as a direct thrust against the clown, in the prologue to *Tamburlaine*. Marlowe announced his stage's withdrawal

> From jigging veins of rhyming mother wits
> And such conceits as clownage keeps in pay.

In 1590 Marlowe's publisher followed his author's preference by omitting the 'fond and frivolous gestures' which despite what the prologue claimed did still accompany the performance.[16] Whetstone and Sidney, objecting to mindless laughter ('mother wits' means moithering or fuddling the wits), now had something from Marlowe to put up against it. The paucity of evidence about audience attitudes in this period, and *Tamburlaine*'s publisher's note, should make us careful not to read too much into Marlowe's prologue. In the long run, though, there is no doubt that audiences followed where Marlowe led.

(C) LYLY'S SPECIAL APPEAL
(1580–89)

The social breadth of Tarlton's popularity has to be set against the continuing competition between the adult companies and the boy choristers. Tarlton and the Queen's Men secured a near-monopoly of adult playing in 1583, but the adults still had rivals in Paul's School and the Chapel Children, who played at Richard Farrant's hall in the Blackfriars precinct. In the years between 1575 when Paul's Boys got their playhouse and the establishment of the Queen's Men when Sussex died in 1583 the honour of performance in the holiday seasons at Court went mostly to the adults. But the child companies were by no means forgotten. Even Richard Mulcaster's boys at the Merchant Taylors' school performed seven or eight times at Court in the decade up to 1583. A Privy Council edict of 1578 lumped boy companies in with adults as professional entertainers. Unlike the adults, who on the whole spent more time in the country than in London, the boys performed exclusively in London. The relative infrequency of their performances – one a week at most compared with the almost daily use of the amphitheatres – together with their more exclusive venues inevitably meant that their audiences came from a narrower and higher social range than went to the amphitheatres. Halls, admitting smaller numbers, all seated, using artificial light, more intimate in scale and proximity to the stage, also had the superior social cachet of the banqueting hall environment which helped to maintain the fiction that the boys played not for money but to demonstrate their educational skills. In practice the boys did get some schooling, two or three hours daily for the Paul's choristers, and their voices were certainly trained for singing. Since the education curriculum in Elizabethan schools aimed at the art of good speaking, performing plays was a logical extension of that aim, and one which an educated audience would have been well trained to appreciate. Inherently the boy chorister performances were far removed from Tarlton's popularism.

Playgoers, however, were demanding paymasters. The Merchant Taylors stopped performances by their boys in 1574, on the grounds of wounded dignity.

... every lewd persone thinketh himself (for his penny) worthye of the chiefe and most comodious place withoute respecte of any other either for age or estimation in the comon weale, whiche bringeth the youthe to such an impudente familiaritie with their betters that often tymes greite contempte of maisters, parents, and magistrats foloweth thereof, as experience of late in this our comon hall hath sufficiently declared.[17]

Disrespectful crowds of Londoners jostling the worshipful masters who were their official hosts mark the end of the banqueting hall tradition. They also promised a better reception for large and loud adult players than for boys.

The outstanding feature of the boy company repertory in the 1580s was the drama of John Lyly. As with Marlowe's work for the adult players in the same decade it is difficult to see exactly how much Lyly's work was original, in that sense of imaginative creation which Coleridge identified with and for his poetry, or how much it was an intelligent and sensitive writer's response to the theatrical opportunities his time offered him. Certainly the style of *Euphues*, set in dialogue, was a novelty to the boys of Paul's, whose plays till then had been a mixture of morality and romance. But its measured, wittily elegant prose was well suited to a company of ten boys trained in elocution rather than swordplay. Lyly's activities, carefully designed and wholly distinctive in the audience they aimed at, and ultimately unsuccessful, carry some intriguing implications about playgoing in the 1580s.

Lyly was almost certainly drawn to write for the theatre by the manoeuvres at Court in the early 1580s when Leicester, Sussex, Oxford and other nobles began using companies of players to exhibit their power and influence. When Walsingham destroyed the rival companies in April 1583 by taking their leaders for the Queen's Men Oxford moved quickly to monopolise the boy players, who had not been touched by Walsingham. In June he took a lease of the Blackfriars playhouse and hired Lyly to write for an amalgamated company of the Blackfriars and Paul's boys. The Paul's master, Sebastian Westcott, had died in 1582 and his successor, Thomas Gyles, was not a producer of plays.[18] Oxford sponsored the amalgamated company at Court in the next two Christmas seasons, where they played Lyly's *Campaspe* and *Sapho and Phao*. In mid 1584, however, the owner regained possession of the Blackfriars playhouse and Lyly had to wait three years before resuming at Paul's, where he produced plays from 1587 to 1590. An ironic letter written in 1585 says that 'my Lord of Oxenfordes man called Lyllie' would be sure to put anything personal or satirical into the mouths of the Paul's boys if he could.[19] Lyly ran the boy company for the intimate world of courtiers and Court gossips. The fact that he failed commercially and died in poverty says something either about the parsimony of Court favours or about the predominant populism of audience tastes up to 1590.

Campaspe was evidently not a popular success, judging from the prologue written for the Blackfriars performances of its successor, *Sapho and Phao*. It set out to offer a distinct contrast with the adult repertory through its elegant prose repartee. It also sought to exploit the distinctive nature of the boys' talents, for instance in V.i., where successively one boy performs a dance, another '*tumbleth*' and a third *'singeth'*. The prologue for Blackfriars of *Sapho and Phao* is defensive:

Our intent was at this time to move inward delight, not outward lightnesse, and to breede, (if it might bee) soft smiling, not loude laughing.
(Complete works, II.371)

There is no doubt here to whom Lyly is appealing for approval. Sidney had completed his *Apology* only a year or two before Lyly wrote *Sapho and Phao*, and it was evidently circulating in manuscript around the Court and the gentry to whom Lyly addressed this prologue. Soft smiling is the gentlemanly alternative to the loud laughter which clowns provoke and which Sidney had attacked in the *Apology* as an 'extreme show of doltishnesse ... fit to lift up a loud laughter and nothing else'. Lyly's plays are a direct response to Sidney's condemnation of the 'mungrell Tragy-comedie' which mingled clowns with kings. Lyly's prologue is an appeal to the Blackfriars audience to adopt Sidney's preference against the fare offered by the adult players.

This appeal was not heard with universal sympathy. Lyly had stressed the gentlemanly composition of the Blackfriars audience and pleaded for gentlemanly restraint if not positive approval of his Sidneian offering in his first Blackfriars prologue, for *Campaspe*.

Onelie this doeth encourage us, that presenting our studies before Gentlemen, though they receive an inward mislike, wee shall not be hist with an open disgrace.   (2.11)

Gentlemen will surely be courteous towards boys. It is a weakly defensive assumption of good behaviour, and does not sound entirely confident that it will prove justified.

Lyly certainly hoped that an audience of Court gentlemen and ladies would attend Blackfriars and behave courteously, without laughing loudly or hissing. If he did get such audience they did not bring him great profit. In 1589 he tangled himself in the Marprelate controversy, writing pamphlets and possibly plays for the Church establishment, with the result that once the government had captured the Marprelate printing press and tried to clamp down on all the controversy it stopped plays at Paul's altogether. Tarlton had also been involved in anti-Marprelate propaganda with the Queen's Men, but they survived. Only Lyly and Paul's, the sole surviving boy company, suffered directly. The gentlemanly appeal of Lyly's plays was not strong enough to gain them any favour in competition with rumbustious popularism, which to the government had begun to seem like bread and circuses. Playgoers were too fond of loud laughter to sustain a gentlemanly repertoire beyond the 1580s.

(D) MASS EMOTION AND THE ARMADA (1588–99)

What seduced playgoers between 1587 and the end of the century was more than anything else an increase in the emotional immediacy of the plays' subject matter. England fought with Spain not only at sea facing the Armada but across the North Sea in the Netherlands. Militarism and hostility to Spain and Spain's Catholicism amongst London audiences found mirrors on stage. For more than ten years wars and stories of wars were the main meal on the broad platforms of the amphitheatres.[20] There were no hall playhouses available to offer more intimate fare, but the mood was in any case right for the drums, swordplay and noise which suited the larger stages and natural daylight of the open playhouses.

The success of swordplay on stage in the 1590s may have been partly a cause and partly an effect of the disappearance of the halls. The evidence is complex and inconclusive. The adults appear to have had access to large rooms at City inns in Gracechurch Street through the winter,[21] and when the City authorities finally blocked that outlet James Burbage tried to build an indoor playhouse to replace his ageing Theatre. The divide between halls for boys and amphitheatres for adults was maintained against the will at least of Burbage, first by the ban on playing at City inns in 1595, and then by the ban on Burbage's new Blackfriars playhouse in 1596. Largely by accident authority connived at maintaining the adults in their open-air playhouses with their battle displays in the militant repertoire which developed with the Armada in 1588.

Swordplay was a standard offering on the amphitheatre platforms in the 1580s, in exhibition bouts and prize fights. It was a simple matter to add it to the plays. Tarlton became a Master of Fence in 1587 by fighting seven other Masters, so he for one had the skill to entertain in this fashion. Others clearly had it too. In *Orlando Furioso* the hero, played by Edward Alleyn, engages in a duel on stage which the quarto text scores with the stage direction *'they fight a good while and then breathe'*. At the Red Bull, where Alleyn's swashbuckling tradition survived right up to the closure, a feltmaker's apprentice in 1622 sitting on the edge of the stage was hurt by a player during a stage swordfight. His pride was more injured than his body, and he held to the spirit of the playgoing occasion by issuing a challenge to the player who wounded him.[22] The duel which concludes *Hamlet* was conceived for the open-air stage used for fencing displays.[23]

Playgoing became a uniform custom in the 1590s for a variety of reasons. The only playhouses available were amphitheatres, which made one kind of choice uniform. Helped by a long closure for the plague in 1593 the government allowed only two companies to flourish in the prosperous years which followed: Shakespeare's company patronised by the Lord Chamberlain, and Alleyn's company under the Chamberlain's rival the Lord Admiral. Henslowe's accounts of the Admiral's Men's activities in these years are the most vivid record we have for the way players and their poets struggled to satisfy playgoers' tastes. Unfortunately the accounts are primarily financial, and only secondarily about the plays which were fed to the playgoers. More than half the plays named in Henslowe's records have vanished, and the only direct evidence he provides about playgoers is the frequency with which some kinds of play were fed to them.

The narrow uniformity of playgoing at this time suggests that playgoers came from all the social strata. What little other evidence there is tends to support this supposition. It does not say whether some playgoers might not have preferred other kinds of fare or other kinds of playhouse. The impresarios who reopened the hall playhouses in 1599 and 1600 clearly thought they would. Nonetheless, a total of two amphitheatres was the sole provision through most of the 1590s. The comments of Sir John Davies and others indicate that the full range of society accepted amphitheatre playgoing in this period. Courtiers, the 'clamorous fry' of law students, citizens, whores, porters and menservants all went to the Rose, Theatre and Curtain.

Nashe did a little sociological delving in *Pierce Penilesse* to identify the kind of people who might be free to attend a play on a working afternoon.

... whereas the after-noone beeing the idlest time of the day; wherein men that are their owne masters (as Gentlemen of the Court, the Innes of the Courte, and the number of Captaines and Souldiers about *London*) do wholy bestow themselves upon pleasure, and that pleasure they devide (howe vertuously it skils not) either into gameing, following of harlots, drinking, or seeing a Playe ...

The players themselves are blameless:

Whereas some Petitioners of the Counsaile against them object, they corrupt the youth of the Cittie, and withdrawe Prentises from their worke; they heartily wishe they might bee troubled with none of their youth nor their prentises; for some of them (I meane the ruder handicrafts servants) never come abroade, but they are in danger of undoing ... (2.15)

A comparatively innocent use of leisure indeed. The other side of that picture should be set alongside Nashe's, because it goes some way towards explaining why the authorities, especially the City fathers whose function was to control civil and criminal trouble, were so concerned about the new institution.

Playhouses are designed to attract crowds, and crowds attract criminals and civil disorders. In a city with no police force and minimal ways of enforcing the law that design created a major headache for the London authorities. The playhouses were in the suburbs where the justices of Middlesex and Surrey ruled, but the Privy Council expected the London authorities to control any riots by Londoners whether in the City or the suburbs. Robert Greene's second cony-catching pamphlet records how playgoers were fair game for criminals in 1591.

... At plaies, the Nip standeth there leaning like some manerly gentleman against the doore as men go in, and there finding talke with some of his companions, spieth what everie man hath in his purse, and where, in what place, and in which sleeve or pocket he puts the boung and according to that so he worketh either where the thrust is great within, or else as they come out at the dores. (2.13)

When Francis Langley proposed building a new playhouse, the Swan, the Lord Mayor wrote to Lord Burghley on 3 November 1594 asking that all of London's playhouses should be pulled down.

... the quality of such as frequent the sayed playes, beeing the ordinary places of meeting for all vagrant persons and maisterles men that hang about the Citie, theeves, horsestealers, whoremoongers, coozeners, connycatching persones, practizers of treason, and other such lyke. (2.21)

He used the same terms in his petition to the Privy Council on 28 July 1597. The City authorities were particularly frustrated by the location of the amphitheatres in the suburbs, where disorders were most likely to break out. Both Shoreditch and the Bankside supported thieves' kitchens and brothels as well as the bear-baiting and playing amphitheatres. When Davies wrote about 'free' Fuscus or Rowlands joked about gallants choosing between a play and a bawdy house (2.19,36) they were lumping together the main activities of London's haunts of pleasure. Even without the outcry from the pulpits it seems reasonable to assume that most playgoers were the 'free' in whose view of life pleasure rated a high priority.

The forms that pleasure in the playhouses took changed quite emphatically by the end of the decade. One of the consequences of having only the one kind of venue seems to have been an intensified pressure to evolve new forms. That pressure affected the evolution of audience likes and dislikes in distinct ways, one of the more striking being a development in the sense of reality in the subjects portrayed on stage.

Reality on stage in the 1590s is a complex thing. It was not simply realism, though that went with it, but something more like an emotional response to staged events which depended for its strength on a conviction that the display was a form of truth. There is a resounding truth in Francis Bacon's recognition of this force in his comment on the minds of men in company (2.57), but in 1605 it was still a new phenomenon.

Whatever the reason – the new poets, the evolution of playgoing and the national shock of the Armada all had a little to do with it – the minds of men in company at plays in the 1590s needed stronger meat for their affections than the 1580s had given them. The 1590s made a great evolutionary leap from the fantastic images so handsomely derided by Gosson in 1582:

Sometime you shall see nothing but the adventures of an amorous knight, passing from countrie to countrie for the love of his lady, encountring many a terrible monster made of broune paper, & at his retorne, is so wonderfully changed, that he can not be knowne but by some posie in his tablet, or by a broken ring, or a hankircher or a piece of a cockle shell ...[24]

The leap was towards what Nashe described in the audience for Shakespeare's 1 *Henry VI* in 1592, the common response to a realistic evocation of a real event:

How would it have joyed brave *Talbot* (the terror of the French) to thinke that after he had lyne two hundred yeares in his Tombe, hee should triumphe againe on the Stage, and have his bones newe embalmed with the teares of ten thousand spectators at least (at severall times) who, in the Tragedian that represents his person, imagine they behold him fresh bleeding.   (2.15)

This is the first description of a mass emotion other than laughter in any London playhouse. If, as is likely, Shakespeare's play about military disasters across the Channel is the 'harey the 6' of Henslowe's *Diary*, then the receipts for its performance at the Rose on Bankside suggest that Nashe underestimated the numbers so moved by at least a half.[25] It was Henslowe's most profitable play after *The Wise Men of Westchester*, a knockabout comedy. Serious matters with an immediate gut appeal to the militarism which set sail in

England against the Armada quickly took hold of the repertory. They gave playgoers the tears of conviction. What the players now had to supply was plausible impersonation. That, along with the emotionalism of Marlowe's mighty line, was what grew from the evolutionary leap of the 1590s.

The great stage figures of this period, Tamburlaine, Faustus and the hero of *The Spanish Tragedy*, share several features. They are all historical or quasi-historical figures with no great claim to a place in the history books. They all speak great verse. They all have powerfully individual personalities, and they all face immense personal challenges. Their verse was mocked by the more advanced tastes as early as 1597 (see 2.25), and it was chiefly their individuality which gave them all such enduring lives on the stage up to 1642, while stereotypes like Tarlton's clown retreated to the fringes or disappeared altogether. Mass emotion in playgoers and powerful 'personation' on stage grew together at the end of the 1580s.

Marlowe's mighty line has been analysed thoroughly, usually as an innovation in the development of spoken verse, as it certainly was. I would add to that analysis two other reasons for its fame, both of them likely consequences of the growth of London playgoing. In varying degrees they are both conjectural, but they fit the other evidence and have strong implications. The first is the extent to which Marlowe's verse was clearly designed to work on the audience's emotions. Marlowe was one of the first university wits to grasp the new opportunities which the willing captives in the London amphitheatres gave poets. He must have recognised his own power to sway audiences with words, that great secret in nature which Bacon saw as the susceptibility of the minds of men in company. Poets had never before been able to grasp the opportunity of moving the 'affections' of three thousand packed and willing hearers at one time. Marlowe was the first poet to grasp that chance.

The second reason is the part played by Tamburlaine, Faustus, and Hieronymo in the growth of 'personation'. The term first came into use in the 1590s, signalling not only the concept of a player pretending to be a real human being (as distinct from Magnificence or a king like Cambyses) but the arrival of stage heroes through whom many of the spectators could identify themselves and their wants. Each of the three characters drew his force from one of the three deepest wells of emotion in the Elizabethan mind. Tamburlaine the shepherd turned conqueror embodied militarism and earthly power. Faustus the sceptic embodied religious doubt. Hieronymo the revenger constructed a model of earthly justice in a corrupt world. Three such potent embodiments of Elizabethan emotions did not evolve and thrive on the stage without strong support from their audiences.

These three wells will be drawn in the next section. One feature of the 1590s which is missing from them should be noted first: all three were peculiarly masculine preoccupations. In all the seventy-five years between 1567 and 1642 no decade supplied less of what was expected to please the women in the audiences. Shakespeare produced his romantic comedies, and a few domestic dramas (considered in a later section) may have been designed to attract women, but the masculine affairs of war and military history, and the bawdy clownings which pervade the repertories show less concern for the women playgoers than any plays before or after.

(E) RULE, RELIGION, AND REVENGE (1588–99)

Tamburlaine launched a fashion for verse which Nashe in 1589 unkindly called 'the swelling bumbast of a bragging blanke verse' (2.12). Appropriately enough Nashe took his metaphor from the fashion in dress favoured by the Spanish enemy, padded or bombasted sleeves and fustian doublets, clothing both exhibitionistic and (by association) militaristic. Alvin Kernan's phrase for Marlowe's style, 'the pathetic fallacy in the imperative mood',[26] nicely captures the assumptions about earthly sympathy and human aggression which Tamburlaine represented to the original playgoers. The imperiousness of his 'stalking and roaring', which half a dozen commentators mention in the 1590s,[27] opened a rich vein for Henslowe and the poets to suck.

There was a plethora of imitations. *Selimus, Alphonsus of Aragon, The Wars of Cyrus,* the two parts of *Tamar Cham,* probably the lost *Cutlack* and *Muly Molloco* which feature as two of Henslowe's more popular plays, *The Battle of Alcazar* and plays about English soldiers abroad such as *Sir Thomas Stukeley,* besides the less battle-ridden plays of national isolationism such as *Friar Bacon and Friar Bungay* all share the narrow nationalism and militancy which Marlowe gave a voice to.

Few of these imitations outlasted the decade in the playwriting fashion, though playgoers were more durable. *Tamburlaine* itself drew mockery both for its verse and for Alleyn's strutting in the title role. It is tempting to assume an evolution in audience taste away from bombast and battle heroics, and certainly some parts of playgoing society went in that direction.[28] It is even more tempting to

18. Edward Alleyn as Tamburlaine in the 1590s. The engraving
appears in Richard Knolles, *A general Historie of the Turkes*,
1597

trace the development in Shakespeare from Talbot to Henry V as the central line of evolution. In the Queen's Men's *Famous Victories* Henry is transformed from dissolute prince to all-conquering king by nothing identifiable in human psychology, whereas the companion of Falstaff in Eastcheap undergoes a complex process of entirely human adaptation. But to fall for such temptations is easy and unhelpful. There were certainly developments in the complexity of character psychology before *Hamlet* broached it as a new interest in 1600, but almost all of them were Shakespeare's own. With the marginal exception of Marlowe in *Edward II* the principal developer of 'personation' besides Shakespeare was Kyd with his mad Hieronymo.

No one feature will explain the unique and lasting popularity of *The Spanish Tragedy* on the Shakespearean stage. Throughout the seventeenth century it was quoted and burlesqued more than any other play, even *Hamlet*. Claude Dudrap[29] has identified quotations from it in fifty-nine plays performed between 1591 and 1642, a startlingly powerful measure of its quotability and its enduring familiarity with playgoers. Its verse alone cannot explain such popularity, and there may well be some cogency in Muriel Bradbrook's suggestion that it is a 'projection of deep fears, the exorcism of guilt which the actors and audience shared'.[30] Revenge is a complex phenomenon psychologically as well as morally, and the conclusion to the play, doing earthly justice through the enactment of a play by the characters on stage, may as Bradbrook suggests be an oblique form of response to the long-lasting assault by the church against the theatre. No Elizabethan could have taken lightly Hieronymo's debate with himself over the morality of revenge in III.xiii, in which he weighs Seneca, ten of whose revenge plays had appeared in English in 1581, against God's word that earthly revenge is wrong and justice sits only in heaven, and chooses Seneca. Bradbrook identifies a Christian context for the play's appeal: 'The figure of the human Revenger represents assimilation and mastery of fear evoked by such a work as Dr Thomas Beard's *Theatre of God's Judgement* (1597), where, upon the stage of the whole universe, God is seen as the supreme Revenger.'[31] Beard's citation of figures well known in the playhouse, such as Tamburlaine, Arden of Feversham, Richard III and Antony and Cleopatra, probably echoed the fears of not a few playgoers. Hieronymo, like Hamlet, appealed because he was hero and victim at once. He enjoyed his revenge and he paid God's price for his pleasure. The play's popularity must have struck chords somewhere in these areas of the ambivalent Elizabethan psyche.

Faustus on the face of it served a much more straightforward religious purpose. Its displays of devilry at work were capable of provoking reactions of mass hysteria in both audience and actors. It was staged in religious technicolour, between the understage area, traditionally the hell which lay under the earth of the stage platform itself, and the heavens of the zodiac-painted stage cover. A description written in 1620 shows that Alleyn's playhouse kept these traditions unchanged for many years.

> ... men goe to the *Fortune* in *Golding-Lane*, to see the Tragedie of Doctor *Faustus*. There indeede a man may behold shagge-hayr'd Devills runne roaring over the Stage with Squibs in their mouthes, while Drummers make Thunder in the Tyring-house, and the twelve-penny Hirelings make artificiall Lightning in their Heavens.   (2.127)

For all the roaring and flashing the play generated plenty of tension. One reference, which has a ring of truth in its offhand delivery, tells of a man with 'a head of hayre like one of my Divells in Doctor *Faustus*, when the olde Theater crackt and frighted the Audience'.[32] There is probably much more truth in that account of audience tension than the story of the players who suddenly noticed during a performance that there was one devil too many in the company, and fled, spending the night in prayer and repentance.[33]

However fanciful such stories seem, the religious power of *Faustus* should not be underestimated. Alleyn played the role in a surplice with a cross stitched on the front, according to a verse by Samuel Rowlands.[34] It is not unlikely that in wearing such a costume he was taking precautions against his own premature damnation. The play was certainly seen as a morality of intellectual pride suffering the pains of hell, just as *Tamburlaine* was seen as its converse, to judge from all the references to 'that Atheist *Tamburlan*'.[35] When Marlowe died so spectacularly in a tavern brawl in 1593, whether or not the knife thrust was aimed by a Privy Council spy, Marlowe's fate was hailed by the pulpits as God's judgement exactly in the form his play seemed to depict. Its popularity very largely depended on audiences viewing the stage spectacle as moralistic and personal.

Henslowe's records confirm what contemporary references would have suggested anyway, that these three plays along with Shakespeare's were the staple fare exciting playgoers, guaranteeing the players' prosperity up to 1600 and indeed fixing the basic lines of taste in plays for generations to come. But there is evidence for other tastes as well, and the broad picture must include more than these main dishes. Comedy also changed rapidly and showed signs of a divergence in audience tastes towards the end of the decade. Perhaps the most illuminating change of all, though, was the arrival of contemporary events openly reproduced on the stages.

In the 1590s the popular playhouses began to tap that reservoir of curiosity about the real lives of living people which is now the chief refreshment in newspapers. Newsworthy people and events, the quotidian gossip of journalism, turned up as stage fare for a wide range of audience appetites. Thomas Platter described Londoners as 'learning at the play what is happening abroad; indeed men and womenfolk visit such places without scruple, since the English for the most part do not travel much, but prefer to learn foreign matters and take their pleasures at home'.[36] The much-travelled Platter might regard this as insularity, but it was also the first great market for daily journalism. The depiction of contemporary affairs in the playhouses, although the evidence is patchy and fragile, does offer a testimony to the increasingly day-by-day ordinariness of playgoing, and its shifts offer some testimony for the social dispositions of the people at whom the players aimed.

Lyly's covert allusions to contemporary affairs were plainly (about the only plain thing about them) in-jokes for the tightly cohesive gossips of the Court and its associated gentlefolk. Jack Roberts' reference in 1585 to Lyly's use of Paul's boys was to his publication on stage of the sort of tattle and scandal which professional letter-writers like Whyte and Chamberlain included in their reports.[37] Their appeal was the same as a tattle-sheet with, in the playhouse, the bonus of wellbeing which comes from feeling part of a crowd collectively deriding its scapegoats. That is always an enticement to a massed audience. But in small and powerful coteries like Elizabeth's Court it was a difficult game to play if you did not have the control and the consequent licence of a Tarlton. The players' involvement in the Marprelate controversy after Tarlton's death burned a few fingers and showed how quickly the licence could be withdrawn.

The Martin Marprelate pamphlets, with their splendidly cutting mockery of the Bishops of London and Winchester and of 'John of Cant' were scandalous, and the players must have been drawn to the scandal for its own sake, without any sponsorship by the authorities, though all their efforts seem to have been on the government side. The utter failure of Elizabeth's officers to track down the Martinists' secret press, and the implicit challenge the controversy put up against political as well as ecclesiastical authority, kept it a sensation for nearly eighteen months. Anti-Martinists, freed to participate by the fact that they were defending the established church and state, poured out pamphlets and stage works in a frenzy of publicity, much as the journalistic media have always done to drum up work for themselves. John Laneham wrote pieces for the Queen's Men at the Theatre which formalised Tarlton's jibes and ballads. Lyly and Nashe both wrote of 'old Lanam' writing 'Jigges and Rimes' against Martin.[38] An anti-Martinist pamphlet of October 1589 describes an allegorical adaptation of the traditional folk-play May-games against Martin. It is a new

> worke ... intituled ... *The May-game of Martinisme.* Verie defflie set out, with Pompes, Pagents, Motions, Maskes, Scutchions, Emblems, Impreases, strange trickes, and devices, between the Ape and the Owle, the like was never yet seene in Paris-garden. Penry the welchman is the foregallant of the Morrice, with the treble belles, shot through the wit with a Woodcocks bill ... *Martin* himselfe is the Mayd-Marian, trimlie drest uppe in a caste Gowne, and a Kercher of Dame Lawsons, his face handsomlie muffled with a Diaper-napkin to cover his beard, and a great Nosegay in his hande ... *Wiggenton* daunces round about him in a Cotten-coate to court him with a Leatherne pudding, and a woodden Ladle ...
> (*The Returne of the renowned Cavaliero Pasquill of England*. Nashe, *Works*, 1.83)

Whether this reports a genuine burlesque staging about the Martinists or is the pamphleteer's fantasy it reflects the terms in which the players choose to represent their audiences' interest in the Marprelate arguments. In a later pamphlet Nashe stressed the traditional May-game framework (*Vetus Comoedia*) and the allegorising:

> Me thought *Vetus Comoedia* beganne to pricke him at London in the right vaine, when shee brought foorth *Divinite* wyth a scratcht face, holding of her hart as if she were sicke, because *Martin* would have forced her.
> (*Works*, 1.92)

What is also significant, whether or not it reflects the burlesque traditions of the May-games, is the physical representation of the Martinists John Penry and Giles Wiggington on stage.[39] It was a relatively short step from such parodic allegorising to more realistic portrayals of newsworthy figures on the popular stage, especially the simple portrayal of battle heroes.

Covert allusions to contemporary people and events have a history almost as long as the stage itself. Nashe's disarming prologue to *Summer's Last Will and Testament*, presented by Paul's boys to the Archbishop of Canterbury in 1592 after he had closed Paul's playhouse, was not the first to suggest that allusion-hunters can find more than is there. He advised 'Moralisers, you that wrest a never meant meaning out of everything, applying all things to the present time' to turn their attention from his play to the 'common stage'.[40] Early in the 1590s, though, the common stages were elaborating the urge to moralise their spectacles by introducing the direct representation of famous or scandalworthy figures. *Arden of Feversham* is a strange play in many respects. Its stage provenance is unknown, though it can be dated close to *Tamburlaine* at the end of the 1580s. Its author is equally unknown, though its theatrical quality is high enough to have produced claims that it must be early Shakespeare. It is also the first play to stage a major domestic scandal. The murder of Arden by his wife and her lover took place forty years earlier, but it was a famous story, and Holinshed's 1587 edition gave four pages of the *Chronicles* to it.[41] Called 'a naked tragedy' in its epilogue, the play is a straightforward dramatisation of Holinshed's account, with some pathos, some sermonising and considerable psychological insight. What is most striking about it is the utter contrast with *Tamburlaine* and its imitations. The emotional force derives from its familiar domestic setting, its claim to be true, the very ordinariness of its world. Even in later years few writers were so willing to let the story speak for itself. If there were any evidence for its impact on contemporary playgoers it would be tempting to call it superlative journalism. Without that, it must stand only as evidence for one writer's sense of what his market would bear.

The taste which evoked *Arden of Feversham* and plays like *A Yorkshire Tragedy* (1606) was possibly satisfied earlier and more often than the evidence surviving in plays can tell us.[42] When the Lord Treasurer ironically told Star Chamber in 1596 that he would like to see the playmakers make a comedy out of a case in front of the Chamber and 'to act it with those names',[43] he was presumably acknowledging a well known practice. Domestic scandals were certainly put on stage in remarkably faithful versions of the known events in two later cases, Chapman's *The Old Joiner of Aldgate* (1602) and a play by Dekker and others, *Keep the Widow Waking* (1624). Neither play text has survived, but court records say enough about them to make it likely that both plays came close to modern newspaper reportage. C. J. Sisson analysed the circumstances in detail, and while his reconstruction of the plays necessarily owes more to what the courts said actually happened than to what Chapman and Dekker wrote, it seems certain that the appeal of the plays for their audiences was meant to lie in the assumption that they were faithful accounts of the events.

Chapman wrote his play for Paul's boys, about a group of people living and working in the immediate neighbourhood of Paul's, who in 1600 became embroiled in manoeuvres which went to litigation over who should marry a wealthy young girl. One of the suitors, a bookbinder named John Flaskett with a shop in Paul's yard, commissioned the play in order to present his version of the quarrel and so influence the court in his favour. In the subsequent court proceedings it was alleged against Flaskett that the play was his idea.

that a stage play should be made and was made by one George Chapman upon a plott given unto him concerning ... Agnes Howe ... (her cause and sutes then depending) & the same under coulorable & fayned names personated, so made & contryved was sold to Thomas Woodford & Edward Pearce for xx markes to be played upon the open stages in divers play houses within the citie of London to resemble and publish the dealing of her father towards her concerning his practize with several sutors to bestow her in marriage with one that might forgoe her portion & that therbie she might shutt up & conclude a match with ... Flaskett rather than to suffer her name to be so traduced in every play house as it was lyke to be.[44]

Flaskett himself took Howe, the father of the girl, to see the play at Paul's. Howe protested in court that he did not realise what the play was about until he was sitting there and heard people around him say it was about the case.

... this defendant thinketh that the same Play was meant by this defendant & his daughter & Mris Sharles John Flaskett & others, att which Play he did once sitt together with Flaskett & sawe the same, being unawares unto him brought to sitt by Flaskett to see the Play. And further he hath heard manie say that the Play was made of this defendant & his daughter & also of others.

(2.48)

Howe, who finally won the legal contest against Flaskett, did not take great offence. He seems almost to have enjoyed the publicity.

Dekker's play was rather different, although its occurrence in 1624 is good evidence for the durability of the journalistic function that the stage established in the 1590s. He worked with Rowley, Ford and Webster to dramatise two sensational cases of felony and murder for the Red Bull players. The play's subplot was again the story of a young woman being exploited for her money, but the main plot was the murder of a widow by her son. The subplot was the subject of a suit in Star Chamber, and the main plot, based on a murder in Whitechapel in April 1624, prompted the publication of ballads and a play by Thomas Drue as well as Dekker's play.[45] The links between broadsheet ballads and the stage were not confined to the clowns with their jigs and endpieces. What they shared was their newsworthy subject matter.

The same newsworthiness led to the conflict between the King's Men and another playhouse in 1634, over the play about the Lancashire witches. This dispute seems to have followed an attempt by the other playhouse, probably Salisbury Court, to cash in on the fuss over the witches by inserting some extra material in another play. The Master of the Revels, who may have been implicated in the Privy Council quarrel over the witches, registered

A peticion of the Kings Players about ye Witches complayning of intermingleing some passages of witches in old playes to ye prejudice of their designed Comedy of the Lancashire witches , and desiring a prohibition of any other till theirs bee allowed and Acted.[46]

The King's Men wanted their scoop. The target of the ban was probably another newsworthy play, *Dr Lambe and the Witches*. Sensational news of this kind evidently appealed to hall playhouse audiences as much as to those who went to the amphitheatres. Paul's and Salisbury Court used the same material as the Red Bull and the Globe, appealing to the same taste for seeing ordinary people doing extraordinary things.

John Howe, the barber surgeon who saw himself staged at Paul's in 1602, was bland about his experience. He was reported to have told the Paul's manager that 'he had no reason to take it to himself for that Kings had been presented on the stage and therefore Barbers might'.[47] Of course a barber who was winning his case could afford to be less sensitive than a king about how the stage portrayed him. The more aristocratic the victim the less complaisant he was likely to be.[48] The letter writer Roland Whyte reported on 26 October 1599 to Sir Robert Sidney that his recent military exploits were in the public eye.

Two daies agoe, the overthrow of *Turnholt* was acted upon a Stage, and all your names used that were at yt; especially *Sir Fra. Veres*, and he that plaid that Part gott a Beard resembling his, and a Watchett Sattin Doublett, with Hose trimmed with Silver Lace. You was also introduced, killing, slaying, and overthrowing the *Spaniards*, and honorable Mention made of your Service, in seconding Sir Francis Vere, being engaged.[49]

There is nothing in Henslowe which indicates responsibility for this, so it may have been put on at the Globe. A few years later it was certainly the Globe players who exploited the interest in Scottish affairs generated by England's new king with an account of the

Gowry conspiracy of 1600. As Chamberlain reported on 18 December 1604,

the tragedie of Gowrie with all the action and actors hath ben twise represented by the Kings players, with exceeding concourse of all sortes of people, but whether the matter or manner be not well handled, or that yt be thought unfit that princes should be plaide on the stage in theyre life time, I heare that some great counsaillors are much displeased with yt: and so is thought shalbe forbidden.   (2.54)

A full set of the 'actors' in the Gowry conspiracy must have included James himself. Displeasure by the great at the portrayal of living people on stage was demonstrated on several occasions besides this, notably over a play at the Curtain in 1601, and over the portrayal of the French king in Chapman's *The Conspiracy of Byron*, which exercised the French Ambassador in 1608.[50]

The greatest sensation of this period was of course the Essex conspiracy in 1601. Essex himself when being tried in 1600 for the failure of his Irish expedition complained to Elizabeth 'shortly they will play me in what forms they list upon the stage'.[51] The relations between Essex and Elizabeth were a notable temptation. In 1604 the Privy Council punished Daniel for representing Essex in *Philotas*, a charge to which the poet gave a wounded and plausible denial, though not many seem to have believed him. The trouble was what Nashe called the common stages' habit of moralising, which led to Jonson's derisive assertion in the dedication to *Volpone* that 'Application is grown a trade.' Elizabeth herself not only applied Shakespeare's *Richard II* to her own position in relation to Essex but complained to Lambarde that the applicable story had been acted forty times in the public playhouses and streets. Everard Guilpin and an enemy of Raleigh both wrote verses applying the Bullingbrook of Shakespeare's play to Essex,[52] like the Essex conspirators when they commissioned Shakespeare's company to perform *Richard II* on the eve of the rebellion. The 'common stages' were the only vehicle for current comment, and they readily supplied the need. Sadly, though, the supply is not often easily identifiable. Even today we can argue over whether Jonson was moralising the Gunpowder Plot in *Catiline*.[53] The closer such sensations came to the pains of possible censorship, the more covert the presentation and consequently the wider the application was likely to be. Events like Middleton's *A Game at Chesse*, burlesquing the Spanish interest at Court in 1624, and running at the Globe to packed audiences for nine days of August before the holidaying authorities got to hear of it, were thoroughly exceptional (2.137). What stands out most clearly is the enthusiasm of London audiences for this kind of journalistic news and topical comment, whether heroic as with Vere and Sidney in 1599 or satirical in the years that followed.

(G) CITIZEN STAPLES AND JULIET'S REBELLION (1588–1605)

In the five years, 1594–99, when the only food for playgoers was provided by the two adult companies playing at the amphitheatres to the north and south of the City, the provision was strikingly similar and surprisingly narrow in its range. The years before were changeable and far less prosperous. The years after, from 1599 to 1605, show a noticeable divergence between the playhouse south of the river and the northern playhouses. But in the central years when Davies and others thought that the amphitheatres contained the whole range of society the players catered chiefly for citizen appetites. As many as 145 plays, more than at any other time, were written for the stage in each of the two five-year periods 1594–99 and 1599–1604,[54] and all the plays of the earlier period reflected citizen tastes. The Robin Hood stories, popular in May-games and traditional festivals, were revamped for the London stage. Maid Marion turns up in Henslowe's *John a Kent and John a Cumber*, which was (if as seems likely it is the play known in his *Diary* as *The Wise Men of Westchester*) the most popular play in the Rose playhouse repertory after 1 *Henry VI.* Henslowe later employed Munday to write a two-part life of Robin Hood, *The Downfall of Robert Earl of Huntingdon* and *The Death of Robert Earl of Huntingdon*, which are complex elaborations for an urban audience of the traditional folk tale evolved in the country areas.[55] Plays about English history were a staple throughout, though their most popular feature by far was Falstaff in Eastcheap. The values characteristically expressed were those of the citizen Simon Eyre in *The Shoemaker's Holiday*. As the Dick Whittington story grew into a legend in prose tales so the citizen values embodied in such topics as the prodigal son story and the fantasies of apprentice heroics dominated the stages.[56]

Speaking in such broad terms, and contrasting this repertory with what came after it, it can be said that the two companies which operated from 1594 ran a similar repertoire of plays. The militancy which Alleyn's company reflected with *Tamburlaine* and its imitations while Burbage's company made use of English history had a similar appeal. Each company was well aware of its rival's offerings, and both companies staged plays about Henry V, Owen Tudor,

Hieronymo, Jack Straw, King John, Richard III and Troilus and Cressida. Both companies offered heroic romances, prodigal plays and citizen comedies such as *Fair Em, The Shoemaker's Holiday, An Englishman for my Money* and *The Merry Wives of Windsor*, a play which in most respects is a model citizen play about virtuous citizen wives resisting lecherous advances from gentlemen, and intermarriage between a citizen daughter and a noble son. Only in one fairly minor way did the interests of the two companies diverge at this time. It was a divergence which intensified quite markedly in the following five years, however, after 1599, and it warrants careful attention.

Lord Howard of Effingham, the Lord Admiral, patron of the Henslowe company, was a powerful figure at Court. His views may well explain the distinctive political allegiance which can be seen in the later repertoire of the Henslowe companies, and may have been an influence earlier. The Burbage company committed a political as well as a social error in making Sir John Oldcastle, the original Falstaff, a figure of vice. Their rivals were quick to capitalise on the error with their own *Sir John Oldcastle*, a play which used the fact that Oldcastle appears as a Protestant martyr in Foxe's *Acts and Monuments*. Foxe was available for reading in churches by government order along with the Bible, and had the status almost of hagiography for the Protestant apologists. The Catholics contrariwise appreciated the Falstaff version. In 1603 Robert Parsons (the Jesuit propagandist Doleman) wrote a pamphlet, *The Third Part of a Treatise, Intituled: of three Conversions of England*, in which he applauded the Falstaffian version of the Protestant martyr: 'Syr John Oldcastle, a Ruffian-knight as all England knoweth, & commonly brought in by comediants on their stages'. So spoke the enemies of the government. Possibly the staging of the Oldcastle play or possibly the influence of Lord Howard prompted the Henslowe companies at the turn of the century to mount a series of plays about Protestant heroes. The 'Elect Nation' plays,[57] and the accompanying celebrations of the heyday of Elizabethan England which Henslowe produced in 1603–05, notably Rowley's *When You See Me You Know Me* (1604?), Dekker and Webster's *Sir Thomas Wyatt* (c.1604), Heywood's *If You Know Not Me* (1605), and other plays by the Henslowe collaborators amount to a small campaign for citizen values. They shed the military heroics of the 1590s, as James's peaceable kingdom of diplomatic saintliness took hold of English politics, but the values they upheld were expressly Protestant and Elizabethan. How much these plays were produced under a stimulus from the company's patron and how much they indicate an allegiance to a particular kind of audience and its values is not clear.

There is little sign that the Shakespeare company followed far along the course of the Henslowe companies after 1600 in upholding such distinctive London values. They burlesqued the speech of Tamburlaine in 2 *Henry IV* as a mark of their divergence from Alleyn's style. Perhaps more to the point they accepted another divergence once they settled on Bankside and the Henslowe companies moved to the northern suburbs. Like the 'Elect Nation' plays this second divergence may have been designed by the Henslowe writers to establish a clearly different identity of the north from the Bankside. It crystallised as a decidedly conservative citizen attitude to love and marriage.

In the 1590s the Shakespeare company became notably popular with the Inns of Court students for its plays about love. Marston's Luscus and his fellows kept commonplace books of verse from Shakespeare's comedies, and echoed Romeo and the 'new pathetique Tragedie' they were then staging at the Curtain. Francis Meres and other young gallants delighted in this attention to love by the author of their favourite *Venus and Adonis*. The Henslowe playwrights made no attempt to copy this newly popular taste. After 1600 they actively opposed it and the challenge to citizen views about marriage which it embodied.

Shakespeare's presentation of marriage was relatively 'new', in that his plays uphold the power of love over parental authority. Juliet's rebellion against the Capulets' insistence that she marry the man of her parents' choice was an act of disloyalty which few London citizens were ready to applaud. Shakespeare's heroines were an alarming novelty. When Beatrice challenged the convention of women undergoing arranged marriages (*Much Ado*, II.i.42–7) and the young lovers in *A Midsummer Night's Dream* rebelled against the harsh Athenian laws they were voicing kinship with Juliet.[58] Even *The Taming of the Shrew*'s marvellously complex reshuffling of the traditional love story, contemplating life after marriage and setting Bianca's conventional posturing in contrast to Katherine, was in its own way a sensational contribution to the debate between young love and parental authority. Heywood's *A Woman Killed with Kindness*, which took the other side in the debate on behalf of the Henslowe companies, probably found its title in Petruchio's derisive use of the proverb about killing a wife with kindness (IV.i.195).

Exactly when the companies began to diverge over this question is not clear, because so much of the Admiral's Company's repertoire from the years up to 1599 has been lost. Possibly lost plays recorded in Henslowe's lists such as *Wonder of a Woman* (1595), *The Chaste Lady* (1595–96), and *A Woman Hard to Please* (1597) may have expressed a view hostile to love, but *The Two Angry Women of Abingdon* ends happily enough in a love-match. The conflict with Shakespeare's company after it settled at the Globe in 1599 was certainly taken up by the second Henslowe company, Worcester's, which began playing, with Shakespeare's former fellow the clown Will Kempe in the company, at the Rose on Bankside and the Boar's Head in 1601. Dekker's lost *Medicine for a Curst Wife* was written for them, followed by *How a Man May Choose a Good Wife from a Bad* and *A Woman Killed with Kindness*. The contention, if that is what it was, ran on into the reign of James, when the Globe staged Wilkins' *The Miseries of Enforced Marriage*, based on pamphlets about the life of Walter Calverley which were printed in 1605. If it was a genuine contention over attitudes to marriage it seems unlikely that it was inspired by political bias like that of the Elect Nation plays. Possibly the whole Henslowe repertoire was mainly inspired by its citizen and conservative allegiance.

The modern assumption that art and commerce are naturally polarised has done some disfavour to Henslowe and his playmakers. His records indicate the constant pressure he was under to acquire new plays as fast as possible. Viewed from the commercial pole the collaborative writing which produced most of his plays can easily seem like hackwork catering for established and familiar tastes, providing what audiences wanted. That this is not the case is evident both in the narrow political bias of the Elect Nation plays and in the sides taken over the marriage debate. On both issues the Henslowe writers chose to take a conservative line supporting Elizabethan values. It was a conservatism which knew what it was doing and which deliberately set the northern playhouses in closer sympathy with predominant citizen interests, so far as we know them, than did the plays of the Globe players. Shakespeare's plays already had a particular appeal for law students and gallants in the 1590s. In the new century the Globe company's allegiance to the specific tastes of the London citizenry drained away.

This divergence between the Henslowe playhouses and the Globe is important, but it is not easily explained. The return of the boy players at Paul's and the Blackfriars in 1599 may have sharpened the sense of loyalty to citizen values in the Henslowe writers. As law students and all the wealthier playgoers began flocking to the new hall playhouses it would be natural for the amphitheatres to narrow their focus onto the citizens who stayed loyal to them. Certainly 1599 can be seen as the beginning of the long run which the Fortune and Red Bull enjoyed as 'citizen' playhouses. James Wright gave them that name in 1699, from a long historical perspective, but it is not inaccurate (2.205). They sustained the repertoire of the 1590s right through to the closure in 1642, with Marlowe at its core throughout. In the 1630s the 'majestic' acting and military trappings of the Red Bull plays, the style set by Alleyn in the 1590s, became a standing joke to the sophisticated, although the plays themselves were occasionally also staged at the indoor Cockpit. The durability of the Marlowe style and repertoire is a testimony to the strength of the citizen enthusiasm for the playhouses most accessible to London's working population.

Far less easy to explain in this time of unprecedented competition at the beginning of the century is the position of the Globe company. Situated next to the baiting houses and whorehouses and little further away across London Bridge from the City it had every reason to expect the same clientele as favoured the northern playhouses. It would probably have expected to lose more of its clientele of Romeo-quoting law students to the boy companies than Henslowe, and Shakespeare did stop writing love comedies after 1600 once the hall playhouses were competing with the Globe. It is true that James Burbage had once thought to provide adult fare at the Blackfriars for the playgoers who now went to the boys there, but in 1600 the Globe players had no reason to expect that they would ever take that playhouse back from the boys. They must have faced a choice, between going the Henslowe way and catering for an increasingly narrow and old-fashioned citizen taste or competing with the boys and their new fashions. With hindsight the wisdom of their preference for a new kind of repertoire seems obvious. It could not have been so then, though, and until *Hamlet* arrived to, in Scoloker's phrase, 'please all' and secure their independent role, they must have had grave doubts about the commercial practicability of their course. Very likely the crux of the matter, and possibly the trigger for their choice, lay in the question of the company's clown. Will Kempe's departure from the Shakespeare company in 1599 was one of a complex series of adjustments which started the company on a road leading firmly away from the jigs and knockabout clowning which stayed on as citizen staples at the northern playhouses until the 1640s. In 1599, when they were just starting in a costly new playhouse, Kempe's departure left the company hazardously poised for a new beginning in conditions of unprecedented competition.

Kempe's 'applauded Merymentes', as they were called on the titlepage of *A Knack to Know a Knave*, were a celebrated feature of the Shakespearean company in the 1590s. Dogberry was written for him, and probably Falstaff. The parts of Launce in *Two Gentlemen of Verona* and Peter in *Romeo and Juliet* were probably added to the original texts to augment Kempe's contribution to the company in which he and Shakespeare became shareholders in 1594. But whether or not he was the first Falstaff, Kempe's real fame lay less in his comic roles in the plays than in his jigs. He was a singing and dancing clown whose talent is probably seen most distinctly in the script for the jig *Singing Simkin*, a piece of knockabout bawdy clowning in rhyming doggerel whose virtue lies more in its energy than its wit.[59] The song and dance jig or endpiece seems to have disappeared from the Globe stage when Kempe left the company, unless Feste's last song in *Twelfth Night* is a kind of singing endpiece. Thomas Platter, seeing *Julius Caesar* at the Globe in September 1599 mentioned the jig which followed the play, but a reference in 1613 to John Shank leaving the Fortune for the Globe suggests that he stopped performing jigs when he joined his new company (2.97). The abandonment of jigs may have been an expression of choice by the company as much as a necessity following Kempe's departure. Shakespeare's fellows may well have shared Hamlet's view of clowns.

The circumstances of Kempe's departure are obscure, though some hints of his own indicate that he may not have gone altogether willingly. On his return from his epic morris dances to Norwich and over the Alps he joined Worcester's Men, working for Henslowe, who approved of jigs, in the winter of 1602–03. Robert Armin, who eventually took Kempe's place in the Shakespeare company, was a singing or Court fool, not a knockabout clown in the Kempe tradition, though he must have taken over Kempe's old parts such as Dogberry and Peter.[60] His acquisition of Kempe's place is a token of the divergent line the Globe company took in 1599, over clowning as well as the priorities of marriage, from its northern rivals. Jigs were always a feature of the northern playhouses, but the Globe seems never to have returned to that kind of clowning.

The years from 1588 to 1605 provide a central focus for playgoing in the whole Shakespearean period. Marlowe's and Kyd's first success helped to create the taste which both companies in the middle years satisfied. Those years also created the tradition which sustained the 'citizen' playhouses for another forty years. The same years prompted Shakespeare's company to move on, partly under their own impetus and no doubt partly also under the stimulus of the boy companies and the new appetites which they identified. What between 1594 and 1599 appears to have been a homogeneous, all-inclusive social range from gallants to grooms and from citizens' wives to whores, in the next years quickly became a stratified social scale divided amongst different playhouses. The northern play-houses then supplied the wants of the lowest social levels, and went on in the same way for forty years. The Globe players and the boy companies aspired higher.

(H) THE WAR OF RAILING
(1599–1609)

Captivating spectacle, the 'theatre of enchantment', as Neil Carson has called it, was the predominant mode in the central five years while the citizen staples ran in the amphitheatres. Towards the end of the period, though, a new mode entered, 'theatre of estrange-ment'.[61] Playwrights writing for the citizen repertory ordinarily spoke of audiences as 'bewitched', believing in the players' imperso-nations, sharing a collective 'charmed soule' which could be subdued to the magic of the stage show.[62] Carson sees this as a characteristic of the 1590s, when as he puts it 'the popular-theatre playwrights had been moving fairly consistently in the direction of what I would call naive illusionism'.[63] Well before 1605 this enchantment was chal-lenged by the sophisticated artifice of the boy companies, making the audience self-conscious, flaunting the artificiality of stage pretence and insisting that audiences became not spell-bound believers but sceptical judges. Jonson's insistence that audiences should function as judges made its mark.

This new anti-mimetic mode in theatre was natural for boy companies, whose 'juniority' made them only approximate physical imitations of adult reality. The new mode also gave them the superior appeal of an evidently more sophisticated concept of drama to set above the adult players' naive illusionism. Its development however is complicated by Jonson's contributions and by Shake-speare's company. The 'humours' plays were making a mark with audiences as early as 1597, when John Chamberlain found the first of them (either Chapman's *An Humorous Day's Mirth* or Jonson's *Every Man in his Humour*) to have been overpraised. Jonson's two 'humours' plays were first staged by Shakespeare's company, intro-ducing not only the comedy of humours but, more to the point, a new expectation of critical alertness in the audience and consequently a

new tone of acerbity in stage comedy. This 'satire' , which Joseph
Hall and John Weever derived by false etymology from *sat irae*, full of
anger,[64] started as an Inns of Court fashion well calculated to appeal
to the audiences already happy to mock their fellows who quoted
Romeo. Jonson's transfer from his early work with Henslowe to the
Chamberlain's Men was dictated more by his killing of Henslowe's
player Gabriel Spencer than by any sense that the other company
would supply a more welcoming audience for his plays, but *Every
Man In* does suggest that he knew what he was doing when he made
the transfer. Opening his play with a father lamenting the way his
student son dreams away his time with 'idle *Poetrie*' was a sure way
to catch the interest of Marston's gull Luscus and his fellow Romeos,
as well as their mockers. The mockery both of the father and of the
student son and his friends which follows is in the vein of Marston
and his fellow satirists.[65] Jonson's play gave Shakespeare's company
the first opportunity to put Inns of Court satire on stage and to broach
the practice of 'railing', as it came to be called.

Railing became the chief and most conspicuous alternative to the
naive illusionism of the heroics of Marlowe and the citizen repertory.
It was taken up quickly by the boy companies which formed soon
after Jonson's first success. They had strong incentives. As Marston
put it, writing for Paul's in 1601,

> This is the straine that chokes the theaters:
> That makes them crack with full stuff't audience,
> This is your humor onely in request
> Forsooth to raile ...   (2.43)

The boys and their liking for railing may have provoked the so-called
'War of the Theatres', which gave a localised point to railing by
turning the device against the playwrights themselves. The War was
a curious little fracas, a wonderful quarry for the trade of application
amongst intimates of the playhouses. Whether it really had much to
do with competition for audiences or not, it was clearly designed to
satisfy a taste for railing.[66] It certainly did have a great deal to do with
some poets' animosity towards Jonson and the new acerbic tone he
brought into comedy. Dekker's *Satiromastix*, using Jonson's tone of
sat-ire against him, reads like the protest of a writer who feels
himself to have been unfairly provoked by a savage mode which he
was quite capable of adopting himself in retaliation.

The boy companies evidently had an interest in fostering satirical
comedy, since it became their most characteristic mode, seen at its
best in *Eastward Ho!*, *The Isle of Gulls*, and *The Knight of the
Burning Pestle*, though all three of these date from the last phase of

the Blackfriars boys, and Paul's never went so far as the Blackfriars. The intensification of Blackfriars railing in their last years brought down James's fury over their *Byron* plays in 1608. Heywood's disavowal of the mode which he wrote at about that time has the air of revulsion against something whose time has passed.

Nowe to speake of some abuse lately crept into the quality, as an inveighing against the State, the Court, the Law, the Citty, and their governments, with the particularising of private mens humours (yet alive) Noble-men, & others. I knowe it distastes many; neither do I any way approve it, nor dare I by any meanes excuse it. The liberty, which some arrogate to themselves, committing their bitternesse, and liberall invectives against all estates, to the mouthes of Children, supposing their juniority to be a priviledge for any rayling, be it never so violent, I could advise all such, to curbe and limit this presumed liberty ...[67]

Heywood was not himself given to railing and his rejection of it here was composed in the heart of the citizen repertory. He was partly commenting on an alternative theatrical tradition and partly on a fashion whose time was now up.

The fashion for railing tried chiefly to appeal to the gallants and law students whose enthusiasm for railing in print was halted by the bishops and their book-burning in 1599.[68] Jonson's transfer of railing to the Shakespeare company's stage is one of the pieces of evidence linking them more with gallant and law student playgoers than with the Henslowe clientele. They did, along with Paul's boys, stage *Satiromastix* as an attack on Jonson after he left them for the Blackfriars boys. There is some point in Brian Gibbons' link between the Globe repertory and that of the boy companies:

Towards the end of Elizabeth's reign, plays at Blackfriars, Paul's, and, increasingly, the Globe, register a note of discontent with public affairs, while the other adult companies at the Red Bull, Swan, Rose and Hope largely continue to evoke an air of cheerful patriotism and national self-satisfaction. It has been surmised that this divergence in attitudes to government and monarchy reflects a progressive split in the political attitudes of the two audiences: the first includes lawyers, members of the Commons, merchants and Inns of Court students, nobility and gentry, the second more predominantly tradesmen, citizens, labourers, carriers, apprentices, servingmen.[69]

Such a surmise is well supported by available evidence both about the social divergence of the boy company audiences from the amphitheatre audiences, and about the divergent repertories. But there are hints in the evidence which indicate that it is not really sufficient to put the Globe company precisely in the same category as the boy companies, or indeed to put the two boy companies exactly together.

The position of Shakespeare's company might more fairly be seen as a neutral one between the polarised Blackfriars and the citizen companies, with Paul's uneasily balanced somewhere between the other hall company and Shakespeare's.

One problem in identifying the kind of playgoer for whom the Shakespeare company prepared itself is the limited evidence about the allegiances implied in its plays. Shakespeare himself wrote more than two thirds of the surviving plays performed by his company between 1599 and 1609, and neither his nor any of the other plays uphold the Protestant patriotism of the elect nation plays on the one hand nor the acerbic railing of the Blackfriars on the other. The company staged Jonson's two humours plays before the boys came back on the scene, and *A Warning for Fair Women* which they performed in 1599 has an elaborate induction voicing discontent over the standard stage fare in comedy and tragedy. Yet Jonson did not hesitate to include them with the other adult companies in his attack in *Poetaster* on the hypocrisy of adult players. They are said to deplore the 'humours, revells and satyres, that girde, and fart at the time', but to corrupt morals with their ribaldry. The player in *Poetaster* proudly boasts that his fellows on Bankside 'have as much ribaldrie in our plaies, as can bee, as you would wish ... All the sinners, i' the suburbs come, and applaud our action, daily.'[70] The Globe as well as Henslowe's Rose is included in this condemnation of Bankside playing which caters for the poor of London's suburbs, 'your tabernacles, ... your *Globes*, and your Triumphs'.[71] What heed the Globe company paid to Jonson's strictures it is not easy to see. They had been mocking fustian plays from the rival adult repertoire with Ancient Pistol since 1597. They did not hesitate to stage *Satiromastix* as Dekker's counterattack against Jonson and the Blackfriars boys in the War of the Theatres. Shakespeare, possibly mindful of Jonson's criticism of romantic comedy in *Every Man Out*, also needled him quietly in *Twelfth Night*. But he then stopped writing in the genre.[72] He also dropped his plan for a new series of history plays about Rome to follow *Julius Caesar*. And yet the plays he wrote instead of these staples were certainly not railing satires. If anything they harked back to the amphitheatre plays of the previous decade. *Hamlet* probably and *King Lear* certainly were rewritings of old Queen's Company plays from 1590 or earlier. None of the company's other plays – *The Devil's Charter* and *The Merry Devil of Edmonton*, for instance – show the least influence from the boy company repertory or the targeted playgoers. By the time Jonson returned to them with *Sejanus* in late 1603 and *Volpone* in 1605 the company's neutrality must have long outweighed the staging of *Satiromastix* as a mark of their position.

By 1605 they were not just neutral between the northern amphi-theatres and the halls but pre-eminent. The Court recognised their lead in 1603 when James made himself their patron while giving the Henslowe companies to his wife and son. The boys' campaign to distinguish themselves from the citizen and artisan tastes of the Henslowe companies had the effect of polarising the two sets of repertories if not their audiences. Remaining neutral, Shakespeare's company avoided the 'public' or popular tag which clung to Hen-slowe's companies and also the risks of being outrageous which the boys ran to get their 'private' or 'select' playgoers into their seats. The taste for railing was shortlived – it did not even last as long as the ten years of the boy companies – partly because satire is by its nature not a durable fashion. Its polarising effect does not seem to have touched the Shakespeare company's repertory. What is not so clear is whether it affected the social composition of the Globe's audiences, and brought back the upper social echelons from the halls to the Bankside.

Marston, Jonson and the other playwrights who praised the select nature of the hall playhouse audiences in 1600 and 1601 all had their reasons. Marston's role as poet-in-chief for Paul's boys made him strident in his insistence on the intimate and clubbable atmosphere at Paul's. Freed not just from the sticky jerkins of artisan brewers but from 'drunken *Censure*' and choked more with tobacco than the smell of garlic (2.40, 43), his audiences could be persuaded to make the smaller size of the Paul's gatherings, no more than two hundred heads at a sitting, into a special mark of superiority. The tobacco-smoking and card-playing gallants now conspicuous at the hall playhouses had previously been noted at the Theatre, Curtain and Globe, so it is likely that the two hundred at Paul's and the eight hundred or so at Blackfriars would have come from the Globe more than from the Fortune, Rose or Boar's Head. That seems to be confirmed by the Player's lament in *Hamlet* at losing custom to the boys, and Jonson's derisive echo of it in *Poetaster*. The Henslowe players make no such complaints. But how long that transfer of allegiance lasted there is no way of telling. The boy companies were a far less healthy commercial operation than the adult companies, and performed far less often. As early as 1604 the Blackfriars impresario was trying to revoke his lease and return the hall to Shakespeare's company. By 1605, when Paul's closed again and the Blackfriars boys were in trouble with the authorities, it seems reasonable to conclude

that the Globe company must have resumed its tradition of catering
for all tastes, and that all social ranks were again represented among
the playgoers at the Globe. It must be admitted, though, that the
evidence is circumstantial. Probably the strongest confirmation is
the company's immediate success when they took over the Blackfriars in 1609.

The humours plays and their railing satire are tightly linked with
the city comedy which flourished from 1599 onwards and reached its
apogee with *Bartholomew Fair* in 1614. City comedy was a variable
thing, though, and so far as possible it should be distinguished from
the satirical railing of the first years of the boy companies. The
development of city comedy is a feature of the ten-year history of the
boy companies from 1599 to 1608, but it appeared on every type of
stage, and its different manifestations are as varied as the different
types of repertory. Before those differences are considered, it is worth
looking more closely at what the targets of the specifically railing
types of comedy were.

Girds at citizens, as Beaumont's Citizen called it, remained a
feature exclusively of the boy company plays. They are mentioned by
Day, Beaumont, Field, Fletcher and others as grounds for a more or
less legitimate if amusing grievance on the part of the wealthier
citizens and merchants.[73] Girds at Puritans also evoked complaint.
Since plays were seen as a corrupting alternative to sermons, some
sermons by the more puritanical preachers in the decade up to 1609
not surprisingly contain violent expressions of hostility to plays
(2.49, 75). Puritanism however was a political question. The satirical
play *The Family of Love* was implicitly endorsed by the attack on
that sect which James wrote for the republication of *Basilikon Doron*
in 1603. Girding at citizens was a smaller matter, a declaration of
social groupings and consequent social alliances. The most distinctive feature about the citizen girds was that they did rouse objections.
Equally derisive satire against gallants and lawyers can be found in
the railing plays, but only merchants seem to have felt themselves
vulnerable enough to warrant a protest. Possibly they felt too far
outside the game, too alien in the intimate and wealthy society of the
boy company playhouses, whereas gallants and law students could
enjoy the jokes against their kind. Beaumont's *Knight of the Burning
Pestle* was certainly written on some such presumption.

The extent to which the targets for railing were social rather than
political is most clearly demonstrated in the satire against James
himself. It was inevitable that any successor to Elizabeth would have
appeared a lesser, more fallible human being. Certainly it is to his

credit, in a way, that most of the satire he attracted was directed at fairly trivial and easily recognisable things like his love of hunting and his Scottish followers.[74] Concern over corruption at Court was a later phenomenon. Satire against James appeared mostly in the period from 1603 (when the Queen was said to be enjoying stage parodies of her husband) to 1608.[75] This fashion in fact coincided with a rising tide of hostility to railing and in some degree marks its furthest extension. The playwrights began increasingly to disclaim railing as a mode – Chapman in 1604, Jonson in 1605, Day and Marston in 1606, Beaumont in 1607 and Barry in 1608 – though by no means all the disclaimers were sincere.[76]

Railing plays were almost exclusively a feature of the boy company repertory, all but twelve of whose fifty-five surviving plays were satirical.[77] Much of the raillery appears in city comedies, for which it was well suited. *Eastward Ho!*, probably the best in the genre, is a sophisticated burlesque of the citizen playhouse repertory and its prodigal son plays, though the fact that its satire against James led to a protest by one of his Scotsmen and punishment for its poets should remind us that the genre was not just a weapon of social class allegiance. It was a fashion, a mode of cynical and acerbic talking, presumably characteristic of the gallant and law student audiences to whom Jonson first appealed with *Every Man In*. The railing plays launched the Blackfriars boys on their brief career and supported the growth of city comedy. The comedies, however, reflect a larger phenomenon, the staging of London life. City comedy gives a broader perspective than railing on the range of the London playhouses between 1599 and 1614.

(1) CITY COMEDY
(1599–1614)

Domestic drama came to the London stages as early as *Arden of Feversham*, and a strengthening of urban comedy is indicated by the change of clowning in about 1590 from rustics to rude mechanicals. In 1597 the citizens of Windsor and Abingdon were put on stage in romantic comedies, one by each of the adult companies. A mode of what Alexander Leggatt calls specifically citizen comedy existed before Jonson transformed it with his humours plays and their Roman New Comedy models. What took over after Jonson's success came out of a mixture of three influences. Romantic comedy about citizens was one. The drama of Plautus, familiar to the university-educated literate in the audiences, was the second. Jonson's own ambition to beat a new path was the third. All three mingled but kept parts of their separate identities in the years that followed. All three seem to have influenced, and no doubt were influenced by, the divergent movement of the various playhouses and their social allegiances.

Leggatt defines 'citizen comedy' as plays about citizens, not necessarily plays written for them or upholding their kind of values.[78] Their main interest was in money and marriage. Much of their incidental comedy lies in the presentation of city types, exaggerated either indulgently (as in Dekker's Simon Eyre) or satirically (as in most of the Blackfriars boys' plays). The social allegiance is obviously important, but easily capable of being misread. Leggatt points out that *Westward Ho!* has been taken as an anti-citizen play by modern critics, presumably because it was a boy company play, whereas its fifth act is, like *Merry Wives*, a triumph for the virtuous citizen women and therefore (presumably) at some remove from the usual boy company anti-citizen play.[79] The two Paul's *Ho!* plays pose some problems which will be looked at shortly. Leggatt's point about *Westward Ho!* serves to emphasise the need to avoid a circular argument and to be cautious both in identifying allegiances in the plays themselves and in deducing from them the bias of the audiences at particular playhouses.

A look at the plays staged by any one company does suggest some conclusions, but most of them are complicated by the special contribution to city comedy that Jonson made. He launched his humours plays, including the first truly railing comedy, *Every Man Out*, with Shakespeare's company. Their developments in *Poetaster* and *Cynthia's Revels*, the first of which is certainly a city comedy although like the early version of *Every Man In* it was set in Rome, were written for Blackfriars boys and develop the acerbic mode of railing to an unprecedented level. Later, for *Volpone*, a city and indeed citizen comedy, he returned to Shakespeare's company. *Epicene* was written for the Blackfriars boys, and then *The Alchemist* for Shakespeare's company after it repossessed the Blackfriars playhouse (the joke realism of its staging partly depends on its performance 'here in the *friers*', a neighbourhood known for its wealthy Lovewits and its puritans as well as its playhouse). Since Jonson laid such intense demands on his audiences, insisting that they should be as acute and judging as Asper, Cordatus and Mitis in *Every Man Out*, it is tempting to see the differences between his plays written for the different companies as at least partly shaped by his idea of their audiences. *Every Man In* as performed by Shakespeare's company had elements of traditional knockabout and other comic features Jonson knew from his years writing for Henslowe. *Every Man Out* abandoned any such physical comedy, and might well have gone to the boy players if they had been operational by then. What Anne Barton calls 'the insupportable weight of its self-commentary',[80] quite apart from its assault on the bases of Shakespearean comedy, looks at least in part like a deliberate test of what the Shakespeare company and presumably its audiences could bear. Jonson's first play for the Blackfriars boys, *Cynthia's Revels*, was composed in the tradition of Lyly's Court plays which had been the staples of the earlier Blackfriars boy company. *Poetaster*, besides its development of the railing mode, was written fast as a pre-emptive strike in the War of the Theatres and offers much more criticism than social allegiance, though it does include a parody of *Romeo and Juliet's* balcony scene. It is the next three comedies, two of them for Shakespeare's company, which show the clearest signs of adaptation to suit the traditions of particular companies.

Volpone was a wholly new departure in comedy for Jonson.[81] Dealing with crimes more than follies, it eschews any specifically London social characterisation except for the gullible English travellers. Its target is human greed, which can only be linked with social divisions in the large-scale terms of L. C. Knights' analysis of economic change and its social consequences.[82] It is completely devoid of any local 'application', at least of the kind which provoked Dekker and Marston in *Poetaster*. The virtuous Celia remains loyal to her citizen husband against Volpone's seductions and her husband's own gross corruption. The virtuous Bonario refuses to flout the authority of his equally corrupt father. In social and theatrical content it has little which might not have been welcomed at one of the northern playhouses. Its social neutrality may very well reflect Jonson's awareness of the neutral position of the Globe repertory. When he wrote his next comedy, *Epicene*, for the Blackfriars boys (now banished, in 1609, to the new Whitefriars hall) he allowed the play to present a much more extreme position. The first play which he openly set in London, it was written entirely in the prose which the boy companies always favoured, and with some evident reservations adopted the New Comedy mode of plays such as Middleton's *A Trick to Catch the Old One*. Like such plays its heroes are a trio of gallants short of money, and the plot turns on their scheme to extract a healthy income from the reluctant uncle of one of them. No wonder Dryden praised it as Jonson's finest comedy, since it anticipates so many features typical of Restoration comedy. Young 'fashionable men' gull the foolish and trick the knavish in order to secure for themselves the style of living – wit allied with money – which was beginning to show itself in the drama as the sole ambition of young gallants about town. The chief gull, Morose, like Hoord in Middleton's play, is a born gentleman turned merchant whose grasping attitude over money poses a direct threat to the liberality which gives the gallants their standard of conduct. Less extreme in its polarisation of attitudes between frugality and prodigality than Beaumont's in *The Knight of the Burning Pestle*, which puts up prodigal 'mirth' as preferable to frugality,[83] it still stands a long way from *Volpone*'s moral rigour.

If Jonson was at all concerned about the kind of playgoer at particular playhouses, *The Alchemist* must have bothered him more than his other plays. Written like *Volpone* for Shakespeare's company, it was also explicitly composed for performance in their newly-acquired hall playhouse before its wealthier clientele. The audience was like the one for which he had written *Poetaster*, the players the company he had condemned in that play. Times had evidently moved on. No doubt he had many reasons for choosing the kind of play he wrote for this new mixture, and no single reason can explain any one of its features. But a poet so sensitive to the interaction between performance and audience and so demanding of his audiences cannot have chosen his setting or his plot without careful calculation. To fix the action on either side of the main door of a private house in the Blackfriars district, to people the play with a full spectrum of London citizenry from Sir Epicure Mammon to Abel Drugger and Jeremy the manservant, was to extend citizen play realism to parodic length,[84] almost as much as the carefully checked-off hours of the day and the location seem to parody the unities of time and place. Like *Volpone* it was written in verse, and like *Volpone* it pillories greed. Unlike *Epicene* it takes no sides, and it gives little more concession to the liberal preferences of the gallant mentality than the name of the character who comes off best in the end, Lovewit. For all the precision of its London locality, it seems as calculatedly neutral in its social allegiance as *Volpone*, certainly far more than *Epicene*. It is a London play for a general audience of Londoners. The only clear sign of its being written especially for a Blackfriars audience is the joke about its location in the '*friers*'.

The effect on Shakespeare's company of their long-delayed acquisition of the Blackfriars playhouse in 1609 is a matter for the next section. Here we need only note how comprehensively Jonson put *The Alchemist*'s social allegiance into a neutral position compared with the alignment he gave *Epicene* the year before. The allowances he made in *Epicene* for the expectation that the Blackfriars boys would appeal to a specifically 'gallant' set of values may throw some light on the differences which appeared earlier in the decade between the two boy companies, which he helped to exploit in *Eastward Ho!* Paul's boys, with much the smaller playhouse, were always a more shaky commercial proposition than the occupants of Blackfriars. From the outset, though, they depended on a similar social cachet as a 'private' playhouse with a 'select' audience and young players. They also seem to have seen the Blackfriars boys as more serious rivals than the adult players. That may be why they staged *Satiromastix* in the War of the Theatres. They seem to have tried to develop a local citizen audience, too, staging Chapman's version of a minor piece of neighbourhood gossip and using two 'citizen' playwrights with citizen antecedents from the Henslowe stable, Dekker and Webster, for the *Ho!* plays in the years immediately before they closed.[85] These citizen interests and the comprehensive burlesque of the *Ho!* plays mounted by the Blackfriars boys suggest that Paul's boys lacked the narrowness of the 'select' social allegiance for which the Blackfriars boys consistently catered. *Eastward Ho!*'s Quicksilver is like the apprentice Ralph of Beaumont's gird at citizens in his enthusiasm for the old citizen repertory, quoting *Tamburlaine* and *The Spanish Tragedy* much as Ralph quotes Hotspur's huffing speech and the Red Bull repertoire of plays. Shakespeare's company had got in first at that game in *2 Henry IV*, of course, but Jonson, Marston and Chapman lumped all their rivals, Henslowe's companies, Shakespeare and Paul's boys, together in their mockery of the prodigal tradition. Their particular trademark was anti-citizen burlesque. Paul's may have started with similar material, but they soon parted company from their boy rivals.

When the Blackfriars boys left the Blackfriars playhouse the fashion for railing and burlesque was dying. The 'salt' had lost its savour. In Brian Gibbons' summary,

as the Jacobean age proceeds, Court corruption and political tyranny cease to be treated in comedy and become increasingly the province of satiric tragedy and tragi-comic romance. Meanwhile in a parallel development, critical comedy concentrates on the city as a setting, depicting the tensions between commercial and social pressures and moral values.[86]

As the Duke in *Measure for Measure* said piously early in the decade, 'Novelty is only in request' (III.ii.210). Fashions were under such constant pressure to change that they were several times compared to fashions in clothing, and it is difficult to see how much of the change was a consequence of tastes evolving and how much was more material factors such as the changes in playhouse conditions. Certainly the Blackfriars boys took their railing off with them when they handed their hall over to Shakespeare's company. Such audiences as stayed with or returned to the Blackfriars under their new management do not seem to have forced many changes in the repertoire of the adult company after 1609. Their most substantial change was the replacement of Shakespeare by Beaumont and Fletcher, though even that adjustment did not take away their staple, the Shakespeare canon.

(j) 1609 AND THE SETTLED HIERARCHY

If we choose to think of the decade from 1599 to 1609 as a period of rivalry between the boy companies and the adult players, 1609 can easily be seen to mark total victory for the adults. After the King's Men took over the Blackfriars it was never again possible to use the social cachet of boy players and their 'private' accommodation as a temptation to the wealthier playgoers. Shakespeare's company with their kingly title and their unique repertoire of Shakespeare's plays became the outstanding company in every way, whether they were performing at the Blackfriars or the Globe. This is rather a narrow view of events, though. Their acquisition of the Blackfriars as their winter playhouse should more properly be seen not as a victory over the boy tenants but as a belated fulfilment of the plan James Burbage originally hatched in 1596. Part of what the Blackfriars boys indirectly accomplished was the renewal by the adults of their old preference for a place to play in winter inside the City. The intervening years had weakened Guildhall's opposition by giving the company its royal title, and silenced the residents of the Blackfriars neighbourhood. Pre-eminence as the King's Men must also have encouraged the company to undertake the extravagance of maintaining two playhouses, something no other company ever did, and indeed to rebuild the Globe richly when the false economy of thatching the original building brought it to the ground in 1613. The culmination of a series of fortunate accidents – fortune more than globe – in 1609 gave the company the three things on which their uniquely long and successful career was based. First, they were the only company in a position to follow the early practice of using the amphitheatre in summer weather and their hall in the winter. Secondly, by the accident of the Burbages being short of cash to build the Globe in 1599 the leading sharers of the playing company were also shareholders in the two playhouses, and presumably took a large part in the decision to operate in the new mode. Thirdly, their possession of the Blackfriars gave them the playhouse situated closest to the Inns of Court, familiar over the ten preceding years as the venue for a repertory aimed precisely at law students and gallants. No other adult company had that resource in 1609, and no hall playhouse existed to rival the Blackfriars for another seven years.

Those seven years fixed the different species of repertory quite distinctly. At the northern playhouses the plays were designed for citizens and the 'porters and carters' whom Galli described at the Curtain in 1613. The Elect Nation plays in the Fortune repertory were reprinted in 1612–13,[87] which suggests the Fortune company revived them at about that time. The Middlesex magistrates complained in 1611 about the tumults which accompanied the jigs still in use to end the day's performances there. Heywood's celebrated plays and displays of the Four Ages for the Red Bull were a variation on the annual City pageants sponsored by the Mayor and guilds. The allegiance is clear. Inhabitants of the suburbs to the north and east of the city, where the Fortune, Curtain and Red Bull operated, were the poorest in London while the Blackfriars was the wealthiest district. The social identity of the different neighbourhoods gradually influenced the reputations of their playhouses. The Blackfriars playhouse, alongside the Inns of Court and central between the City of London and the aristocratic housing developments in the City of Westminster, was joined in 1616 by Beeston's Cockpit in Drury Lane, just to the west of the City of London boundary. The Cockpit shared the Blackfriars' superior reputation along with its superior neighbourhood, and became the only alternative to the Blackfriars in term time for student playgoers such as Edward Heath and John Greene, who regularly went to both. Gentry like Sir Humphrey Mildmay went primarily to the Blackfriars, secondly to the Cockpit. Unlike the law students, whose terms coincided with the period when the King's Men were using their hall playhouse, Mildmay also went to the Globe in the summer months. His loyalty to the company was greater than to its neighbourhood. Gondomar's visit to the Fortune in 1621 when he gave a banquet for the players seems in the broad context of this growing social polarisation to have been a calculated piece of political slumming. The King's Men drew gentry to the Globe every year, but there is less and less evidence that people like Mildmay visited the northern playhouses after 1609.

More obviously than any other change, the King's Men's takeover of the Blackfriars altered the pattern of playgoing towards a more socially stratified distribution. But they altered far more than just their venue, and the effects on playgoing were complex. Most substantially they increased the supply of Blackfriars performances sixfold. The boys kept to one performance a week despite all the commercial incentives they had to increase their revenue. The epilogue to *Eastward Ho!* voices the modest hope that its pleasures might 'attract you hither once a week'. No bar was placed against the King's Men using Blackfriars for their customary six afternoons a week. Despite that increase in the availability of performances at the most gentrified playhouse, however, the transfer did cut off the King's Men's performances for more than half the year from more than half of the playgoers who had visited them, on the Bankside. The sixfold increase in the price of admission at Blackfriars over the Globe minimum plus the reduction in the capacity of its auditorium by two thousand or more places altered at a stroke the nature of the audience for whom Shakespeare's company performed through nearly eight months of the year. And those were only the material changes. For a playing company to be allowed to use Blackfriars daily indicates a profound change in the status of the players. In 1596 the Lord Chamberlain himself supported the petition blocking the players from using their new playhouse. In 1609 nothing was said. The Liberty of the Blackfriars had long been popular with the aristocracy not just as a handsome residential area but for its church services. Stephen Egerton's sermons at St Anne's in the precinct, for instance, were extremely popular, especially with ladies. Margaret Hoby, a Puritan lady, daughter of one of the signatories of the 1596 petition, recorded in her diary for 30 November 1600 that 'after I was come home and had dined, I went to the blake friers, from whence I returned home and set downe in my testement the chieffe notes delivered by Mr. Egertone'.[88] In the circumstances it is a little surprising that the escalation of playgoing in competition with churchgoing in 1609 did not provoke a petition of protest until the adult players had been there for all of ten years. Only the prestige of the King's Men in society at large can explain the painless acquisition of their new playhouse. That prestige, based principally on Shakespeare's plays written for the Globe, set the other companies their standard. The northern companies now more openly kept clear of the privileged in the centre of the City, leaving them to the King's Men. Records of performances at Court confirm the Blackfriars players' ascendancy. Not until 1616 did Christopher Beeston mount a challenge for that end of the market.

The King's Men's repertoire of plays from 1609 onwards aspired to satisfy the top of the social hierarchy, but it still based itself centrally on the plays of Shakespeare. His major plays remained staples for the next thirty years, if the lists of plays offered at Court are any indicator. And the flow of new plays initiated by the success of Beaumont and Fletcher once they transferred from the boy company repertory secured its head of pressure largely by redeploying Shakespearean elements. *Philaster, The Maid's Tragedy,* and *A King and No King* came to rival *Pericles* as the characteristic style of the King's Men, and all three plays are infused with Shakespearean situations and characters to a degree which shows not just their authors' but their audiences' familiarity with the originals.[89] Playgoers at both the Blackfriars and the Globe took enthusiastically to the Arcadian style of the so-called 'Beaumont and Fletcher' canon[90] as an outgrowth of its Shakespearean base.

The Beaumont and Fletcher plays along with Shakespeare's own last plays were not so much a new playgoing fashion as an extension of the supremely popular old one at the Globe. The company did not radically alter its repertory when it moved into Blackfriars. There has been much dispute since Gerald Bentley first broached the idea that Shakespeare's last plays differ from their predecessors because they were written for the newly-acquired hall playhouse and its new clientele, and that the company hired Beaumont and Fletcher to write for them because the younger men had experience writing for the previous tenants.[91] This ignores the fact that *Pericles*, certainly a play in Shakespeare's late style, was on stage at the Globe in 1607, before the company had any reason to expect that they might repossess the Blackfriars, and that *The Winter's Tale* and *Cymbeline* were staged at the Globe in 1611 when Simon Forman saw them. It also ignores the fact that Beaumont and Fletcher, whether writing together or separately, were noted chiefly for plays which failed utterly when performed by the boys. More likely in 1609 Shakespeare, preparing for his retirement to Stratford, revoked his longstanding contract to provide the company with their ration of two new plays a year and left an opening for a new resident playwright which the company did not like entrusting to Jonson and which Fletcher eventually filled. *Philaster*, the first play Beaumont and Fletcher wrote for the King's Men at Blackfriars, opens with what looks like an uneasily self-conscious joke about the audience for the old company in its new venue.

CLE. Here's nor lords, nor ladies.
DION. Credit me, gentlemen, I wonder at it. They received strict charge from the King to attend here . . .

Possibly when Fletcher penned this opening for his new employers he was unsure whether the top of the social range would come to see the adults in the boys' playhouse. Jonson, writing *The Alchemist* for the same venue a little later, had fewer doubts. He expected his Blackfriars audience to be familiar with *The Spanish Tragedy* and with the Globe repertoire, and indeed to be largely the same as the King's Men had always entertained. *Philaster*, which is a rewriting of *Cupid's Revenge*, a boy company play, eliminating its gods and simplifying its staging, may reflect Fletcher's uncertainty about the readiness of the Blackfriars audience to receive the King's Men's offerings. Its echoes of *Hamlet* and *Othello* may well have been emphasised for the sake of the former Globe audience which they hoped would stay loyal to the company at its new venue, as Jonson expected. Fletcher's uncertainty was probably ill-advised. The next Beaumont and Fletcher play, *The Maid's Tragedy*, shifted in the other direction far enough to include a masque, in explicit imitation of the Court's most distinctive pastime. Shakespeare's late plays in any case made far more extravagant demands of the company in staging and of the audience in suspending their disbelief at the surreal events on stage. He definitely was happy to accept the challenge of a Blackfriars audience long accustomed to the sophisticated games of the 'theatre of estrangement'. Still, that was a minor change from his previous practices. His Globe plays transplanted to the Blackfriars unchanged, as his Blackfriars plays transplanted to the Globe. Audience expectations seem largely to have been transplanted with them. Beaumont and Fletcher's nearly fifty plays written for the King's Men exploited a fashion first created by Shakespeare for the Globe. The addition to the company's resources of the Blackfriars playhouse may have helped the development of the fashion but it cannot be said to have created it.

This is not the place to examine the nature of the fashion which Shakespeare's last plays generated. Its closest affinities are to Sidney's *Arcadia*, the favourite reading of young gallants and university men. That affinity together with the availability of the plays at the venue most convenient for the Inns of Court no doubt helped to confirm the King's Men in their grip on the upper sections of the playgoing market. It does not, however, tell anything like the whole story of the King's Men's audiences after 1609.

In 1596 James Burbage had planned to replace his old amphitheatre with the Blackfriars, and to keep only the hall with its fewer but wealthier patrons for his company. In 1609 his sons and their fellows were not under any pressure to relinquish the Globe as old Burbage had been with the Theatre. They might have kept the Globe and leased out the Blackfriars to another boy company. They might have taken on the Blackfriars with its law student clientele and leased the Globe to another adult company. Seemingly it was not only their pre-eminence as the best company with the best plays, attracting the widest range of audiences, but their desire to stay loyal to their Globe clientele which made them choose to divide their time between both playhouses. When the first Globe burned down in 1613 they could have simply reverted to the Blackfriars, which was now securely theirs. Instead they spent £1,400 to build a second Globe on the same foundations. This was more than either the first Fortune in 1600 or its replacement in 1622 cost, and probably more than the Hope, which replaced the old Beargarden near the Globe in 1614.

That sum was a substantial commitment to continuing the tradition established at the Globe through the previous decade. *Henry VIII*, the play which caused the Globe to burn, has distinct affinities with the plays of nostalgia for Elizabeth's England which the square amphitheatres of the northern suburbs were also performing in 1613. Its epilogue condemns the practice of girding at citizens. To some extent the Globe clearly was a citizen playhouse. But it also offered Blackfriars plays, and there is no evidence before the late 1630s to suggest that the company chose to stage some plays at one venue and not the other. Even *Hamlet*'s duel must have been accommodated indoors somehow. Nothing in the available evidence suggests that the King's Men's pre-eminence and their possession of the playhouse most frequented by the privileged altered in any way their assumption that they catered for the whole range of society. Standing at the top of the hierarchy of players they could still revive an old citizen favourite, *Mucedorus*, to offer the king in the Christmas revels of 1610. Their appeal was wider than any of their rivals, and their repertory more wide-ranging. Under James they kept a stable formula sustained by the input from the Beaumont and Fletcher canon. The only evidence for change turns up under Charles, when the company seems to have begun to acknowledge a difference in tastes between the Blackfriars gentry and the Globe's citizenry, though even that may be rather more a matter of adapting styles between the hall and the open amphitheatre than of catering to different clientele. Before the 1630s, and certainly in the years from 1609 till Richard Burbage died in 1619, the company saw itself as catering for the whole of society, and it offered the same fare at both playhouses.

(K) BEESTON'S COCK AND BULL
(1616–30)

Christopher Beeston was London's cleverest innovator in theatre affairs between 1609 and his death in 1638. He began as a player apprenticed to Augustine Phillips in Shakespeare's company, appearing in *Every Man in his Humour* in 1597. He transferred to the Henslowe enterprises by 1602 and became a leader of the Queen's Men, taking over management of its business affairs in 1612. He lived in Clerkenwell near the Red Bull where his company performed, and was a friend as well as a colleague of Heywood, who wrote his citizen pageant plays for him. The citizen repertory however did not satisfy Beeston. He had considerable skill as a manager, and saw the way forward as an upward social shift like the King's Men in their use of the Blackfriars. By 1616 he had the resources to take a thirty-one year lease on a property in Drury Lane, half a mile north-west of the Blackfriars, an equal distance north-east of Whitehall Palace, and close to the Inns of Court. The property was 'All that edifices or building called the Cockpits, and the Cockhouses and shed thereunto adjoining'.[92] The original cock-fighting pit had its own circular auditorium, which Beeston probably retained as the basic structure for the new hall playhouse while extending one side of the circle to make a stage and boxes, with a tiring-house behind the extension. James had forbidden new building in the district, and the enlargement of existing buildings by more than one third, so Beeston calculated his development nicely. If, as seems very likely, he did use the surviving Inigo Jones drawings of an adapted cockpit for his new playhouse its auditorium would probably have resembled the curved galleries of the Blackfriars, though its seating capacity was rather smaller.[93] Restricted though the income was, Beeston evidently felt there would be more profit from imitating the Blackfriars than he could get at the Red Bull. He evidently expected to have the only hall playhouse operating through the summer months.

Beeston's subsequent career does not impinge directly on the question of audience composition and allegiances, though the link he maintained in the 1620s between the Red Bull and Cockpit raises some intriguing questions which will be considered below. The immediate question is how he succeeded with his attempt to rival the Blackfriars, and what effect it might have had on the repertory.

From the time Beeston's new playhouse opened when the law term had commenced late in 1616, the Revels Office allowed four companies to work in London. The King's Men as the leading company were followed by the Queen's at the Cockpit, the Palsgrave's at the Fortune and Prince Charles's, who took over the Red Bull when Beeston transferred the Queen's Men to the Cockpit. The Queen's company's transfer to the Cockpit was not quite the same as the King's Men's transfer from the Globe to the Blackfriars. Beeston's company, much less prosperous than the King's Men,[94] did not copy them by retaining an amphitheatre for the summer season, and they paid a peculiar price for not doing so. The Queen's company had a drum and trumpet repertory designed for the 'fishwives' and artisans of the City. When they left the Red Bull they took those plays with them to the Cockpit. Although a new company started playing at the Red Bull, its plays were different. And the apprentices and fishwives could hardly make the same transfer to the Cockpit as the players, because its prices were six times higher. They lost their favourite repertory. Consequently it is something less than a coincidence that on the following Shrove Tuesday holiday early in 1617 a mob of apprentices went to the Cockpit and wrecked it. The fact that they chose to attack the Cockpit ahead of the northern amphitheatres and the Blackfriars, and that they destroyed Beeston's new house next door, suggests that they were taking revenge for the loss of their plays. John Chamberlain's colourful account of the riot confirms this evidence of animus against the newly-installed Cockpit company. Although the players defended their playhouse and shot some of the attackers, 'yet they entered the house and defaced yt, cutting the players apparell all to pieces, and all other theyre furniture, and burnt theyre play bookes and did what other mischeife they could'.[95] Playbooks and apparel were a playing company's most valuable possessions. The attack was pointedly against the company rather than against playhouses in general. On Shrove Tuesday the following year they tried again, planning to assemble at the Fortune and to attack both the Cockpit and the Red Bull, but the Privy Council was forewarned and stopped them. Since this time they used the Fortune as their assembly point their animus was evidently not against playhouses in general but against the two which had disrupted their pleasures. It can only have been Beeston and his removal of the Red Bull repertoire to the more expensive Cockpit which stirred these acts of revenge.

There is regrettably little direct evidence about the plays Beeston took to the Cockpit. Webster had been writing for the Queen's Men at the Red Bull, and after the success of his *Duchess of Malfi* at the Blackfriars *The White Devil* and *The Devil's Law-Case* might have seemed useful hall playhouse fodder. More surprisingly Heywood, who wrote regularly for the Cockpit in the 1620s, may have gone with his pageant plays to Beeston's new hall. *The Iron Age*, dealing with the Trojan War and originally composed for the Queen's Men at the Red Bull, might have been one play to make the transfer. The epistle which accompanied its publication in 1632 claimed that at different times it had 'thronged three severall Theaters, with numerous and mighty Auditories'. The Red Bull was certainly one of the three. The Curtain may have been a second, and it is difficult to ignore the circumstantial evidence of the Red Bull company's transfer and Heywood's subsequent association with the Cockpit which suggests that it must have been the third.[96] Almost nothing is known for certain about the early Cockpit repertoire, but since play-texts were a major part of a playing company's assets, and since the Red Bull company did make the transfer, it seems likely that the first years there saw the performance of plays originally written for the Red Bull. Some plays which had been Henslowe's property when he ran the Queen's Men do turn up later in the Cockpit repertoire. The most notable of these is Marlowe's *Jew of Malta*, which was printed in 1633 with an epistle by Heywood and a prologue praising Richard Perkins, the Cockpit's leading man, in the title role. It, and perhaps other Marlowe plays, would most likely have moved to the Cockpit when the Queen's Men first went there in 1616. Heywood's *If You Know Not Me* also transferred there at some point. So the second hall playhouse sustained an older and more openly citizen repertoire than its rival at Blackfriars.

Beeston's enterprise at the Cockpit was in some respects a rather shady operation. He was accused by the Queen's Men after they separated from him in 1619 of milking their funds to feed his own interests. There was a good deal of acrimony over the Cockpit, which may have blocked his return to the Red Bull after the Shrove Tuesday riot destroyed his new house. In the event he rebuilt it – evoking its alternative name, the Phoenix – and ran it with the Queen's Men until his patron died in 1619. He then took over Prince Charles's Men, who had taken the Queen's Men's place at the Red Bull. Once again a Red Bull company supplied the wants of the Cockpit audiences. No plays of theirs from their first Red Bull period have survived, though Middleton and Rowley appear to have written for them at about this time.[97] Certainly Beeston himself felt, on the evidence of this readiness to use Red Bull players and repertoires, that the King's Men's seasonal transfers between the Globe and Blackfriars could be imitated in some respects. If he was wrong, it was not because of the repertoire of plays but because his kind of

SVVETNAM,

THE

VVoman-hater,

ARRAIGNED BY

WOMEN.

A new Comedie,

Acted at the *Red Bull*, by the late
Queenes Seruants.

LONDON,
Printed for *Richard Meighen*, and are to be fold at his Shops
at Saint *Clements* Church, ouer-againft *Eſſex* Houſe, and
at *Weſtminſter* Hall. 1620.

19. The titlepage of *Swetnam the Woman Hater*, 1620. This
picture probably is not a reproduction of the stage performance,
since the room shown has windows, so it cannot represent the
tiring-house wall behind the stage. But the seat of justice may
well have been imitated on stage for the 'state' or throne of a
judge or a king, and the women shown all wear citizen dress of
the time, including their hats

transfer was permanent. The apprentices in 1617 were objecting to the permanent removal of a Red Bull repertoire beyond their final reach.

From 1616 onwards the supply of new plays to the four repertories slowed down markedly, and many of the new plays never reached print and have been lost, particularly those belonging to the Red Bull and Fortune companies. The King's Men were taking only four new plays a year by the 1630s, when more than 80% of the plays offered at Court were old favourites. Consequently it becomes more and more difficult to identify a particular repertoire at a particular playhouse. To some extent the repertories were particular, and playhouses did have distinct reputations, presumably based chiefly on their stock of old plays, which attracted particular types of audience. The Red Bull players developed a reputation as 'terrible teare-throats', speaking and strutting more vigorously than their rivals.[98] The Bull played the man while the Globe and Blackfriars told tricks of love. From 1616 on the reputations of the different playhouses are more revealing than their repertoires. It is this which makes the continuing series of transfers from the Red Bull to the Cockpit so intriguing.

From the time when Beeston's reborn Phoenix started performing in 1617 until at least 1630 the repertoires of the two playhouses were similar, though their reputations diverged. The Red Bull staged *Swetnam the Woman Hater* in 1617, a play designed in part to please the sort of ladies who wrote pamphlets refuting Joseph Swetnam's misogynistic charges against women.[99] Like Middleton and Rowley's *A Fair Quarrel* it looks entirely suitable for the ladies in the boxes at the Cockpit. It hardly deserves the jibe Thomas Tomkis levelled against the citizen playhouses in 1614 in his Cambridge play *Albumazar*, an imitation of *The Alchemist* and *The Tempest*, that at 'the Plaies I see at the Fortune and Red Bull … I learne all the words I speake and understand not' (2.111). Tomkis wrote academic plays which assumed that his audience would be familiar with London playgoing and current reputations. In *Lingua* (1607), for instance, he commented on the abuse to be expected in boy company plays, 'when Boys dare traduce men in authority'.[100] The Red Bull's reputation for overdoing was evidently current well before Beeston found its company a new home. And odd though it seems, that reputation stayed with the Red Bull tenants even though the actual players transferred every few years to the Cockpit.

In 1625 when the companies resumed playing under the new king Beeston reopened the Red Bull with Queen Henrietta's Men. Following what had by now become his standard practice he soon acquired

20. The Duke of Buckingham, from a painting (NPG 3840)

for his new company Perkins and other leading players who had been notable at the Red Bull.[101] They did well, if the fact that Beeston kept them together much longer than any of his other companies is anything to go by. In August 1628 the Duke of Buckingham, greatest grandee in the country and soon to be assassinated, visited the Cockpit to see Heywood's *Rape of Lucrece*, a play originally written for the Red Bull. The Cockpit company performed ten times at Court in the festive season over Christmas 1629, while the Blackfriars company played twelve. In the following season they played sixteen times. Not surprisingly in 1630 the Blackfriars playwrights complained that they were losing customers to the rival hall. Thomas Carew condemned the alternative attraction for its rowdiness and the declining standards of recent audiences in a verse epistle for a play of Davenant's written for the Blackfriars. He lumped the Cockpit and Red Bull tastes together, in a complaint clearly designed to be offensive to the Cockpit.

> I have beheld, when pearched on the smooth brow
> Of a fayre modest troope, thou didst allow
> Applause to slighter workes; but then the weake
> Spectator gave the knowing leave to speake.
> Now noyse prevayles, and he is taxed for drowth
> Of wit, that with the crie, spends not his mouth.
> Yet aske him, reason why he did not like;
> Him, why he did; their ignorance will strike
> Thy soule with scorne, and Pity: marke the places
> Provoke their smiles, frownes, or distorted faces,
> When, they admire, nod, shake the head: they'le be
> A scene of myrth, a double Comedie.
> But thy strong fancies (raptures of the brayne,
> Drest in Poetique flames) they entertayne
> As a bold, impious reach; for they'l still slight
> All that exceeds Red Bull, and Cockpit flight.   (2.148)

Implicit in this is Carew's belief that the new poetry and wit of the Blackfriars writers was superior to the old-fashioned noise and 'double Comedie' of the citizen and Cockpit repertory. This charge the Cockpit's supporters promptly challenged, calling it 'a discourse of cock and bull', and Heywood a little later also spoke out against Carew. Modern commentators have found it harder to accept this lumping together of the tear-throats at the Red Bull with the Cockpit than writers of the time did.[102] Beeston's repertory was evidently not so ready to accept innovation as the Blackfriars, and while the volume and overdoing for which the Red Bull was notorious could not have adjusted easily to the Cockpit the plays and even the players clearly did. This suggests that the two playhouses became distinct in the social composition of their audiences more through their prices and their locality than their repertoire. Printers named the Cockpit nearly as often as they proclaimed the Blackfriars as the place of first publication for plays, often concealing their origin as Red Bull products. If printers thought the social status of the playhouse mattered, so presumably did audiences.

(L) THE BLACKFRIARS IN THE 1630S

In the last twelve years before the closure the social prestige of particular playhouses settled into a distinct hierarchy. The Blackfriars' pre-eminence was never shaken after 1630, though for different reasons the Cockpit and the Globe served as respectable alternatives. The third hall playhouse, the Salisbury Court in Whitefriars, which opened in 1629, was smaller than the two older halls, and remained self-consciously inferior to them in status if not in what it offered on its stage. Bankside continued to be the resort for bear-baiting and brothels throughout the year, but kept some attraction for playgoers as the suburb where the Blackfriars players held their summer season. The Swan, and the Hope after its first few years with both bears and players, never gave the Globe any competition, so in a way the King's Men were as distinct on the Bankside as they were in Blackfriars. The two square amphitheatres in the northern suburbs were lumped together and strengthened their identity as popular venues catering primarily for the masses, artisans, apprentices and the lowest levels of the hierarchy of wealth. Some evidence links all three amphitheatres as providers of vigorous drum and trumpet plays of a simpler make than the halls provided – or could provide, given their smaller size and enclosed shape with the consequent acoustic constraints. How consistently the amphitheatres aimed to supply heartier appetites than those of the ladies and their escorts in the boxes at the hall playhouses remains to some extent an assumption based on the physical conditions of the different venues.

Francis Lenton's cheerful verses about the rise and fall of a young prodigal gallant coming as an Inns of Court student to London, written in 1629, show how closely social standing and the choice of playhouse went together. Initially the young man goes to the Cockpit. Soon though, in 'silken garments, and ... sattin robe' he starts attending the Blackfriars and, staying in town out of term, to the Globe. With his copy of Jonson's 'booke of Playes' he seems to ally social pretensions with intellectual as he ascends from the Cockpit repertory to that of the King's Men.

> The Cockpit heretofore would serve his wit,
> But now upon the Fryers stage hee'll sit. (2.145)

No doubt both his progress and his pretensions were characteristic of the time, though in 1629 it may have been intellectual pretensions to 'wit' which drew him to the Blackfriars rather than the social ladder. In the years from the late 1620s to 1636, despite the divergent repertoire of plays which led to the dispute between Carew and the Cockpit writers, the two playhouses were almost equal in social standing. Shackerley Marmion, writing for the smaller Salisbury Court hall in 1631, praised them equally.

> ... on each hand
> To over-top us, two great Lawrels stand;
> The one, when she shall please to spread her traine,
> The vastnesse of the Globe cannot containe;
> Th' other so high, the Phoenix does aspire
> To build in ... (2.154)

Ladies in this period went as readily to the Cockpit as the Blackfriars, and both repertories began to run plays aimed specifically at what were thought to be female tastes.[103] This equivalence, which led Inns of Court gentry like John Ford to write for both playhouses, lasted until the long closure of 1636–37, when the ten-year run of Beeston's company came to an end, and he replaced them with the odd group of youngsters known as 'Beeston's Boys'. The Blackfriars then ran unchallenged till all playing was stopped.

In the 1630s prologues written for the Blackfriars and the Cockpit began to develop a language of their own. Addressing themselves to any or all of the four categories they identified in the hall audiences, gentry, ladies, wealthy merchant citizens and 'wity young masters o' the *Innes o' Court*',[104] they indicate that a new currency of judicious criticism was being minted.

> Let some say *This was flat*; Some here *the Sceane*
> *Fell from its height*; Another that the Meane
> Was *ill observ'd*, in such a growing passion.[105]

All these new prologues and epilogues were probably themselves a consequence of the settled sense which audiences now had of themselves as judges. This, sadly though understandably, came too late for Jonson. He attacked the Blackfriars audiences in 1635 bitterly for being no better than the 'understanders' at the amphitheatres:

> ... those deepe-grounded, understanding men,
> That sit to censure *Playes*, yet know not when,
> Or why to like ...[106]

But Alexander Gill mocked Jonson for sending his *Magnetic Lady* to the Blackfriars instead of the Fortune and its apple-wives.

> ... when as silkes and plush, and all the witts
> Are calde to see, and censure as befitts,
> And yff your follye take not, they, perchance,
> Must here themselfes stilde, gentle ignorance. (2.158)

The self-conscious function of gentle audiences at the hall play-houses was to 'censure'. For the first time plays had become respectable matter for serious discussion. The king himself made critical notes in the margins of his playbooks and more than once interceded on a matter of critical judgement with the Master of the Revels. It became the mode of the town.

On the whole, audiences at the Blackfriars and Cockpit seem to have been much more akin than their two repertoires. In some respects both playhouses shaped their offerings to suit the new Caroline respectability and showed a new respect for the ladies in the boxes.[107] The main shifts in taste reflected the female presence and called for refinements in the verbal crudities of the older repertory. The Master of the Revels, Sir Henry Herbert, was himself a crude censor, taking a narrow line over oaths and profanity and insisting that revivals of old plays like *The Taming of the Shrew* and Fletcher's sequel *The Woman's Prize* should be freshly 'purged' before they could be performed. His objection to Charles's more liberal idea of what was an oath shows that he was not just led to this stand by his need of the fee for reading the playbooks. He gave unctuous praise to Shirley's innocuous *Young Admiral*, a play slickly adapted from Lope de Vega's *Don Lope de Cardona*, and urged other playwrights to copy Shirley's moderation. Abraham Wright also liked *The Young Admiral*, so what prompted Herbert's judgement was not merely an officious idea of censorship.[108]

A large contribution to this shift in taste came from the circle of gallants who attended Henrietta Maria and who wrote for the Blackfriars. The courtier poet Lodowick Carlell, who wrote for Court performance but passed his work on to the King's Men, along with the pushing young gallants Davenant, Suckling and Rutter, did most to fix the concept of 'wit' as the test of quality in the Blackfriars repertoire. Their style was controversial, and made enemies of Massinger and Shirley, who wrote in an older tradition. Two of

Massinger's plays written for the Blackfriars failed between 1630 and 1633, at least one of them because it was decried by a faction of gallants in the audience. Massinger did not like Carew's verses in 1630 attacking the Cockpit and Red Bull. One of Carew's supporters in turn condemned him for bringing

> : his flat
> dull dialogues frought with insipit chatt
> Into the scale with thy Sweet Muse, which sings
> ditties fit only for the eares of Kings.[109]

Shirley, chief victim of the Carew attack, was appointed to Henrietta Maria's household in 1632, and may have felt that he was joining not so much the opposition as a superior and select company. But in November of that year Herbert censured him severely for *The Ball*, played at the Cockpit, where 'ther were divers personated so naturally, both of lords and others of the court, that I took it ill'.[110] Shirley never again ventured into the intimate satire which this charge implies. He fell out of favour as Davenant rose. A sharp comment in *The Bird in a Cage* (1633) about 'the flattering tribe of courtiers . . . glow worms' indicates his uneasiness in such company. It may be too simple to see Davenant and his allies making a concerted attempt to displace Massinger from the Blackfriars to join Shirley at the Cockpit, where a less innovative repertoire was more welcome, but the circumstantial evidence does suggest that a campaign aimed at some such change did run for a while at the Blackfriars. The transfer of writers like Ford from the Blackfriars to the Cockpit, the failure of several Massinger plays and Shirley's difficulties, including his brief transfer from the Cockpit to Salisbury Court, in the period from 1629 to 1633, offer confirmation that some upheavals in taste did take place when Davenant and his allies established themselves at the Blackfriars.

Conservatism in the playgoing tastes of the gentry was probably one factor which kept the Cockpit in strong competition with the Blackfriars up to 1636. Traditional preferences lingered on, sustained by the quality of the old repertoire which made it good policy to mount such revivals as Shakespeare's and Fletcher's Shrew plays in 1633. In explicit contrast to this pleasure in the old plays, and possibly to emphasise their own originality, Davenant and his allies distanced themselves carefully from them. In the prologue to his *Unfortunate Lovers* at Blackfriars Davenant characterised the habits of amphitheatre audiences, dominated by citizens, as out of date.

> Good easy judging souls, with what delight
> They would expect a jig, or target fight.

Blackfriars audiences of 1638 were required to be more severe judges, and to enjoy witplay, not swordplay.

There is a good deal of evidence suggesting that the Cockpit plays were far more traditional and less innovatory than the Blackfriars throughout this period. The plays which Beeston took from the Red Bull to the Cockpit stayed in the hall's repertoire, and as late as 1639 Beeston's son was protecting numbers of Red Bull plays for his Cockpit company. This protection, which took the form of an edict issued on 10 August 1639 by the Lord Chamberlain, was designed to stop illegal performance or publication of plays in the Cockpit repertoire. They were still valuable commodities to the Cockpit.

It also seems that at least some of the gentry visiting the Cockpit maintained citizen-like preferences for the knockabout comedy of jigs. So Shirley claimed in *The Changes*, in 1631:

> Many gentlemen
> Are not, as in the days of understanding,
> Now satisfied without a Jig, which since
> They cannot, with their honour, call for after
> The play, they look to be serv'd up in the middle.   (2.153)

In other words gentry (or that combination of gallants, country squires and merchants who expected by the 1630s to be called gentlemen) in the halls yearned for the amphitheatre practice of jigs performed as afterpieces for the 'understanders', and hoped to see them in respectable disguise as a play-within-the-play or dance in Cockpit plays. Heywood expressed a version of that sentiment himself when he grumbled about the passing of the Red Bull tradition and the history plays of the 1590s in favour of the lesser things which the Blackfriars now offered.

> ... where before great Patriots, Dukes and Kings
> Presented for some hie facinorious things,
> Were the Stage-Subject; now we strive to flie
> In their low pitch, who never could soare hie:
> For now the common argument intreats,
> Of puling Lovers, craftie Bawdes or cheates.   (2.170)

Heywood did not like the new Blackfriars plays, including pastorals and the Platonic love interest which the Queen's circle fostered.

The new Blackfriars fashion was not itself entirely new. It rested on elements of the Fletcher canon, for instance. The terms in which Marmion praised the King's Men in 1634 for their revival of Fletcher's early play *The Faithful Shepherdess* indicate both a source for the new taste and the self-conscious pride in critical judgement which nurtured it. Addressing the company's chief player, Joseph Taylor, Marmion wrote

> When this smooth Pastorall was first brought forth,
> The Age twas borne in, did not know it's worth.
> Since by thy cost, and industry reviv'd,
> It hath a new fame, and new birth atchiv'd.   (2.166)

The play appeared at Court at the end of the Christmas festivities in January 1634. Rutter wrote an imitation of it for the Blackfriars. A careful combining of the old repertoire, knowing the Queen's liking for romantic and pastoral drama, was all to the good for the company's status. Novelty, not in the plays but in taste, was the new requirement at Blackfriars.

Early Beaumont and Fletcher matched the new critical sense nicely. *The Knight of the Burning Pestle*, revived in 1635–36 and performed at Court, had now a much better reception for its mockery of the old tastes than it received in 1607. This kind of mockery, some of which will be considered in the next section, was an important feature of the attitudes voiced at the hall play-houses in these last years. Even the least of the three, Salisbury Court, was happy to signal the gulf in tastes between a gallant on the one hand and a country gentleman and a merchant on the other. The Praeludium to Goffe's *The Careless Shepherdess*,[111] written for a revival in about 1638 which was probably trying to join the Blackfriars fashion for pastorals, makes fun of three such stereotypes. A money-conscious citizen named Thrift, a courtier named Spruce and a 'landlord' from the country come on stage to discuss their preferences as playgoers. The citizen finally decides to retrieve his shilling and instead 'go to th' Bull or Fortune, and there see / A Play for two pence, with a Jig to boot'. The 'landlord', although he does stay to watch the pastoral, has similar likes. He and Thrift exchange reminiscences of clowns they have enjoyed, especially Timothy Reade, who was the Salisbury Court's clown at the time and probably playing one of the speakers. 'I would have the Fool in every Act, / Be't Comedy, or Tragedy', says the country landowner. Insistent mockery of this kind, aimed at the debased standards of playgoing amongst the wealthier citizenry and lesser gentry, is a feature of the hall playhouses in the last years. Partly it grew out of the self-consciously judgemental role which audiences starting with Charles himself felt to be their proper function. Partly it was an effect of the long divergence in tastes which began in 1599.

(M) CITIZENS IN THE LAST YEARS
(1630–42)

In a section of *The Jacobean and Caroline Stage* entitled 'The Reputation of the Red Bull Theatre',[112] G. E. Bentley lists twenty jibes about the low theatrical standards of the Red Bull and its various companies. 'As the Curtain falls into disuse', he concludes, 'the Red Bull reigns supreme in ignominy.' This view takes too readily as an absolute the dismissive statements made by gentlemanly commentators. It ignores the fact that in numbers if not in revenue the northern playhouses did more business than the halls. It certainly ignores the close association which Beeston maintained between the Cockpit and the Red Bull. The twenty jibes need to be set in the context of a vigorous and far from mindlessly traditional citizen repertory. The principal question is the extent to which the social polarisation between the halls and amphitheatres in the 1630s evoked a similar polarisation of social and political allegiances in the repertories.

The jibes against the Red Bull fall into three categories. Mostly, like Tomkis in *Albumazar*, Carew in his defence of Davenant's *Just Italian*, and the Praeludium to *The Careless Shepherdess*, they voiced derision at its debased standards of literary sophistication. These jibes began as early as 1614 and ran for more than half a century, mocking its 'musty phrases' and old-fashioned clowning. A second kind of charge was directed against noisy overacting. Jonson in *Timber* (1632) scorned the '*Tamerlanes*, and *Tamer-chams* of the late Age, which had nothing in them but the *scenicall* strutting, and furious vociferation, to warrant them to the ignorant gapers'. Its players were 'terrible teare-throats', its clown a 'roaring Rimer', its tragedians created a simile for roaring 'like *Tamerlin* at the Bull'.[113] Its kings and queens spoke 'in a *Majestick tone*' of exaggerated loftiness.[114] The third charge, a little more neutral, concerned its repertoire of plays about war. Its audiences were 'Turmoyl'd with Battailes'. 'Drums, Trumpets, Battels, and Hero's' were the trappings of '*Red-Bull* wars', with their 'sieges laid to the *Musique-Roome*'. Davenant claimed that citizen audiences for Heywood's *The Iron Age* were happy with 'a furious Tale of *Troy* which they ne're thought / Was weakly Writ, if it were strongly *Fought*'.[115] All the claims about exaggeration and battles relate to the last fifteen years of the Red Bull, after Beeston had taken his last contingent of players from it. The tradition of playing Tamburlaine loudly and vigorously had started however with Alleyn, who played the part originally.

Marlowe's opus and the tradition of playing it with 'furious vociferation' stayed in the Red Bull's repertoire and seems to have been
identified as its most typical offering particularly in those last years.
The very fact that it stayed on as Red Bull fare when the companies
themselves moved elsewhere and other Marlowe plays like *The Jew
of Malta* were transferred to the Cockpit implies that, however the
ownership of the playbook may have changed hands, the play itself
was thought to belong at that particular playhouse. The fact that the
Cockpit used so much from the Red Bull repertory in the 1630s
implies that it was the style of playing, and probably the plays with
battles in them, which most distinguished the Red Bull.

As *Tamburlaine* became a feature at the Red Bull, so *The Spanish
Tragedy* seems to have been identified with the Fortune, in ways
which suggest there was a broadly similar style of acting at those two
playhouses. At the end of the decade the two companies developed
some hostility to one another. The animosity blew up when the
Prince's Men exchanged playhouses with the Red Bull-King's
Company at Easter 1640. If we can judge from John Tatham's
prologue, written for the company which was displaced from the
Fortune, the Red Bull was much the less prestigious playhouse. He
complained that the Fortune's owners had 'thrust us out of doore /
For some peculiar profit', and voiced his angry contempt for the
debased following which the former Red Bull company would leave
behind them at the Fortune.

> ... shee has t'ane
> A course to banish Modesty, and retaine
> More dinn, and *incivility* than hath been
> Knowne in the *Bearward Court*, the *Beargarden*.   (2.196)

The Fortune audience, not its actors, are here accused of being more
noisy and barbaric than the bears. Such a reputation was apparently
not shared by the Red Bull. Tatham, of course, may well have been
exaggerating, since a reverse exchange took place with no acrimony
six years earlier.[116] Curiously, that exchange may have taken the Red
Bull style of overacting to the Fortune, because in 1639 the Red Bull
players themselves accused the Fortune players and especially their
leading player, Richard Fowler, of overdoing *The Spanish Tragedy*. A
clownish tailor in Thomas Rawlins' *The Rebellion* demands to act
Jeronimo, declaring 'Marke if I doe not gape wider than the widest /
Mouth'd Fowler of them all.'[117] Fowler, who was known for his
'Conquering parts',[118] cannot have used an acting style widely
different from the tear-throat fashion attributed to the Red Bull.

This kinship, even in hostility, between the two northern amphitheatres provides some justification for James Wright's statement in *Historia Histrionica* that the Fortune and Red Bull were 'mostly frequented by Citizens, and the meaner sort of people' (2.205). Wright must have been at least a little influenced by the jibes against their old-fashioned repertories. It is difficult to ignore the implication that a meaner sort of audience was poor not only in financial resources but in taste, and it is not clear which form of poverty influenced Wright. The co-existence of Red Bull plays at the Cockpit may indicate that the differences in the types of playhouse were beginning to alter the image which the public had of their repertories. The Red Bull's name for plays with battles in them signals the extent to which they exploited the open conditions of a large stage and daylight for swordfighting, which the Cockpit, staging former Red Bull plays, could not. There are no swordfights in *The Jew of Malta*. If so, the Fortune's open stage would naturally have put it nearer to the Red Bull than to the hall playhouses.

The citizens' continued liking for the repertoire of the 1590s has several possible causes. One is the recurrent waves of militarism which swept London at fairly regular intervals. Another is a similar recurrence of nostalgia for the golden age of Elizabeth, which was particularly strong in the 1630s.[119] This was certainly not a feeling shared by the Blackfriars poets. Both of these possible causes of the apparent conservatism of citizen taste emphasise the extent to which audiences became polarised socially between the different kinds of playhouse. The trouble is that the argument is nearly circular. Battle plays belonged on open stages which, being cheaper, were attended by the poorer sort. Which chose which? The fact that the amphitheatres played mainly older plays, which apart from being cheaper to produce offer less clear evidence about how tastes were evolving, is no help. The best evidence about the division between the two kinds of repertoire probably lies in the evidence about what, in a time of growing political strain, was picked out for censorship.

Herbert did not like satirical in-jokes about courtiers, or profane language. Little else sent him by the King's Men or Beeston gave him concern. Charles intervened occasionally, once with his rather more benign ruling than Herbert's about what constituted an oath, and once objecting to a rash declaration in a Massinger play about unjust taxation. The poets writing for gallants and courtiers knew how to be cautious over affairs of state.[120] Two major misfortunes visited by censorship on the northern playhouses in 1639 suggest they were less cautious. These two incidents are not matched by any comparable cases in the whole of the previous seventy years, so far as records show, except for *The Isle of Dogs* in 1597 and *A Game at Chesse* in 1624. Both of these also happened at amphitheatres, though only the Middleton play, with its onslaught on the government's foreign policy, bears any relation to the two incidents of 1639. Middleton's play, in any case, seems to have had the connivance of people in high places, a privilege which the northern playhouses certainly did not enjoy. Their offences say something specific about playgoing at the citizen places of this last phase.

The first offence occurred in May, in the performance of a lost play, *The Cardinal's Conspiracy*, at the Fortune. The players evidently used it for an attack on the high-church Arminianism of the establishment. In a letter reporting the case, Edmond Rossingham wrote

Thursday last the players of the Fortune were fined 1,000£. for setting up an altar, a bason, and two candlesticks, and bowing down before it upon the stage, and although they allege it was an old play revived, and an altar to the heathen gods, yet it was apparent that this play was revived on purpose in contempt of the ceremonies of the church.   (2.188)

Application was still, up to a point, a profitable trade. The company had evaded the censor by using an old play, and applied it to a current cause for anger in the City.[121] The intention was to feed popular hatred of Romanism. Then in September the Red Bull players staged another cause for anger, this time about the City's own affairs. *The Whore New Vamped*, the text of which is also understandably lost, attacked the new duty on wines, called the monopolist Sir William Abell, a City alderman, a knave and drunkard, and the proctors of the probate Court dishonest. The play was extremely popular and had a run of 'many days together' before the Privy Council intervened on 29 September. The Council's minutes report that

complaint was this day made to his Majestie sitting in Councell, that the Stage Players of the Red Bull have lately for many days to gether acted a scandalous and Libellous play wherein they have audaciously reproached, and in a Libellous manner traduced and personated some persons of quality, and scandalised, and defamed the whole profession of Proctors belonging to the Court of the Civill Lawe, and reflected upon the present Government.
                                                                       (2.189)

The author, the players and the censor were all examined to see whose fault it was that the offensive play appeared on stage. The offences show hostility to the government's practice with monopolies and the City figures and their agents who made profitable use of the monopolies. It was a feeling natural to the 'meaner sort' of citizens.

These were both local matters, of religious prejudice and City misgovernment. They differ from the matters for which the hall playhouse companies were censured in their distance from the affairs of the Court. When Beeston's company at the Cockpit suffered in 1640, the charge was over a much more direct political comment than those at the Fortune and Red Bull. The Cockpit's offending play, as Herbert reported, 'had relation to the passages of the K.s journey into the Northe, and was complayned of by his Majestye to mee, with commande to punishe the offenders'.[122] The royal conduct of government was not a central subject in the citizen playhouses. Their repertory generally shows hostility to the counsellors of government and its City agents rather than to the king himself.[123]

Finally in this hardly strange but not uneventful history, its acts being seven decades, comes the question of the closing years at the Globe. Its repertory differed from the Fortune and Red Bull as the Blackfriars differed from the Cockpit. When the company moved to it for the summer it enjoyed the continued custom of the Mildmays and the gallants who stayed in town out of term, but its locality was no more respectable than the Red Bull's, and its open stage invited the staging of the battle plays which had financed its original construction in 1599. What is not clear is whether it altered its repertoire of plays from the Blackfriars range to satisfy the larger numbers of playgoers paying lower prices through the summer, and whether the lower prices at the Globe did significantly alter the social or the mental composition of its audiences.

Contemporary comment on the Globe's playgoers suggests little change from the Blackfriars clientele, either in gallants or ladies. Nicholas Goodman in 1632 wrote that 'halfe the yeere a World of *Beauties* and brave *Spirits* resorted unto it' (2.155). A few references do suggest that citizens were preponderant in the summer, but they belong to the fashion of witty contempt for slow and old-fashioned citizen tastes, and say little about the real composition of the audiences or about the favoured repertoire of plays. Henry Glapthorne's poem 'To a Reviv'd Vacation Play' carries in its title the implication that summer was the season for an older style of play. The poem, written as a prologue, probably for the Cockpit, ironically praises citizen wit and begs the citizens present to forget their business cares.

> And now we hope you've leisure in the Citie
> To give the World cause to suspect you witty. (2.180)

Such mockery had been customary in the hall playhouses for forty years.

Possibly more revealing than the gentry's usual prejudice is a point implied by Lovelace, who wrote only for the Blackfriars, about the divisions within the hall audiences. The epilogue to his lost play *The Scholars*, printed with his poems in 1649, notes how distinct was the division made by money even inside the hall playhouse. The gentry in the Blackfriars pit want different things from the lesser beings in the upper gallery.

> His *Schollars* school'd, sayd if he had been wise,
> He should have wove in one two comedies.
> The first for th' gallery, in which the throne
> To their amazement should descend alone,
> The rosin-lightning flash and monster spire
> Squibs, and words hotter than his fire.
> Th'other for the gentlemen of the pit
> Like to themselves all spirit, fancy, wit   (2.199)

The upper gallery, he claims, the sixpence-payers, like precisely the same visual spectacles and hot words for which the amphitheatre playhouses were noted. This implies that the seasonal transfer of gentry from the Blackfriars to the Globe and back might have been accompanied by more of the Globe clients than the prejudice of the Blackfriars writers normally allowed them to admit. If so, it calls into question the one truly explicit piece of evidence from a King's Men's playwright which suggests that the Globe playgoers were treated to a repertoire of the King's Men's plays distinct from those the Black-friars playgoers enjoyed.

Shirley's *The Doubtful Heir* was probably written in Dublin, where Shirley went during the long closure because of plague in 1636–37. It was performed in Dublin in about 1638. In April 1640, when Shirley returned to London, he offered it to the Blackfriars. Massinger had just died, and the post of resident playwright therefore becoming vacant, it probably went to Shirley. In May, as usual, the company transferred to the Globe, and it was there that the play first appeared, after Herbert licensed it on 1 June. Shirley, it is thought, was upset by the change in venue. For more than a decade he had written two plays a year for Beeston at the Cockpit. He had been away from London for another four years. Now he had secured London's outstanding playhouse for his work, only to find himself overtaken by the seasonal change to the Globe. In his 'distress', as Bentley calls it,[124] he wrote a heavily sarcastic prologue telling the Globe playgoers what not to expect in a play designed for a hall playhouse. The prologue was published with his poems in 1646, with the title '*A Prologue at the Globe to his Comedy call'd* The Doubtful Heire, *which should have been presented at the Black-Friers*'. The text is worth quoting in full.

Gentlemen, I am onely sent to say,
Our Author did not calculate his Play,
For this Meridian; The Bank-Side he knowes
Is far more skilful at the ebbes and flowes
Of water then of Wit: He did not mean
For the elevation of your Poles this Scene.
No shews, no frisk, and what you most delight in,
(Grave understanders) here's no Target fighting
Upon the Stage, all work for cutlers barrd,
No Bawd'ry, nor no Ballads; this goes hard.
The wit is clean, and (what affects you not)
Without impossibilities the plot;
No Clown, no squibs, no Divells in't; oh now
You Squirrels that want nuts, what will ye do?
Pray do not crack the benches, and we may
Hereafter fit your palats with a Play.
But you that can contract your selves, and fit
As you were now in the *Black-Friers* pit,
And will not deaf us with lewd noise, or tongues,
Because we have no heart to break our lungs,
Will pardon our vast Scene, and not disgrace
This Play, meant for your persons, not the place.   (2.195)

This, I think, does not have the note of distress that Bentley hears in it. Most of the elements contained in the jibes at the Red Bull are there, even an allusion to overloud speaking. We players, says Shirley, being from the Blackfriars, will not 'break our lungs' in the 'vast Scene' of the Globe's much larger stage. He implies that a good proportion of the Globe audience must be familiars of the Blackfriars, and that the play is meant for their persons, not the Globe place. It is the open amphitheatre which generates the 'understanders' who crack nuts and make lewd noises because the players are not speaking loudly and providing them with bawdy song-and-dance jigs, fireworks and sword fighting. Kathleen McLuskie hears no distress and calls the prologue 'reverse flattery',[125] telling the audience what good taste it has approving a play which lacks the stigma of the traditional amphitheatre plays.

Shirley prepared this prologue only a month or so after his return from a four-year absence. He probably had not yet encountered a Globe audience when he wrote it. Therefore it makes rather tenuous evidence to hang much weight on, especially when its tone can be interpreted as differently as Bentley's and McLuskie's readings. Nonetheless it does carry implications about the Globe audience, especially in its closing lines (which neither Bentley nor McLuskie quote). The arch tone of the opening may well be ironically amusing flattery, enough to indicate that Shirley did really expect the Globe

audience to enjoy the prologue's exaggerated apprehension over the
nutcrackers' anger at receiving food prepared for different appetites.
The final appeal to 'you that can contract your selves, and fit / As you
were now in the *Black-Friers* pit', the equivalent position in the hall
to the Globe's standers, is confident. He expects that the Blackfriars
'persons', presumably even the wealthy persons of the pit, will after
all be at the Globe 'place'. The only difficulty seems to be the different
style of acting and the old-fashioned repertoire to be expected at an
amphitheatre. From Shirley's concern about the 'vast Scene' and the
extra noise the players were expected to generate on it we might
conclude that the style of acting did differ enough between the two
types of venue to require different types of play. Perhaps the fact that
the Red Bull and Cockpit used the same plays while only the Red Bull
developed a reputation for its players tearing their throats can be put
down to the effect on playing style not of the repertoire of plays but of
the types of playhouse. If so, the King's Men must have developed two
acting styles, one for winter and the other for summer. The only
evidence for that is Shirley's prologue, and this, given his years away
in Dublin and the arch tone, may not be entirely trustworthy.

If it is true, though, it might explain the rather heavy-handed
byplay in the epilogue to Davenant's *News from Plymouth*. The play
was licensed on 1 August 1635, and the epilogue was printed in the
1673 edition of Davenant's poems under the title 'To a Vacation Play
at the Globe'. The speaker, renewing his part as a comic country
gentleman from the play itself, enters holding a heavy old longsword,
and threatens to 'mowe you off' if the audience, 'Yeo'man and Squire,
Knight, Lady, and her Lord', do not pay their respects to the king by
respecting the King's Men. The sword was typical of Globe plays
according to Shirley. This audience apparently had made the transfer
from Blackfriars. Davenant, no friend of Shirley judging from the
1630 Cock and Bull quarrel, appears to have taken a rather similar
view to his of the summer clientele at the Globe.

The only conclusion I would draw from Shirley's verses is that he
expected the Globe's playgoers to include a substantial number from
the Blackfriars, and that he did not expect them to take offence at the
kind of jibe which was voiced in the halls against the amphitheatres.
The latter suggests that a preference for drum and trumpet plays and
jigs was not in fact part of the chemistry of Globe tastes. As always
the Globe, its offerings and its playgoers stood midway between the
familiar extremes of amphitheatre reputation and hall playhouse
snobbery which first began to show themselves in the year the Globe
was built.

Playgoers 1567–1642

Abdy, Sir Christopher. Brother-in-law to Humphrey Mildmay, recorded as accompanying him to a play. His family were merchants in the Clothworkers' Guild.

Alderson, Thomas. Sailor, of Stepney. On 16 May 1626 he was bound over for the sum of 100 marks (£33) for his part in an affray at the Fortune.

Alleyn, Edward. Actor and impresario. After he left acting in 1602 and went fully into theatre management with the Fortune and the Hope, he still attended other playhouses. On 1 October 1617 he made a note 'I came to London in ye coach & went to ye red bull. 0.0.2.' (i.e. for twopence).

Banfield, Mr. A lawyer, who accompanied Mildmay to a play in November 1639.

Beeston, Christopher. Theatre manager and impresario. He wrote a poem for Heywood's *Apology for Actors* which says 'of playes I make best use ... Two hours well spent'.

Bestney, Nicholas. A 'junior gentleman' stabbed at the Fortune in 1614.

Blount, Sir Christopher. Younger brother of the Earl of Devonshire, he fought in the Netherlands, and at Cadiz and in Ireland with the Earl of Essex, whose father-in-law he was. He went with other conspirators to the Globe on 7 February 1601 to see *Richard II*. He was executed on 18 March of that year.

Boteler, or Butler, Ned. Accompanied Mildmay and a group of others on 21 May 1634 to a play by the King's Men, probably *The Lover's Progress*.

Boyle, Elizabeth, nee Killigrew. Sister-in-law of Mary Rich, with whom she frequently went to plays in about 1640.

Bradley, Richard. Yeoman who knifed Nicholas Bestney at the Fortune in 1614.

Brathwait, Richard. Author of 50 or more publications, many pseudonymous, between 1611 and 1662. A student of Oriel College, Oxford and Gray's Inn, he claimed in 1614 that Thomas Heywood was his friend. References in his writings show him to be a frequenter of playhouses, and in his account of his life he claimed to have stopped writing for the stage because writing for money was beneath him.

Brewyn, Ralph. A butcher in an affray at the Fortune in 1611.

Brian, Edward. A feltmaker involved in an affray at the Red Bull in May 1610.

Brown, R. Mentioned in a letter by James Howell as a keen playgoer at the Blackfriars and Cockpit in the early 1620s.

Browne, Thomas. A 'serving man in a blew coat' accused of stirring trouble amongst some 'handicraft prentises' at the door of the Theatre in 1584.

Browne, Valentine. An Inns of Court student, admitted to Gray's Inn in 1639. In 1642 at a play he took offence over a mistaken piece of horseplay by the MP Peter Legh, and subsequently killed him in a duel. He was a nephew of the Herbert brothers.

Brunswick, Duke of. A visitor to London in January 1625, when he went to a play at the Blackfriars.

Buckingham, Duke of. In August 1628, shortly before he was assassinated, he went to the Globe to see *Henry VIII*. The next day he saw Heywood's *Rape of Lucrece* at the Cockpit.

Bushell, Edward. Accompanied other Essex conspirators to the Globe on 7 February 1601.

Busino, Orazio. Chaplain to the embassy of Venice. He visited the Fortune with his ambassador in 1617.

Butler, James, twelfth Earl, first Duke of Ormonde. As Lord Thurles, became involved in an affray with Charles Essex at the Blackfriars in January 1632, when he was standing on stage in front of one of the boxes. His biographer described him as 'a great admirer of plays, and acquainted with all the good actors of the stage. He took such delight in the theatre, that it scarce ever wanted his presence.' (Carte, 1.17). His education was in the hands of the Archbishop of Canterbury, who, according to the same biographer, was a man 'who, whatever learning he had himself, shewed very little concern to encourage it in others' (Carte, 1.12). In the 1640s Ormonde commanded the king's army.

Caldwell, Mary, of Essex. Attended a play with George Evelyn, brother of the diarist, and some ladies, in November 1639.

Carver, James. Sailor, of Shadwell. Bound over for 100 marks (£33) on 16 May 1626 for an affray at the Fortune.

Cary, Lucius, Lord Falkland. He was cited in the publisher's address in the Folio edition of Henry Killigrew's *The Conspiracy* as attending the first performance of the play at the Blackfriars, probably in 1630 or 1631. Writing to Thomas Carew returning a playbook, he asked for a copy on the grounds that 'if I valued it so high at the single hearing, when myne eares could not catch half the wordes, what must I do now, in the reading when I may pause uppon it' (Kurt Weber, *Lucius Cary*, 1940, p. 63).

Cavendish, Margaret, nee Lucas, Duchess of Newcastle. With her sisters she was used 'in winter time to go sometimes to plays, or to ride in their coaches about the streets to see the concourse and recourse of people' (*The Life of William Cavendish ...*, ed. C. H. Firth, 1886, p. 285).

Chamberlain, John. Professional letter writer. He saw 'a new play of humors' in midsummer 1599, 'drawne alonge to yt by the common applause', but was not impressed (*Letters*, ed. McClure, 1.32).

Charles, Prince of the Palatinate. Accompanied the queen to a performance at Blackfriars, 5 May 1636. This may have been a special evening performance rather than a normal commercial afternoon. Charles's mother had been patron of the Lady Elizabeth's Men.

Cholmley, Sir Richard. In 1603, aged 23, he went to a play at Blackfriars, where being late he had to take a stool on the stage. When, 'as the custom was', he 'stood up to refresh himself', a young gallant took over his stool. Cholmley led the young man outside and challenged him. When the youngster said he had no sword Sir Richard offered to buy him one. A constable appeared, and Sir Richard had to be content with giving the gallant 'two or three good blows'. The young man was 'my Lady's eldest son' according to his manservant, who fetched the constable.

Clifford, Ann. Her diary records that she saw Fletcher's *The Mad Lover* at Court, 5 January 1617.

Collison, William. Sailor, of Blackwall in Stepney. He was bound over for £50 on 16 May 1626 for an affray at the Fortune.

Constable, Sir William. Fought in Ireland with Essex, who knighted him there. On 7 February 1601 went to the Globe with other Essex conspirators. In the 1640s he fought on the Parliamentary side, and sat as a regicide in 1648.

Crofts, Will. A gentleman involved in an affray with Lord Digby at the Blackfriars in 1635. His father, Henry Crofts, was Humphrey Mildmay's brother-in-law. His mother was sister to Francis Wortley, a minor poet, 'son of Ben' and nephew to Mildmay's wife.

Davies, Sir John. Gallant and Inns of Court man. His epigrams indicate that he was a frequent playgoer in the 1590s.

Davies, Sir John, of Oxford. He held office in the Tower, and was known as a necromancer. Accompanied other Essex conspirators to the Globe on 7 February 1601. He was sentenced to death for his part in the plot, but pardoned.

Davies, John, of Hereford. An epigram in his *Scourge of Folly* hails Shakespeare's playing of kingly roles.

Davige, Lawrence. Gentleman of St Andrew's, Holborn. He was bound over on 16 May 1626 for £5 over his part in an affray at the Fortune.

Dekker, Thomas. Playwright. In 1624 in a lawsuit over a play of his, *Keep the Widow Waking*, performed at the Red Bull, he deposed that he 'did often see the said play or part thereof acted but how often he cannot depose'.

Dering, Sir Edward. Author of the first adaptation of Shakespeare's *Henry IV* plays, a regular playgoer in the 1620s according to his diary. In December 1623 he attended six plays in seven days. He was MP for Kent in 1640–42 and introduced the Root and Branch Bill into Parliament.

De Witt, Johannes. A Dutch visitor to London in 1596. He described the playhouses and sketched the Swan, then the most newly built of the amphitheatres.

Digby, John. Younger brother of Sir Kenelm Digby. He was waylaid by Suckling as he left a play at the Blackfriars in November 1634, and involved in an affray which injured both parties.

Digges, Leonard. In his verses published in 1640 but probably written for the First Folio of Shakespeare's works in 1623 (he died in 1635) he claims familiarity with *Julius Caesar, Othello*, Falstaff, *Much Ado* and *Twelfth Night*.

Donne, John. Poet, known as 'a great frequenter of Playes' (Baker, *Chronicle*, 1696, p. 450). He writes of *Tamburlaine* in *The Calme*.

Doricla (Dorislaus), Isaac. A Dutch historian resident in England from 1628, friend of Kenelm Digby and Selden, an anti-monarchist. He accompanied Mildmay to playhouses in November 1634, November 1635, February 1638, February 1639 and February 1640.

Drayton, Michael. Poet. In *Idea*, Sonnet 47 speaks of attending his own plays in 'thronged Theaters'. He wrote for Henslowe at the turn of the century.

Ellice, Thomas. Possibly related to Robert Ellice, of Gray's Inn, a friend of John Ford and a dedicatee of Ford's *Lover's Melancholy* (1629). Thomas wrote a verse for the publication of *'Tis Pity She's a Whore* (1633) indicating he had seen the play in performance.

Essex, Captain Charles. In a brawl with James Butler, Lord Thurles, at the Blackfriars in 1632.

Essex, Countess of. In a box at Blackfriars in 1632 when her escort was in a brawl.

Evelyn, George. Brother of the diarist. He attended his beloved, Mary Caldwell, and other ladies to the playhouses in November 1639.

Fennor, William. In *Fennors Descriptions* (1616) he indicates familiarity with the Fortune playhouse.

Fitzgeoffery, Henry. Inns of Court student. He describes an audience at the Blackfriars in *Satyres and Satyricall Epigrams*, 1617.

Flaskett, John. A bookbinder. He visited Paul's Boys in 1603 to see himself portrayed as Touchbox the suitor in Chapman's *The Old Joiner of Aldgate*.

Fletcher, John. Lowin and Taylor's dedication to the 1652 edition of his *Wild Goose Chase* (1621?) says that he attended its performance: 'The Play was of so Generall a receiv'd Acceptance, that (he *Himself a Spectator*) we have known him un-concern'd, and to have wisht it had been none of His; He, as well as the *throng'd Theatre* (in despight of his innate Modesty) Applauding this *rare issue of his Brain.*'

Florio, John. In his *First Fruites*, an English–Italian conversation book, he has a dialogue inviting a lady to see a play at the Bull Inn or other playhouse.

Forman, Simon. Necromancer. He saw four plays at the Globe in the summer of 1611, including *Macbeth, The Winter's Tale*, and *Cymbeline*.

Foscarini, Ambassador of Venice. Recorded as visiting the Curtain, the Fortune and possibly other playhouses three or four times.

Foster, William. Cordwainer of Stepney. Bound over on 16 May 1626 for £50 for an affray at the Fortune.

Francke, Robert. Sailor, of Blackwall in Stepney. Bound over on 16 May 1626 for £50 for an affray at the Fortune.

Frith, Marion. Transvestite, who attended a performance of a play about her, *The Roaring Girl*, at the Fortune in 1611.

Fryne, John. A feltmaker involved in an affray at the Red Bull in May 1610.

Fulsis, Alexander. Stole a purse containing £3 from Alexander Sweet at the Red Bull in 1614.

Gee, John. A student of Brasenose College, Oxford in 1613, briefly a Roman Catholic in the early 1620s. In *New Shreds of the Old Snare* (1624) he writes of Burbage having been the 'lodestone' of his audience. He also refers familiarly to the Fortune, Red Bull, Cockpit and Globe, and knew the ghosts in *The Spanish Tragedy* and *Hamlet*, and Moonshine with his lantern in *A Midsummer Night's Dream* as well as *The Alchemist*.

Gerschow, Frederic. In the train of the Duke of Stettin-Pomerania, and attended a play at the Blackfriars on 18 September 1602, about which he commented on the exquisite singing and the hour-long concert before the play (*Transactions of the Royal Historical Society* n.s. 6 (1892), pp. 26–8).

Gilbye, John. Purser, of Blackwall in Stepney. Bound over on 16 May 1626 for an affray at the Fortune.

Gill, Alexander. Wrote hostile verses about Jonson's *Magnetic Lady* at Blackfriars in 1632.

Gill, John. An apprentice, wounded at the Red Bull by the player Richard Baxter during a performance in March 1622. He sent a challenge to Baxter.

Giustinian, Ambassador of Venice. Together with the Secretary of Florence and the French Ambassador and his wife he saw *Pericles* at the Globe in 1607–08 (*C.S.P. Venetian* xiv, p. 600).

Gondomar, Ambassador of Spain. He went with his train to the Fortune in 1621, and subsequently banqueted with the players (Chamberlain, *Letters*, ii.391).

Gosson, Stephen. A playwright turned Puritan attacker of plays in *Playes Confuted in Five Actions*, 1582.

Gray, Patrick. Sailor, of Blackwall in Stepney. Bound over on 16 May 1626 to answer charges for an affray at the Fortune.

Greene, John. Student of Lincoln's Inn. His diary records numerous visits to plays, including on 8 November 1635 a day when all 'ther batchelors' went either to the Cockpit to see *The Lady of Pleasure* or to the Blackfriars to see *The Conspiracy*. Amongst the plays he records seeing are *Rule a Wife and Have a Wife*, *The Elder Brother* (both Blackfriars plays), *Truth's Triumphs*, *The Malcontent*, *The Changeling*, *The Inconstant Lady*, *'Ffalstafe'*, *Wit Without Money*, *The Lady of Pleasure* and *The Conspiracy*, all Blackfriars or Cockpit plays.

Guilpin, Everard. Satire V in *Skialetheia* (1598) mentions going to the Rose or Curtain. Other satires and epigrams echo plays such as *Richard II*.

Habington, William. In verses prefixed to Davenant's *Madagascar* (1638) he claimed that he was "mongst the first, to see the Stage / (Inspired by thee) strike wonder to our Age' (Davenant, *Shorter Poems*, ed. Gibbs, p. 8).

Halkett, Lady Anne. Born 1622. In her *Autobiography* she states that she never disobeyed her parents before 1644: 'so scrupulous I was of giving any occasion to speake of mee, as I know they did of others, that though I loved well to see plays and to walke in the Spring Garden sometimes (before itt grew something scandalous by ye abuse of some), yett I cannot remember 3 times that ever I wentt with any man besides my brothers; and if I did, my sisters or others better than myselfe was with mee. And I was the first that proposed and practised itt for 3 or 4 of us going together withoutt any man, and every one paying for themselves by giving the mony to the footman who waited on us, and he gave itt to the play-house, And this I did first upon hearing some gentlemen telling what ladys they had waited on to plays, and how much itt had cost them; upon which I resolved none should say the same of mee.'

Hall, Dr Joseph, later Bishop. In *Virgidemiarum* he indicates that he had seen *Tamburlaine*.

Harvey, Gabriel. In *Foure Letters and certeine Sonnets*, 1592 (3rd letter), he writes of the chance of seeing Tarlton's 'famous play of the seaven Deadly sinnes' in London, and of being invited to it in Oxford by Tarlton himself. His reference to *Hamlet* in his copy of Speght's Chaucer (1598) most likely indicates that he had seen the play, possibly the Cambridge performance mentioned in the Q1 titlepage.

Hawkins, William. A barber caught at the Curtain in 1600 stealing a purse and £1.6.6.

Heath, Edward. A student of the Middle Temple. His accounts show that he attended 49 plays in eighteen months through 1628–29, and bought ten playbooks.

Henrietta Maria, Queen. The accounts of the Master of the Revels include 13 May 1634: 'the Queene was at Blackfryers, to see Messingers playe ... Blake Friers, where the Queene saw Lodwick Carlile's second part of Arviragus and Felicia acted, which is hugely liked of every one' (a performance in early 1636 when she was accompanied by Prince Charles of the Palatinate) ... 'The 5th of May at the Blackfryers for the Queene and the prince elector ... Alfonso ... At the blackfryers the 23 of Aprill (1638) for the queene ... the unfortunate lovers'. The referral of the bills to the Chamberlain's office indicates that these were probably special performances.

Herringe, Robert. A surgeon of Shadwell in Stepney, bound over on 16 May 1626 for £50 after an affray at the Fortune.

Hobart, Sir John. Mentioned in Dering's diary as accompanying him to plays. He was of a Norfolk family which supported the Parliamentary side in the 1640s.

Holland, the Earl of. He attended *Henry VIII* at the Globe in August 1628.

Howe, John. A barber surgeon, who visited Paul's Boys in 1603 to see himself portrayed as Snipper-Snapper in Chapman's *The Old Joiner of Aldgate*.

Howell, James. In a letter to R. Brown of 20 January 1624, he writes 'I pray make haste, for *London* streets, which you and I have trod together so often, will prove tedious to me else. Among other things, *Black-Friars* will entertain you with a Play spick and span new, and the *Cockpit* with another; nor, I believe, after so long Absence, will it be an unpleasing object for you to see.' (*Epistolae Ho-Elianae*, p. 214).

Jacob, Thomas. Arrested for brawling at the Red Bull in 1638.

James, Mrs. She accompanied Mildmay to a playhouse in February 1639, and with 'her goodman' to *The Alchemist* in May 1639.

Jones, Captain Ellis. Accompanied other Essex conspirators to the Globe on 7 February 1601.

Jonson, Ben. Playwright. He was satirised in *Satiromastix* for exchanging 'curtezies, and complements with Gallants in the Lordes roomes'. He evidently also saw Shakespeare's *Pericles, The Tempest, Julius Caesar,* and *The Winter's Tale.*

Kerbye, John. A victualler of Blackwall in Stepney. He was bound over on 16 May 1626 for an affray at the Fortune.

Kiechel, Samuel. A merchant of Ulm, visiting London in 1584, he noted the playhouses in his diary.

Lake, Sir Thomas. He is in the list of people Chamberlain mentioned as attending performances of *A Game at Chesse,* in August 1624.

Lambarde, William. Keeper of the Tower of London. He mentions the Bel Savage and the Theatre as London playhouses in the revised edition, published in 1596, of his 1576 *Perambulation of Kent.*

Lambe, Dr. In a notorious case, he was killed by a mob after a visit to the Fortune, 13 June 1626.

Lea, Captain Thomas. Went with other Essex conspirators to the Globe on 7 February 1601. He was executed for his part in the plot on 17 February.

Leak or Leke, Father Thomas. A Catholic priest imprisoned in the Clink for his religion in 1618. He regularly went to plays at the nearby Bankside playhouses while in the Clink, and challenged his Archpriest's right to forbid his playgoing.

Legh, Sir Peter. An 18-year-old MP from Cheshire, killed in a duel after a quarrel at a playhouse in February 1642. 'Being at a play, he hurled a piece of tobacco-pipe at a man, thinking he had known him; but, being mistaken, they fell out in words, and so challenged one another.' His opponent was a Gray's Inn student, twenty-three-year-old Valentine Browne from Lincolnshire (Martin Butler, 'Two Playgoers, and the Closing of the London Theatres, 1642', *Theatre Research International* 9 (1984), pp. 93–9).

Lennox, Duke of. Embroiled in a quarrel with Pembroke, the Lord Chamberlain, over the possession of a box at Blackfriars for a new play in January 1636.

Lewis, Prince of Anhalt-Cöthen. A visitor to London in 1596, he mentions four amphitheatres.

Lewis, Prince Frederick of Württemberg. A visitor to London in 1610, he went to the Globe to see *Othello* (William B. Rye, *England as Seen by Foreigners in the Days of Elizabeth and James I,* London 1865, p. 61).

Lynsey, John. A butcher in an affray at the Fortune in 1611.

Madox, Richard. On 22 February 1583 he 'went to the theater to see a scurvie play set out al by one virgin, which there proved a fyemartin without voice, so that we stayed not the matter' (B. L. Cotton MS App. xlvii, f. 6).

Margrave, Richard. A sailor of Wapping, bound over on 16 May 1626 for 100 marks over an affray at the Fortune.

Marmion, Shackerley. Playwright at the Salisbury Court and Cockpit in the 1630s, and a Son of Ben. He wrote verses to Joseph Taylor for his revival of Fletcher's *Faithful Shepherdess* at Court in 1633.

Marston, John. His *Antonio's Revenge* (1601) seems indebted to *Hamlet,* which was not yet in print.

Matthew, Sir Toby. Son of the Archbishop of York, who turned Jesuit. Chamberlain (II.137) reported seeing him, when a newly made Catholic

21. Father of Toby Matthew (NPG 1048)

priest, on his way to a play at Blackfriars on 6 February 1618. He was then aged about fifty.

Melton, John. In *Astrologaster*, 1620, he mentions *Faustus* at the Fortune, and also *Alphonsus of Aragon, Friar Bacon and Friar Bungay, Byron*, and a player speaking a prologue.

Meres, Francis. In his book *Palladis Tamia*, 1598, culled from his wide reading, he mentions several of Shakespeare's plays which were not yet in print, notably *Two Gentlemen of Verona, Comedy of Errors, A Midsummer Night's Dream* and *King John*.

Merrick, Sir Gilly. An Essex conspirator, he attended the Globe on 7 February to see *Richard II*.

Middleton, Thomas. Playwright. A lawsuit of 8 February 1601 testified that he 'remaynethe heare in London daylie accompaninge the players'.

Mildmay, Anthony. Recorded as accompanying his brother Humphrey to Blackfriars to see *Volpone* and other plays in 1634, 1638 and other dates. The brothers were closer to each other than to their third brother Sir Henry. All three became Parliamentarians in 1642. Sir Henry was a judge at the trial of Charles I. Anthony was King Charles's gaoler in 1648. He described himself as 'a great opposer of tyranny and Popery'. His wife Grace wrote in her memoirs that she refused to go to 'the Court, to feastes, marryages, and plays' when asked by Court ladies.

Mildmay, Sir Humphrey. The eldest of three brothers and a sister, grandchildren of the Puritan founder of Emmanuel College, Cambridge. He was born in 1592, knighted in 1616 and married in the same year. His wife, Jane or Joan, was of the famous Crofts family of Saxham, which regularly entertained royalty during its visits to Newmarket. Her sister Ann married Wentworth, the Earl of Cleveland. Mary married Christopher Abdy and Cicely married Thomas Killigrew. She was literate. Mildmay began the diary at the age of 40 in 1633. On Saturday 3 February 1638 he failed to get in to a play, 'being full', after supper with Coke. But he saw many other plays at Court and in the playhouses. Mostly he went to the Blackfriars, but also the Cockpit and the Globe. In September 1648, when the playhouses were officially closed, he saw a performance at the Red Bull. The plays he saw during the years of regular playgoing included Mabbe's *Spanish Bawd* on 18 May 1632, Fletcher's *Rollo* at the Globe on 23 May 1633, Davenant's *The Wits* at Blackfriars on 22 January 1634, Shirley's *The Gamester* at Whitehall on 6 February 1634, *Lysander and Calista* on 21 May 1634, *Catiline* at Court on 9 November 1634, Davenant's *Love and Honour* on 12 December 1634, Fletcher's *Elder Brother* at Blackfriars on 25 April 1635, *Othello* at Blackfriars on 6 May 1635, Shirley's *Lady of Pleasure* on 8 December 1635, and Fletcher's *Mad Lover* on 21 May 1639.

Mildmay, Lady Jane. Recorded by her husband as accompanying him to a playhouse six times between 1632 and 1640.

Mildmay, Nan. Accompanied Mildmay and his wife to *The Lover's Progress*, a King's Men's play, 21 May 1634.

Milton, John. Went to the Fortune at the age of twelve, in 1621. In 1623 he was again in London attending the amphitheatre playhouses. His first

Elegy to Charles Diodati mentions *sinuosi pompa theatri*, the splendour of the curved theatre. (See R. Hosley, *Renaissance Drama Supplement* 10 (1967), p. 14.)

More, James. A secretary to William Darrell of Littlecote, he attended a play at Paul's in 1589 at a cost of sixpence to his master. (see H. Hall, *Society in the Elizabethan Age*, 1888, pp. 101, 211, 206–33, reprinting Darrell's accounts.)

Morton, Sir Albert. Went to *A Game at Chesse* at the Globe in August 1624.

Newport, Lady. The scandal over her conversion to Catholicism includes mention of her at the Cockpit in November 1637 (*Earl of Strafford's Letters*, ed. Knowles, II.128)

Overall, Mrs. Wife of John Overall, Regius Professor of Theology at Cambridge 1596–1607, Dean of St Paul's 1602–18. Aubrey writes 'She had (they told me) the loveliest Eies that were ever seen, but wondrous wanton. When she came to Court, or to the Play-house, the Gallants would so flock about her.' (*Brief Lives*, ed. O. L. Dicks, p. 226).

Parker, William, fourth Baron Monteagle. Attended the Globe on 7 February 1601 as an Essex conspirator. He paid a heavy fine for his part in the plot. In 1605 he received a warning not to attend Parliament, and prompted an investigation which led to the discovery of the Gunpowder Plot.

Peacham, Henry. Saw *Titus Andronicus* in about 1595, and drew a scene together with an extended quotation from the play.

Pembroke, fourth Earl of. The Lord Chamberlain, in a quarrel with the Duke of Lennox over a box at Blackfriars for a new play, January 1636.

Percy, Sir Charles. In a letter of 27 December 1600 he refers to Justice Silence and Justice Shallow (*C.S.P. Dom. Eliz. 1598–1601*, p. 502). He attended the Globe on 7 February 1601 as an Essex conspirator. A short, plump man, he was one of the two horsemen who raced to Edinburgh to tell James of Elizabeth's death.

Perkins, Richard. Principal player at the Red Bull. In his poem 'To my loving Friend and Fellow, Thomas Heywood', prefixed to *An Apology for Actors* (1612), he writes 'when I come to playes, I love to sit / That all may see me in a publike place'.

Philip Julius, Duke of Stettin-Pomerania. Visited London in 1602 and went to both the boys' and the adult playhouses, including the Fortune on 14 September (*Transactions of the Royal Historical Society* n.s.6 (1892), p. 29).

Pinnocke, Thomas. Silkweaver arrested in 1638 for menaces, at the Red Bull.

Platter, Thomas. Swiss scholar who visited England in 1599. His travels included a visit to the Globe to see *Julius Caesar* on 21 September.

Prince, Mr. Accompanied Mildmay to a play at Blackfriars, 7 February 1634.

Prynne, William. Author of *Histriomastix*, 1633. In his Epistle Dedicatory he writes of 'having upon my first arrival here in London, heard and seene in foure severall Playes (to which the pressing importunity of some ill acquaintance drew me whiles I was yet a novice) such wickednes, such lewdnes as then made my penitent heart to loath, my conscience to *abhorre all Stage-playes ever since*'.

Pudsey, Edward. His commonplace book (Bodleian Library MS Eng. poet.

D.3) contains quotations from Jonson's *The Case is Altered, Every Man Out of his Humour, Cynthia's Revels*, and *Poetaster*, Marston's *Antonio* plays and *Jack Drum's Entertainment*, Chapman's *Blind Beggar of Alexandria, The Merchant of Venice*, and Dekker's *Satiromastix*. Most of the quotations are inaccurate, and must have been jotted down during or soon after a performance in the years around 1600.

Purfet, Edward. A feltmaker, one of four involved in an affray at the Red Bull, May 1610.

Reynolds, Henry, esq. A friend of Drayton, who writes of reminiscing with him and hearing him quote from stage plays. He wrote *Torquato Tasso's Aminta Englisht* (1628).

Rich, Mary, nee Boyle. The Countess of Warwick, her autobiography records her staying in London in about 1640 with her sister-in-law, who enticed her 'to spend (as she did) her time in seeing and reading plays and romances' (*Autobiography of Lady Warwick*, Percy Society no. 74 (vol. xx), 1848, p. 4).

Rich, Sir Robert. Accompanied the Marchese di Villa, the Savoy Ambassador, with Sir Henry Wotton to 'the public plays, where anyone at all can go for a few pence', in May 1613 (John Orrell, 'The London Stage in the Florentine Correspondence, 1604–1618', *Theatre Research International* 3 (1977–78), p. 169).

Richards, Nathanael. Author of *Messallina*. His commendatory verses to *Women Beware Women* say that he had seen the play on stage.

Rowlands, Samuel. Several of his verses refer to plays. His references to Pope and Singer as clowns confirm his familiarity with the public stages.

Ruddier, Sir Benjamin. According to John Chamberlain he saw *A Game at Chesse* at the Globe in August 1624.

Savoy, Ambassador of. In company with the Duke of Buckingham he saw *Henry VIII* at the Globe in August 1628.

Scoloker, Antony. In *Daiphantus*, 1604, he refers to a man wearing only his shirt, like mad Hamlet, and echoes passages not in the 1603 quarto of the play.

Sewster, Mr. Herbert records him as taking exception to a play performed at Salisbury Court in October 1633. Herbert stopped the play on Sewster's complaint.

Sidney, Sir Philip. In his *Apology for Poetry* he writes about *Gorboduc* and other plays in ways which indicate he must have been to the amphitheatres.

Skipwith, Sir Henry. Accompanied Mildmay to a play, probably *The Lover's Progress*, in May 1634.

Smyth, William. Yeoman of St Margaret's, Westminster, bound over on 16 May 1626 for an affray at the Fortune.

Spenser, Edmund. Gabriel Harvey wrote to Spenser in the 1580s, about 'sum maltconceivid comedye fitt for the Theater, or sum other paintid stage whereat thou and thy lively copesmates in London maye laughe ther mouthes and bellyes full for pence or twopence apeece' (*Letter Book*, ed. E. J. L. Scott, Camden Soc. Publications n.s. 33 (1884), pp. 67–8).

Stafferton, Parr. A student of Gray's Inn, he led a 'dysordered companye of

22. Bulstrode Whitelocke, from a painting in St John's College,
Oxford

gentlemen of the Innes of Court' to attack players of Lord Berkeley's Men in 1581.

Sweet, Alexander. He was robbed of a purse containing £3 by Alexander Fulsis at the Red Bull in 1614.

Tatham, John. The author of *Fancies Theater*, 1640. It has a poem about meeting a friend at the Globe, and a subsequent meeting being hindered by rain. He also wrote a prologue for the Fortune players on their transfer to the Red Bull in 1639.

Taylor, John. The water poet. He describes a visit on 14 October 1618 to a play by Derby's Men about Guy of Warwick. The Globe and Fortune are frequently mentioned in his writings.

Tedcastle, William. A yeoman involved in an affray in May 1610 at the Red Bull, with four feltmakers.

Thules. One of the three Catholic priests named as a playgoer in 1618, in correspondence between William Harison and Thomas Leke (Folger MS 4787).

Tofte, Robert. In *The Months Minde of a Melancholy Lover*, 1598, he writes 'Loves Labour Lost, I once did see a Play / Y-cleped so.' The titlepage calls him 'gentleman'.

Tomkyns, Nathaniel. He wrote an account of *The Late Lancashire Witches*, which he saw at the Globe on about 14 August 1634. Tomkyns had been an MP, and was then clerk and registrar of the Queen's council. In 1643 when his plot to raise London for the king was betrayed by his brother-in-law, the poet Edmund Waller, he was executed.

Tufton. A husband and wife who accompanied Dering to a playhouse. One of them was related to Dering's wife.

Vennar, Richard. A member of Lincoln's Inn, and author of a notorious trick about an advertised extravaganza 'England's Joy' at the Swan in 1602. In his pamphlet *Apology* of 1614 defending his conduct he wrote that in 1602 'I saw a daily offring to the God of pleasure, resident at the Globe on the Banke-side'. The same passage refers to his pursuit as 'the hunting of the fox' (as in *Volpone*), and of another failed play, the 'burning pestle'. Beaumont's play had been published the year before with a note about its failure when first staged (*An Apology*, 1614, B6r).

Villa, Marchese di. Ambassador Extraordinary from Savoy, in London in early 1613. Sir Robert Rich and Sir Henry Wotton took him to 'the public plays'.

Webster, John. Playwright, described by Henry Fitzgeoffery in 1617 as in the audience at Blackfriars ('Crabbed *Websterio* / The *Play-wright Cartwright*).

Weever, John. An epigram (1599) indicates that he had attended a performance of *The Spanish Tragedy*. He seems also to have known Shakespeare.

Wenman, Sir Richard. Reported by Chamberlain (II.181) as attending Blackfriars for 'an ordinarie play' in November 1618.

Whitelocke, Bulstrode. Lawyer and politician. Of his life in the 1630s, he wrote 'I was so conversant with the musicians, and so willing to gain their favour, especially at this time, that I composed an air myself, with the assistance of Mr. Ives, and called it *Whitelock's Coranto*, which being cried up, was first played publicly by the Blackfriars Music, who were then esteemed the best of the common musicians in London. Whenever I came to that house (as I did sometimes in those days), though not often, to see a play, the musicians would presently play *Whitelock's Coranto*, and it was so often called for that they would have played it twice or thrice in an afternoon.' (Charles Burney, *A General History of Music from the Earliest Ages to the Present Period*, London 1782–89, II.299).

Williams, Elizabeth. Married sister of Alice, wife of Sir Dudley Carleton. On 30 June 1614 Chamberlain wrote to Alice Carleton saying that he had tried twice to see her sister, but 'the first time she was at a neighbours house at Cards, and the next she was gon to the new Globe to a play' (Letters, I.544)

Williams, Thomas. One of four feltmakers in an affray at the Red Bull, May 1610.

Wilson, George. A note for March 1634 says 'George Wilson kild at ye play house in salesburie court' (Guildhall MS 6538).

Wortley, Sir Frank. Recorded as accompanying his cousin Humphrey Mildmay to Blackfriars to see *Volpone* and other plays in January 1632 and October 1638.

Wotton, Sir Henry. Accompanied the Ambassador of Savoy to 'the public plays' in 1613, and went to *A Game at Chesse* at the Globe in August 1624. His account of the burning of the Globe in 1613 does not make it clear that he was present for the performance of *Henry VIII* which caused the fire.

APPENDIX 2

References to playgoing

References are arranged by date, or approximate date.

1. 1563
[An Idle noble man] licenciously roames in ryot, coasting the stretes with wavering plumes, hangd to a long side blade, & pounced in silkes ... haunteth plaies, feastes, bathes and bankettings ... I allowe him not so much as one ynche of Nobility.

Laurence Humphrey, *The Nobles, or of Nobilitye*, Iɪɪ–2ɪ

2. 1574
... the present time requirithe yowe to have good care and use good meanes towchinge the contagion of sickenes, that the sicke be kept from the whole, that the places of persons infected be made plaine to be knowen and the more releeved; that sweetenes and holsomnes of publique places be provided for; that unnecessarie and scarslie honest resorts to plaies, to shewes to thoccasion of thronges and presse, except to the servyce of God; and especiallie the assemblies to the unchaste, shamelesse and unnaturall tomblinge of the Italian Weomen maye be avoided.

Thomas Norton, 'An Exhortation or Rule wherbie the L. Maior of London is to order him selfe and the Citty' (J. P. Collier, *Illustrations of the Old English Literature*, ɪɪɪ.14)

3. 1577
If you will learne howe to be false and deceyve your husbandes, or husbandes their wyves howe to playe the harlottes, to obtayne one's love, howe to ravishe, howe to beguyle, howe to betraye, to flatter, lye, sweare, forsweare, how to allure to whoredome, howe to murther, howe to poyson, howe to disobey and rebell against princes, to consume treasures prodigally, to moove to lustes, to ransacke and spoyle cities and townes, to bee ydle, to blaspheme, to sing filthie songs of love, to speake filthily, to be prowde, howe to mocke, scoffe, and deryde any nation ... shall not you learne, then, at such enterludes howe to practise them?

John Northbrook, *A Treatise wherein Dicing, Dauncing, Vaine playes, or Enterluds, with other idle pastimes, & c., commonly used on the Sabbath day, are reproved by the Authorities of the word of God and the aunteint writers*, p. 92 (mentions 'the Theatre and Curtaine' p. 82)

4. 1578
The Englishman in this quallitie, is most vaine, indiscreet, and out of order: he fyrst groundes his worke, on impossibilities; then in three howers ronnes he throwe the world: marryes, gets Children, makes Children men, men to conquer kingdoms, murder monsters, and bringeth Gods from Heaven, and fetcheth Divels from Hel. And (that which is worst) their ground is not so

unperfect, as their working indiscreete: not waying, so the people laugh,
though they laugh them (for theyr folleys) to scorne: Manye tymes (To make
mirthe) they make a Clowne companion with a Kinge: in theyr grave
Counsels, they allow the advise of fooles.

George Whetstone, *Promos and Cassandra*, prefatory Epistle

5. 1578

Where shall we goe?
To a playe at the Bull, or else to some other place.
Doo Comedies like you wel?
Yea sir, on holy dayes.
They please me also wel, but the preachers wyll not allowe them.
Wherefore, knowe you it:
They say, they are not good.
And wherefore are they used?
Because every man delites in them.
I beleeve there is much knavery used at those comedies:
So beleeve I also.

John Florio, *First Fruites*, 1578, A11 (an English–Italian conversation book)

6. 1580

Some citizens wives, upon whom the Lord for ensample to others hath laide
his hands, have even on their deathbeds with teares confessed, that they have
received at those spectacles such filthie infections, as have turned their
minds from chast cogitations, and made them of honest women light
huswives ...

Whosoever shal visit the chappel of Satan, I meane the Theater, shal finde
there no want of yong ruffins, nor lacke of harlots, utterlie past al shame:
who presse to the fore-front of the scaffoldes, to the end to showe their
impudencie, and to be as an object to al mens eies.

Anon (Anthony Munday), *A third blast of retrait from plaies and Theaters*,
1580, pp. 125, 139

7. 1581

Parr Stafferton gentleman of Grayes Inne for that he that daye brought a
dysordered companye of gentlemen of the Innes of Court & others, to assalte
Arthur Kynge, Thomas Goodale, and others, servauntes to the Lord Barkley,
& players of Enterludes within the Cyttye.

City order & Lord Berkeley letter, July 1581 (*ES* IV.282)

8. 1582

The argument of Tragedies is wrath, crueltie, incest, injurie, murther eyther
violent by sworde, or voluntary by poyson. The persons, Gods, Goddesses,
juries, friendes, kinges, Quenes, and mightie men. The grounde worke of
Commedies, is love, cosenedge, flatterie, bawderie, slye conveighance of
whoredome; The persons, cookes, knaves, baudes parasites, courtezannes,
lecherous olde men, amorous young men ...

Sometime you shall see nothing but the adventures of an amorous knight,
passing from countrie to contrie for the love of his lady, encountering many a
terrible monster made of broune paper, and at his retorne, is so wonderfully
changed, that he cannot be knowne but by some posie in his tablet, or by a
broken ring, or a handkircher or a piece of a cockle shell, what learne you by

that? When ye soule of your playes is eyther mere trifles, or Italian bawdery, or cussing of gentlewomen, what are we taught? ...

The ancient Philosophers ... called them a monster of many heades ... The common people which resorte to Theatres being but an assemblie of Tailors, Tinkers, Cordwayners, Saylers, Olde Men, yong Men, Women, Boyes, Girles, and such like ...

So in Comedies delight being moved with varietie of shewes, of eventes, of musicke, the longer we gaze, the more we crave ...

As at the first, so nowe, theaters are snares unto faire women. And as I toulde you long ago in my schoole of abuse, our Theaters, and play houses in London, are as full of secrete adulterie as they were in Rome ... In the playhouses at London, it is the fashion of youthes to go first into the yarde, and to carry theire eye through every gallery, then like ravens where they spye the carion thither they flye, and presse as nere to ye fairest as they can. In stead of pomegranates they give them pippines, they dally with their garments to passe ye time, they minister talke upon od occasions, & eyther bring them home to theire houses on small aquaintance, or slip into taverns when ye plaies are done ...

The *Poets* send their verses to the Stage upon such feete as continually are rowled up in rime at the fingers endes, which is plaucible to the barbarous, and carrieth a stinge into the eares of common people.

> Stephen Gosson, *Playes Confuted in Five Actions*, C6r, D1r, D4r, F1r, F6r

9. 1584
Uppon Weddensdaye one Browne, a serving man in a blew coat, a shifting fellowe having a perrelous witt of his owne, entending a spoile if he cold have browght it to passe, did at Theatre doore querell with certen poore boyes, handicraft prentises, and strook some of theym, and lastlie he with his sword wonded and maymed one of the boyes upon the left hand; where upon there assembled nere a ml people.

... This Browne is a common cossiner, a thieff, & a horse stealer, and colloreth all his doynges here about this towne with a sute that he haithe in the lawe agaynst a brother of his in Staffordshire. He resteth now in Newgate
...

> Letter of William Fleetwood to Lord Burghley (*ES* IV.297–8)

10. c.1584
[Prologue at Blackfriars concludes] ... wishing that although there bee in your precise judgementes an universall mislike, yet wee maye enjoy by your woonted courtisies a general silence.

> John Lyly, *Campaspe* (*Complete Works*, II.315)

11. c.1589
[Prologue at Paul's] ... Onelie this doeth encourage us, that presenting our studies before Gentlemen, thogh they receive an inward mislike, wee shall not be hist with an open disgrace.

> John Lyly, *Midas* (*Complete Works*, III.115)

12. 1589
I am not ignorant how eloquent our gowned age is grown of late; so that every mechanical mate abhorres the English he was borne too, and plucks, with a solemne periphrasis, his *ut vales* from the inkehorne: which I impute, not so

much to the perfection of Arts, as to the servile imitations of vain-glorious Tragedians, who contend not so seriously to excell in action, as to embowell the cloudes in a speech of comparison, thinking themselves more than initiated in Poets immortality, if they but once get *Boreas* by the beard and the heavenly bull by the deaw-lap. But herein I cannot so fully bequeath them to folly, as their idiot Art-Masters, that intrude themselves to our eares as the Alcumists of eloquence, who (mounted on the stage of arrogance) Think to out-brave better pennes with the swelling bumbast of a bragging blanke verse. Indeede it may bee the ingrafted overflow of some kil-cow conceit, that overcloyeth their imagination with a more then drunken resolution, being not extemporall in the invention of any other meanes to vent their manhoode, commits the digestion of their cholericke incumbrances to the spacious volubilitie of a drumming deca-sillabon.

> Thomas Nashe, epistle 'To the gentlemen Students of Both Universities', prefixed to Greene's *Menaphon* (*Works*, ed. McKerrow, 1311)

13. 1590
At plaies, the Nip standeth there leaning like some manerly gentleman against the doore as men go in, and there finding talke with some of his companions, spieth what everie man hath in his purse, and where, in what place, and in which sleeve or pocket he puts his boung and according to that so he worketh either where the thrust is great within, or else as they come out at the dores.

> Robert Greene, *The Second part of Conny Catching*, 1591 (*Life and Works*, ed. Grosart, x.105)

14. 1592
The next, by his sute of russet, his buttond cap, his taber, his standing on the toe, and other tricks, I knew to be either the bodyer resemblaunce of Tarlton, who living for his pleasant conceits was of all men liked, and dying for mirth left not his like.

... lette ... the young people of the Cittie, either abstaine ... altogether from playes, or at their comming thither to use themselves after a more quiet order ... The beginners are neither gentlemen, nor citizens, nor any of both their servants, but some lewd mates that long innovation; & when they see advantage that either Servingmen or Apprentises are most in number, they will be of either side, though indeed they are of no side, but men beside all honestie, willing to make boote of cloakes, hats, purses, or what ever they can lay holde on in a hurley burley. These are the common causes of discord in publike places.

> Henry Chettle, *Kind-Harts Dreame*, B2v, D4v

15. 1592
whereas the after-noone beeing the idlest time of the day; wherein men that are their owne masters (as Gentlemen of the Court, the Innes of the Courte, and the number of Captaines and Souldiers about *London*) do wholy bestow themselves upon pleasure, and that pleasure they devide (howe vertuously it skils not) either into gameing, following of harlots, drinking, or seeing a Playe.

How would it have joyed brave *Talbot* (the terror of the French) to thinke that after he had lyne two hundred yeares in his Tombe, hee should triumphe againe on the Stage, and have his bones newe embalmed with the teares of ten thousand spectators at least, (at severall times) who, in the Tragedian that represents his person, imagine they behold him fresh bleeding!

Whereas some Petitioners of the Counsaile against them object, they corrupt the youth of the Cittie, and withdrawe Prentises from their worke, they heartily wishe they might bee troubled with none of their youth nor their prentises; for some of them (I meane the ruder handicrafts servants) never come abroade, but they are in danger of undoing ...

Thomas Nashe, *Pierce Penilesse*, F3r–3v

16. 1592

... it is the lucke of some pelting Comedies, to busy the Stage, as well as some graver Tragedies.

Gabriel Harvey, *Foure Letters and certeine Sonnets*, the fourth letter

17. 1593?

For as we see at all the play house dores,
When ended is the play, the daunce, and song,
A thousand townsemen, gentlemen, and whores,
Porters and serving-men together throng ...

Sir John Davies, *Epigrammes* 17, 'In Cosmum' (*The Poems*, ed. Kruger)

18. 1593?

Rufus, The Courtier, at the Theater,
Leaving the best and most conspicuous place,
Doth either to the stage himselfe transferre,
Or through a grate, doth shew his double face,
For that the clamorous fry of Innes of court
Fills up the private roomes of greater price:
And such a place where all may have resort,
He in his singularity doth despise.

Sir John Davies, *Epigrammes* 3, 'In Rufum'

19. 1593?

Fuscus is free and hath the world at will,
Yet in the course of life that he doth leade,
He's like a horse which turning rounde a mill,
Doth alwaies in the selfe same circle treade:
First he doth rise at 10 and at eleven
He goes to *Gyls*, where he doth eate till one,
Then sees a play til sixe, and sups at seaven,
And after supper, straight to bed is gone,
And there till tenne next day he doth remaine,
And then he dines, then sees a commedy,
And then he suppes, and goes to bed againe:
Thus rounde he runs without variety:
Save that sometimes he comes not to the play,
But falls into a whore-house by the way.

Sir John Davies, *Epigrammes* 39, 'In Fuscum'

20. 1594
>   ... toies
>   Or needlesse antickes imitations,
>   Or shewes, or new devices sprung a late,
>   we have exilde them from our Tragicke stage.
>   Anon, *The Wars of Cyrus*, prologue

21. 1594
... the quality of such as frequent the sayed playes, beeing the ordinary places of meeting for all vagrant persons & maisterles men that hang about the Citie, theeves, horsestealers, whoremoongers, coozeners, connycatching persones, practizers of treason, & other such lyke ...

> Lord Mayor to Lord Burghley, 3 November 1594 (repeated in petition for abolition of playhouses 28 July 1597 to the Privy Council) (*ES* IV.317)

22. 1595?
>   A Lady of great Birth, great reputation,
>   Clothed in seemely, and most sumptuous fashion,
>   Wearing a border of rich Pearl and stone,
>   Esteemed at a thousand crowns alone,
>   To see a certaine Interlude, repaires
>   To shun the press, by dark and privat staires.
>   Her page did beare a Torch that burnt but dimly.
>   Two cozening mates, seeing her deckt so trimly,
>   Did place themselves upon the stayres to watch her,
>   And thus they laid their plot to cunny-catch her:
>   One should as 'twere by chance strike out the light;
>   While th'other that should stand beneath her, might
>   Attempt (which modestie to suffer lothes)
>   Rudely to thrust his hands under her clothes.
>   That while her hands repeld such grosse disorders,
>   His mate might quickly slip away the borders ...
>   Sir John Harington, *Letters and Epigrams*, ed. McLure, pp. 245–6

23. 1596
>   All suddenly they heard a troublous noyes,
>   That seemd some perilous tumult to desine,
>   Confusd with womens cries, and shouts of boyes,
>   Such as the troubled Theaters oftimes annoyes.
>   Edmund Spenser, *The Faerie Queene*, IV.iii.37

24. 1596
the said Burbage is now altering and meaneth very shortly to convert and turne the same into a comon playhouse, which will grow to be a very great annoyance and trouble, not only to all the noblemen and gentlemen thereabout inhabiting but allso a generall inconvenience to all the inhabitants of the same precinct, both by reason of the great resort and gathering togeather of all manner of vagrant and lewde persons that, under cullor of resorting to the playes, will come thither and worke all manner of mischeefe, and allso to the great pestring and filling up of the same precinct, yf it should please God to send any visitation of sicknesse as heretofore hath been, for that the same precinct is allready growne very populous; and besides, that

the same playhouse is so neere the Church that the noyse of the drummes and trumpetts will greatly disturbe and hinder both the ministers and parishioners in tyme of devine service and sermons.

Petition to the Privy Council from the inhabitants of Blackfriars (*ES* IV.320)

25. 1597

One [poet] higher pitch'd doth set his soaring thought
On crowned kings that Fortune hath low brought:
Or some upreared, high-aspiring swaine
As it might be the Turkish *Tamberlaine.*
Then weeneth he his base drink-drowned spright,
Rapt to the threefold loft of heavens hight,
When he conceives upon his fained stage
The stalking steps of his great personage,
Graced with huf-cap termes, and thundring threats,
That his poore hearers hayre quite upright sets.
Such soone, as some brave-minded hungry youth,
Sees fitly frame to his wide-strained mouth,
He vaunts his voyce upon an hyred stage,
With high-set steps, and princely carriage;
Now soouping in side robes of Royalty,
That earst did skrub in lowsie brokery.
There if he can with termes Italianate,
Big-sounding sentences, and words of state,
Faire patch me up his pure *Iambicke* verse,
He ravishes the gazing Scaffolders:
Then certes was the famous *Corduban*
Never but halfe so high *Tragedian.*
Now, least such frightfull showes of Fortune fall,
And bloudy Tyrants rage, should chance appall
The dead stroke audience, mids the silent rout,
Comes leaping in a selfe-misformed lout,
And laughes, and grins, and frames his Mimick face,
And justles straight into the princes place.
Then doth the Theatre eccho all aloud,
With gladsome noyse of that applauding crowd.
A goodly *hoch-poch*, when vile *Russettings,*
Are match'd with monarchs, & with mighty kings.
A goodly grace to sober *Tragick Muse,*
When each base clown, his clumbsie fist doth bruise,
And show his teeth in double rotten-row,
For laughter at his selfe-resembled show.

Joseph Hall, *Virgidemiarum* II, Liber I, Satire iii

26. 1597

We have here a new play of humors in very great request, and I was drawn alonge to yt by the common applause, but my opinion of yt is (as the fellow sayde of the shearing of hogges) that there was a great crie for so litle wolle.

Chamberlain to Carleton, *Letters* 132 (11 June 1597)

27. 1598

> Luscus what's playd to day? faith now I know
> I set thy lips abroach, from whence doth flow
> Naught but pure *Juliat* and *Romio*.
> Say, who acts best? *Drusus*, or *Roscio*?
> Now I have him, that nere of ought did speake
> But when of playes or Plaiers he did treate.
> H'ath made a common-place booke out of plaies,
> And speakes in print, at least what ere he sayes
> Is warranted by Curtaine *plaudeties*.
> If ere you heard him courting *Lesbias* eyes;
> Say (Curteous Sir) speakes he not movingly
> From out some new pathetique Tragedie?
> He writes, he railes, he jests, he courts, what not,
> And all from out his huge long scraped stock
> Of well penn'd playes ... O ideot times,
> When gawdy Monkeyes mowe ore sprightly rimes!
> O world of fooles, when all mens judgements set
> And rests upon some mumping Marmoset!
> You Athens Ape (that can but simperingly
> Yaule *auditores humanissimi*,
> Bound to some servile imitation,
> Can with much sweat patch an Oration,
> Now up he comes, and with his crooked eye
> Presumes to squint on some faire Poesie;
> ... O what a tricksie lerned nickering straine
> Is this applauded, sencles, modern vain
> When late I heard it from sage *Mutius* lips,
> How il me thought such wanton Jigging skips
> Beseem'd his graver speech.
> John Marston, *The Scourge of Villainy*, G7v, H4r

28. 1598

> And she with many a salt *La volto* jest
> Edgeth some blunted teeth, and fires the brest
> Of many an old gray-bearded Citizen,
> *Medea* like making him young againe;
> Who comming from the Curtaine sneaketh in
> To some odde garden noted house of sinne.
> Everard Guilpin, *Skialetheia*, Satyre Preludium

29. 1598

> See you him yonder, who sits o're the stage,
> With the Tobacco-pipe now at his mouth?
> It is *Cornelius* that brave gallant youth,
> Who is new printed to this fangled age;
> He weares a Jerkin cudgeld with gold lace,
> A profound slop, a hat scarce pipkin high,
> For boots, a paire of dagge cases; his face,
> Furr'd with Cads-beard: his poynard on his thigh.
> Guilpin, *Skialetheia*, Epigram 53, 'Of Cornelius'

30. 1598

    How some damnd tyrant, to obtaine a crowne,
    Stabs, hangs, imprisons, smothers, cutteth throats,
    And then a Chorus too comes howling in,
    And tels us of the worrying of a cat,
    Then of a filthie whining ghost,
    Lapt in some fowle sheete, or a leather pelch,
    comes skreaming like a pigge half stickt,
    And cries *Vindicta*, revenge, revenge:
    With that a little Rosen flasheth forth,
    Like smoke out of a Tabacco pipe, or a boyes squib:
    Then comes in two or three like to drovers,
    With taylers bodkins, stabbing one another,
    Is not this trim? is not here goodly things?
    That you should be so much accounted of ...
    Enter Comedie at the other end.

TRAGEDIE What yet more Cat guts? O this filthie sound
    Stifles mine eares:
    More cartwheeles craking yet?
    A plague upont, Ile cut your fiddle strings,
    If you stand scraping thus to anger me.

    Anon, *A Warning for Fair Women*, Induction

31. 1599

    It chaunced me gazing at the Theater,
    To spie a Lock-Tobacco-Chevalier
    Clowding the loathing ayr with foggie fume
    Of Dock-Tobacco, friendly foe to rume.

    Henry Buttes, *Dyets Dry Dinner*, P3v

32. 1599

On September 21st after lunch, about two o'clock, I and my party crossed the water, and there in the house with the thatched roof witnessed an excellent performance of the tragedy of the first Emperor Julius Caesar with a cast of some fifteen people; when the play was over, they danced very marvellously and gracefully together as is their wont, two dressed as men and two as women.

On another occasion not far from our inn, in the suburb of Bishopgate, if I remember, also after lunch, I beheld a play in which they presented diverse nations and an Englishman struggling together for a maiden; he overcame them all except the German who won the girl in a tussle, and then sat down by her side, when he and his servant drank themselves tipsy, so that they were both fuddled and the servant proceeded to hurl his shoe at his master's head, whereupon they both fell asleep; meanwhile the Englishman stole into the tent and absconded with the German's prize, thus in his turn outwitting the German; in conclusion they danced very charmingly in English and Irish fashion. Thus daily at two in the afternoon, London has two, sometimes three plays running in different places, competing with each other, and those which play best obtain most spectators. The playhouses are so constructed that they play on a raised platform, so that everyone has a good view. There are different galleries and places, however, where the seating is better and more comfortable and therefore more expensive. For whoever cares to stand below only pays one English penny, but if he wishes to sit he enters by another door, and pays another penny, while if he desires to sit in the most comfortable seats which are cushioned, where he not only sees everything well, but can also be seen, then he pays yet another English penny at another door. And during the performance food and drink are carried round the audience, so that for what one cares to pay one may also have refreshment. The actors are most expensively and elaborately costumed; for it is the English usage for eminent lords or knights at their decease to bequeath and leave almost the best of their clothes to their serving men, which it is unseemly for the latter to wear, so that they offer them for sale for a small sum to the actors ...

Good order is also kept in the city in the matter of prostitution, for which special commissions are set up, and when they meet with a case, they punish the man with imprisonment and fine. The woman is taken to Bridewell, the King's palace, situated near the river, where the executioner scourges her naked before the populace. And although close watch is kept on them, great swarms of these women haunt the town in the taverns and playhouses.

> Thomas Platter, *Travels in England*, trans. Clare Williams, pp. 166–75

33. 1599

>   ... in all this front,
>   You can espy a gallant of this marke,
>   Who (to be thought one of the judicious)
>   Sits with his armes thus wreath'd, his hat pull'd here,
>   Cryes meaw, and nods, then shakes his empty head.
>   Jonson, *Every Man Out of his Humour* (*Works*, iii.434)

34. 1599

>   *Ruffinus* lost his tongue on stage,
>   And wot ye how he made it knowne?
>   He spittes it out in bloudy rage,
>   And told the people he had none:
>   The fond spectators said, he acted wrong,
>   The dumbest man may say, he hath no tongue.
>   John Weaver, *Epigrammes, 6, In Ruffinum*, C1v

35. 1600

Gentlemen, Gallants, and you my little Swaggerers that fight lowe ... I recant, beare witness all you Gentle-folkes (that walke i'th Galleries) I recant the opinions which I helde of Courtiers, Ladies, and Citizens, when once (in an assembly of Friars) I railde upon them.

> Dekker, *Satiromastix*, Epilogus

36. 1600

>   Speak gentlemen, what shall we do today? ...
>   Or shall we to the Globe to see a play?
>   Or visit Shoreditch for a bawdy house?
>   Samuel Rowlands, *The Letting of Humours Blood in the Head-Vaine*,
>   Epigram 7

37. 1600

I rembred one of them to be a noted Cut-purse, such a one as we tye to a poast on our stage, for all people to wonder at, when at a play they are taken pilfring.

William Kempe, *Kemps nine daies wonder*, B1r

38. 1600

[If he could paint spotless Chastity truly]
Then light-taylde huswives which like *Syrens* sing,
And like to *Circes* with their drugs enchant,
Would not unto the Banke-sides round house fling,
In open sight themselves to show and vaunt:
Then then I say they would not marked goe,
Though unseene to see those they faine would know.

John Lane, *Tom Tell-Troths Message, and His Pens Complaint*, F3r

39. 1600

... the gentlewoman that sware by her trouth, *That she was as much edefied at a play as ever she was at any sermon, &c.* will, ere she die, be of another minde, though it may be shee saied true then, in regard of her owne negligence and backwardnes in not giving eare to the word of God with reverence. The like may fall out also to those men too, that have not bene afraid of late dayes to bring upon the Stage the very sober countenances, grave attire, modest and matronlike gestures & speaches of men & women to be laughed at as a scorne and reproch to the world ... Well to heale, if it may be, or at least, to correct the bad humour of such humorists as these (who in their discovery of humours doe withall fouly discover their own shame and wretchednes to the world) here is now laied before thee (good Reader) a most excellent remedie and receipt.

Richard Schilders, The Printer to the Reader, in Rainolds, *The Overthrow of Stage Playes*, A3v–4r

40. 1600

[The author's] violence proceeds not from a minde
That grudgeth pleasure to this generous presence,
But doth protest all due respect and love
Unto this choise selected influence ...
And vowes not to torment your listning eares
With mouldy fopperies of stale Poetry ... (Prologue)
... I saw the Children of *Powles* last night ...
Ifaith I like the Audience that frequenteth there
With much applause: A man shall not be choakte
With the stench of Garlicke, not be pasted
To the barmy Jacket of a Beer-brewer ...
... Tis a good gentle Audience ... (Act V)

Marston, *Jack Drum's Entertainment*

41. 1600?

With those the thronged Theaters that presse,
I in the Circuit for the Lawrell strove:
Where, the full Prayse I freely must confesse,
In heat of Bloud, a modest Mind might move.
With Showts and Claps at ev'ry little pawse,

> When the proud Round on ev'ry side hath rung,
> Sadly I sit, unmov'd with the Applause,
> As though to me it nothing did belong.

Drayton, *Idea*, Sonnet 47, *Works*, ed. Hebel, II.334

42. 1601

> If thousands flocke to heare a Poets pen,
> To heare a god, how many millions then? ...
> Wit, spend thy vigour, Poets, wits quintessence,
> *Hermes*, make great the worlds eies with teares:
> *Actors* make sighes a burden for each sentence:
> That he may sob which reades, he swound which heares.

John Weever, *The Mirror of Martyrs*, A3v, F3v

43. 1601

... *sineor Snuffe, Mounsieur Mew*, and *Cavaliero Blirt*, are three of the most to bee fear'd Auditors ...

> ... beleeve it *Doricus* his spirit
> Is higher blouded then to quake and pant
> At the report of *Skoffes* Artillery;
> Shall he be creast-falne, if some looser braine,
> In flux of witte uncively befilth
> His slight composures? shall his bosome faint
> If drunken *Censure* belch out sower breath,
> From *Hatreds* surfet on his labours front?
> Nay say some halfe a dozen rancorous breasts
> Should plant them-selves on purpose to discharge
> Impostum'd malice on his latest Sceane
> Shall his resolve be struck through with the blirt,
> Of a goose breath? What imperfect borne?
> What short-liv'd *Meteor*? what cold-harted Snow
> Would melt in dolor? cloud his mudded eyes
> Sinck downe his jawes, if that some juicles husk
> Some boundlesse ignorance should on sudden shoote
> His grosse knob'd burbolt, with *that's not so good,*
> *Mew, blirt, ha, ha, light Chaffy stuff?*

[the Prologue protests that he will be put off by] ... the female presence; the Genteletza; the women will put me out ... [to which Doricus replies] ... and so we leave thee to the kinde Gentlemen, and most respected Auditors.

> This is the straine that chokes the theaters:
> That makes them crack with full stufft audience,
> This is your humor onely in request
> Forsooth to raile, this brings your eares to bed,
> This people gape for, for this some doe stare
> This some would heare, to crack the Authors neck,
> This admiration and applause persues.

Marston, *What You Will*, Induction; III.ii

44. 1602

At our feast wee had a play called 'twelve Night, or what you will'; much like the commedy of errores, or Menechmi in Plautus, but most like and neere to that in Italian called *Inganni*. A good practise in it to make the Steward beleeve his Lady widdowe was in Love with him, by counterfayting a letter as from his Lady, in generall termes, telling him what shee liked best in him, and prescribing his gesture in smiling, his apparaile, &c., and then when he came to practise, making him beleeve they tooke him to be mad.

> John Manningham, *Diary*, ed. R. Parker Sorlien, p. 48

45. 1602
... they did not only presse gentlemen, and sarvingmen, but Lawyers, Clarkes, country men that had lawe causes, aye the Quenes men, knightes, and as it was credibly reported one Earle, quight contrary to that the councell, and especyally my L. Cheif Justice intended.

> Philip Gawdy, *Letters*, ed. Jeayes, pp. 120–1

46. 1602
[At Richard Vennar's Swan extravaganza] there was great store of good companie and many noble men.

> John Chamberlain, *Letters*, 1.172

47. 1602
MISTRESS PURGE. Hither I come from out the harmless fold
>   To have my good name eaten up by wolves:
>   See, how they grin!

> Middleton (?), *The Family of Love*, V.iii

48. 1603
there was a stage Play plaied by the children of Powles concerning a barber & others & this defendant thinketh that the same Play was meant by this defendant & his daughter & Mris Sharles John Flaskett & others, att which Play he did once sitt together with Flaskett & sawe the same, being unawares unto him brought to sitt by Flaskett to see the Play. And further he hath heard manie say that the Play was made of this defendant & his daughter & also of others.

> John Howe, deposition in Star Chamber, quoted by C. J. Sisson, *Lost Plays of Shakespeare's Age*, p. 77

49. 1603
... a Play is like a sincke in a Towne, whereunto all the filth doth runne: or a byle in the body, that draweth all the ill humours unto it ... is it fit that the infirmities of holy men should be acted on a Stage ... there is no passion wherwith the king, the soveraigne majestie of the Realme was possest, but is amplified and openly sported with, and made a May-game to all the beholders.

> Henry Crosse, *Vertues Commonwealth*, P3r

50. 1603
The second moneth of *February* is more fertile of rubricate Martyrs, then *January*, for that yt hath 8 in number, two Wickliffians, *Syr John Oldcastle*, a Ruffian-knight as all England knoweth, & commonly brought in by comediants on their stages: he was put to death for robberyes and rebellion under the foresaid *K. Henry* the fifth

> Robert Parsons (Dolman), *The Third Part of a Treatise, Intituled: of three Conversions of England*, D2v

51. 1603
my very fine Heliconian gallants, and you my worshipful friends in the middle region . . .

Marston, *The Dutch Courtesan*, V. iii

52. 1604
the whole Neast of Ants . . . made a Ring about her and their restored friend, serving in stead of a dull Audience of Stinkards sitting in the Penny Galleries of a Theater, and yawning upon the Players, whilst the Ant began to stalke like a three Quarter sharer . . .

the Campe had bene supplied with Harlots too, as wel as the Curtaine . . . [a gallant after dinner] must venture beyond sea, that is, in a choice paire of Noble mens Oares, to the Bank-side, where he must sit out the breaking up of a Comedie, or the first cut of a Tragedie; or rather (if his humour so serve him) to call in at the Black-fryers, where he shall see a neast of Boyes able to ravish a man.

Middleton (?), *Father Hubburds Tale*, B4r, C1v, D1r

53. 1604
> Faith, that same vein of railing
> Becomes now most applausive; your best poet is
> He that rails grossest.

Chapman, *All Fools*, II.i

54. 1604
. . . the tragedie of Gowrie with all the action and actors hath ben twise represented by the Kings players, with exceding concourse of all sortes of people, but whether the matter or manner be not well handled, or that yt be thought unfit that princes should be plaide on the stage in theyre life time, I heare that some great counsaillors are much displeased with yt: and so is thought shalbe forbidden.

Chamberlain to Winwood, *Letters*, 1.199

55. 1605
> [of a burlesque City pageant]
> O may you find in this our pageant, here,
> The same contentment which you came to seek,
> And as that show but draws you once a year,
> May this attract you hither once a week.

Jonson, *Eastward Ho!* epilogue

56. 1605
> Yet, thus much I can give you, as a token
> Of his PLAYES worth, No egges are broken;
> Nor quaking Custards with feirce teeth affrighted,
> Wherewith your rout are so delighted;
> Nor tales hee in a *Gull*, old ends reciting,
> To stop gappes in his loose writing;
> With such a deale of monstrous, and forc'd *action*
> As might make *Bethlem* a faction . . .
> All gall, and coppresse, from his inke, he drayneth,
> Onelie, a little salt remaineth.

Jonson, *Volpone*, prologue

57. 1605

The action of the theatre, though modern states esteem it but ludicrous, unless it be satirical and biting, was carefully watched by the ancients, that it might improve mankind in virtue; and indeed many wise men and great philosophers have thought it to the mind as the bow to the fiddle; and certain it is, though a great secret in nature, that the minds of men in company are more open to affections and impressions than when alone.

Francis Bacon, The Advancement of Learning, Bk II Ch. 13

58. 1605

> One tould a Drover that beleev'd it not,
> What booties at the playes the Cut-purse got,
> But if twere so my Drovers wit was quicke,
> He vow'd to serve the Cut-purse a new tricke.
> Next day unto the play, pollicy hy'd,
> A bagge of fortie shillings by his side,
> Which houlding fast hee taketh up his stand,
> If stringes be cut his purse is in his hand.
> A fine conceited Cut-purse spying this,
> Lookt for no more, the fortie shillings his,
> Whilst my fine Politique gazed about,
> The Cut-purse feately tooke the bottom out.
> And cuts the strings, good foole goe make a jest,
> This Dismall day they purse was fairely blest.
> Houlde fast good Noddy tis good to dread the worse,
> Your monie's gone, I pray you keepe your purse.
> The Play is done and foorth the foole doth goe,
> Being glad that he cousned the Cut-purse soe.
> He thought to jybe how he the Cut-purse drest.
> And memorize it for a famous jest.
> But putting in his hand it ran quight throw
> Dash't the conceite, heele never speake on't now,
> You that to playes have such delight to goe,
> The Cut-purse cares not, still deceive him so.

Samuel Rowlands, Humors Antique Faces, D11

59. 1606

... their houses smoakt every after noone with Stinkards who were so glewed together in crowdes with the Steames of strong breath, that when they came foorth, their faces lookt as if they had beene per boylde ... tis given out that *Sloth* himselfe will come, and sit in the two-pennie galleries amongst the Gentlemen.

Dekker, Seven Deadly Sinnes (Non Dramatic Works, II.53)

60. 1606

2 GENT. And where sits [the author's] friends? hath he not a prepard company of gallants, to aplaud his jests, and grace out his play.

PROL. None I protest: Doe Poets use to bespeake their Auditory.

2 GENT. The best in grace doe, and but for that, some that I know, had never had their grace in Poetry till this day ...

PROL. Alas Gentlemen, how ist possible to content you? you will have rayling, and invectives, which our Author neither dares, nor affects: you baudy and scurrill jests, which neither becomes his modestie to write, nor the eare of a generous Auditory to heare: you must ha swelling comparisons, and bumbast Epithetes, which are as fit for the body of a Comedie, as *Hercules* shooe for the foote of a Pygmey ...

> Neither quick mirth, invective, nor high state,
> Can content all: such is the boundless hate
> Of a confused audience.

John Day, *The Isle of Gulls*, Induction

61. 1606

At this time there was much speech of a play in the Black Friars, where, in the 'Isle of Gulls', from the highest to the lowest, all men's parts were acted of two divers nations: as I understand sundry were committed to Bridewell.

Sir Thomas Edmondes, February 1606 (*Court and Times of James I*, ed. T. Birch, 1.60–1)

62. 1606

> And if yee list to exercise your Vayne,
> Or in the Sock, or in the Buskin'd Strayne, ...
> The thick-brayn'd Audience lively to awake,
> Till with shrill Claps the Theater doe shake.

Michael Drayton, 'The Sacrifice to Apollo', ode (*Works*, ed. Hebel, II.358)

63. 1606

> Spectators know, you may with freest faces
> Behold this Scene, for here no rude disgraces
> Shall taint a publique, or a privat name.

John Marston, *The Fawn*, Prologue

64. 1606

Hell being under everie one of their *Stages*, the Players ... might with a false Trappe doore have slipt [the devil] downe, and there kept him, as a laughing stocke to al their yawning Spectators.

Dekker, *Newes from Hell* (*Non-Dramatic Works*, II.92)

65. 1606

> If sceans exempt from ribaldrie or rage
> Of taxinges indiscreet, may please the stage,
> If such may hope applause, he not commandes
> Yet craves as due, the justice of your hands.

John Marston, *Sophonisba*, Epilogue

66. 1606

... though *bodies* oft-times have the ill luck to be sensually preferr'd, they find afterwards, the good fortune (when *soules* live) to be utterly forgotten. This it is hath made the most royall *Princes*, and greatest *persons* (who are commonly the *personators* of these *actions*) not onely studious of riches, and magnificence in the outward celebration, or shew: (which rightly becomes them) but curious after the most high, and heartie *inventions*, to furnish the inward parts: (and those grounded upon *antiquitie*, and solid *learnings*) which, though their *voyce* be taught to sound to present occasions, their *sense*, or doth, or should alwayes lay hold on more remov'd *mysteries*.

Jonson, *Hymeniae*, preface

67. c.1606

NOBODY ... *somebody* once pickt a pocket in this Play-house yard,
Was hoysted on the stage, and shamd about it.

Anon, *No-body and Some-body*, I1v

68. 1607

If there be any amongst you, that came to heare lascivious Scenes, let them
depart: for I doe pronounce this, to the utter discomfort of all two peny
Gallerie men, you shall have no bawdrie in it: or if there bee any lurking
amongst you in corners, with Table bookes, who have some hope to find fit
matter to feede his – mallice on, let them claspe them up, and slinke away, or
stay and be converted. For he that made this Play, meanes to please Auditors
so, as hee may bee an Auditor himselfe hereafter, and not purchase them
with the deare losse of his eares.

Francis Beaumont, *The Woman Hater*, Apologetical prologue

69. 1607

A Wench having a good face, a good body, and good clothes on, but of bad
conditions, sitting one day in the two-penny roome of a play-house, & a
number of yong Gentlemen about her, against all whom she maintaind
talke, One that sat over the stage, sayd to his friend: doe you not thinke that
yonder flesh will stincke anon, having so many flyes blowing upon it. Oh
(quoth his friend) I thinke it stinckes already, for I never saw so many crowes
together but there was some carion not far off.

Dekker, *Jests to Make You Merry* (*Non-Dramatic Works*, II.292)

70. 1607

... the basest stinkard in London, whose breth is stronger then Garlicke, and
able to poison all the 12. penny roomes.

Dekker, *The Ravens Almanacke* (*Non–Dramatic Works* IV.194)

71. 1608

Pay thy two-pence to a *Player*, in his gallerie maist thou sitte by a harlot.

Dekker, *Lanthorne and Candlelight* (*Non-Dramatic Works*, III.216–17)

72. 1608

His ma' was well pleased with that which your lo. advertiseth concerning
the committing of the players yt have offended in ye matters of France, and
commanded me to signifye to your lo. that for ye others who have offended in
ye matter of ye Mynes and other lewd words which is ye children of ye
blackfriers That though he had signified his mynde to your lo. by my lo. of
Montgommery yet I should repeate it again That his G. has vowed they
should never play more but should first begg their bred and he wold have his
vow performed. And therefore my lo. chamberlain by himselfe or your ll.
at the table should take order to dissolve them, and to punish the maker
besides.

Sir Thomas Lake to Lord Salisbury, 11 March 1608 (*M.S.C.* II.2, 1923, p. 149)

73. 1608

... satiric inveighing at any man's private person (a kind of writing which of
late seems to have been very familiar among our poets and players, to their
cost).

H. Parrott, *The More the Merrier*, epistle

74. 1608

[The Profane] ... comes to Church as to the Theater, saving that not so willinglie, for companie, for custome, for recreation, perhaps for sleepe; or to feed his eyes or his eares.

Joseph Hall, *Characters of Vertues and Vices*, H1r

75. 1608

[referring to *The Puritan*, 1607] ... now they bring religion and holy things upon the stage ... Two hypocrites must be brought foorth; and how shall they be described but by these names, *Nicholas S. Antlings, Simon S. Maryoveries* ... by these miscreants thus dishonoured, and that not on the stage only, but even in print.

William Crashaw, *The Sermon preached at the Crosse, Feb. xiiij, 1607* (i.e. 1608)

76. c.1608

[Spongus] Plays at Primero over the stage.

Farmer-Chetham manuscript (*ES* 11.535)

77. 1609

Ile thinke
As abjectly of thee, as any Mongrill
Bred in the Citty; Such a Citizen
As the Playes flout still.

Nathaniel Field, *A Woman is a Weathercock*, 11.i

78. 1609

... when at a new play you take up the twelve-penny room next the stage; (because the Lords and you may seeme to be haile fellow wel-met) there draw forth this booke, read alowd, laugh alowd, and play the *Antickes*, that all the garlicke mouthd stinkards may cry out, *Away with the fool* ... The Theater is your Poets Royal Exchange ... Your Gallant, your Courtier, and your Capten, had wont to be the soundest paymaisters ... your *Groundling*, and *gallery-Commoner* buyes his sport by the penny ... Sithence then the place is so free in entertainment, allowing a stoole as well to the Farmers sonne as to your Templer: that your Stinkard has the selfe-same libertie to be there in his Tobacco-Fumes, which your sweet Courtier hath: and that your Car-man and Tinker claime as strong a voice in their suffrage, and sit to give judgement on the plaies life and death, as well as the prowdest *Momus* among the tribe of *Critick*: It is fit that hee, whom the most tailors bils do make roome for, when he comes, should not be basely (like a vyoll) casd up in a corner ...

Dekker, *The Gull's Hornbook*, Proemium and Chapter 6 (*Non-Dramatic Works*, 11.203, 246–7)

79. 1609

The quick eares [of a Court audience contrast with] those sluggish ones of Porters, and Mechanicks, that must be bor'd through, at every act, with Narrations.

Jonson, *The Masque of Queens*, 107–10

80. 1609

Amazde I stood, to see a Crowd
Of *Civill Throats* stretcht out so lowd;

(As at a *New Play*) all the Roomes
Did swarme with *Gentiles* mix'd with *Groomes*,
So that I truly thought all These
Came to see *Shore* or *Pericles*.
         Anon, *Pimlyco, or Runne Red-Cap*, Cɪɪ

81. 1609

Tearme times, when the *Two-peny Clients*, and *Peny Stinkards* swarme
together to heere the *Stagerites*.
         Dekker, *Worke for Armourers* (*Non-Dramatic Works*, ɪv.96)

82. c.1609

It is a pastorall Tragie-comedie, which the people seeing when it was plaid,
having ever had a singuler guift in defining, concluded to be a play of country
hired Shepheards in gray cloakes, with curtaild dogs in strings, sometimes
laughing together, and sometimes killing one another: And missing whitsun
ales, creame, wassel and morris-dances, began to be angry.
         John Fletcher, *The Faithful Shepherdess*, epistle

83. c.1609

The wise, and many headed *Bench*, that sits
Upon the Life, and Death of *Playes*, and *Wits*,
(Composed of *Gamster, Captaine, Knight, Knights man,*
Lady, or *Pusill*, that weares maske or fan,
Velvet, or *Taffeta* cap, rank'd in the darke
With the shops *Foreman* or some such *brave sparke*,
That may judge for his *six-pence*) had, before
They saw it halfe, damd the whole Play ...
         Jonson, *The Faithful Shepherdess*, commendatory verses

84. c.1609

... since it was thy happe to throw away,
Much wit, for which the people did not pay,
Because they saw it not, I not dislike
This second publication, which may strike
Their consciences, to see the thing they scornd,
To be with so much will and art adornd.
Bisides one vantage more in this I see,
Your censurers must have the quallitie
Of reading, which I am afraid is more
Then halfe your shreudest judges had before.
         Beaumont, *The Faithful Shepherdess*, commendatory verses

85. c.1609

Such art, it should me better satisfie,
Then if the monster clapt his thousand hands,
And drownd the sceane with his confused cry ...
         Nathaniel Field, *The Faithful Shepherdess*, commendatory verses

86. 1610

Momus would act the fooles part in a play,
And 'cause he would be exquisite that way,
Hies me to London, where no day can passe,
But that some play-house still his presence has.

Now at the *Globe* with a judicious eye,
Into the Vice's action doth he prie.
Next to the *Fortune*, where it is a chaunce,
But he marks something worth his cognisance.
Then to the *Curtaine*, where, as at the rest,
He notes that action downe that likes him best.
Being full fraught, at length he gets him home,
And *Momus* now, know's how to play the Mome . . .
Fie on this Mimick still, it marres his part:
Nature would doe farre better without art.

John Heath, *Two Centuries of Epigrammes*, E3r–v

87. 1610

. . . in Playes: wherein, now, the Concupiscence of Daunces, and Antickes so raigneth, as to runne away from Nature, and be afraid of her, is the onely point of art that tickles the *Spectators*. (To the Reader)
. . . 'Judging Spectators . . .' (Prologue)

Jonson, *The Alchemist*

88. 1611

[Marion Frith] . . . being at a play about three quarters of a yeare since at ye Fortune in man's apparel and in her boots and with a sword at her syde she told the company then present yt she thought many of them were of opinion that she was a man, but if any of them would come to her lodging they should finde she is a woman, and some other immodest and lascivious speaches she also used at yt time. And also sat upon the stage in the public viewe of all the people there present in man's apparel and played upon her lute and sange a song.

Consistory of London Correction Book, 1611–12 (*JCS* VI.147)

89. 1612

The fashion of play-making, I can properly compare to nothing, so naturally, as the alteration in apparell. For in the time of the Great-crop-doublet, your huge bombasted plaies, quilted with mighty words to leane purpose was onely then in fashion. And as the doublet fell, neater inventions beganne to set up. Now in the time of sprucenes, our plaies followe the nicenes of our Garments, single plots, quaint conceits, letcherous jests, drest up in hanging sleeves, and those are fit for the Times and Tearmers   (Epistle)

      Within one square a thousand heads are laid
      So close, that all of heads, the roome seemes made.   (I.ii)

Middleton and Dekker, *The Roaring Girl*

90. 1612

      If then the world a Theater present,
      As by the roundnesse it appeares most fit,
      Built with starre-galleries of hye ascent,
      In which, *Jehove* doth as spectator sit.
      And chiefe determiner to'applaud the best . . .

Heywood, 'The Author to his Booke', *An Apology for Actors*

91. 1612

Now to speake of some abuse lately crept into the quality, as an inveighing against the State, the Court, the Law, the Citty, and their governements, with the particularising of private mens humours (yet alive) Noble-men, & others. I know it distastes many; neither do I any way approve it, nor dare I by any meanes excuse it. The liberty, which some arrogate to themselves, committing their bitternesse, and liberall invectives against all estates, to the mouthes of Children, supposing their juniority to be a priviledge for any rayling, be it never so violent, I could advise all such, to curbe and limit this presumed liberty within the bands of discretion and government.

> Thomas Heywood, *An Apology for Actors*, G3v.

92. 1612

... it was acted, in so dull a time of winter, presented in so open and black a theatre, that it wanted (that which is the only grace and setting out of a tragedy) a full and understanding auditory: and that since that time I have noted, most of the people that come to that playhouse, resemble those ignorant asses (who visiting stationers' shops, their use is not to inquire for good books, but new books) I present it to the general view.

> John Webster, *The White Devil*, Epistle

93. 1612

But tis with *Poets* now, as tis with Nations,
Th'il-favouredst *Vices*, are the bravest *Fashions*.
A Play whose *Rudenes, Indians* would abhorre,
Ift fill a house with Fishwives, *Rare, They All Roare*.
It is not Praise is sought for (Now) but *Pence*,
Tho dropd, from Greasie-apron *Audience* ...
[the verse] Can call the *Banishd* Auditor home, And tye
His Eare (with golden chaines) to his Melody:
Can draw with *Adamantine Pen*, (even creatures
Forg'de out of *th'Hammer*,) on tiptoe, to *Reach*-up,
And (from *Rare silence*) clap their *Brawny hands*,
T' *Applaud*, what their *charmd* soule scarce understands.
That Man give mee; whose Brest fill'd by the *Muses*,
With Raptures, Into a second, them infuses:
Can give an Actor, Sorrow, Rage, Joy, Passion,
Whilst hee againe (by selfe-same Agitation)
Commands the *Hearers*, sometimes drawing out *Teares*,
Then smiles, and fills them both with *Hopes* and *Feares* ...

> Dekker, *If This Be Not a Good Play, the Devil is in it*, prologue

94. 1612

I wish a *Faire* and *Fortunate Day*, to your *Next New-Play* (for the *Makers-sake* and your *Owne*), because such *Brave Triumphes of Poesie*, and *Elaborate Industry*, which my *Worthy Friends Muse* hath there set forth, deserve a *Theater* full of very *Muses* themselves to be *Spectators*. To that *Faire Day* I wish a *Full, Free*, and *Knowing Auditor*. And to that *Full Audience, One Honest Doore-Keeper*.

> Dekker, *If This Be Not a Good Play*, dedication to the Queen's Men

95. 1612

An Order for suppressinge of Jigges att the ende of Playes – Whereas Complaynte have beene made at this last Generall Sessions, that by reason of certayne lewde Jigges songes and daunces used and accustomed at the playhouse called the Fortune in Goulding lane, divers cutt-purses and other lewde and ill disposed persons in great multitudes doe resorte thither at the end of everye playe, many tymes causinge tumultes and outrages ...

Middlesex General Session of the Peace, 1 October 1612 (*ES* IV.340–1)

96. 1613?

>   All we have done we aim at your content,
>   Striving to illustrate things not known to all,
>   In which the learn'd can censure right;
>   The rest we crave, whom we unletter'd call,
>   Rather to attend than judge; for more than sight
>   We seek to please.

Heywood, *The Brazen Age*, prologue

97. 1613

>   That's the fat foole of the Curtin,
>   and the leane foole of the Bull:
>   Since *Shanke* did leave to sing his rimes,
>   he is counted but a gull.
>   The players of the Banke side,
>   the round Globe and the Swan,
>   Will teach you idle trickes of love,
>   but the Bull will play the man.

William Turner, *A Dish of Lenten Stuffe* (*A Pepysian Garland*, ed. Rollins, p. 35)

98. 1613

>   His Poetry is such as he can cul,
>   From plaies he heard at *Curtaine* or at *Bul*,
>   And yet is fine coy Mistres *Marry Muffe*,
>   The soonest taken with such broken stuffe.

George Wither, *Abuses Stript and Whipt*, first satire

99. 1613

These are the youths that thunder at a playhouse, and fight for bitten apples: that no audience but the tribulation of Tower Hill, or the limbs of Lime-house, their dear brothers, are able to endure.   (V.iv)

>   'Tis ten to one this play can never please
>   All that are here: some come to take their ease
>   And sleep an hour or two; but those we fear
>   W'have frighted with our trumpets, so 'tis clear
>   They'll say 'tis naught: others to hear the City
>   Abus'd extremely, and to cry 'That's witty',
>   Which we have not done neither.   (Epilogue)

Fletcher, *Henry VIII*

100. 1613

The Kings Players had a new Play, called *All is true*, representing some principal pieces of the Reign of *Henry* the 8*th*, which was set forth with many extraordinary Circumstances of Pomp and Majesty, even to the matting of the Stage; the Knights of the Order, with their Georges and Garter, the Guards with their embroidered Coats, and the like: sufficient in truth within a while to make Greatness very familiar, if not ridiculous. Now,

King *Henry* making a Masque at the Cardinal *Wolsey*'s House, and certain Cannons being shot of at his entry, some of the Paper, or other stuff, wherewith one of them was stopped, did light on the Thatch, where being thought at first but an idle smoak, and their Eyes more attentive to the show, it kindled inwardly, and ran round like a train, consuming within less than an hour the whole House to the very ground.

> Henry Wotton, letter to Edmund Bacon, *Reliquiae Wottoniae*, 1685, pp. 425–6

101. 1613

... my Pantalone often goes out now all alone, though with a faithful interpreter who walks a little in front to show him the way. He goes about saying that he's travelling incognito, and goodness knows where he ends up. He often goes to the plays in these parts. Among others, he went the other day to a playhouse called the Curtain, which is out beyond his house. It is an infamous place in which no good citizen or gentleman would show his face. And what was worse, in order not to pay a royal, or a scudo, to go in one of the little rooms, not even to sit in the degrees that are there, he insisted on standing in the middle down below among the gang of porters and carters, giving as his excuse that he was hard of hearing – as if he could have understood the language anyway! But it didn't end there because, at the end of the performance, having received permission from one of the actors, he invited the public to the play for the next day, and named one. But the people, who wanted a different one, began to call out 'Friars, Friars' because they wanted the one that they called 'Friars'. Then, turning to his interpreter, my Tambalone asked what they were saying. The interpreter replied that it was the name of a play about friars. Then, he, bursting out of his cloak, began to clap his hands as the people were doing and to yell 'Friars, Friars'. But at this racket the people turned on him, thinking him to be a Spaniard, and began to whistle at him in such a fashion that I don't think he'll ever want to go back there again. But that doesn't stop him frequenting the other theatres, and almost always with just one servant.

> Antimo Galli, in Orrell, 'Letters from the Florentine Correspondence', p. 171

102. 1614

... you think you have undone me, think so still, and swallow that belief, till you be company for Court-hand Clarks, and starved Atturnies, till you break in at playes like Prentices for three a groat, and crack Nuts with the Scholars in peny Rooms again, and fight for Apples, till you return to what I found you ...

> Fletcher, *Wit Without Money*, IV.i

103. 1614

Hee that will sweare, *Jeronimo*, or *Andronicus* are the best playes, yet, shall passe unexcepted at, heere, as man whose Judgement shewes it is constant, and hath stood still, these five and twentie, or thirtie yeeres.

> Jonson, *Bartholomew Fair*, Induction

104. 1614

The Players have all (except the King's Men) left their usuall residency on the Banke-side, and doe play in Middlesex farre remote from the Thames, so that every day in the weeke they doe drawe unto them three or four thousand people, that were used to spend their monies by water, (to the reliefe of so many thousands of poore people, which by Players former playing on the Banke-side are encreased) so that oft-times a poore man that hath five or sixe children, doth give good attendance to his labour all day, and at night (perhaps) hath not gotten a Groat to relieve himselfe, his wife and family.

John Taylor, *The True Cause of the Water-mens Suit* ... (*Works*, 1630, p. 172)

105. 1614

... a *Water-bearer* on the floore of a *Play-house* [admires] a wide-mouth'de *Player*. (*An Hypocrite*)

he hath heard one mooting, and seen two plaies. (*A Fantasticke Innes of Court man*)

He hath sworn to see *London* once a yeare, though all his businesse be to see a Play, walke a turne in *Paules*, and observe the fashion (*A meere Fellow of an House* [i.e. a College])

eates Ginger bread at a Play-house. (*A Puny-Clarke*)

He withers his Cloathes on the Stage, as a Sale-man is forc't to doe his Suits in Birchin-Lane; and when the Play is done, if you but mark his rising, 'tis a kind of walking Epilogue between the two Candles, to know if his Suite may passe for currant (*A Phantastique*)

The Play-houses only keepe him sober; and as it doth many other Gallants, make him an afternoones man. (*A Water-Man*)

Thomas Overbury, *Characters*, ed. Paylor, pp. 41, 45, 46, 52, 60, 68

106. 1615

[at university plays] And who are the spectators? but such like as both Poets and Actors are, even as such as reckon no more of their studies, then spend-all Gentlemen of their cast sutes ... [against Heywood's *Apology*] In what a doubtfull case would the use of playes then stand, if none but fooles (as commonly they are) or none but blindmen were their auditors? the one kind could not understand, the other could not see, and consequently neither give right judgement of them.

I.G., *A Refutation of the Apology for Actors*, C2r, F1v

107. 1615

And when hee heares his play hissed, hee would rather thinke bottle-Ale is opening. (*A base Mercenary Poet*)

John Stephens, *Satyrical Essayes Characters and Others*, p. 292 (V4v)

108. 1615

When he doth hold conference upon the stage; and should looke directly in his fellows face; hee turnes about his voice into the assembly for applause-sake, like a Trumpeter in the fields, that shifts places to get an eccho.

J. Cocke, 'A Common Player', in Stephens, *Satyrical Essayes*, p. 297 (V7r)

109. 1615

Sit in a full Theater, and you will thinke you see so many lines drawne from the circumference of so many eares, whiles the *Actor* is the *Center* ... what we see him personate, we thinke truely done before us: a man of deepe thought might apprehend, the Ghosts of our ancient *Heroes* walk't againe, and take him (at severall times) for many of them ... He entertaines us in the

best leasure of our life, that is betweene meales, the most unfit time, either
for study or bodily exercise.

Anon (Webster?), *New Characters*, 'An Excellent Actor', M5v–M6v

110. 1615

    Ide have a plaie could I but to my mind
    Good actors gett, but thats not now to find
    For (oh) thare dead; this age afordeth none,
    Good actors all longe since are dead and gone
    For beggars parte a Courtyer I would have ...
    But oh the Divell! I am graveld nowe
    To finde a Divell out I knowe not howe
    And with out one my plaie shall nere come forth
    For with out Divells, plaies are nothing worth
       Mas I have thought of one for gold heel come
       An exlent actor is the Pope of Rome ...   (Epigram 12)
    Wouldst thou turne Rorer boye? wouldst growe in fashon
    Learne this garbe then, shalt gaine faire reputation
    Tobacco take; run in each mercers score
    Visit plaies, be seene to court thy whore
    Laughe at learning ...   (Epigram 36)
    Goe to your plaie-howse you shall actors have
    Your baude, your gull, your whore, your pandar knave
    Goe to your bawdie howse, y'ave actors too
    As bawdes, and whores, and gulls: pandars also.
    Besides, in eyther howse (yf you enquire)
    A place there is for men themselves to tire
       Since th'are soe like, to choose ther'es not a pinn
       Whether bawdye-howse or plaie-howse you goe in. (Epigram 64)
    William Goddard, *A Neaste of Waspes*

111. 1615

[a rustic clown, Trincalo, woos his mistress] then will I confound her with
complements drawn from the Plaies I see at the Fortune and the Red Bull,
where I learne all the words I speake and understand not.

    Thomas Tomkis, *Albumazar*, C1r

112. 1615?

    Now talk of this, and then discoursed of that,
    Spoke our owne verses, 'twixt our selves, if not
    Other men's lines, which we by chance had got,
    Or some Stage pieces famous long before,
    Of which your happy memory had store ...

Michael Drayton, 'To my most dearely-loved friend, HENERY REYNOLDS
Esquire, of Poets & Poesie' (*Minor Poems*, ed. Cyril Brett, p. 108)

113. 1615?

    He rather prayes, you will be pleas'd to see
    One such, to day, as other playes should be.
    Where neither *Chorus* wafts you ore the seas,

Nor creaking throne comes downe, the boyes to please;
Nor nimble squibbe is seene, to make afear'd
The Gentlewomen ...

Jonson, prologue to *Every Man in his Humour,* 1616 Folio

114. 1616

                    ... sweet Poesye
Is oft convict, condem'd, and judg'd to die
Without just triall, by a multitude
Whose judgements are illiterate and rude.
Witnesse *Sceianus,* whose approved worth,
Sounds from the calme South, to the freezing North.
And on the perfum'd wings of *Zephorus,*
In triumph mounts as farre as *Aeolus,*
With more then humane art it was bedewed,
Yet to the multitude it nothing shewed;
They screwed their scurvy jawes and look't awry,
Like hissing snakes adjudging it to die:
When wits of gentry did applaud the same,
With silver shouts of high lowd sounding fame:
Whil'st understanding grounded men contemn'd it,
And wanting wit (like fooles to judge) condemn'd it.
Clapping, or hissing, is the onely meane
That tries and searches out a well writ *Sceane.*
So is it thought by *Ignoramus* crew,
But that good wits acknowledge's untrue;
The stinkards oft will hisse without a cause,
And for a baudy jeast will give applause.
Let one but aske the reason why they roare
They'll answere, cause the rest did so before.

William Fennor, *Fennors Descriptions,* epistle, *The Description of a Poet',*
B2r–3r

115. 1616

Player is much out of countenance, if fooles doe not laugh at them, boyes
clappe their hands, pesants ope their throates, and the rude rascal rabble cry
excellent, excellent: the knaves have acted their parts in print.

T. G[ainsford], *A Rich Cabinet,* Q5r–5v

116. 1616

Or why are *women* rather growne so mad,
That their *immodest feete* like *planets* gad
With such *irregular motion* to base *Playes,*
Where all the *deadly sinnes* keepe *hollidaies*
There shall they see the *vices* of the *times,*
Orestes incest, *Cleopatres* crimes.

Robert Anton, *The Philosopher's Satyrs,* p. 46

117. 1616

Today I goe to the *Black-fryers Play-house,*
Sit i'the view, salute all my acquaintance,
Rise up between the *Acts,* let fall my cloake,
Publish a handsome man, and a rich suite

(As that's a speciall end, why we goe thither,
All that pretend, to stand for't o' the *Stage*)
The Ladies aske who's that?
>Jonson, *The Devil is an Ass* (*Works* VI.178)

118. 1617

These theatres are frequented by a number of respectable and handsome ladies, who come freely and seat themselves among the men without the slightest hesitation. On the evening in question [at the Fortune] his Excellency and the Secretary were pleased to play me a trick by placing me amongst a bevy of young women. Scarcely was I seated ere a very elegant dame, but in a mask, came and placed herself besides me ... she determined to honour me by showing me some fine diamonds on her fingers, repeatedly taking off no fewer than three gloves, which were worn one over the other ... This lady's bodice was of yellow satin richly embroidered, her petticoat of gold tissue with stripes, her robe of red velvet with a raised pile, lined with yellow muslin with broad stripes of pure gold. She wore an apron of point lace of various patterns: her head-tire was highly perfumed, and the collar of white satin beneath the delicately-wrought ruff struck me as extremely pretty.
>Orazio Busino, *C.S.P. Venetian 1617–19*, pp. 67–8

119. 1617

Wee are informed that there are certayne Players or Comedians wee knowe not of what Company, that goe about to play some enterlude concerning the late Marquesse d'Ancre, wch for many respectes wee thincke not fitt to be suffered.
>Privy Council Order, 22 June 1617, to the Master of the Revels (*JCS* v.1371)

120. 1617

See (*Captain Martio*) he ith' *Renounce me* Band,
That in the middle Region doth stand ...
Look next to him to, *One* we both know well,
(Sir *Iland Hunt*) a Travailer that will tell
Of stranger Things then *Tatterd Tom* ere li't of,
Then *Pliny*, or *Herodotus* e're writ of ...
But stay! see heere (but newly Entred,)
A *Cheapside* Dame, by th' Tittle on her head!
Plot (Villain!) plot! Let's lay our heads together!
We may devise perchance to get her hither.
(If wee to-gether cunningly compact)
Shee'l holde us dooing till the Latter *Act*
And (on my life) Invite us Supper home,
Wee'l thrust hard for it, but wee'le finde her rome,
Heer *Mrs* – (pox ont! she's past, she'l not come ore,
Sure shee's bespoken for a box before ...
Knowest thou yon world of fashions now comes in
In *Turkie* colours carved to the skin.
Mounted *Pelonianly* untill hee reeles,
That scornes (so much) plaine dealing at his heeles.
His Boote speakes *Spanish* to his *Scottish* Spurres,

His Sute cut *Frenchly*, round bestucke with Burres ...
Now *Mars* defend us! seest thou who comes yonder?
Monstrous! A *Woman* of the *masculine Gender*.
Looke! thou mayst well descry her by her groath,
Out, point not man! Least wee be beaten both.
Eye her a little, marke but where shee'l goe,
Now (by this hand) into the Gallants Roe.
Let her alone! What ere she gives to stand,
Shee'l make her selfe a gayner, *By the Hand* ...
What think'st thou of yon plumed *Dandebrat*,
Yon Ladyes *Shittle-cocke, Egyptian Rat:*
Yon *Musk-ball, Milke-sop:* yon *French Sincopace:*
That Ushers in, with a *Coranto* grace.
Yon Gilded *March-pane:* yon *All Verdingall*,
This is the *Puppet*, which the Ladyes all
Send for of purpose and solicite so
To *daunce* with them ...
A Stoole and Cushion! Enter *Tissue slop!*
Vengeance! I know him well, did he not drop
Out of the *Tyring-house*? Then how (the duse)
Comes the mishapen *Prodigall* so spruce,
His year's *Revenewes* (I dare stand unto't,)
Is not of worth to purchase such a *Sute* ...
Who woo'd not all his Land spend had hee more,
Then in a day a *Kite* could hoover ore ...
T'injoy the pleasant *Harmony* that wee
Finde in this *Microcosme*, Man's societie ...
... yon Spruse *Coxcombe*, yon Affecting *Asse*,
That never walkes without his *Looking-glasse*,
In a *Tobacco* box, or *Diall* set,
That he may privately conferre with it ...
But h'st! with him Crabbed (*Websterio*).
The *Play-wright Cart-wright:* whether? either! ho –
No further. Looke as yee'd bee look't into:
Sit as ye woo'd be *Read*: Lord! who woo'd know him?
Was ever man so mangled with a *Poem*?
See how he drawes his mouth awry of late,
How he scrubs: wrings his wrests: scratches his Pate.
A *Midwife!* helpe!

H[enry] F[itzgeoffery], *Satyres: and Satyricall Epigrams: with Certaine Observations at Blackfryers*, E8v–F2v, F4v, F6v–7r

121. 1617

Fourth dutie is, to love her owne house best,
And be no gadding gossippe up and downe,
To heare and carry tales amongst the rest.
That are the newes reporters of the towne:
A modest womans home is her delight,
Of businesse there, to have the oversight.

At publike plays she never will be knowne,
And to be taverne guest she ever hates,
Shee scornes to be a streete-wife (Idle one,)
Or field wife ranging with her walking mates.
She knows how wise men censure of such dames ...

> Rowlands, *The Bride*, EII–IV

122. 1618

[Of Robert Shute, the King's candidate for Recorder] I am sory that Shute was brought upon the stage ...

> Chamberlain to Carleton, *Letters*, II.181

123. 1618

Mine host was full of ale and history ...
Besides what of his knowledge he could say,
He had authenticke notice from the Play;
Which I might guesse, by's mustring up the ghosts,
And policyes, not incident to hosts;
But cheifly by that one perspicuous thing,
Where he mistooke a player for a King.
For when he would have sayd, King Richard dyed,
And call'd – A horse! a horse! – he, Burbidge cry'de.

> Richard Corbet, 'Iter Boreale', *Poems*, 1807, pp. 193–4

124. 1619

oft have I seene him, leap into the Grave
suiting the person, wch he seem'd to have
of A sadd Lover, with soe true an Eye
that theer I would have sworne, he meant to dye,
oft have I seene him, play this part in jeast,
soe livly, that Spectators, and the rest
of his sad Crew, whilst he but seem'd to bleed,
amazed, thought even then hee dyed in deed.

> Funeral elegy for Richard Burbage (C. M. Ingleby, *Shakespeare, the Man and the Book* II.180)

125. 1619

He had ane intention to have made a play like Platus Amphitrio but left it of, for that he could never find two so like others that he could persuade the Spectators they were one.

> Jonson, *Conversations with Drummond of Hawthornden*, p. 18

126. 1619

We hope, for your owne good, you in the Yard
Will lend your Eares, attentively to heare
Things that shall flow so smoothly to your ear;
That you returning home, t'your Friends shall say,
How ere you understand't, 'Tis a fine Play:
For we have in't a Conjurer, a Devill,
And a Clowne too; but I feare the evill,
In which perhaps unwisely we may faile,
Of wanting Squibs and Crackers at their taile ...

> I.C., *The Two Merry Milkmaids*, prologue

127. 1620

Another will fore-tell of Lightning and Thunder that shall happen such a day, when there are no such Inflamations seene, except men goe to the *Fortune* in *Golding-Lane*, to see the Tragedie of Doctor *Faustus*. There indeede a man may behold shagge-hayr'd Devills runne roaring over the Stage with Squibs in their mouthes, while Drummers make Thunder in the Tyring-house, and the twelve-penny Hirelings make artificial Lightning in their Heavens.

> John Melton, *Astrologaster*, E4r

128. 1620

[Every poet] must govern his Penne according to the Capacitie of the Stage he writes too, both in the Actor and the Auditor.

> The printer, *The Two Merry Milkmaids*

129. 1620

> Nor Lord, nor Lady we have tax'd; nor State,
> Nor any private person.

> Fletcher, *The Custom of the Country*, prologue

130. 1620

(in the midst of his pride or riches) at a Play house ... (before he dare enter) with the *Jacobs*-Staffe of his owne eyes and his Pages, hee takes a full survay of himselfe, from the highest sprig in his feather, to the lowest spangle that shines in his Shoo-string.

> Anon, *Haec-Vir: or the Womanish-Man*, C2r

131. 1620

Our pulpits ring continually of the insolence and impudence of women: and to helpe the matter forward the players have likewise taken them to taske, and so to the ballades and ballad-singers.

> Chamberlain to Carleton, *Letters*, II.289

132. 1621

> fly to ye Globe or Curtaine with your trul,
> Or gather musty phrases from ye Bul.
> This was not for your dyet he doth bring
> what he prepar'd for our Platonique King.

> Peter Heylyn, verse on the performance of *Technogamia*, for the king at Woodstock (*JCS* VI.135)

133. 1623

... no true Puritanes will endure to bee present at playes ... few of either sex come thither, but in theyr holy-dayes appareil, and so set forth, so trimmed, so adorned, so decked, so perfumed, as if they made the place the market of wantonnesse, and by consequence to unfit for a Priest to frequent.

> William Harison (quoted in Harbage, *Shakespeare's Audience*, pp. 71, 113)

134. 1623

> So have I seene, when Cesar would appeare,
> And on the Stage at halfe-sword parley were,
> Brutus and Cassius: oh how the Audience,
> Were ravish'd, with what wonder they went thence,
> When some new day they would not brooke a line,
> Of tedious (though well laboured) Catilines;
> Sejanus too was irksome, they priz'de more

Honest Iago, or the jealous Moore.
And though the Fox and subtill Alchimist,
Long intermitted could not quite be mist ...
Yet these sometimes, even at a friend's desire
Acted, have scarce defraied the Seacoale fire
And doore-keepers: when let but Falstaffe come,
All is so pester'd: let but Beatrice
And Benedicke be seene, loe in a trice
The Cockpit Galleries, Boxes, are all full
To heare Malvolio that crosse garter'd Gull ...
But if you needs must write, if poverty
So pinch, that otherwise you starve and die,
On Gods name may the Bull or Cockpit have
Your lame blancke Verse, to keepe you from the grave:
Or let new Fortunes younger brethren see,
What they can picke from your leane industry.
I do not wonder when you offer at
Blacke-Friers, that you suffer.

Leonard Digges, Commendatory verses for the First Folio, published with Shakespeare's *Poems*, 1640 (*WS* II.233)

135. 1624

Here are no Gipsie Jigges, *no* Drumming stuffe,
Dances, *or other* Trumpery *to delight,*
Or take, by common way, the common sight.

W. B., commendatory verses to Massinger's *The Bondman*

136. 1624

[to the ladies in the audience]
Nor blame the Poet if he slip aside,
Sometimes lasciviously if not too wide.
But hold your Fannes close, and then smile at ease,
A cruell Sceane did never Lady please.

Fletcher, *Rule a Wife and Have a Wife*, prologue

137. 1624

I doubt not but you have heard of our famous play of Gondomar, which hath ben followed with extraordinarie concourse, and frequented by all sorts of people old and younge, rich and poore, masters and servants, papists and puritans, wise men *et.ct.*, churchmen and statesmen as Sir Henry Wotton, Sir Albert Morton, Sir Benjamin Ruddier, Sir Thomas Lake, and a world besides; the Lady Smith would have gon yf she could have persuaded me to go with her. I am not so sowre nor severe but that I wold willingly have attended her, but I could not sit so long, for we must have ben there before one a clocke at farthest to find any roome. They counterfeited his person to the life, with all his graces and faces, and had gotten (they say) a cast sute of his apparell for the purpose, and his Lytter, wherin the world sayes lackt nothing but a couple of asses to carry yt, and Sir G. Peter or Sir T. Mathew to beare him company.

Chamberlain to Carleton, 21 August 1624, *Letters*, II.577–8

138. 1625

> A worthy story, howsoever writ
> For Language, modest Mirth, Conceit or Wit,
> Meets oftentimes with the sweet commendation
> Of hang't, 'tis scurvy, when for approbation
> A Jigg shall be clapt at, and every rhime
> Prais'd and applauded by a clamorous chime.
> Let ignorance and laughter dwell together,
> They are beneath the Muses pity. Hither
> Come nobler Judgements, and to those the strain
> Of our inventions is not bent in vain.

> Fletcher, *The Fair Maid of the Inn*, prologue

139. 1625

... the hearers and beholders, who being baptised into the name of Christ are brought into danger of Gods wrath, and theire owne condemnation, in as much as they are partakers of the sinnes of the Players and of the Playes in approving them.

> Anon, *A Shorte Treatise of Stage-Playes*, Ch.4

140. 1625?

> [A youth from Cornwall]
> Most of my money being spent,
>   To *S. Johns* street to the *Bull* I went,
> Where I the roaring Rimer saw,
>   And to my face was made a daw:
> And pressing forth among the folke,
>   I lost my purse, my hat and cloke.

> Anon, '[Dice, Wine, and Women] or the Unfortunate Gallant Gulled at London', (in *The Pepysian Ballads*, ed. Rollins, 1.239)

141. 1626

> For your owne sakes, not his, he bad me say,
> Would you were come to heare, not see a Play.
> Though we his *Actors* must provide for those,
> Who are our guests, here, in the way of showes,
> The maker hath not so; he'ld have you wise,
> Much rather by your eares, then by your eyes.

> Jonson, *The Staple of News*, prologue

142. 1626

Whereas wee are informed that on thursday next, divers loose and Idle persons, some Saylors, and others, have appointed to meete at the Playhouse called the Globe, to see a Play (as it is pretended) but their ende is thereby to disguise some Routous and Riotous action ...

> Privy Council to Surrey Justices of the Peace, 17 May 1626 (*JCS* 1.21)

143. 1628

[a gallant] his business is the street: the Stage, the Court, and those places where a proper man is best showne ...

[Paul's Walk is] the other expence of the day, after Playes, Taverne, and a Baudy house ... [a player] The waiting-women Spectators are over-eares in

love with him, and Ladies send for him to act in their Chambers. Your Innes
of Court men were undone but for him, hee is their chiefe guest and
imployment, and the sole business that makes them Afternoones men.

John Earle, *Microcosmographie,* 1629, D4r, H3v

144. 1629?
... you may now at last falsifie that ignominious Censure which some
English Writers in their printed Workes have passed upon Innes of Court
Students; of whom they record: ... (p) That Innes of Court men were undone
but for Players, that they are their chiefest guests and imployment, & the
sole busines that makes them afternoons men; (q) & take smoke at a
Play-house, which they commonly make their Studie ...

William Prynne, *Histriomastix,* 1633, Epistle Dedicatory

145. 1629

> [A young gallant loves Jonson's] booke of Playes ...
> The Cockpit heretofore would serve his wit,
> But now upon the Fryers stage hee'll sit ...
> His silken garments, and his sattin robe,
> That hath so often visited the Globe,
> And all his spangled rare perfum'd attires
> Which once so glistred in the Torchy Fryers,
> Must to the Broakers ...

F[rancis] L[enton], *The Young Gallants Whirligig,* C3r–4v

146. 1629
... that last daye certaine vagrant French players, who had beene expelled
from their owne contrey, *and those women,* did attempt, thereby giving just
offence to all vertuous and well-disposed persons in this town, to act a
certain lacivious and unchaste comedye, in the French tonge at the Black-
fryers. Glad am I to saye they were hissed, hooted, and pippin-pelted from the
stage ...

Letter by Thomas Brande, 8 November 1629 (*JCS* 1.25)

147. 1629

> [Joseph Taylor complains against]
> some sowre censurer who's apt to say
> No one in these times can produce a Play
> Worthy his reading since of late, 'tis true
> The old accepted are more than the new.

Massinger, *The Roman Actor,* I.i

148. 1630

> ... they'll still slight
> All that exceeds Red Bull, and Cockepit flight.
> These are the men in crowded heapes that throng
> To that adulterate stage, where not a tong
> Of th'untun'd Kennell, can a line repeat
> Of serious sence: but like lips, meet like meat;
> Whilst the true brood of Actors, that alone
> Keepe naturall unstrayn'd Action in her throne

Behold their Benches bare, though they rehearse
The tearser *Beaumonts* or great *Johnsons* verse.

Thomas Carew, verses for Davenant's *The Just Italian*, A3v–4r

149. 1630

You've seen the Muses Looking Glass, ladies fair,
And gentle youths: and others too whoeer
Have fill'd this orb: it is the end we meant:
Yourselves unto your selves still to present.
A soldier shall himself in Hector see;
Grave councillors, Nestor, view them selves in thee;
When Lucrece' part shall on our stage appear,
Every chaste lady sees her shadow there.
Nay, come who will, for our indifferent glasses
Will show both fools and knaves, and all their faces,
To vex and cure them: but we need not feare
We do not doubt but each one now thats here
That has a fair soul and a beauteous face,
Will visit of the Muses Looking Glass.

Thomas Randolph, *The Muses' Looking Glass*, 1638, epilogue

150. 1631

[A yong Innes a Court Gentleman]: His Recreations and loose expence of time, are his only studies (as Plaies, Dancing, Fencing, Taverns, Tobacco,) and Dalliance ...

Francis Lenton, *Characterismi*, F5r

151. 1631

[A Ruffian] ... To a play they will hazard to go, though with never a rag of money: where after the *second Act*, when the *Doore* is weakly guarded, they will make *forcible entrie*, a knock with a Cudgell is the worst; whereat though they grumble, they rest pacified upon their admittance. Forthwith, by violent assault and assent, they aspire to the two-pennie roome; where being furnished with Tinder, Match, and a portion of decayed *Barmoodas*, they smoake it most terribly, applaude a prophane jest unmeasurably, and in the end grow distastefully rude to all the Companie. At the Conclusion of all, they single out their *dainty Doxes*, to cloze up a fruitlesse day with a sinnefull evening.

Clitus-Alexandrinus (i.e. Richard Brathwait), *Whimzies: or a New Cast of Characters*, pp. 134–5

152. 1631

In this following *Act*, the *Office* is open'd, and shewn to the *Prodigall*, and his *Princesse Pecunia*, wherein the *allegory*, and purpose of the *Author* hath hitherto beene wholly mistaken, and so sinister an interpretation beene made, as if the soules of most of the *Spectators* had liv'd in the eyes and eares of those ridiculous Gossips that tattle betweene the *Acts*.

Jonson, Address to the reader, before Act III, *The Staple of News*

153. 1631

Many gentlemen
Are not, as in the days of understanding,
Now satisfied without a Jig, which since

> They cannot, with their honour, call for after
> The play, they look to be serv'd up in the middle
>> James Shirley, *The Changes*, IV.ii

154. 1631

> ... though on each hand
> To over-top us, two great Lawrels stand;
> The one, when she shall please to spread her traine,
> The vastness of the Globe cannot containe;
> Th'other so high, the Phoenix does aspire
> To build in, and takes new life from the fire
> Bright Poesie creates.
>> Shackerley Marmion, *Holland's Leaguer*, prologue for Salisbury Court

155. 1632

Especially, and above all the rest, she was most taken with the report of three famous *Amphytheators*, whicstood so neere scituated, that her eye might take view of them from the lowest *Turret*, one was the *Continent of the World*, because halfe the yeere a World of *Beauties*, and brave *Spirits* resorted unto it; the other was a building of excellent *Hope*, and though *wild beastes* and *Gladiators* did most possesse it, yet the Gallants that came to behold those combats, though they were of a mixt Society, yet there were many Noble worthies amongst them.

>> Nicholas Goodman, *Holland's Leaguer*, F2v

156. 1632

[Players] love not the company of Geese or Serpants, because of their hissing.

>> Donald Lupton, *London and the Countrey Carbonadoed*, G1v

157. 1632

... the faeces or grounds of your people, that sit in the oblique caves and wedges of your house, your sinful sixpenny mechanicks.

>> Jonson, *The Magnetic Lady*, Induction

158. 1632

> Is this the childe of your bed-ridden witt,
> An none but the Black-friers foster ytt?
> If to the Fortune you had sent your ladye,
> Mongst prentizes and apell-wyfes, ytt may bee
> Your rosie foole might some sport have gott.
> But when as silkes and plush, and all the witts
> Are calde to see, and censure as befitts,
> And yff your follye take not, they, perchance,
> Must here them selfes stilde, gentle ignorance.
>> Alexander Gill, verses against *The Magnetic Lady*

159. 1632

> [Ann Frugal, a city magnate's wife, wants to imitate a Court lady]
> ... A friend at court to place me at a masque;
> The private box took up at a new play
> For me, and my retinue; a fresh habit,
> (Of a fashion never seen before) to draw
> The gallants' eyes that sit on the stage upon me ...
>> Massinger, *The City Madam*, II.ii

160. 1632

This Captaine attending and accompanying my Lady of Essex in a boxe in the playhouse at the blackfryers, the said lord coming upon the stage, stood before them and hindred their sight. Captain Essex told his lordship they had payd for their places as well as hee, and therefore intreated him not to deprive them of the benefitt of it. Whereupon the lord stood up yet higher and hindred more their sight. Then Capt. Essex with his hand putt him a little by. The lord then drewe his sword and ran full butt at him, though he missed him, and might have slaine the Countesse as well as him.

> *P.R.O.* CI15/8391 (quoted by Herbert Berry, 'The Stage and Boxes at Blackfriars', p. 165)

161. 1632

Item: That no tobacco be taken in the Hall nor anywhere else publicly, and that neither at their standing in the streets, nor before the comedy begin, nor all the time there, any rude or immodest exclamations be made; nor any humming, hawking, whistling, hissing, or laughing be used, or any stamping or knocking, nor any such other uncivil or unscholarlike or boyish demeanour, upon any occasion; nor that any clapping of hands be had until the *Plaudite* at the end of the Comedy, except his Majesty, the Queen, or others of the best quality here, do apparently begin the same.

> Order to Cambridge students over play for royal visit, March 1632 (quoted in Masson, *Life of Milton*, I.218)

162. 1632?

> ... yet had hee longer sin'd I doubt
> he had but foold this long life out,
> as other Courtiers spend their dayes
> wearing good clothes, seeing bad Playes,
> In Courting Ladyes, begging favours,
> in perfuming 'gainst ill savours,
> powdring his hayre, ruffing his boote,
> matching points unto his suite,
> all the morning spent in dressing,
> all the afternoone in kissing,
> or to Hide parke his mistresse squiring,
> or with his tayler is Conspiring ...

> John Earle, mock epitaph on Viscount Falkland, Malone MS 13, 29 (quoted in Kurt Weber, *Lucius Cary*, pp. 43–4)

163. 1633

The comedy called *The Yonge Admirall*, being free from oaths, prophaness, or obsceanes, hath given mee much delight and satisfaction in the readinge, and may serve for a patterne to other poetts, not only for the bettring of maners and language, but for the improvement of the quality, which hath received some brushings of late.

When Mr. Sherley hath read this approbation, I know it will encourage him to pursue this beneficial and cleanly way of poetry, and when other poetts heare and see his good success, I am confident they will imitate the original for their own credit, and make such copies in this harmless way, as shall speak them masters in their art, at the first sight, to all judicious spectators ... [3 July]

Exception was taken by Mr. Sewster to the second part of The Citty Shuffler, which gave me occasion to stay the play till the company had given him satisfaction; which was done the next day, and under his hande he did certifye mee that he was satisfyed ...

On friday the nineteenth of October, 1633, I sent a warrant by a messenger of the chamber to suppress The Tamer Tamd, to the Kings players, for that afternoone, and it was obeyd; upon complaints of foule and offensive matters conteyned therein.

They acted The Scornful Lady instead of it ...

On saterday morninge followinge the booke was brought mee, and at my lord of Hollands request I returned it to the players ye monday morninge after, purgd of oaths, prophaness, and ribaldrye ...

All ould plays ought to bee brought to the Master of the Revells, and have his allowance to them for which he should have his fee, since they may be full of offensive things against church and state; ye rather that in former time the poetts tooke greater liberty than is allowed by me.

> Henry Herbert, *Diary*, pp. 19–21

164. 1633

> Blesse mee you kinder Stars! How are wee throng'd?
> Alas! whom, hath our long-sick-Poet wrong'd,
> That hee should meet together in one day
> A Session, and a Faction at his Play?
> ... But 'bove the mischiefe of these feares, a sort
> Of cruell Spies (we heare) intend a sport
> Among themselves; our mirth must not at all
> Tickle, or stir their Lungs, but shake their Gall.

> Davenant, *The Wits*, prologue

165. 1633

> ... If I winne
> Your kinde commends, 'twill bring more *custome* in.
> When others fill'd *Roomes* with neglect disdaine ye
> And if such *Guests* would dayly make it shine,
> Our POET should no more drinke *Ale*, but *Wine*.

> Nabbes, *Tottenham Court*, 1638, epilogue

166. 1633

> When this smooth Pastorall was first brought forth,
> The Age twas borne in, did not know it's worth.
> Since by thy cost, and industry reviv'd,
> It hath a new fame, and new birth atchiv'd.

> Shackerley Marmion, 'Unto his worthy friend Mr. *Joseph Taylor* upon his presentment of the *Faithfull Shepherdesse before the King and Queene, at the Whitehall, on Twelfth night last* 1633.' Prefatory verses, 1634

167. c.1634

... it is the *Ingeniousness* of the Speech, when it is fitted to the Person; and the *Gracefulness* of the *Action*, when it is fitted to the Speech; and therefore a Play *read*, hath not half the pleasure of a Play *Acted:* for though it have the pleasure of *ingenious Speeches*, yet it wants the pleasure of *Gracefull action:* and we may well acknowledg, that *Gracefulness* of *action*, is the greatest pleasure of a Play, seeing it is the greatest pleasure of (the Art of pleasure)

Rhetorick in which we may be bold to say; there never had been so good Oratours, if there had not first been Players.

> Richard Baker, *Theatrum Redivivum*, 1662

168. 1634

Here hath been an Order of the Lords of the Council hung up in a Table near *Paul's* and the *Black-Fryars*, to command all that Resort to the Play-House there to send away their Coaches, and to disperse Abroad in *Paul's Church-Yard*, *Carter-Lane*, the Conduit in *Fleet-Street*, and other Places, and not to return to fetch their Company, but they must trot afoot to find their Coaches, 'twas kept very strictly for two or three Weeks, but now I think it is disorder'd again.

> 9 January, *Strafforde's Letters*, 1.175–6

169. 1634

> [The players reject]
> All bitter straines, that suit a Satyr Muse:
> And that which so much takes the Vulgar Eare,
> Loosenes of speech, which they for jests do heare.

> William Rutter, *The Shepherd's Holiday*, Prologue to the Stage

170. 1634

> ... where before great Patriots, Dukes and Kings
> Presented for some hie facinorious things,
> Were the Stage-Subject; now we strive to flie
> In their low pitch, who never could soare hie:
> For now the common argument intreats,
> Of puling Lovers, craftie Bawdes or cheates.

> Heywood, *A Challenge for Beauty*, prologue

171. 1634

> If any meete here, as some men i'th age
> Who understand no sense, but from one stage,
> And over partiall will entaile like land
> Upon heires male all action, and command
> Of voice and gesture, upon whom they love,
> These, though cal'd Judges, may delinquent's prove.

> Shirley, *The Example*, prologue

172. 1634

> [female Prologue at the Cockpit]
> ... is there not
> A blush upon my cheekes that I forgot
> The Ladies, and a Female Prologue too?
> Your pardon noble Gentlewomen, you
> Were first within my thoughts, I know you sit
> As free, and high Commissioners of wit ...
> You are the bright intelligences move,
> And make a harmony this sphere of Love.

> Shirley, *The Coronation*, prologue

173. 1635

> For all your pretious Morning-hours are given
> For you to paint and decke you till eleven;

And then an houre or two must be the least
To jeere your foolish Lover, or to feast,
Or court your amorous cringing Favorite
With a bare-bathed breast to feed delight,
And purchase more Spectators: — but time's lost
Till a Play-bill be sever'd from the Post
T'informe you what's to play; then comes your Coach,
Where numerous light-ones, like your selfe approach,
But where's Devotion all this while? asleepe,
And for her selfe sole Centinall may keepe.
But now you'r seated, and the Music sound
For th'Actors entry; pleasures doe abound
In ev'ry Boxe; sometimes your eye's on th' Stage,
Streight on a lighter Object, your loose *Page*,
Or some phantastike *Gallant*, or your *Groome*,
But when this Embleme of your life is done,
This piece of witty art, what doe you then?
To your sinne-shrouding Coaches streight againe,
You make repaire, where you relaters bee
Of what your Eare did heare, or Eye could see.
Then to a luscious Supper, after this
To a reere banket, or to some quaint dish
To move a sensuall slumber, and delight
But never sate your boundless appatite.
Thus you in painted joyes mis-spend your dayes
More to your *Suiters* than your *Makers* praise.

Richard Brathwait, *Anniversaries upon his Panarete; Continued*, A6r–6v

174. 1635
These things now we that live in *London* canot help, and they are as great news to men that sit in Boxes at *Black-Fryars*, as the affairs of Love to Flannel-Weavers.

John Suckling, letter to Mary and Anne Bulkeley (*Works*, 1.134)

175. 1635
The places thou dost usually frequent,
Is to some Play-house in an afternoone.
And for no other meaning, and intent,
But to get company to sup with soone,
More changeable, and wavering then the moone.
And with they wanton lookes, attracting to thee,
The amorous spectators for to wooe thee.
Thether thou com'st, in severall formes, and shapes,
To make thee still a stranger to the place:
And traine new lovers, like young Birds to scrapes ...
Now in the richest colours maybe had,
The next day, all in mourning blacke, and sad.
In a Stuffe Wastcote, and a Peticote
Like to a chamber-mayd, thou com'st to day:
The next day after thou dost change thy note,

Then like a countrey wench, thou com'st in gray,
And sittest like a stranger at the Play.
The morrow after that, thou comest then
In the neate habit of a Citizen.
The next time, rushing in thy Silken weeds,
Embroyder'd, lac't, perfum'd, in glittering shew,
Rich like a Lady, and attended so,
As brave as any Countesse dost thou goe.

> Thomas Cranley, *Amanda, or The Reformed Whore*, F2r

176. 1635

Here hath bin lately a newe comedie at the globe called *The Witches of
Lancasheir*, acted by reason of ye great concourse of people 3 dayes togither:
the 3rd day I went with a friend to see it, and found a greater apparence of
fine folke gentmen and gentweomen then I thought had bin in town in the
vacation.

> Thomas Tomkyns, letter to Robert Phelips, quoted in Berry, 'The Globe
> Bewitched and *El Hombre Fiel*', in *Medieval and Renaissance Drama in
> England* 1 (1984), p. 215

177. 1635

The Gallants of the Court are more impatient to hear the News of a Battle,
than they are to have a Play begin at *Black-Fryars*.

> Viscount Conway, 14 November, *Strafforde's Letters*, 1.478

178. 1635

> *The speaker enter'd with a Sword drawne*
> For your owne sakes (Poore Soules!) you had not best
> Beleeve my fury was so much supprest
> I'th'heat of the last Scene, as now you may
> Boldly, and safely too, cry downe our Play!
> For you if you dare but Murmure one false Note,
> Here in the House, or going to take Bote,
> By Heav'n I'le mowe you off with my long Sword;
> Yeo'man, and Squire, Knight, Lady, and her Lord!

> William Davenant, epilogue to *News from Plymouth*, at the Globe

179. 1636

A little Pique happened betwixt the Duke of Lenox and the Lord Chamberlain about a Box at a new Play in the *Black Fryars*, of which the Duke had got
the Key; Which if it had come to be debated betwixt them as it was intended,
some Heat or perhaps other Inconvenience might have happen'd. His
Majesty hearing of it, sent the Earl of *Holland* to commend them both not to
dispute it, but before him, so he heard it and made them Friends.

> 25 January, *Strafforde's Letters*, 1.511

180. 1636?

> [Applauds the audience, despite]
>   ... this long neglect
> Of Court and Citie Gentry, that transfer
> In Terme their visits to our Theater ...
> And now we hope you've leisure in the Citie
> To give the World cause to suspect you witty.

We would intreat you then put off a while
That formall brow you wear when you beguile
Young Chapmen with bad wares; pray do not look
On us, as on the Debtors in your Book.
                                    ... tis your care
To keepe your Shops, 'lesse when to take the Ayr
You walke abroad, as you have done to day,
To bring your Wives and Daughters to a play.
          Henry Glapthorne, 'To a Reviv'd Vacation Play' (*Plays and Poems*, II.194–5)

181. 1638
    Thine were *land-Tragedies*, no Prince was found
    To swim a whole *Scoene* out, then oth' *Stage* drown'd;
    Pitch'd fields, as *Red-Bull* wars, still felt thy doome,
    Thou laidst no sieges to the *Musique-Roome* ...
          Jasper Mayne, *Jonsonus Virbius*, E4r

182. 1638
    [Twenty years ago] ... they ... to th' Theatre would come
    Ere they had din'd to take up the best room;
    Then sit on benches, not adorn'd with mats,
    And graciously did vail their high-crowned hats
    To every half dress'd Player, as he still
    Through th'hangings peep'd to see how th'house did fill.
    Good easy judging souls, with what delight
    They would expect a jig, or target fight.
          Davenant, *The Unfortunate Lovers*, prologue

183. 1638(?)
          How is't possible to suffice
          So many Ears, so many Eyes?
          Some in wit, some in shows
          Take delight, and some in Clothes;
          Some for mirth they cheifly come,
          Some for passion, for both some,
          Some for lascivious meetings, that's their arrant;
          Some to detract and ignorance their warrant ...
          How is't possible to please
          Opinion toss'd in such wild seas?
          Yet I doubt not, if attention
          Seize you above, and apprehension
          You below, to take things quickly,
          We shall both make you sad, and tickle ye.
          Anon, *No Wit, No Help Like a Woman's*, prologue

184. 1638
    The sneaking Tribe, that drinke and write by fits,
    As they can steale or borrow coine or wits,
    That Pandars fee for Plots, and then belie
    The paper with – *An excellent Comedie,
    Acted* (more was the pitty) *by th' Red Bull
    With great applause*, of some vaine City Gull;

That damne Philosophy, and prove the curse
Of emptinesse, both in the Braine and Purse;
These that scrape legs and trenchers to my lord,
Had starv'd but for some scraps pick'd from thy board ...
R. Bride-oake, *Upon Mr. Randolph's Poeme, collected and published after
his death,* ** II

185. 1638

[To the Clown]
LETOY. But you Sir are incorrigible, and
Take licence to your selfe, to adde unto
Your parts, your owne free fancy; and sometimes
To alter, or diminish what the writer
With care and skill compos'd: and when you are
To speake to your coactors in the Scene,
You hold interloqutions with the Audients.
BIPLAY. That is a way my Lord has bin allow'd
On elder stages to move mirth and laughter.
LETOY. Yes in the dayes of *Tarlton* and *Kempe*,
Before the stage was purg'd from barbarisme,
And brought to the perfection it now shines with.
Richard Brome, *The Antipodes*, D3v

186. c.1638

LANDL. Why I would have the Fool in every Act,
Be't Comedy or Tragedy, I'ave laugh'd
Untill I cry'd again, to see what Faces
The Rogue will make: O it does me good
To see him hold out's Chin hang down his hands,
And twirle his Bawble. There is nere a part
About him but breaks jests.
THRI. ... his part has all the wit,
For none speaks Craps and Quibbles besides him:
I'd rather see him leap, laugh, or cry,
Then hear the gravest speech in all the *Play*.
I never saw Rheade peeping through the Curtain,
But ravishing joy enter'd into my heart ...
[The Courtier and gallant leave, and the country gentleman
follows]
I'le follow them, though't be into a Box.
Though they did sit thus open on the Stage
To shew their Cloak and Sute, yet I did think
At last they would take sanctuary 'mongst
The Ladies, lest some Creditor should spy them.
'This better looking o're a Ladies head,
Or through a Lettice-window, then a grate.
Thomas Goffe, *The Careless Shepherdess*, 1656, Praeludium

187. 1639

Troth Gentlemen, we know that now adayes
Some come to take up Wenches at our Playes;

It is not in our power to please their sence,
We wish they may go discontented hence.
And many Gallants do come hither, we think
To sleep and to digest there too much drink:
We may please them; for we will not molest
With Drums and Trumpets any of their rest.
If perfum'd Wantons do for eighteen pence,
Expect an Angel, and alone go hence;
We shall be glad with all our hearts: for we
Had rather have their Room then companie;
For many an honest Gentleman is gon
Away for want of place, as looke you yon!
We guess some of you Ladies, hither come
To meet your Servants, wh'are at dice at home:
You'l be deceiv'd ...

> Aston Cockayne, *The Obstinate Lady*, prologue

188. 1639

Thursday last the players of the Fortune were fined 1,000 £ for setting up an altar, a bason, and two candlesticks, and bowing down before it upon the stage, and although they allege it was an old play revived, and an altar to the heathen gods, yet it was apparent that this play was revived on purpose in contempt of the ceremonies of the church.

> Edmond Rossingham to Viscount Conway, 8 May 1639 (*JCS* v.1300)

189. 1639

Order of the King in Council. Complaint was this day made that the stage-players of the Red Bull have for many days together acted a scandalous and libellous play in which they have audaciously reproached and in a libel represented and personated not only some of the aldermen of the city of London and some other persons of quality, but also scandalised and libelled the whole profession of doctors belonging to the Court of Probate, and reflected upon the present Government.

> *C.S.P. Dom*, 29 September 1639 (*JCS* v.1441–2). See also *Malone Society Collections*, 1.4 & 5, pp. 394–5.

190. 1639

Here are no bumbast raptures swelling high,
To pluck *Jove* and the rest downe from the sky.
Here is no sence that must be thee be scann'd,
Before thou canst the meaning understand.
Here is not any glorious Scene of state;
Nor Christning set out with the Lottery plate.
There's no disguise in't; no false beard, that can
Discover severall persons in one man.
No politician tells his plots unto
Those in the Pit, and what he meanes to doe.
But now me thinkes I heare some Criticke say,
All these left out there's nothing in the play.
Yes: Thou shalt find plaine words, and language cleane;
That *Cockram* needs not tell thee what they meane.

Shalt find strict method in't, and every part
Severely order'd by the rules of Art.
A constant Scene: the business it intends
The two houres time of action comprehends.

Thomas Nabbes, *The Unfortunate Mother*, Proeme To the Reader

191. 1639?

... The Company's my Merchant, nor dare they
Expose my weak frame on so rough a Sea,
'Lesse you (their skilful Pilots) please to stear
By mild direction of your Eye and Ear
Their new rigg'd Bark ...

Henry Glapthorne, 'For *Ezekiel Fen* at his first Acting a Mans Part', *Poems*,
1639 (prologue spoken by Fenn)

192. 1640

You shall not here be feasted with the sight
Of anticke showes; but Actions, such as might
And have beene reall, and in such a phrase,
As men should speake in ...

Glapthorne, *The Ladies Privilege*, prologue

193. 1640

Wee've cause to fear yours, or the Poets frowne
For of late day's (he know's not how) y'are grown,
Deeply in love with a new strayne of wit
Which he condemns, at least disliketh it,
And solemnely protests you doe expect the same;
Hee'l tread his usuall way, no gaudy Sceane
Shall give instructions, what his plot doth meane;
No handsome Love toy shall your time beguile
Forcing your pitty to a sigh or smile,
But a slight piece of mirth ...   (prologue)

Ladyes ... Cavaliers and Gentry ... the City friends ... my
Countrey folkes too if here be any o'em.   (epilogue)

Brome, *The Court Beggar*

194. 1640

... others that have seen,
And fashionably observ'd the English scene,
Say (but with lesse hope to be understood)
Such titles unto Playes are now the mood,
Aglaura, *Claracilla*, names that may
(Being Ladies) grace, and bring guests to the Play.

Shirley, prologue for the Dublin performance of *The Doubtful Heir*

195. 1640

Gentlemen, I am onely sent to say,
Our Author did not calculate his Play,
For this Meridian; the Bank-side he knowes
Is far more skilful at the ebbes and flowes
Of water then of Wit: He did not mean
For the elevation of your Poles this Scene.

No shews, no frisk, and what you most delight in,
(Grave understanders) here's no Target fighting
Upon the Stage, all work for cutlers barrd,
No Bawd'ry, nor no Ballads; this goes hard.
The wit is clean, and (what affects you not)
Without impossibilities the plot;
No Clown, no squibs, no Divell's in't; oh now
You Squirrels that want nuts, what will ye do?
Pray do not crack the benches, and we may
Hereafter fit your palats with a Play.
But you that can contract your selves, and fit
As you were now in the *Black-Friers* pit,
And will not deaf us with lewd noise, or tongues,
Because we have no heart to break our lungs,
Will pardon our vast Scene, and not disgrace
This Play, meant for your persons, not the place.

    Shirley, *The Doubtful Heir*, prologue, *Poems*, 1646, D4v–5r

196. 1640

Who would rely on Fortune, when *shee's* knowne
An *enemie* to Merit, and hath shewne
Such an example here? Wee that have pay'd
Her tribute to our losse, each night defray'd
The charge of her attendance, now growne poore,
(Through her expences) thrusts us out of doore.
For some peculiar profit; shee has t'ane
A course to banish Modesty, and retaine
More dinn, and *incivility* than hath been
Knowne in the *Bearward Court*, the *Beargarden*.
Those that now sojourne with *her*, bring a noyse
Of *Rables, Apple-wives* and Chimney-boyes,
Whose shrill confused Ecchoes loud doe cry,
Enlarge your *Commons*, We hate *Privacie*.
Those that have plots to *undermine*, and strive
To blow their Neighbours up, so *they* may thrive,
What censure they deserve, *wee* leave to you,
To whom the judgement on't belongs as due.
Here Gentlemen, our Anchor's fixt; And wee
(Disdaining Fortune's mutability)
Expect your kinde acceptance; then wee'l sing
(Protected by your smiles our ever-spring;)
As pleasant as if wee had still possest
Our lawfull Portion out of Fortunes brest:
Onely wee would request you to forbeare
Your wonted custome, banding *Tyle*, or Peare,
Against our *curtaines*, to allure *us* forth,
I pray take notice *these* are of more Worth,
Pure Naples silk, not *Worsted*, we have ne're
An Actour here has mouth enough to teare

Language by th'eares; this forlorne Hope shall be
By Us refin'd from such grosse injury.
And then let your judicious Loves advance
Us to our Merits, them to their Ignorance.

John Tatham, 'A Prologue spoken upon removing of the late Fortune Players
to the Bull', *The Fancies Theater*, H2v–3r

197. 1640

When last we did encounter with the GLOBE,
The Heav'ns was pleas'd to grace us with his robe
Of settled motions; but *Aquarius*, hee,
Like an ambitious Churle, disdaines that wee
Should have another meeting . . .

Tatham, 'Upon the hinderance of meeting by raine, sent to his friend Mr.
W. B.', *The Fancies Theater*, C1v

198. 1641

[Plays are] First for strangers, who can desire no better recreation, then to
come and see a Play: then for Citizens, to feast their wits: then for Gallants,
who otherwise perhaps would spend their money in drunkennesse, and
lasciviousnesse, doe find a great delight and delectation to see a Play: then
for the learned, it does increase and adde . . . to their knowledge.

Anon, *The Stage-Players Complaint*, p. 24

199. 1641?

His *Schollars* school'd, sayd if he had been wise
He should have wove in one two comedies.
The first for th' gallery, in which the throne
To their amazement should descend alone,
The rosin-lightning flash and monster spire
Squibs, and words hotter than his fire.
Th'other for the gentlemen o' th' pit
Like to themselves all spirit, fancy, wit.

Richard Lovelace, *The Scholars*, epilogue, in *Poems*, 1649

200. 1643

. . . we shall for the future promise, never to admit into our sixpenny-roomes
those unwholesome inticing Harlots, that sit there meerely to be taken up by
Prentizes or Lawyers Clerks; nor any female of what degree soever, except
they come lawfully with their husbands, or neere allies: the abuses in
Tobacco shall be reformed, none vended, not so much as in three-penny
galleries, unlesse of the pure *Spanish* leafe. For ribaldry, or any such paltry
stuffe, as may scandall the pious, and provoke the wicked to loosenesse, we
will utterly expell it, with the bawdy and ungracious Poets, the authors to
the *Antipodes*.

Anon, *The Actors Remonstrance, or Complaint*, conclusion

201. 1654

The players have been appointed, notwithstanding their bills to the contrary,
to act what the major part of the company had a mind to. Sometimes
Tamerlane, sometimes *Jugurtha*, sometimes *The Jew of Malta*, and sometimes parts of all these; and at last, none of the three taking, they were forced
to undress and put off their tragick habits, and conclude the day with *The*

Merry Milkmaides And unless this were done, and the popular humour satisfied (as sometimes it so fortun'd that the players were refractory), the benches, the tiles, the laths, the stones, oranges, apples, nuts, flew about most liberally; and as there were mechanicks of all professions, who fell every one to his trade, and dissolved a house in an instant, and made a ruin of a stately fabric.

Edmund Gayton, *Pleasant Notes upon Don Quixot*, p. 272

202. 1659
The chief of the Spectators sit in *the Gallery* ... the common sort stand on *the ground* ... and clap the hands if anything please them.

Comenius, *Orbis Sensualium Pictus*, English Edition, 1659, p. 264

203. 1671
We may remember that the Red Bull writers, with their Drums, Trumpets, Battels, and Hero's, have had this success formerly.

Edward Howard, *The Six Days' Adventure*, A4v

204. 1673
[An appendix] without which a Pamphlet now a dayes, finds as small acceptance as a Comedy did formerly, at the *Fortune* Play-house, without a Jig of *Andrew Kein's* into the bargain.

Henry Chapman, *The City of Bath Described*, epistle

205. 1699
Before the Wars, there were in being all these Play-houses at the same time. The *Black-friers*, and *Globe* on the *Bankside*, a Winter and Summer House, belonging to the same Company called the King's Servants; the *Cockpit* or *Phoenix*, in *Drury-lane*, called the Queen's Servants; the private House in *Salisbury-court*, called the Prince's Servants; the Fortune near *White-cross-street*, and the *Red Bull* at the upper end of St. *John's-street:* The two last were mostly frequented by Citizens, and the meaner sort of People. All these Companies got Money, and Liv'd in Reputation, especially those of the *Blackfriars*, who were Men of grave and sober Behaviour.

James Wright, *Historia Histrionica*, B3r

Notes

1. INTRODUCTION

1 See David Bevington, *Action is Eloquence: Shakespeare's Language of Gesture*, Cambridge, Mass. 1984; Alan C. Dessen, *Elizabethan Stage Conventions and Modern Interpreters*, Cambridge 1984; Jean E. Howard, *Shakespeare's Art of Orchestration*, Urbana 1984.

2 Alfred Harbage, *Shakespeare's Audience*, New York 1941; *Shakespeare and the Rival Traditions*, New York 1952.

3 Ann Jennalie Cook, 'The Audience of Shakespeare's Plays: A Reconsideration', *Shakespeare Studies* 7 (1974) pp. 283–305.

4 *The Privileged Playgoers of Shakespeare's London, 1576–1642*, Princeton 1981, p. 272.

5 Ibid., p. 93. The most detailed challenge to her conclusions is in Martin Butler, *Theatre and Crisis 1632–1642*, Cambridge 1984, Appendix 2.

6 Some work has been done on particular sections or periods of London playgoing. The most valuable is Michael Neill's '"Wit's most accomplished Senate": The Audience of the Caroline Private Theaters', *Studies in English Literature* 18 (1978), pp. 341–60.

7 See Martin Butler, 'Two Playgoers and the Closing of the London Theatres, 1642', *Theatre Research International* 9 (1984), pp. 93–9.

8 See Janet S. Loengard, 'An Elizabethan Lawsuit: John Brayne, his Carpenter, and the Building of the Red Lion Theatre', *Shakespeare Quarterly* 35 (1984), pp. 298–310.

9 The principal sceptic, although he directs his evidence mainly against critics who see complexities of allusion and allegory in the plays, is Richard Levin, 'The Relation of External Evidence to the Allegorical and Thematic Interpretation of Shakespeare', *Shakespeare Studies* 13 (1980), pp. 1–29. One different view among many is that of Ralph Berry, *Shakespeare and the Awareness of the Audience*, London 1984.

2. PHYSICAL CONDITIONS

1 See map, p. 14, and Glynne Wickham, *Early English Stages 1300 to 1600*, 4 vols., London 1959–, II.2, pp. 60–78, 101–16 (*EES*). All the evidence about the first playhouse, the Red Lion, is given by Janet S. Loengard, 'An Elizabethan Lawsuit: John Brayne, his Carpenter, and the Building of the Red Lion Theatre', *Shakespeare Quarterly* 35 (1984), pp. 298–310.

2 See Glynne Wickham's discussion of the relationship between the baiting houses and the playhouses, *EES* II.1, pp. 161–3, 204–5.

3 Samuel Kiechel, quoted in E. K. Chambers, *The Elizabethan Stage*, 4 vols., Oxford 1923, II.358 (*ES*).

4 The evidence about the entranceways is considered thoroughly by Richard Hosley, *The Revels History of Drama in English III, 1576–1613*, pp. 157–64 (*Revels History*). The phrase 'twopenny galleries' came into existence at the end of the century, suggesting that a single payment of twopence for the galleries replaced the penny by penny system at about the time the Globe was built.

5 John Orrell, *The Quest for Shakespeare's Globe*, Cambridge 1982, p. 136, allows 1,848 square feet for the Globe yard, almost exactly the Fortune space, but for this calculation he ignores the area flanking the stage platform.

6 John Marston, *Jack Drum's Entertainment*, 1600, V.i; Thomas Dekker, *Seven Deadly Sins* (1606), *The Ravens Almanacke* (1609), *Worke for Armourers* (1609), and *The Gull's Hornbook* (1609), where the Proemium refers to 'all the garlic-mouthed stinkards'.

7 Orrell, *The Quest for Shakespeare's Globe*, p. 135.

8 G. E. Bentley, *The Jacobean and Caroline Stage*, 7 vols., Oxford 1942–68, IV.871 (*JCS*).

9 Richard Hosley has suggested that the balcony rooms should strictly be called 'lord's rooms' (in the singular) on the grounds that they were officially set aside for the one lord who was the company's patron. But only the Globe playhouse was actually owned by the players who used it and so could assume that the same lord would consistently patronise the same company at the same playhouse. Moreover all the playhouses seem to have had several such rooms. It was something of a courtesy title for whoever chose to separate himself from the crowd in that way.

10 John Harington, *Letters and Epigrams*, ed. N. E. McLure, Philadelphia 1930, pp. 245–6. The epigram is addressed to Sir John Lee in the autograph (B. L. Add. MS 12049). As a whole, the epigrams date from between about 1585 and 1603.

11 *Henslowe's Diary*, ed. R. A. Foakes and R. T. Rickert, Cambridge 1961, pp. 22–30 (*Diary*); J. Leeds Barroll, *Revels History*, III.48. Extrapolating from the *Diary* figures, it seems that in 1594–95, with two amphitheatres offering plays, about 15,000 people attended each week. With three or more amphitheatres and two indoor playhouses open in 1605, the attendance would have been nearer 21,000 a week.

12 Orrell, *The Quest for Shakespeare's Globe*, p. 137.

13 The term 'standing', as used by Lambarde and others, usually indicated a seat. A modern equivalent might be 'standpoint'.

14 *ES* II.535. Harington's Epigram 195 (*Letters and Epigrams*, pp. 227–8) describes the game succinctly.

15 Cook, *The Privileged Playgoers*, p. 187, notes a comment by Middleton about the Fortune, that 'Within one square a thousand heads are laid' (*The Roaring Girl*, I.ii), and concludes that it indicates the capacity of the yard. I would be inclined to doubt whether the galleries, also in the square, could be ignored in such a calculation. The number more likely indicates the expected total attendance.

16 See Orrell, *The Quest for Shakespeare's Globe*, p. 129.

17 See Reavley Gair, *The Children of Paul's*, Cambridge 1982, Chapter 2.

18 *EES*, II.2, p. 99.

19 For the details of this arrangement, whereby five of the sharers became

'housekeepers', see Andrew Gurr, *The Shakespearean Stage 1574–1642*, 2nd edition, Cambridge 1980, p. 46.

20 Thomas Platter in 1599 distinguished the Bankside playhouse where he saw *Julius Caesar* as 'the house with the thatched roof'. We know the Swan had a tiled roof from De Witt's drawing, and can assume from Platter's statement that the Rose was also tiled. Since thatch was markedly cheaper than tiles, we must assume that in this feature if no other the Globe was a cut-price job.

21 The most comprehensive survey of the evidence for the design of the second Blackfriars is by Richard Hosley, *Revels History* III.197–226.

22 The evidence about pricing is summarised in Gurr, *The Shakespearean Stage*, pp. 197–8.

23 In the prologue to *Jack Drum's Entertainment* (1600) they are addressed as 'this choise selected influence'.

24 Hosley, *Revels History* III.212. See also John Orrell, 'The Private Theatre Auditorium', *Theatre Research International* 9 (1984), pp. 79–94.

25 Letter by John Pory. See Herbert Berry, 'The Stage and Boxes at Blackfriars', *Studies in Philology* 63 (1966), pp. 163–86.

26 In 1603 at Blackfriars Sir Richard Cholmley, then aged twenty-three, discovered some of the problems of using stools. He took only one because he arrived late at a full playhouse, '... and as the custom was, between every scene stood up to refresh himself'. When he did so another young gallant took the stool for himself. The number of available stools was fixed, and when demand was high it seems that latecomers stood amongst the stool-sitters. In the smallest hall playhouse in 1639 the king banned stools from the stage altogether.

27 *The Gull's Hornbook*, 1610, Chapter 6.

28 John Marston, *The Malcontent*, 1604, Induction.

29 Beeston's hall playhouse was probably called the Cockpit because it was adapted from an old game house in Drury Lane. Inigo Jones's drawings seem to be an enlargement of the originally circular building. It was burned down in a riot by apprentices in 1617, and may have gained its alternative name, the Phoenix, from the incident and the speed with which Beeston rebuilt it.

30 *ES* IV.36.

31 George Whetstone, prefatory epistle to *Promos and Cassandra*, 1578; Thomas Dekker, *The Ravens Almanacke, Non-Dramatic Works*, ed. A. B. Grosart, 5 vols., London 1884–86, IV.194.

32 *ES* II.543.

33 *JCS* I.5.

34 Ibid., VI.34–5.

35 See 2.52. John Taylor the water-poet, in his 1614 pamphlet *The True Cause of the Water-mens Suit concerning Players*, probably exaggerated the numbers ferried to the Bankside playhouses: 'the Players have all (except the King's men) left their usuall residency on the Banke-side, and doe play in Middlesex farre remote from the Thames, so that every day in the weeke they doe draw unto them three or four thousand people, that were used to spend their monies by water'. (*Works*, 1630, p. 172). Overbury's Character 'A Water-Man', also published in 1614, suggests that his element was stronger than water. 'The Play-houses only keepe

him sober; and as it doth many other Gallants, make him an afternoones man.' (*Characters*, ed. W. J. Paylor, Oxford 1936, p. 68). The term 'afternoon's man' was a euphemism for a drunkard.

36 *JCS* I.4–5. According to Edmund Howes' additions to Stow's *Annales*, the 'ordinary use of Caroaches' began in 1605 (*Annales*, 1631, p. 867).

37 John Tatham, in a poem 'Upon the hinderance of meeting by raine, sent to his friend Mr. W. B.', exonerates the Globe in verses punning heavily on the signs of the zodiac which decorated the stage cover at the playhouse. The hindrance seems rather to have been over travelling to the playhouse in the rain than standing in its open yard.

38 See John Orrell, 'Sunlight at the Globe', *Theatre Notebook* 38 (1984), pp. 69–76.

39 *The City Match*, 1639, prologue.

40 *Travels in England*, p. 176.

41 One of the riverside views of Lambeth engraved by Hollar seems to show a row of privies on the riverbank. See Graham Parry, *Hollar's England*, London 1980 (Parthey catalogue no. P1038). The engraving is reproduced on page 37.

42 *The Seven Deadly Sins*, 1606; *Worke for Armourers*, 1609; *The Gulls Hornbook*, 1609; *The Raven's Almanacke*, 1609, in *Non-Dramatic Works*, II.53; IV.96; II.203; IV.194.

43 Epigram 36, 'Of Tobacco', in *The Poems*, ed. Robert Kruger, Oxford 1975, p. 144.

44 *Travels in England*, pp. 170–1.

45 Caps were also worn by women, children, old men and lawyers. Bonnets or brimmed hats might be worn on top of such caps. Harrison's *Description* says of the artisan class, 'They also wore flat Caps, both then and many yeares after, as well Apprentizes as Journey-men and others, both at home and abroad, whom the Pages of the Court in derision called "Flat Caps".'

46 'To the Gentleman Reader', *The Letting of Humours Blood in the Head-Vaine*, 1600. Rowlands also has a verse in 1619 in which a gallant demands that the feather-maker 'plume my head with his best Estridge tayle' (*A pair of Spy-knaves*, 1619).

47 Dekker, *If This Be Not a Good Play*, 1612, prologue. Donald Lupton acknowledged the practice of hissing as a mark of disapproval when he wrote (*London and the Countrey Carbonadoed*, 1631, G1v) '[players] love not the company of Geese or Serpents, because of their hissing'.

48 Fletcher wrote bitterly of the angry reception his innovatory *Faithful Shepherdess* received at a hall playhouse in about 1608 (2.82). Edmund Gayton wrote sarcastically of an audience at an amphitheatre demanding a change of play and later wrecking the playhouse (*Pleasant Notes upon Don Quixot*, 1654, p. 272).

49 The original order was issued in Latin. It is translated and quoted in David Masson, *Life of Milton*, I.218.

50 *Jests to make you Merie*, 1607, F3r.

51 There are several records of affrays at playhouses, in addition to the fight over the Countess of Essex's box at the Blackfriars in 1632 and a quarrel over the Lord Chamberlain's box at Blackfriars in 1636. In 1584 there was a riot involving apprentices outside the Theatre or Curtain (*ES* IV.297–8).

In 1626 the Privy Council warned the Surrey magistrates about an intended riot by sailors meeting at the Globe (*JCS* 1.21). They had similarly headed off a riotous assembly of apprentices meeting at the Fortune to wreck the Red Bull and Cockpit in 1618 (*JCS* 1.222). In between there is occasional evidence of other squabbles or riots which exercised the civic authorities. Considering the alarm which the authorities periodically voiced about the playhouses as sources of civic disorder the number of affrays was remarkably small. Chettle in *Kind-Harts Dreame* (1592) suggested that 'some lewd mates that long for innovation' might provoke fights between apprentices and servingmen, and that 'These are the common cause of discord in publike places', like the opening of *Romeo and Juliet*. But if such affrays did happen in the playhouses few of them came to the notice of the authorities. A good deal of the Lord Mayor's agitation over playhouse riots may have had its origin in the fact that although the suburbs were technically outside his jurisdiction the Privy Council held him responsible for putting down any civil disorders there.

3. SOCIAL COMPOSITION

1 Lawrence Stone, *Family and Fortune: Studies in Aristocratic Finance in the Sixteenth and Seventeenth Centuries*, Oxford 1973, pp. 59–61. Other London wage rates are in *Proclamations*, ed. P. L. Hughes and J. F. Larkin, 2 vols., New Haven 1964, II.22–3.
2 Louis B. Wright, *Middle-class Culture in Elizabethan England*, Chapel Hill 1935. The broad notion of an identifiable category of 'middle class' coming into existence in the sixteenth century is too gross an oversimplification to be of any use. Ann Jennalie Cook's second chapter in *The Privileged Playgoers*, on the privileged class, offers a useful correction to Wright.
3 Sir Thomas Smith, *De Republica Anglorum*, 1583. Mary Dewar's edition (1982) discusses in detail the date of original composition and the relationship of Smith's description to Harrison's. She dates both in the early 1560s, and regards Smith as the borrower from Harrison.
4 William Harrison, 'A Description of England', in Rafael Holinshed, *The Chronicles of England, Scotlande, and Irelande*, 2 vols., 1577. Harrison's 'Description' is near the beginning of vol. 1.
5 Thomas Wilson, 'The State of England (1600)', ed. F. J. Fisher, *Camden Miscellany*, 3rd ser. 52 (1936), pp. i–vii, 1–47.
6 Keith Wrightson, *English Society 1580–1680*, London 1981, p. 13, emphasises two major social developments in this period. The first was an enhanced sense of national identity, and the second an intensified polarisation between the poor and the wealthy.
7 The young Earl of Southampton in the six years up to his arrest for involvement in the Essex conspiracy spent over £40,000, more than half of it from the sale of land. See Stone, *Family and Fortune*, pp. 217–19.
8 Roger Finlay, *Population and Metropolis: The Demography of London 1580–1650*, Cambridge, 1981, p. 6.
9 Holinshed, *Chronicles*, 1577, vol. 1, Bk. II, Chapter 5. All the quotations from Harrison are taken from this chapter.
10 See Samuel Schoenbaum, *William Shakespeare: A Compact Documentary Life*, London 1977, pp. 277–31.

11 Wilfred R. Prest, *The Inns of Court under Elizabeth I and the Early Stuarts*, London 1972, pp. 6–8.

12 Of the major playwrights whose plays were published with their names on the titlepages before 1642, Armin, Brome, Day, Dekker, Field, Glapthorne, Heywood, Jonson, Marston, Nabbes, Peele, the Rowleys, Shakespeare, Tourneur, Webster, Wilkins and Robert Wilson were never called 'Gent.' Beaumont and Fletcher ocasionally had the honour, as did Chapman in 1598, Daborne, Ford in 1638, Lodge, Marlowe, Massinger, Thomas May, Middleton (occasionally), Shirley (once) and Whetstone. Daborne, Goffe, Greene, William Hemminges, Lyly and Marmion were implied as being gentlemen by the award 'M.A.' Perhaps the most intriguing evidence of the care with which this line was drawn is in the award of 'Gent.', to Middleton, on the titlepage of *A Chaste Maid* and *A Fair Quarrel*, and its absence from Webster's titlepages. Middleton came from London gentry, and made a good deal of theatrical capital from social climbing in his city comedies, especially *A Trick to Catch the Old One* and *A Chaste Maid*. Webster's citizen links with the family coachbuilding firm were derided by Fitzgeoffery, who called him a '*Play-wright Cart-wright*', in 1617. It is difficult to be sure how deliberate these titlings were. Day, who was the son of a husbandman and who never completed his degree at Cambridge because he was expelled for stealing a book, was never called 'Gent.' On the other hand Marston, whose presence as an Inn of Court student was well publicised, never received the title either. The use could be quite specific, as with Tom May and Lodowick Carlell, who were called 'esq.' But that was in the 1630s, by when even Shakespeare was accorded a 'Gent.'

13 Wrightson, *English Society 1580–1680*, p. 28.

14 A. L. Beier, 'Social problems in Elizabethan London', *Journal of Interdisciplinary History* 9 (1978), pp. 209, 214.

15 Ibid., p. 204.

16 David Cressy, *Literacy and the Social Order: Reading and Writing in Tudor and Stuart England*, Cambridge 1980, p. 129. Cressy's basis for his calculations is the ability to sign a name rather than using a cross. It is not an entirely dependable basis for determining true literacy, since illness or similar difficulties might have hindered the use of a complete signature, particularly in making wills, which are the chief data for Cressy's calculations. The printer Lionel Snowdon, who must surely have been more than moderately literate, signed his will with a cross in 1616 (Peter Blayney, *The Texts of 'King Lear' and their Origins*, Cambridge 1982, p. 19). The prologue to Davenant's *Platonic Lovers*, a Blackfriars play of 1635, claims a high proportion of illiterates amongst the citizenry: 'Bove half our City audience would be lost, / That knew not how to spell [the play's title] on the post.'

17 Ibid., p. 134.

18 Ibid., p. 128. The taste for prose romances exhibited by Beaumont's City madam in *The Knight of the Burning Pestle* was normative. The publishing of escapist prose fiction increased threefold in the forty years up to 1600.

19 J. H. Wiffen, *Historical Memoirs of the House of Russell*, 2 vols., 1833, I.499.

20 Henry Peacham, *The Compleat Gentleman*, 1622, p. 36.
21 The play may have been 2 *Tamburlaine*. Gawdy's letter says that 'My L.
    Admyrall his men and players having a devyse in ther playe to tye one of
    their fellowes to a poste and so to shoote him to deathe, having borrowed
    their callyvers one of the players handes swerved his peece being charged
    with bullet missed the fellowe he aymed at and killed a chyld, and a
    woman great with chyld forthwith, and hurt an other man in the head
    very soore.' *Letters of Philip Gawdy*, ed. I. H. Jeayes, London 1906, p. 23.
22 *The Autobiography of Anne Lady Halkett*, Camden Society, 1875, p. 3.
23 Quoted by Cyrus Hoy, *Introductions, Notes and Commentaries to Texts
    in 'The Dramatic Works of Thomas Dekker'*, 4 vols., Cambridge 1980,
    III.2
24 *JCS* VI.146.
25 *ES* I.264, II.447.
26 *ES* III.387.
27 *ES* IV.280.
28 Frederic Gerschow, printed and translated in *Transactions of the Royal
    Historical Society* n.s.6 (1892), p. 29. Gerschow also states that there
    were 'many respectable women' at Blackfriars.
29 Sir Hugh Cholmley, *Memoirs*, 1787, p. 18.
30 E. K. Chambers, *William Shakespeare*, 2 vols., Oxford 1930, II.335 (*WS*).
31 William B. Rye, *England as Seen by Foreigners in the Days of Elizabeth
    and James 1*, London, 1865, p. 61.
32 The principal exponent of this view was Alfred Harbage. His book on
    audiences, elaborated in *Shakespeare and the Rival Traditions*, New
    York 1952, overstates its case but assembles so much evidence that it can
    hardly be ignored. G. E. Bentley introduced consideration of historical
    changes with his assertion in 1948 that Shakespeare's last plays were
    influenced by his company's acquisition of the Blackfriars ('Shakespeare
    and the Blackfriars Theatre', *Shakespeare Survey* 1, 1948, pp. 38–50).
33 *The Knight of the Burning Pestle*, Induction, 1–3. The first quarto text,
    1613, mispunctuates these lines, putting the comma which should end
    the first line at the end of the second. See J. C. Maxwell, 'Conservative
    Principles', *Essays in Criticism* 21 (1971), p. 389.
34 *An Apology for Actors*, 1611, G3v; Anon., *Mucedorus*, 1611, epilogue.
    See *ES* IV.35–6.
35 *Middlesex County Records*, II.71, cited by Cook, *The Privileged Play-
    goers*, p. 137.
36 *JCS* VI.225.
37 E. M. Symonds, 'The Diary of John Greene (1635–1657)', *English His-
    torical Review* 43 (1928), pp. 385–94.
38 B. L. MS Egerton 2983.
39 B. L. MS Harleian 454, summarised in *JCS* II.673–81.
40 *The Guardian*, 1650, C3v.

4. MENTAL COMPOSITION

 1 *Discoveries, Works* VIII.578.
 2 *The Diary of John Manningham of the Middle Temple, 1602–1603*, ed.
    R. Parker Sorlien, Hanover, N. H. 1976, p. 202.

3 This is implicit in Puttenham, Gascoigne and Campion, for instance, despite Puttenham's acknowledgement of the device of writing verses in geometrical shapes on the page.

4 Kurt Weber, *Lucius Cary*, New York 1940, p. 63.

5 See Martin Butler, 'Massinger's *The City Madam* and the Caroline Audience', *Renaissance Drama* n.s.13 (1982), pp. 157–88.

6 *The Complete Works of John Webster*, ed. F. L. Lucas, 4 vols., London 1927, III.327. I am indebted to Michael Neill for drawing my attention to this reference.

7 T. W. Baldwin, *William Shakespeare's Small Latine and Lesse Greeke*, 2 vols., Urbana 1944, 1.344.

8 See Jacqueline Pearson, *Tragedy and Tragicomedy in the plays of John Webster*, Manchester 1980, pp. 94–5. 'Integer vitae' is the most readily recognisable of all tags from Horace. Shakespeare quotes it in *Titus Andronicus* II.ii. Chapter 1 of Simon Raven's first novel, *The Feathers of Death* (1959), has a discussion between army officers about a jungle expedition: ' "pleasure ... will not be plentiful for a bit. *Integer vitae*, whether we like it or not, is what each of us is going to be." "In which case, if we are to believe Horace, we shall at least have nothing to fear from the wild animals." "Do not rely too much on one of his less happy efforts. I suspect that ode of having been written by Dr Arnold and smuggled into the canon by way of a school edition." ' There is perhaps some justification for the view that Horace wrote the ode with his tongue in his cheek. Webster, however, like Shakespeare, probably read it straightforwardly, judging by his re-use of it in *Monuments of Honour*.

9 George Puttenham, *The Arte of English Poesie*, ed. Gladys Willcock and Alice Walker, Cambridge 1936, p. 145. Puttenham condemned the rhetorical figure of '*Barbarismus* or Forrein speech' (p. 250). He represents the hostility, current in his time because of anti-Catholic prejudice, against the use of Latinisms and neologisms based on Latin. He wrote (p. 36) of the 'beholders' of ancient tragedies, and translated *theatrum* as 'a beholding place'. He also refers (p. 291) to 'the hearer or beholder'. But by the time his book was published Sidney had already introduced the word 'spectator', and the Latin term easily prevailed. A preference in an anti-playing pamphlet of 1625 to 'hearers and beholders' is a sign of its derivation from the pamphlets of the 1580s (*A Shorte Treatise of Stage Playes*, 1625, Chapter 4).

10 The most elegant assessment of the quarrel, presenting Jones's side as well as Jonson's, is Donald Gordon's essay 'Poet and Architect: The Intellectual Setting of the Quarrel between Ben Jonson and Inigo Jones', first published in 1949 and reprinted in *The Renaissance Imagination*, ed. Stephen Orgel, Berkeley 1975, pp. 77–101.

11 'An Expostulation with Inigo Jones', *Works*, VIII.402.

12 Ibid., IV.43. In *The Masque of Queens* (1609), lines 107–10, Jonson contrasted the 'quick eares' of a Court audience with 'those sluggish ones of Porters, and Mechanicks, that must be bor'd through, at every act, with Narrations'.

13 See 2.141. The point about poets preferring the ear to the eye has been made by Alan C. Dessen, *Elizabethan Drama and the Viewers's Eye*, Chapel Hill 1977, p. 11. Some playgoers of course also preferred the

poetry. Lord Falkland, writing in the 1630s about a playbook in manuscript, asked for a copy on the grounds that 'if I valued it so at the single hearing, when myne eares could not catch half the wordes, what must I do now, in the reading when I may pause uppon it'. It might be argued that Falkland viewed the stage presentation of poetry as inadequate compared with reading. Sir Richard Baker in the same decade took the opposite view, affirming his preference for the stage over reading. He also affirmed that sight is more influential than hearing. Both writers are cited by Martin Butler, *Theatre and Crisis 1632–1642*, Cambridge 1984, pp. 106–7.

14 Robert Burton, *The Anatomy of Melancholy*, Part 1, Section 1, Memb.2, Subsection 6. The author of *A third blast of retrait from plaies*, 1580, attacked playgoing for its effect on the eyes: 'There commeth much evil in at the eares, but more at the eies, by these two open windowes death breaketh into the soule.' Gosson even included music in the visual seductions. 'In Comedies delight beeing moved with varietie of shewes, of eventes, of musicke, the longer we gaze, the more we crave.' *Playes Confuted in Five Actions*, 1582, 4th Action.

15 I am grateful to Alan Wardman for pointing out to me the uses in *Amphitruo* and in the *Confessions* (3.2).

16 Puttenham, *The Arte of English Poesie*, p. 55.

17 T. G., *The Rich Cabinet*, 1616, Q4r. In the epistle to *The Fawn*, 1606, Marston had put 'action' as the poet's main objective. Apologising for the play's appearance in print, he acknowledged that '*Comedies* are writ to be spoken, not read: Remember the life of these things consists in action.' Puttenham in the 1570s had suggested how much at odds 'action' could be with careful listening. The common people, he wrote, 'rejoyse much to be at plaies and enterludes, and besides their naturall ignorance, have at all such times their eares so attentive to the matter, and their eyes upon the shewes of the stage, that they take little heede to the cunning of the rime, and therefore be as well satisfied with that which is grosse, as with any other finer and more delicate' (*The Arte of English Poesie*, p. 82). Puttenham is presumably contrasting the poulter's rhyme used by the stage clown with less emphatic rhythms.

18 *The Works of Geoffrey Chaucer*, ed. F.N. Robinson, London 1933, Canterbury Tales Fragment III, lines 1935–7.

19 Quoted by David Bevington, *From 'Mankind' to Marlowe*, Cambridge, Mass. 1962, p. 41. Despite the emphatically English lexis, 'audiens' is the classical Latin for a single hearer. In this context where the term is clearly plural it presumably is a variant spelling for 'audience', from Latin *audientia*, an audience or attention.

20 See 2.34. Other writers who use 'spectator' include Daniel, *The Civil Wars*, 1595, II.58; anon, *A Warning for Fair Women*, 1599, prologue; *The Fair Maid of the Exchange*, c.1602, G2r; and most pointedly William Percy, who begins *Cuckqueans and Cuckolds Errant*, 1600, with a prologue spoken by Tarlton's ghost, who begins by addressing the audience as 'Spectators', and goes on to claim that who he is must be visible to all so that he need not 'recapitulate into your eares now, either my name or my Person'. The only writer who does not seem to have been sensitive to the distinction between seeing or hearing is William Corn-

wallis, who wrote in his *Essayes*, 1600, H3r: 'Let ape-keepers and players catch the eares of their Auditory and Spectators with faire bumbaste words, & set speeches.'

21 See Andrew Gurr, 'The Bear, the Statue, and Hysteria in *The Winter's Tale*', *Shakespeare Quarterly*, 34 (1983), pp. 420–5.

22 III.ii.35–7. The contrast between a told tale which is incredible and a visual presentation which convinces is reaffirmed by Paulina when the statue comes to life, V.iii.115–17.

23 V.ii.15–18. Shakespeare sometimes did use Puttenham's term. In *Richard III* he combined Puttenham's word with Spenser's phrase: 'The beholders of this tragic [F: frantic] play' (IV.iv.68).

24 *Lingua*, 1602, IV.ii. The association of women with seeing can also be found in John Earle, *Microcosmographie*, 1628, 'Of a Player': 'The waiting-women Spectators are over-eares in love with him.' Aston Cockayne's 1639 *Masque* speaks of 'spectator ladies'.

25 See 2.87. In the epistle 'To the Reader' Jonson echoed *Hamlet*, writing that 'the Concupiscence of Daunces, and Anticks ... is the onely point of art that tickles the Spectators'.

26 *The Dramatic Records of Sir Henry Herbert*, ed. J. Q. Adams, Newhaven 1917, p. 20 (*Herbert*).

27 *A Short Treatise of the Stage*, printed in *Love's Kingdom*, 1664, G7v.

28 T. G., *The Rich Cabinet*, of a player: 'if there be not a facility in his deliverance, and as it were a naturall dexteritie, it must needes sound harsh to the auditour'.

29 Prefatory epistle, *The Two Merry Milkmaids*, 1620: Every poet 'must govern his Penne according to the Capacitie of the Stage he writes too, both in the Actor and the Auditor'.

30 *New Shreds of the Old Snare*, 1624, p. 21. Gee was sensitive to the distinction, and used 'auditory' for orators and lawyers. When he writes of the Jesuits deceiving a young girl with an apparition he calls her a 'spectator' – in fact once (p. 19) a 'Spectatrix'.

31 J. H., *This World's Folly*, 1615. The same author writes of an 'Oyster-crying Audience' and a 'Monster-headed Multitude' (B2v). Richard Baker, writing a reply to Prynne's *Histriomastix* of 1633, was an unashamed beholder rather than hearer. He used the term 'spectator' regularly, along with 'beholders' and 'the seeing of plays'. He also claimed that 'a Play *read*, hath not half the pleasure of a Play *Acted*: for though it have the pleasure of *ingenious Speeches*, yet it wants the pleasure of *Gracefull action*'. *Theatrum Redivivum*, 1662, p. 33.

32 John Stephens, epistle, in Henry Fitzgeoffery, *Satyres and Satyricall Epigrams*, 1616; Richard Brome, *The Antipodes*, 1638, II.ii. Shakespeare also makes use of 'audience', but always for hearers and usually with a legal implication. The watchers who are 'mutes or audience' to the tragedy of Hamlet (V.ii.337) are legal witnesses. Polonius spying on Hamlet in Gertrude's closet becomes 'some more audience than a mother' by overhearing their talk. In *King Lear* the blinded Gloster is literally Lear's 'audience' or 'hearer' as a witness in the mock trial of Lear's daughters.

33 The anti-democratic image of the 'many-headed monster' lay behind the term 'multitude'. As early as 1582 Gosson wrote of playhouse audiences

that 'the auncient Philosophers ... called them a monster of many heades' (*Playes Confuted in Five Actions*, 2nd Action). Nathaniel Field in verses for *The Faithful Shepherdess* wrote of the Blackfriars audience as a 'monster' clapping its 'thousand hands' (2.85).

34 *A Treatise at Playe*, 1598, reprinted in *Nugae Antiquae*, 1804, 1.186–232, pp. 190–1.

35 Cecil certainly attended plays at Court, and was entertained with them privately, by for instance Sir Edward Hoby in 1596 at his house in the Strand, when *Richard II* seems to have been on the menu. Harington was enthusiastic enough about plays to have collected 90 of the 110 plays published in quarto in the decade up to 1610, including 18 copies of the 15 quartos of Shakespeare's plays. He is unlikely to have been quoting anything other than a memory of performance to Cecil.

36 *Letters and Epigrams*, p. 31.

37 Richard Levin, 'The Relation of External Evidence to the Allegorical and Thematic Interpretation of Shakespeare', *Shakespeare Studies* 13 (1980), pp. 1–29.

38 R. H. MacDonald, *The Library of Drummond of Hawthornden*, Edinburgh 1971. Drummond's reading is strikingly similar in its range if not in detail to Gabriel Harvey's, judging from Harvey's marginalia made in the years 1582–99.

39 Sir Dudley Carleton, quoted in Ralph Winwood, *Memorials of Affairs of State*, 2 vols., London 1725, 11.44; Orazio Busino, quoted in *C.S.P. Venetian 1617–19*, pp. 67–8.

40 Beaumont expected there to be gentry sitting on stage with the Grocer and his wife. In the interval after Act III she asks for beer and talks to the 'Gentlemen' next to her, and in the Epilogue she does the same.

41 See John Doebler, 'Beaumont's *Knight of the Burning Pestle* and the Prodigal Son Plays', *Studies in English Literature* 5 (1965), pp. 333–44.

42 The Citizen wants a play called 'The Grocer's Honour' to proclaim citizen pretensions to aristocratic honour. The boy Prologue's suggestion, 'The Knight of the burning pestle', both parodies the Palmerin romances of the Knight of the Ardent Sword and hints at bawdy exploitation of the pestle/pizzle joke.

43 Levin, 'The Relation of External Evidence'.

44 The practice of memorising quotable passages from plays has been noted already. The commonplace book of Edward Pudsey (Bodleian MS Eng. poet d.3) records passages from a number of plays performed at about the time Hamlet was using his 'tables' for memorable jottings, including four of Jonson's plays, one by Chapman, Marston's *Antonio* plays and *Jack Drum's Entertainment, The Merchant of Venice* and *Satiromastix*. The mix includes plays at Paul's, the Blackfriars and the Globe.

45 See 2.44. Jarold Ramsay conjectures that Malvolio's 'gesture in smiling' should read 'gesture in suiting'. See 'The Importance of Manningham's Diary', *Shakespeare Studies* 7 (1974), p. 329.

46 Forman's text is given in *WS* 11.337–41. Since the company was evidently performing at the Globe throughout April, and *Cymbeline* was one of their plays, it must have been staged there along with the other three. For an analysis of Forman's account of *Macbeth*, see Leah Scragg, 'Macbeth on Horseback', *Shakespeare Survey* 26 (1973), pp. 81–8.

47 The text is transcribed and its content superbly analysed by Herbert Berry, 'The Globe Bewitched and *El Hombre Fiel*', in *Medieval and Renaissance Drama in England* I (1984), pp. 211–30.

48 Ibid., p. 223. My reading of Tomkyns' account differs from Professor Berry's to the extent that I would question Tomkyns' knowledge of any division in Privy Council views about the trial.

49 Ibid., p. 229 note 17.

50 Levin, 'The Relation of External Evidence', p. 10.

51 Ibid., p. 21.

52 See H. S. Bennett, *English Books and Readers 1558–1603*, Cambridge 1965, p. 260.

5. THE EVOLUTION OF TASTES

1 Anne Righter, *Shakespeare and the Idea of the Play*, London 1962, p. 53. A good account of the 'romantic narrative' plays of 1570–90 is Patricia Russell's essay in *Elizabethan Theatre*, ed. J. R. Brown and Bernard Harris, London 1966, pp. 106–29.

2 Anne Righter (Barton) has an admirable summary of the changing idea of the play, pp. 15–78. A special category of play which also evolved at this time was the Protestant morality, of which eight or so survive from the period 1550–75. According to P. K. Ayers, they suffer from the inherently undramatic nature of Protestant theology. See 'The Protestant Morality Play and Problems of Dramatic Structure', *Essays in Theatre* 2 (1984), pp. 94–110.

3 J. Leeds Barroll, in *Revels History III, 1576–1613*, pp. 4–14.

4 At the height of the demand on the repertoires that could entail a comparable number of new plays in a year. In 1596 the total of plays not previously recorded was thirty-five. The convenience of travelling with a small repertoire was noted by Donald Lupton, *London and the Country Carbonadoed*, 1632, G1v. Travelling players, he wrote, 'do as some wandring Sermonists, make one Sermon travaile and serve twenty Churches'.

5 *Es* IV.280.

6 See Marie Axton, *The Queen's Two Bodies*, London 1977, pp. 70–2.

7 Pistol's fortuitously searching question to the disguised king, *Henry V*, IV.i.38.

8 The phrase is Antony Scoloker's, of *Hamlet*, in *Daiphantus*, 1604. A2r.

9 Gabriel Harvey, *Foure Letters and certeine Sonnets*, 1592, p. 19. Harvey writes in the third letter of being invited by Tarlton to see his *Seven Deadly Sins* at Oxford.

10 *Tarltons Jestbook*, titlepage. The only extant edition was printed in 1611, but editions had appeared before 1600.

11 The only surviving fragment of this publication is in the Folger Shakespeare Library. It is described and quoted in M. C. Bradbrook, *The Rise of the Common Player*, London 1964, pp. 173–6.

12 *C.S.P. Dom 1581–90*, pp. 541–2. Walsingham was Sidney's father-in-law. His role in promoting plays and players is a little ambivalent. He was the dedicatee of Gosson's *Plaies Confuted in Five Actions*. Tarlton certainly had social pretensions. Gabriel Harvey (see note 9) speaks of him calling himself a gentleman, no light word for Elizabethans.

13 Both passages are quoted in Gurr, *The Shakespearean Stage*, p. 86

14 See 2.14. If it were not for Tarlton's use of it very possibly the word 'clown' would now be no more in use than the alternative word 'swad', which also meant a yokel. Gabriel Harvey writes at the beginning of his commonplace book of being 'drowsely or swaddishly affected' (*Gabriel Harvey's Marginalia*, p. 87), and Sir John Davies had an epigram about a 'countrey swadd' whose behaviour to his lady is more direct than a courtier's. 'The Courtier first came lepping in, / And tooke the Lady by the chin, / The cuntry swadd as he was blunt / Came tooke the lady by the elbow.' (*Poems*, ed. Robert Kruger, Oxford 1975, p. 181). The currency Tarlton gave to 'clown' as the word for a stage yokel might have promoted 'swad' because it avoided the stage associations of the other word. The new term 'clown' was distinct enough for Jonson to invent an etymology for it. In *A Tale of a Tub* I.iii.40–1 a clown is described as a rustic, the Roman 'colonus', a colonist or farmer. '*Colonus* is an Inhabitant: /A Clowne originall.'

15 Samuel Rowlands, *The Letting of Humours Blood in the Head-Vaine*, Sat. 4, D8r.

16 Richard Jones in the 1590 edition wrote of the omissions as 'far unmeet for the matter ... though haply they have been of some vain conceited fondlings greatly gaped at'.

17 *ES* II.75.

18 Reavley Gair, *The Children of Paul's*, Cambridge 1982, p. 98.

19 Quoted by Gair, ibid., p. 109.

20 A brief look through those curiosities of the history of journalism, G. B. Harrison's *The Elizabethan Journals*, London 1928, and its successors *The Jacobean Journals*, will show how much current news up to 1603 was about military dispositions and skirmishes on land and sea against the Spanish.

21 See O. L. Brownstein, 'A Record of London Inn Playhouses from c. 1565–1590', *SQ* 22 (1971), p. 22. Richard Flecknoe, however, writing in the 1660s, declared that the Bull and Cross Keys both had innyards still in existence (*A Discourse of the English Stage*, p. 2). Glynne Wickham discounts Flecknoe's comment (*EES* II.1, pp. 190–1).

22 *JCS* II.361.

23 Since fencing bouts only took place in the open air, at places like the Bel Savage Inn and the Swan and Curtain playhouses, we might well wonder what happened when *Hamlet* was performed at the Blackfriars in the winter months after 1609.

24 See 2.8. Sidney is equally derisive in his *Apology*. The 'gallimaufrey' or romantic narrative plays seem to have created the first public division of elite taste from popular.

25 Alfred Harbage, *Shakespeare's Audience*, New York, 1941, p. 49. *Harey the 6* appears in Henslowe's records from their commencement in 1592 until 1594, when it probably accompanied Shakespeare to the rival Chamberlain's Men.

26 *Revels History III, 1576–1613*, p. 256.

27 See Richard Levin, 'The Contemporary Perception of Marlowe's Tamburlaine', *Medieval and Renaissance Drama in England* 1 (1984), pp. 51–70. He was universally seen as a mighty conqueror, and some

commentators emphasised his rise from Scythian shepherd to great king. Donne in *The Calme* (1597), Rowlands in 1605 and Middleton in a City pageant of 1623 all emphasised his social climb. For imitations of *Tamburlaine* see Peter Berek, '*Tamburlaine's* Weak Sons; Imitation as Interpretation before 1593', *Renaissance Drama* n.s. 13 (1982), pp. 55–82.

28 Beside Joseph Hall, others who made *Tamburlaine* a joke include Marston (*Histriomastix*, c. 1597, G1r); *Antonio and Mellida*, 1599, Induction; E.S., *The Discovery of the Knights of the Post*, 1597, C2v; Dekker, *the Wonderfull Yeare*, 1603, C4v; T. M., *The Blacke Booke*, 1604, D1r; and of course Ancient Pistol.

29 'La "Tragédie Espanole" face à la Critique Elisabethaine et Jacobéene', in *Dramaturgie et Societé*, ed. Jean Jacquot, 2 vols., Paris 1968, II.607–31.

30 Bradbrook, *The Rise of the Common Player*, p. 130.

31 Ibid., p. 131.

32 T. M., *The Blacke Booke*, B4r.

33 Quoted in *ES* III.425.

34 *The Knave of Clubs*, 1609, p. 29. Aubrey cites a legend that Alleyn was frightened by a devil when playing Faustus and vowed to found Dulwich College as a result.

35 Starting with Greene, *Perimedes the Blacksmith*, 1588, preface.

36 *Thomas Platter's Travels in England*, p. 170.

37 Newspapers were invented to feed this appetite early in the seventeenth century, as Jonson's *Staple of News* very strongly registers. The aristocracy paid professional letter-writers to keep them informed. Roland Whyte, for the Sidney family, and John Chamberlain for the English Ambassador to France, are the best known. Pamphlets of 'News' became commonplace in the 1590s. See H.S. Bennett, *English Books and Readers 1558–1603*, Cambridge 1965, pp. 220–47.

38 Lyly, *A Whip for an Ape* (*Complete Works*, III.421); Nashe, *Martins Months Minde* (*Works*, ed. R. B. McKerrow, 10 vols., London 1904, I.166).

39 The fourth Martinist tract, *Hay any worke for Cooper*, issued early in 1589, cheekily proposed candidates for Martin's identity, including both Penry and Wiggington (p. 31).

40 Moralising the great was a practice going back at least to great house drama like Skelton's *Magnyfycence*. In the prologue to *Damon and Pithias* Richard Edwardes protested 'Wherein talking of Courtly toyes, we doo protest this flat, / Wee talke of *Dionysius* Courte, wee meane no Court but that.'

41 *Chronicles of England, Scotlande and Irelande*, 2nd edition, 1587, III.1062–6.

42 Besides *Arden* and *A Yorkshire Tragedy*, domestic dramas which have survived include *A Warning for Fair Women, A Woman Killed with Kindness, How a Man May Choose a Good Wife from a Bad, The Witch of Edmonton, The English Traveller, The Miseries of Enforced Marriage*, and of course *The Merry Wives of Windsor*.

43 *ES* I.267 note 4.

44 Quoted by C. J. Sisson, *Lost Plays of Shakespeare's Age*, London 1936, p. 58.

45 One ballad was entered in the Stationers' Register in July 1624, as *The*

repentance of NATHANAEL TINDALL that killed his mother, and the other in September as *A Most bloudy unnaturall and unmatchable murther Committed in Whitechappel by NATHANAELL TINDALL upon his owne mother.* See *JCS* III.186 [i.e. 286].

46 *JCS* III.75–6.
47 Sisson, *Lost Plays of Shakespeare's Age,* p. 78.
48 William Crashaw preached a sermon at Paul's Cross on 14 February 1608 in which he protested at the labelling of puritans by their churches as real people in *The Puritan,* played at Paul's and recently published. '... now they bring religion and holy things upon the stage ... Two hypocrites must be brought foorth; and how shall they be described but by these names, *Nicholas S. Antlings, Simon S. Maryoveries* ... by these miscreants thus dishonoured, and that not on the stage only, but even in print.' Crashaw had the support of the 1606 Statute against profanity on stage. Possibly Paul's was in Henry Parrott's mind along with the Blackfriars boys who evoked the French Ambassador's protest, when he noted in his epistle to *The More the Merrier* (1608) how much there had been of 'satiric inveighing at any mans private person (a kind of writing which of late seems to have been very familiar among our poets and players, to their cost)'. The 'railing' vein which opened with the boy companies at the turn of the century was running fairly dry by that time.
49 Quoted in *ES* I.322 note 2.
50 On 10 May 1601 the Privy Council instructed the Middlesex magistrates to suppress a play at the Curtain because it portrayed 'the persons of some gentlemen of good desert and quality that are yet alive, under obscure manner, but yet in such sort as all the hearers may take notice both of the matter and of the persons that are meant thereby'. (*ES* I.324). The 'obscure manner' of their representation probably meant that the persons portrayed were notable enough for the players to anticipate censure. The offence over Chapman's *Byron* was committed by the boys of Blackfriars. Sir Thomas Lake wrote to Lord Salisbury on 11 March 1608 that 'His ma' was well pleased with that which your lo. advertiseth concerning the committing of the players that have offended in the matters of France, and commanded me to signifye to your lo. that for the others who have offended in the matter of the Mynes and other lewd words which is the children of the blackfriers That though he had signified his mynde to your lo. by my lo. of Montgommery yet I should repeat it again That his G. had vowed they should never play more but should first begg their bred and he would have his vow performed.' *Malone Society Collections,* II.2, 1923, p. 149.
51 *C.S.P. Dom Eliz,* CCLXXIV.138.
52 Guilpin, *Skialetheia,* Sat. 1, "In Foelix', C3v; the attack on Raleigh, 1603, is in *Poetical Miscellanies,* ed. J. O. Halliwell, London 1845, p. 17.
53 See for instance B. de Luna, *Jonson's Romish Plot,* Oxford 1967.
54 See L. G. Salingar, Gerald Harrison and Bruce Cochran, 'Les Comédiens et leur Public en Angleterre de 1520 à 1640', *Dramaturgie et Societé* II.553 (Table 10).
55 See John C. Meagher, 'Hackwriting and the Huntingdon Plays', in *Elizabethan Theatre,* ed. Brown and Harris, pp. 197–219.
56 Citizen values were not just a matter of making citizens like Simon Eyre

or nobly-born apprentices into heroes for stage purposes. See Laura Caroline Stevenson, *Praise and Paradox: Merchants and Craftsmen in Elizabethan Popular Literature*, Cambridge 1984, especially pp. 19–21, 73–4 and 126–7.

57 See Judith Doolin Spikes, 'The Jacobean History Play and the Myth of the Elect Nation', *Renaissance Drama*, n.s.8 (1977), pp. 117–49.

58 A succinct account of the background to Juliet's rebellion is G.R. Hibbard, 'Love, Marriage and Money in Shakespeare's Theatre and Shakespeare's England', *Elizabethan Theatre* 6 (1978), pp. 134–55.

59 *Singing Simkin* is reprinted in C.R. Baskerville, *The Elizabethan Jig*, Chicago 1929, pp. 444–9.

60 C. S. Felver, *Robert Armin, Shakespeare's Fool*, Kent State University Bulletin Research Series 5, 1961.

61 Neil Carson, 'John Webster: the Apprentice Years', *Elizabethan Theatre* 6 (1978), pp. 76–87.

62 Heywood wrote of bewitched spectators in his *Apology*, Dekker of the 'charmed soule' in the prologue to *If This Be Not a Good Play*. See Carson, ibid., p. 80.

63 Ibid., p. 79.

64 See Frank Kerins, 'The Crafty Enchaunter: Ironic Satires and Jonson's *Every Man Out of his Humour*', *Renaissance Drama* n.s. 14 (1983), pp. 132–3.

65 Jonson's thinking was close enough to Marston's for him also to parody *Romeo and Juliet* in *Every Man Out*.

66 A level-headed assessment of the main points at issue in the War of the Theatres can be found in David Bevington, *Tudor Drama and Politics*, Cambridge, Mass. 1968, pp. 262–88.

67 See 2.91. Heywood's pamphlet was probably originally written in 1607–08. Marston in *Jack Drum's Entertainment* aims Heywood's kind of animus directly at Jonson, who, he claims, takes pleasure 'to Gull / Good honest soules, and in thy arrogance / And glorious ostentation of thy wit, / Thinke God infused all perfection / Into thy soule alone ...' (V, conclusion).

68 See Raman Selden, *English Verse Satire, 1590–1765*, London 1978, p. 72.

69 Brian Gibbons, *Jacobean City Comedy*, 2nd edition, London 1980, p. 34.

70 *Poetaster*, III.iv. See Bevington, *Tudor Drama and Politics*, p. 285.

71 III.iv.201. This reference is followed in the play by an extended burlesque of the Player's speech and other passages in *Hamlet*, and concludes with the player lamenting the loss of his audience to the boys: 'No bodie comes at us; not a gentleman, nor a – ' (329–30).

72 I am inclined to think that *Twelfth Night* was written after *Every Man Out* and partly as a reply to the idea of dramaturgy expressed in that play.

73 Dekker, *Satiromastix*, 1601, epilogue; *The Knight of the Burning Pestle*, Induction; Field, *A Woman is a Weathercock*, 1609, II.i; Fletcher, *Henry VIII*, 1613, epilogue.

74 Beside the jibes about the 'few industrious Scots' and the 'thirty pound knights', in *Eastward Ho!*, a letter of Sir Thomas Edmondes (February

1606) testifies to the satirical basis and particularly the Scottish accents which Day exploited in 1606. 'At this time there was much speech of a play in the Black Friars, where in the "Isle of Gulls", from the highest to the lowest, all men's parts were acted of two diverse nations: as I understand sundry were committed to Bridewell.' (*Court and Times of James I*, ed. Thomas Birch, 2 vols., London 1848, 1.60–1). The satire was not so much directed at James's policy of union between the two countries which he ruled as at the introduction of his Scottish followers into the Court and positions of power.

75 Henry Crosse, *Vertues Commonwealth*, 1603, P3r, complained that 'there is no passion wherwith the soveraigne majestie of the Realme was possest, but is amplified, and openly sported with, and made a May-game to all the beholders'. Anne of Denmark was reported by the French Ambassador in 1604 to have attended plays in order to enjoy the mockery of her husband (*ES* 1.325). Possibly her giving her name to the Blackfriars boys (the Children of the Queen's Revels) means that they were the company who provided her with that kind of entertainment.

76 Chapman, *All Fools*, II.i; Jonson, *Volpone*, prologue: Day, *Isle of Gulls*, prologue; Marston, *The Fawn*, prologue; *Sophonisba*, epilogue; Beaumont, *The Woman Hater*, Apologetical prologue; Barry, *Ram Alley*, prologue; *Mucedorus* (1610), epilogue.

77 According to Alfred Harbage, *Shakespeare and the Rival Traditions*, p. 71.

78 Alexander Leggatt, *Citizen Comedy in the Age of Shakespeare*, Toronto 1973, p. 4.

79 Ibid., p. 130.

80 Anne Barton, *Ben Jonson, Dramatist*, Cambridge 1984, p. 68.

81 Its place in the sequence of Jonson's writing is finely examined by Anne Barton, ibid., pp. 105–19.

82 L. C. Knights, *Drama and Society in the Age of Jonson*, London 1937, especially Chapter 7.

83 Beaumont was a close follower and ally of Jonson from 1605 onwards, judging from the commendatory verses each wrote for the publication of the other's plays.

84 Barton, *Ben Jonson, Dramatist*, pp. 137–40, examines the wide social range of the characters in *The Alchemist*.

85 The most detailed study of Chapman's lost play *The Old Joiner of Aldgate* is Sisson's *Lost Plays of Shakespeare's Age*, pp. 12–79. For the *Ho!* plays see Gair, *The Children of Paul's*, Chapter 5. Neil Carson, 'John Webster: the Apprentice Years' makes some good points about the complexities involved in changing from a 'citizen' repertory to a boy company repertory. See especially pp. 81–6.

86 Gibbons, *Jacobean City Comedy*, pp. 76–7.

87 *Sir Thomas Wyatt*, 1607 and 1612; *Thomas Lord Cromwell*, 1602 and 1613; *When You See Me*, 1605, 1613; and *If You Know Not Me*, 1605, 1608, 1610 and 1613. See Spikes, 'The Jacobean History Play', p. 142.

88 *The Diary of Lady Margaret Hoby 1599–1605*, ed. Dorothy M. Meads, London 1930, p. 49.

89 On the use of Shakespeare in *The Maid's Tragedy*, see H. Neville Davies, 'Beaumont and Fletcher's *Hamlet*', in *Shakespeare, Man of the Theater*,

ed. Kenneth Muir, Jay L. Halio and D.J. Palmer, Newark, 1983, pp. 173–81. Clifford Leech has an excellent analysis of the Fletcherian style in *The John Fletcher Plays*, London 1962, pp. 24–40.

90 Beaumont collaborated with Fletcher only until 1613. Fletcher continued as a kind of resident playwright, collaborating with Field, Massinger and others. The standard identification of a specific type of King's Men's play as by 'Beaumont and Fletcher', which eventually stretched to over fifty plays, indicates how popular the fashion was, and how prescriptive its style, a point affirmed by the amount of collaborative writing in the canon.

91 G. E. Bentley, 'Shakespeare and the Blackfriars Theatre', *Shakespeare Survey* 1 (1948), pp. 38–50. See also Andrew Gurr, ed. *Philaster*, pp. xliii–l, and J. A. Lavin, 'Shakespeare and the Second Blackfriars', *Elizabethan Theatre* 3 (1973), pp. 66–81.

92 *JCS*, II.365.

93 John Orrell, *The Theatres of Inigo Jones and John Webb*, Cambridge 1985, Chapter 3. For the argument that the Blackfriars' galleries were curved although the hall was rectangular, see Orrell, 'The Private Theatre Auditorium', *Theatre Research International* 9 (1984), pp. 79–94.

94 Beeston's tangled finances and the litigation they involved him in are explained by C. J. Sisson, 'Notes on Early Stuart Stage History', *Modern Language Review* 37 (1942), pp. 25–36.

95 *Letters*, II.59–60.

96 This is Chambers' conclusion. See *ES* III.346.

97 See *JCS* I.214–17. The only title to have survived from the first period is the lost play *The Younger Brother. A Fair Quarrel* and *All's Lost by Lust* can reasonably be identified as Red Bull plays of this period.

98 The phrase is Edmond Gayton's. See 2.201.

99 Joseph Swetnam's pamphlet appeared in 1615. By the time the play, a romance based on a Spanish novella with a subplot making comic use of the controversy, had reached the stage at the Red Bull three women had answered Swetnam. Rachel Speght used her own name, but the other two, Ester Sowerman and Constantia Munda, were probably pseudonyms.

100 *Lingua*, 1607, D4v.

101 *JCS* I.219–22.

102 Leonard Digges, in verses prefixed to the 1640 edition of Shakespeare but probably written in 1622 for the first Folio, wrote of poetasters 'On Gods name may the Bull or Cockpit have / Your lame blancke Verse, to keepe you from the grave: / Or let new Fortunes younger brethren see, / What they can picke from your leane industry.' The reference to the 'new' Fortune places this close to its rebuilding, in 1622. Evidently Digges regarded the Cockpit and Red Bull as equivalent venues in their judgement of poetry.

103 Michael Neill, '"Wits most accomplished Senate": The Audience of the Caroline Private Theaters', *Studies in English Literature* 18 (1978), pp. 341–60. This is an admirable account of gallant interests and thinking in the 1630s.

104 The phrase is Jonson's, from *Bartholomew Fair*, Induction. Brome

addresses the three main categories, plus 'my Countrey folkes too if here be any o' em' in the epilogue to *The Court Beggar*, written for the Cockpit in 1639–40. Shirley's *The Coronation*, written for the Cockpit in 1634–35, has a prologue addressing the 'noble Gentlewomen'.

105 Ford, *The Broken Heart*, 1633, epilogue. Ford's play was written for the Blackfriars. Michael Neill, '"Wit's most accomplished Senate"', pp. 353–8, analyses the new critical sense in detail.

106 Jonson, 'Ode to Joseph Rutter', *Works*, VIII.414–15.

107 On the repertoires of plays and the private playhouse audiences, see Martin Butler, *Theatre and Crisis 1632–1642*, and Michael Neill, '"Wit's most accomplished Senate"'. Both writers have excellent sections on the hall playhouse audiences. Kathleen McLuskie's comment is also pertinent: 'There is little point in deploring or mocking the conventional quality of much Stuart drama. To understand its cultural impact one must link that conventionality to the emergence of a fully professional theatrical organisation with a huge turnover of plays catering for a clearly defined audience who might recognise and enjoy varied treatments of familiar formulas.' *Revels History IV*, pp. 257–8.

108 Abraham Wright's reading of plays in the 1630s is examined by James McManaway, 'Excerpta Quaedam per A. W. Adolescentem', in *Studies in Honor of DeWitt T. Starnes*, ed. Thomas P. Harrison et al., Houston 1967, pp. 117–29. Humphrey Mildmay occasionally commented on the plays he saw. He saw 'a base play att the Cockpitt' in March 1634, but also at the Cockpit 'a pretty & Merry Comedy' in June 1633, and Shirley's *Lady of Pleasure*, 'that rare play', in 1635. Three plays he marked down as 'foolish'. *JCS*, II.673–81.

109 Peter Beal, 'Massinger at Bay: Unpublished Verses in a War of the Theatres', *Yearbook of English Studies* 10 (1980), pp. 190–203, especially p. 194.

110 *Herbert*, p. 19. See Marvin Morillo, 'Shirley's "Preferment" and the Court of Charles I', *Studies in English Literature* 1 (1961), pp. 101–17.

111 Goffe was a clergyman, who died in 1629, the year Salisbury Court first opened. The Praeludium refers to Brome's *Antipodes*, produced at Salisbury Court in 1638. Either Shirley or Brome (as G. E. Bentley suggests, *JCS* IV.504) revised the play and inserted the Praeludium.

112 *JCS* VI.238–47.

113 *Timber*, in *Works* VIII.587; Gayton, *Pleasant Notes*, p. 24; anon, 'The Unfortunate Gallant Gulled at London', *The Pepys Ballads*, ed. Rollins, 1.239; Abraham Cowley, *The Guardian*, 1650, C3v.

114 Richard Flecknoe, *AEnigmaticall Characters*, 1658, I8r.

115 Anon, *The Two Merry Milkmaids*, 1620, prologue; Davenant, *The Unfortunate Lovers*, 1673, prologue. See also 2.181, 203.

116 *JCS* 1.274–5.

117 *The Rebellion*, 1639, V.ii.

118 *Knavery in All Trades*, 1664, III, E1r.

119 Butler, *Theatre and Crisis*, pp. 198–203, 206–10.

120 Margot Heinemann in her adroit analysis of censorship in the political aspects of Jacobean and Caroline drama runs the risk of assuming the absence of comment is a token of censorship. See *Puritanism and*

Theatre, Cambridge 1980, especially Chapters 9–12. Annabel Patterson, *Censorship and Interpretation,* Wisconsin 1984, provides some striking examples of tacit censorship in Sidney and in seventeenth-century writers. Much of this is likely to remain unknown territory.

121 See Butler, *Theatre and Crisis,* p. 194.
122 *Herbert,* p. 66.
123 Butler, *Theatre and Crisis,* p. 207.
124 *JCS* v.1106.
125 *Revels History IV,* p. 167.

Index

Puritan, The, 222, 266
Puttenham, George, 85, 89, 90, 91, 259, 260

Queen Henrietta's Men, 174–7
Queen's Men, 117, 118, 125, 128, 129, 142
Queen's Men (Red Bull Company), 95, 170, 171, 172, 225

railing comedy, 47, 153–9, 216, 218, 220, 224–5, 266
Rainolds, John, 215
Raleigh, Sir Walter, 146
Ram Alley, 159
Randolph, Thomas, 78, 238
Rape of Lucrece, The, 78, 176, 192
Rawlins, Thomas, 184
Reade, Timothy, 182, 246
Rebellion, The, 184
Red Bull playhouse, 14, 15, 31, 36, 44, 46, 60, 64, 65, 71, 72, 76, 78, 79, 82, 93, 95, 97, 104, 132, 144, 145, 151, 155, 165, 170–7, 181, 182, 183–7, 190, 191, 194, 195, 196, 199, 200, 201, 203, 204, 226, 229, 234, 235, 236, 237–8, 245, 247, 249, 251
Red Bull-King's Men, 184
Red Lion playhouse, 10, 11, 13, 14, 15, 26, 115
Revels, Master of the, 34, 96, 117, 120, 145, 170, 179, 196, 231, 240–1
Reynolds, Henry, 80, 201, 229
Rich, Barnaby, 51, 52
Rich, Mary, 191, 201
Rich, Sir Robert, 70, 201, 203
Richard II, 113, 146, 191, 195, 199, 262
Richard III, 111–12, 139, 233, 261
Richards, Nathanael, 201
Rival Friends, The, 46
Roaring Girl, The, 61–3, 65, 194, 253
Roberts, Jack, 130, 141
Rollo, 199
Roman Actor, The, 237
Romeo and Juliet, 69, 100, 149–50, 151, 152, 161, 212, 267

Rose playhouse, 13, 14, 16, 19, 20, 34, 45, 69, 133, 150, 155, 156, 157, 195
Rossingham, Edmond, 186, 247
Rowlands, Samuel, 41, 43, 56, 64, 65, 68, 134, 140, 201, 214, 219, 232–3, 265
Rowley, Samuel, 148, 257
Rowley, William, 172, 257
Roxana, 77
Ruddier, Sir Benjamin, 201, 235
Rule a Wife and have a Wife, 43, 195, 235
Russell, Lord John, 55
Rutter, William, 179, 182, 242

Salisbury, Earl of, *see* Cecil
Salisbury Court playhouse, 14, 31, 44, 78, 110, 145, 177, 178, 180, 182, 204, 239, 251
Sapho and Phao, 120, 130
satire against James, 158–9
Satiromastix, 74, 154, 155, 156, 159, 163, 196, 201, 214
Savoy, Ambassador of, 205
scaffold, *see* playhouse galleries
Schilders, Richard, 215
Scholars, The, 188
Scoloker, Antony, 201
Sejanus, 156, 234
Selimus, 137
servingmen, 52, 53, 60, 64, 65, 66, 119–20, 133, 155, 208, 209, 217
Sewster, Mr, 201, 241
Shakespeare, William, xiii, xiv, 1, 2, 12, 24, 26, 33, 45, 51, 52, 69, 70, 87, 90, 100, 135, 156, 193, 203, 257
Shank, John, 152, 226
sharers, 26, 30, 218, 253–4
Shirley, James, 96, 179, 180, 181, 188–90, 240, 248–9, 257
Shoemaker's Holiday, The, 147, 148, 160
shows, *see* spectacle
Shute, Robert, 233
Sidney, Sir Philip, 83, 91–2, 100, 106–7, 116, 122, 128, 201
Sidney, Sir Robert, 145, 147
Singing Simkin, 152